SAGA of CHIEF JOSEPH

Oil painting by Rowena Lung Alcorn

Chief Joseph, the Nez Perce

Saga of Chief JOSEPH

By

Helen Addison Howard

MAPS AND ILLUSTRATIONS BY
GEORGE D. McGRATH

UNIVERSITY OF NEBRASKA PRESS
LINCOLN AND LONDON

First Bison Book printing: 1978

Most recent printing indicated by first digit below:
3 4 5 6 7 8 9 10

Library of Congress Cataloging in Publication Data

Howard, Helen Addison.
Saga of Chief Joseph.

Reprint of the 1971 ed. published by Caxton Printers, Caldwell, Idaho; first published in 1941 under title: War Chief Joseph.
Bibliography: p. 381
1. Joseph, Nez Percé chief, 1840–1904. 2. Nez Percé Indians—Wars, 1877. 3. Nez Percé Indians—Biography. I. Title.
[E99.N5J584 1978] 970'.004'97 [B] 78–16138
ISBN 0–8032–7202–2

Reprinted by arrangement with The Caxton Printers, Ltd.
Manufactured in the United States of America

TO THE ORIGINAL AMERICANS—
THE RED INDIANS OF NORTH AMERICA

Acknowledgments

THE AUTHOR gratefully wishes to acknowledge the help and cooperation of the many people who so willingly and generously aided her in obtaining source material for this biography. She is especially indebted to the late Dan L. McGrath who assisted her in the original research in 1933-34 for WAR CHIEF JOSEPH; to the late William Andrews Clark, Jr., whose splendid collection of Americana made it possible to study the subject thoroughly; and to Dr. Clifford M. Drury for his constructive criticism.

Among those to whom special credit is due are: Mrs. Rowena Lung Alcorn, the well-known artist of Tacoma, Washington, for permission to reproduce her fine oil portrait of Chief Joseph; and to the following who assisted in the preparation of the original volume during the 1930's: Chief James Allicott, Umatilla Reservation; Mr. Omar Babcock, superintendent of the Umatilla Indian Reservation, Pendleton, Oregon; Mr. Jean Baptiste, Flathead Indian Reservation, Arlee, Montana; Mr. Joseph Blackeagle, Nez Perce Reservation, Lapwai, Idaho; Martin L. Brown, Missoula, Montana; Mr. John Collier, Commissioner of Indian Affairs, Washington, D.C.; Mr. John Connolly, Long Beach, California; the late Mr. Bernard DeVoto; Mr. George W. Fuller, former librarian, Public Library, Spokane, Washington; Dr. Garland Greever, Professor of English, University of Southern California, Los Angeles; Mr. J. H. Horner, Enterprise, Oregon; Judge William I. Lippincott, Butte, Montana; Mr. George D. McGrath, Columbia Studio, Hollywood, California; the late Dr. Edmond S. Meany, Professor of History, University of Washington, Seattle; Dr. Harold

G. Merriam, chairman of the English Department, University of Montana, Missoula; Miss Cora Sanders, librarian, Clark Memorial Library, Los Angeles; Chief Nipo Strongheart of the Yakima tribe, Hollywood, California; Mrs. Adeline Stumph, Los Angeles; Mr. Samuel Tilden, Flathead Indian Reservation, Arlee, Montana; Mr. W. Joseph Williams, Umatilla Reservation, Pendleton, Oregon; the staffs of the public libraries of Los Angeles, California; Portland, Oregon; and Spokane, Washington; Mrs. Esther Hanifen, former assistant librarian, Idaho State Historical Library, Boise, Idaho; the staff of the Huntington Library, San Marino, California; Clark Memorial Library, and to the Library of the University of California at Los Angeles. The author also wishes to express her gratitude to Mrs. Charlotte Tufts, Western Americana Librarian, Public Library, Burbank, California, for recent assistance in supplying additional materials.

Foreword

ONE of the most romantic and important figures in the history of the Pacific Northwest is Chief Joseph, the reluctant but highly effective leader of the Nez Perce uprising of 1877. He has been called the "Indian Napoleon." Endowed with unusual abilities, well informed in Indian lore, gifted with a forceful physique and a magnetic personality, Chief Joseph was by nature destined to be the leader of his people in their futile struggle against the encroachments of the whites.

The tragic and dramatic story of Chief Joseph has never been told in its fullness. Many have written about him, dwelling upon some particular episode in his eventful life. He has been the subject of several magazine articles, and he moves across the pages of many a book on Northwest history. A few have endeavored to set forth his story in more completeness, but such works have been open to the criticism of inaccuracy and partiality. Now for the first time serious-minded and well-trained students have set themselves to the task of telling a story that needs to be told.

Mr. Dan McGrath, whose parents were witnesses of some of the stirring events of those times, assisted in the assembling of the necessary historical data. Miss Helen Addison Howard, also a native of the Northwest and a historian in her own right, began this project several years ago. She has added new material to the work of her collaborator and has done the final writing of the original manuscript. Deliberately and conscientiously, the author has sought to tell the story of Chief Joseph with strict historical accuracy and in all of its details.

Every known source bearing upon this episode has been examined. Old-timers whose memories go back to those stirring days have been interviewed. With literary skill Miss Howard has woven a multitude of widely scattered facts into an absorbing story.

While this book will no doubt stand for years as the authoritative life of Chief Joseph, at the same time it will have a fascination for those who are not historically minded. Let the reader get but a few pages into this book and, if he has any compassion in his heart for the mistreated red men, or any interest in a dramatic story, he will be loath to lay the book aside until he has read the full account. No novelist could ever have conceived such a tale. This book gives proof to the old adage that truth is sometimes stranger than fiction.

CLIFFORD M. DRURY,
San Anselmo, Calif.

Contents

PART IV—LATER HISTORY

APPENDICES:

Illustrations

Prologue

THIS is the biography of Hin-mut-too-yah-lat-kekht, known to the whites as Young Joseph, Nez Perce chief, diplomat, and warrior. His story is the tragic and epic struggle of the American Indians who were relentlessly, fraudulently, and treacherously dispossessed of their hunting, fishing, and grazing grounds to satisfy the white man's greed for more land. The conflict in which Joseph was forced to engage against the whites, known as the Nez Perce War of 1877, was the last important contest between the Indians and the United States Army. Dr. Cyrus T. Brady has called Joseph's struggle "the story of the bitterest injustice toward a weak but independent people to which the United States ever set its hand."[1] Buffalo Bill also put the matter succinctly when he said: "They [the Indians] never broke a treaty, and we never kept one."

Joseph, it has been stated by earlier writers, conducted the most scientific campaign against the United States Army ever generaled by an Indian. No one knew better than he the tremendous odds against him, yet, for the freedom of his people, he fought with a puny force of never more than three hundred warriors against superior forces of a mighty nation of millions. He stood up in battle array against veteran troops, fresh from the victory of Appomattox, who were considered the "greatest soldiers in the world." He has been called the "Red Napoleon of the West," and his march toward Canada has been likened to Xenophon's March of the Ten Thousand.

However, more recent available data based on the

---

[1] Dr. Cyrus T. Brady, *Northwestern Fights and Fighters*, p. 3.

Indian testimony so painstakingly collected over a period of thirty-six years by the late L. V. McWhorter and published in his *Hear Me, My Chiefs!* caused him to conclude that "Chief Joseph was not a military genius," or was he the "war chief" during the retreat, although he did fight as a warrior. Indians were individualists; they recognized no supreme head chieftain. Thus, Nez Perce tribal organization precluded this rank. Unlike the chain of command in the white man's military organization, they had no commander in chief serving continuously throughout the campaign. Chief Looking Glass, though, along with Poker Joe (Lean Elk), did act as a war leader during much of the march. On the other hand, Joseph, according to McWhorter's two dozen sources, was the camp guardian during the war, protector of the women and children and old men. His was a "sacred trust," in McWhorter's words. In the battles Joseph fought only in self-defense when the families of the five warring bands were hard pressed by the soldiers.

But few men in the world's history have fought for the cause of liberty on both the diplomatic and military fronts as long as this Nez Perce chief. For thirty-three years—from 1871 until 1904—Chief Joseph carried the burdens of his people and used every resource to win what he believed to be justice for his tribe. He tried every kind of peaceful means to gain his ends. Like Ghandi, he pursued a policy of noncooperation, and when this failed, he unwillingly sought recourse to arms.

His valiant efforts, unparalleled in the Indian annals of America, gained for him an immortal place among the heroes of the West. Far more remarkable, however, was the chief's strict adherence to the white man's civilized code of war. The evidence shows that all the atrocities committed against civilians were perpetrated by White Bird's band before Joseph reluctantly cast his lot with the hostiles.

His character fulfilled the fondest desires of novelists who would depict the "noble red man." Colonel G. O. Shields, who knew Joseph, rated him as "easily the peer of Red Cloud in courage and daring, of Logan or Tecumseh, or John Grass in oratory; of Spotted Tail in craftiness; of Crazy Horse or Gall in strategy and generalship in battle; of Quanah Parker in statesmanship and diplomacy. He combined within himself all these attributes in a degree that made him greater than them all."[2]

His leadership won plaudits from his enemies. Brigadier General Oliver O. Howard, hero of Antietam and Gettysburg, and Joseph's most persistent foe, declared, "The leadership of Chief Joseph was indeed remarkable. No general could have planned a battle more skilfully."[3] Colonel Nelson A. Miles, the most famous of the Indian fighters, and victorious Union leader at the battle of Fredericksburg, wrote: "Chief Joseph was the highest type of Indian I have ever known."[4]

Yet beneath the chief's bravery, whether he is to be considered as a "war" chief or as a "camp guardian," there beat a heart of kindliness. White men who expected to meet a fierce and warlike savage were amazed to find Joseph cordial and gentle in manner. Judge William I. Lippincott, in a personal interview with Dan McGrath and the author at Los Angeles, California, said: "I have never before witnessed such tenderness and solicitude on the part of a man as Chief Joseph exhibited toward two Nez Perce women who were ill."[5] Among his own people the famous Nez Perce was given the place of honor wherever he appeared. Until his death he remained their recognized leader.

When the Great Spirit Above[6] beckoned this Indian patriot to enter the Spirit Lodge, a white man, Judge C.

---

[2] Col. G. O. Shields, *Blanket Indians of the Northwest*, p. 90.

[3] *Ibid.*, p. 117.

[4] Col. Nelson A. Miles, *Serving the Republic*, p. 181.

[5] Interview with Judge Lippincott, April, 1934. The judge was then a resident of Butte, Montana.

[6] The "Great Spirit [Chief] Above" is the name used by the Nez Perces to refer to a Supreme Being. Other tribes refer to the Deity as the "Great Manitou." See "An Indian's Views of Indian Affairs," *North American Review*, April, 1879, p. 430; and James Mooney, "The Ghost Dance Religion," *Fourteenth Annual Report, Bureau of American Ethnology*, Part I, p. 719.

C. Goodwin, penned his eulogy: ". . . No son of the Northwest will ever be braver than he, more true to his native land than he; more self-controlled under terrible dangers than was he." His character, Judge Goodwin continues, "will be an everlasting challenge to the schools to present a braver or more self-contained hero, or one with more native genius or more tenacity of purpose."[7]

This revised edition of the former volume is a reappraisal of the story of Young Joseph and of his people, an intelligent, peace-loving, and trustworthy tribe which preferred to "suffer wrong, rather than do wrong." A new interpretation of Joseph's war leadership is needed as a consequence of much significant material made available in the last twelve years through additional Indian sources.

---

[7] Al J. Noyes, *The Story of Ajax*, p. 37.

PART I
Early History

CHAPTER I

The Valley of Winding Waters

MANY, many moons ago, so many moons that not even the oldest people of the tribe could remember, the Nez Perces[1] wandered, a free and happy people, over a vast area of mountains, plains, valleys, and sagebrush plateaus. Their hunting and fishing grounds extended throughout what is now north central Idaho, southeastern Washington, and northeastern Oregon. For generations these healthy red men and women had been bred in the mountains, and they had become a tall, big-boned race whose erect and dignified carriage betokened their heritage of liberty. Their handsome features displayed intelligence and a gentle disposition. Like all free peoples they possessed an independent nature, as individuals as well as a tribe. The religion of their fathers held a powerful sway over their tribal life, which tended to make them strongly ethical.

As the Great Spirit Above intended they should, these peace-loving and carefree Nez Perces roamed the grassy plateaus and valleys during the spring, summer, and fall, seeking pasturage for their large herds of well-bred horses. The men and boys devoted their days to hunting and fishing, while the women and girls gathered berries and herbs and made buckskin clothing out of deer hides, or wove baskets and mats out of rushes. In the spring and fall the Nez Perces migrated across the Bitterroot Mountains to engage in hunting buffalo on the plains of

[1] The name "Nez Perce," being of French origin, was formerly written with the final *e* accented (Nez Percé). However, since the name is no longer pronounced in the French manner, the Anglicized form of spelling will be used throughout this text.

eastern Montana. But the cold storms of winter found their lodges in sheltered valleys.

After Lewis and Clark passed through their country (about which more later), French-Canadian trappers came to trade the white man's guns, cloth, metal articles, and trinkets for their pelts of beaver. The French traders, it is claimed, applied the name "Nez Percé" (Pierced Nose) to these Indians because a few members of the tribe used to pierce their noses to insert a shell for ornament. This habit was not a tribal custom, but the name clung to them. Young Joseph corroborates this theory:

> These men were Frenchmen, and they called our people "Nez Perces," because they wore rings in their noses for ornaments. Although very few of our people wear them now, we are still called by the same name.[2]

The Nez Perces called themselves "*Numípu,* or *Nimípu,* a word formed on the pronoun *nun,* we, with the addition of *pu* . . . commonly added to a place-name in forming the name of the inhabitants. Numípu, then, is equivalent to 'we people.' The name by which the tribe is known to us is the French equivalent of the appellation given to them by some other native tribes . . . in reference to a former custom of wearing a dentalium shell transversely in the septum of the nose."[3] Their language belongs to the Sahaptian (Shahaptin) group.

Regarding their name, Herbert J. Spinden, who has written the only standard authority on the ethnology of the Nez Perce Indians, states:

> The word Shahaptin, which now supplies this need, [*i. e.* a native term embracing the whole stock] is of Salish origin and was used by the earliest fur traders as the name for both the Nez Percé nation and Snake river. . . . The word takes different forms . . . Chute-pa-lu, Chohoptins, Shawhaptins, etc. The word Chopunnish, much used by Lewis and Clark, may have been obtained from the eastern Salish or corrupted from the Indian

[2] "An Indian's Views of Indian Affairs," *North American Review,* April, 1879, p. 416. An interview with Chief Joseph.

[3] Edward Curtis, *The North American Indian,* VIII, 4.

word Tsupnitpelun. The word Chopunnish seems not to have been used after Lewis and Clark except on their authority. . . . Lewis and Clark sometimes call the tribe Pierced Noses, and mention explicitly the occasional wearing of the shell.[4]

For a brief span the Nez Perces had intercourse with the traders of John Jacob Astor's fur company. These traders were followed by the North West Company, a British firm, which took over the fort at Astoria and later merged with the Hudson's Bay Company. This latter concern soon spread a chain of forts and trading posts throughout the Northwest.

Then in 1832 Captain B. L. E. Bonneville's expedition came into the country of the Nez Perces. These peaceful Indians hospitably received the Americans and gave aid to the leader on his journey to the Columbia River. Bonneville made an extended stay in the valley of Imnaha, near the Wallowa valley of winding waters, where he presumably became the guest of Old Joseph. Young Joseph had not yet been born.

In return for the Indians' kindness to him, Captain Bonneville treated the ailing and sick of the tribe. He found the Nez Perces eager to trade with the Americans, whom they called the "Big Hearts of the East." They even requested a trading post to be established among them. Bonneville found these Indians "among the gentlest and least barbarous people of these remote wildernesses," and also some of the most religious.[5]

Their piety, according to a well-established account, caused them to send a delegation in 1831 to St. Louis in search of the white man's teachers and Book. Although the authenticity of this spiritual quest by the Nez Perces

[4] H. J. Spinden, "The Nez Percé Indians," *Memoirs of the American Anthropological Society*, II, 171-72.

[5] Washington Irving, *Adventures of Captain Bonneville*, Part II, pp. 56-57. It is the belief of Mr. J. H. Horner, pioneer and historian of Wallowa Valley, Oregon, that Captain Bonneville camped "at Joseph's main winter camp, just below the mouth of Joseph Creek on the Welleweah, now called Grand Ronde River."

has been doubted by some writers,[6] a recent historian, after extensive and painstaking investigations, has presented conclusive documentary evidence that three Nez Perces and one Flathead did make the trip to St. Louis.[7]

Arriving there, they were directed to Captain William Clark, who, since the expedition, had become governor of Missouri and superintendent of Indian Affairs. During the visit both Speaking Eagle and Man-of-the-morning died and were buried by Catholic priests. The third Indian, No-horns-on-his-head, died on the return journey near the mouth of the Yellowstone, and the fourth warrior, Rabbitskin-leggings, met a band of his tribespeople in the buffalo country of the present western Montana. He told them that the white men were coming and would bring the Book. But several years were to elapse before his words came true. The important thing was that the delegation's journey brought the Western tribes to the attention of the missionaries as a fertile soil for their efforts.

Meanwhile, the tribal life of the Nez Perces repeated its generations-old routine. In the summer camp of Chief Tu-eka-kas (Old Joseph)[8] on the shores of Lake Wallowa in northeastern Oregon, the herald of the morning sun mounted his pony. According to ancient custom, when the first rays of the sun burst over the mountains to shed

---

[6] Francis Haines, "The Nez Perce Delegation to St. Louis in 1831," *Pacific Historical Review*, VI (March, 1937), 78. See also his *Red Eagles of the Northwest*, pp. 59-60, where he says: "They [the Nez Perces] were not divinely inspired toward Christianity, nor were they seeking for a higher moral standard. They wanted better 'medicine' to increase their prestige and power. They did not seek reading and writing as tools but as magic formulae to aid their 'medicine.' Hence it is absurd to argue whether they were seeking Catholic or Protestant teachers, or whether they really asked for the white man's 'Book of Heaven.' They were looking for new incantations to use on this earth, and not seeking information on a possible world to come."

[7] C. M. Drury, *Henry Harmon Spalding*, pp. 72-74, 79 ff.

[8] To avoid confusion, the old chief's Indian name, Tu-eka-kas, will be used, although his Christian name was Joseph. His son, the subject of this biography, will be designated as Young Joseph where there is danger of ambiguity. Regarding the name, see Kate McBeth, *Nez Percés Since Lewis and Clark*, pp. 63-64.

its golden warmth on the valley of winding waters and to light the copper skin of the herald, he rode through the village, shouting the morning speech:

> I wonder if every one is up! It is morning. We are alive, so thanks be! Rise up! Look about! Go see the horses, lest a wolf have killed one! Thanks be that the children are alive!—and you, older men!—and you, older women! —also that your friends are perhaps alive in other camps. But elsewhere there are probably those who are ill this morning, and therefore the children are sad, and therefore their friends are sad.[9]

His circuit of the village completed, the sun herald rode to his lodge to await his breakfast. Indian women soon emerged from the buffalo-hide tepees to stir the dying embers of the fires. The men came out later to stand around the flames, warming themselves, while their women prepared serviceberry cakes, blueback salmon, wild carrots and onions, roast fawn, or kouse gruel.[10]

From the center of the encampment Tu-eka-kas, chief of the Wal-lam-wat-kin band of "Lower" Nez Perces in the Wallowa Valley, looked on the familiar village scene. He, son of a Cayuse chief and a Nez Perce mother,[11] was a "sturdy, strong-built man with a will of iron and a foresight that never failed him, save when he welcomed the Americans to his country."[12] His best qualities he would impart to his sons; also the idea, which he clung to throughout his life, that "no man owned any part of the earth, and a man could not sell what he did not own."[13] At this early date the chief wore the barbaric costume of his tribe—a loose, long-sleeved shirt decorated with beads and elk teeth and a collar of otter skin, the tail hanging in front. Over his chest hung two long braids of shiny hair.

---

[9] Franz Boas, *Folk-Tales of Salishan and Sahaptin Tribes*, p. 201.

[10] Spinden, *op. cit.*, pp. 200-215. The information in this chapter concerning the habits and customs of the Nez Perces is based upon Spinden's study of their tribal life and upon Boas' collection of myths.

[11] For further discussion see Genealogy chart (Appendix).

[12] Norman B. Wood, *Lives of Famous Indian Chiefs*, p. 498.

[13] *Ibid.*

A belt around his waist gave support to his deerskin leggings. On his feet were the traditional moccasins of the same material, the flaps snugly knotted by a double thong.

Peace and a happy content shone in the dark eyes of Tu-eka-kas as his gaze roved from the camp to linger on the hills encircling his ancestral home. In the mountains to the west jagged ridges with forested slopes darkly blue-green in the early morning sunlight girdled the valley. To the south and east lofty peaks rose thousands of feet into the sky. Snowfields, which would remain unmelted by the July sun, sparkled among the crags of the Wallowa Mountains on the south. Closer by, bunchgrass and sage cloaked the floor of the valley, broken by the meandering course of streams where the first run of blueback salmon were fighting their way to the spawning grounds. Sage dotted the foothills. Here and there the chief's eye caught the gleam of a tiny waterfall. Near the village the mountain-rimmed surface of Lake Wallowa lay as placid as a mirror until its waters were rippled by trout leaping for flies. The chief's gaze studied the vast herd of ponies grazing on the nutritious grass among the sage as they roamed the plain guarded by young boys a mile or more from the camp. Life was good in this valley, a land of plenty.

Nor did the scene materially change after the missionaries had come to the Northwest. The people of Tu-eka-kas continued to live in their primitive valley of winding waters, a happy, healthy, and contented band. By the year 1844 the chief had become the father of two sons by his Nez Perce wife. The elder, who was to become known as Young Joseph, was born in 1840—probably in the summer, as in 1878 he made the following statement: "I was born in eastern Oregon, thirty-eight winters ago";[14] and it was

---

[14] "An Indian's Views . . . ," *op. cit.*, p. 415. Dr. C. M. Drury believes it likely that the Rev. H. H. Spalding baptized young Joseph on April 12, 1840, as 'Ephraim.' See Drury, *The Diaries and Letters of Henry H. Spalding and Asa Bowen Smith, Relating to the Nez Perce Mission, 1838-1842* (Glendale, Calif.: The Arthur H. Clark Company, 1958), p. 288, note 90.

during the summer that his father's band visited the Wallowa Valley. The younger son, Alokut, was born two or three years after his brother. They grew to look so much alike that white people thought them twins.

As documentary records are lacking, the following account of Young Joseph's probable early life is drawn from material in H. J. Spinden's "The Nez Percé Indians." Without doubt the age-old life of the summer camp went on. Little Joseph rambled about the village, a naked, copper-skinned boy, and his beady black eyes sharply observed its every detail. He watched the women busy with pestle and mortar grinding flour from the roots of camas, and others placing berries on tule mats to dry in the sun. A few would pause in their work to smile at the chief's little son. Several of the women had sharp, disk-shaped fragments of boulders picked up in the near-by streams, and with these they were scraping the hides of deer and elk.

With childish curiosity the lad stared at young men fashioning spearheads and arrow points of obsidian rock found in the John Day region of Oregon. One young man, noticing the boy's interest, showed him an arrowhead. The child fondled the smooth symmetry of it, running his chubby palm over its hard, shiny surface.

Curiosity led the boy to the outskirts of the village where two warriors were plucking from captive eagles their first feathers, which they would use to adorn their warbonnets. Later, the choice feathers of second growth would be taken and the bird then given its freedom. Other eaglets, though, would be stolen from their nests and raised until the feathers had been obtained.

During his wanderings about the camp, little Joseph passed old men and women who sat outside their lodges to bask in the afternoon sun, while they dreamed perhaps of battles with the fierce Blackfeet in the buffalo country, or gossiped about their friends and relatives in other villages. A few grandmothers were busy sewing beads on buckskin garments for their grandchildren.

Then a group of little girls and small boys, naked like

himself, attracted the sharp, bright eyes of the lad. The children sat in a circle about an aged warrior, listening to his tale of the white men with beards and glass eyes that came into their country many moons ago. Little Joseph, delighted, squatted among the group to hear again the story of Lewis and Clark—the first whites ever to be seen by the Nez Perces—although his father had recited it so many times that he already knew it by heart.

These strange white people came in September, the month of the hunting moon, the old warrior told his young listeners, and met Chief Twisted Hair's band on the Weippe prairie in what is now northern Idaho. The Nez Perces gave the strangers supplies of camas root and held a big feast for them and exchanged presents. After a short stay the visitors left their horses and saddles to be cared for by Chief Twisted Hair's tribe while they sailed down the great river to the ocean. Upon their return the following spring, everything they had left with the Indians was returned to them in good condition.

The leaders of these white people were great men, the old warrior declared, and not like the whites who now traveled in wagons through the Grande Ronde country to the northwest. Lewis and Clark did not wish to buy furs, to teach "spirit law," or to plow up the Earth-Mother for farms. They were content with the friendship of the Nez Perces, and as proof of their good will, they gave each chief a bronze disk with curious symbols carved upon it. Peace between red and white men was their message, which the Nez Perces cherished in their hearts. Although little Joseph did not know it, Patrick Gass recorded in his *Journal:* "The Nez Perce were better than the Flatheads, and the Flatheads were the whitest Indians Lewis and Clark had ever seen before . . . Weippe Prairies."

In speaking of this expedition years later, Young Joseph said:

> All the Nez Percés made friends with Lewis and Clarke, and agreed to let them pass through their country, and never to make war on white men. This promise the Nez

Percés have never broken. No white man can accuse them of bad faith, and speak with a straight tongue.[15]

All the testimony bears out the truth of these words of Young Joseph. Truly, he, at least, spoke "with a straight tongue."

Summer evenings were long in the valley of winding waters. Slowly the sun disappeared behind the mountains, its last rays flecking the peaks to the east with tints of burnished gold that gradually faded to purple in the afterglow. Breezes sprang up to rustle through the prairie grass, and the women built up the fires before the lodges, while the men wrapped buffalo robes about them to ward off the evening chill.

It was especially around the campfires inside the lodges on winter nights that little Joseph and other children would gather to hear the old men tell tribal legends. In answer to such questions as have been asked by children of all races since the beginning of time, of whence the people came, these tellers of tales would recite the myth of the origin of the Nez Perces.

A huge monster from the sea, the great Iltswetsix,[16] roamed the Kamiah Valley in north Idaho. So enormous was his appetite that he sucked everything into himself, and was soon devouring all the animals in the land. When Spi-li-yai,[17] or Coyote (the fabled knave of Indian mythology), heard of this, he left the Umatilla country to engage in a test of strength with the monster. Upon reaching Kamiah, Coyote concealed himself under a grass bonnet and tied his body down with a wild grapevine. Then he defied Iltswetsix to pull him into his cavernous mouth. The great beast sucked and sucked, until slowly

[15] *Ibid.*, p. 416.

[16] Spinden, *op. cit.*, p. 268. Nipo Strongheart, a chief of the Yakimas and an ethnologist of note, in a personal conversation with Dan McGrath and the author, gave the spelling of the monster's name, as Ilt-swi-tsichs. The *ch* is pronounced as in German. There are various versions of the legend. This one is from Boas' collection of folk tales.

[17] Chief Nipo Strongheart in an interview, December 10, 1934, gave Spi-li-yai as the Nez Perce name for Coyote.

the ropes gave way and Coyote was drawn into the monster's stomach. But Coyote had not yet lost the contest. Taking a knife that he had concealed in his belt, he began to cut out the sea demon's heart, and so killed him. Then Coyote carved his way out of the monster's body.

At once Fox, who had witnessed the duel, joined him. Since Coyote did not know what to do with the body, Fox suggested that they cut it up and make people. So, from the head came the Flathead Indians; from the feet, the Blackfoot tribe; and thus from each part they made a different nation of Indians. Finally, only the heart remained. As Coyote held it aloft, the beast's blood dropped to the ground and from these drops more people sprang up. They were taller, stronger, nobler, and wiser than the others—these were the Nez Perces. The Great Spirit Chief, who rules above, was well pleased with Coyote, and, lest the people forget this wonderful deed, he turned the heart into a large stone, and it may be seen yet in the Kamiah Valley.

After the storyteller had finished, little Joseph stretched out on his bed of buffalo robes, lying beside his younger brother, Alokut. The older people retired, and the fires died down to glowing embers. From somewhere in the darkness the brothers heard the soft tones of a wooden flageolet as some brave played and chanted his love song to the maiden of his choice. The young man would be standing in the cold and snow outside her father's lodge. Then the high-pitched howl of a coyote, long-drawn and weird, sounded from the dark, wooded hills and lulled little Joseph and Alokut to sleep.

CHAPTER II

The Coming of the Missionaries

THE NEZ PERCES waited three years for the white men to bring them the teachings of the "spirit law." The Methodist Church was the first to respond. That denomination sent out Jason Lee and his associates, among whom was his nephew, Daniel Lee. The party of missionaries traveled into the Northwest with the trading expedition of Nathaniel J. Wyeth and William L. Sublette. Early in July, 1834, they met Lawyer's band of Nez Perces in the vicinity of Fort Hall on Snake River. But Lee and his assistants did not tarry long among these Indians, for they had instructions to make their way to the Willamette Valley in Oregon.

The next missionaries to arrive were Dr. Marcus Whitman, a physician, and the Reverend Samuel Parker. They came in August of the following year and held a religious council with the Nez Perces at the rendezvous on Green River. So delighted and impressed was Dr. Whitman with these Indians that he returned East to make arrangements for founding a mission, while Parker continued to the settlements on the lower Columbia. Whitman was accompanied to the States by two Nez Perce boys, one the son of a chief. The youths wished to learn the English language.

The American Board of Commissioners for Foreign Missions, which then included the Presbyterian and Congregational denominations, commissioned Whitman for missionary work among the Nez Perces. In the spring of 1836 he again started West, bringing as his assistants his bride, the former Miss Narcissa Prentiss, the Reverend and Mrs. Henry H. Spalding, and W. H. Gray. A party of Nez Perces met them at the Green River rendezvous in the present state of Wyoming, and some of the Indians accompanied the missionaries to the Columbia River Valley.[1]

At Fort Vancouver they visited Dr. John McLoughlin, chief factor of the Hudson's Bay post, who advised them to devote their religious efforts to the Cayuse Indians and the Nez Perces. So Dr. Whitman built his mission in the fertile Walla Walla Valley at a place called Waiilatpu.

Acting on the request of Tack-en-su-a-tis, a Nez Perce chief, also called Rotten Belly, Spalding located his home November 29, 1836, on Lapwai Creek near its confluence with the Clearwater River in the present north Idaho. During that winter he built the Presbyterian mission house. Besides teaching the "spirit law," Spalding also taught the Indians how to till the soil and how to raise crops of wheat, corn, potatoes, and other foods. His wife opened a mission school to teach the youngsters the elementary essentials of "readin', 'ritin', and 'rithmetic," while their elders learned the principles of agriculture. Spalding also introduced cattle, sheep, and hogs.

Then in December, 1842, all the far-flung bands composing the Nez Perce nation held a council at Lapwai with Dr. Elijah White, subagent of Indian Affairs west of the Rocky Mountains; Thomas McKay, a stepson of Dr. McLoughlin; Cornelius Rogers; Baptiste Dorion; and the Hudson's Bay trader, Archibald McKinley. At this council Dr. White proposed a system of criminal laws, to which the Indians agreed by acclamation. He then suggested that they elect a head chief over all the bands of the Nez Perce nation. Their tribal custom had never recognized the rule by majority, even within the various bands. Members of each band voluntarily followed the counsel and advice of their chief, who was assisted by

---

[1] Haines in *Red Eagles of the Northewst*, p. 73, states that Old Joseph or Tu-eka-kas was a member of this welcoming party upon Whitman's return. However, Haines mistakes Tak-en-sue-tis (Samuel), who was present at the rendezvous, for Tu-eka-kas. See McBeth, *The Nez Percés Since Lewis and Clark*, pp. 38-39.

minor chiefs or headmen under him, and by medicine men. But anyone could dissent and do as he pleased, and still remain a member of the band. Each tribe had its war chief, subject to the head chief, the position being granted by majority vote.

It is important to understand the Nez Perces' idea of political economy, because of the tragic misunderstanding it brought upon Joseph's band in his dealings with the government officials, when Lawyer's decisions, expressed in the Treaty of 1863, were accepted by the various commissions as representing the wishes of the entire Nez Perce nation. Thus the adoption of Dr. White's proposal to elect a tribal head not only violated tribal custom, but also laid the foundation for the troubles which culminated in the Nez Perce War of 1877.

Ellis, secretly sponsored by Dr. White, received the election as head chief. He had been educated at the mission school on the Red River. In addition, twelve subchiefs were chosen, among whom was Tu-eka-kas.

Meantime, the influx of American settlers into the Oregon country, dominated by the British-owned Hudson's Bay Company, promoted dissatisfaction and unrest among emigrants as well as among the Indian tribes of the Columbia Basin.

Dr. White was relieved of his post by a new administration in Washington and returned East. After he left in August of 1845, the provisional legislature of Oregon elected Governor Abernethy to the newly created office of Superintendent of Indian Affairs. With the passing of White, the Nez Perces disregarded their laws and reverted to the aboriginal customs of their forefathers. Ellis was killed in the buffalo country in 1848, which left the position of head chief vacant.[2] Lawyer, the son of Chief Twisted Hair who befriended the Lewis and Clark expe-

[2] Drury, *Henry Harmon Spalding*, p. 296. For a detailed account of Nez Perce missionary history see C. M. Drury's trilogy, *Henry Harmon Spalding; Marcus Whitman, M.D.;* and *Elkanah and Mary Walker*.

dition, was afterwards elected, but not with the nation's full sanction.

During the time that the Reverend Henry Spalding and his wife continued to preach the gospel to the Nez Perces at Lapwai (Place Where the Butterfly Dwells),[3] Chief Tu-eka-kas visited the mission and listened to the words of the Presbyterian missionary. The chief desired his people to learn the "white man's Book" and the many useful things taught the Indians by these strangers. A few Nez Perces were learning to write their own language from the grammar Spalding had devised, and some could read the Gospel of St. Matthew which he had translated into their native tongue.

Tu-eka-kas gravely embraced the "spirit law." Indeed, he and Chief Timothy were Spalding's first two converts. In his diary for November 17, 1839, the missionary reports: "I proceeded to marry Joseph & his wife lawfully his wife taking the name of Arenoth."[4] Tu-eka-kas appears to have been devoutly religious, and used his influence among his people to spread the teaching of Christianity. He even "assisted in the teaching and took the responsibility for the discipline."[5] Spalding baptised him, giving him the name of Joseph, and in 1845 the chief's eldest son, then five years of age, was also given the same name.

By this time little Joseph and his brother, Alokut, were going to the day school,[6] while their parents attended the religious services. The boys were not old enough to learn to read and write much English, but they no doubt enjoyed being with the older students.

Until the fall of 1847, except for minor difficulties, the Spaldings continued to reap a spiritual harvest among the peace-loving Nez Perces. But the course of Whitman's

---

[3] Crawford, *The Nez Percés Since Spalding*, p. 8.

[4] Drury, *op. cit.*, p. 234. Tu-eka-kas' wife was admitted into the church on May 14, 1843. *Op. cit.*, p. 304.

[5] Drury, *op. cit.*, p. 299.

[6] O. O. Howard, *Chief Joseph; His Pursuit and Capture*, p. 9. Joseph's father-in-law made this statement to Howard.

efforts at the Cayuse mission, 120 miles to the south and west, did not fare so well. The dreaded measles broke out among his Indians during the autumn. Ignorant of the cause, the superstitious Cayuses believed the missionary was making bad medicine for them. With savage treachery they fell upon Dr. Whitman on November 29, 1847, killing him and fourteen other whites, including Mrs. Whitman. Those whom they spared—mostly women and children—they took as prisoners. They then proceeded to loot or destroy the mission buildings.

Upon learning of the massacre, Spalding, who had just left the Walla Walla settlement, hurried home to his wife and children at Lapwai. When he arrived, he asked for an escort to the nearest fort, since he feared that all the Northwestern Indians would start a wholesale murder of the whites. He accepted the offer of forty Nez Perce warriors who volunteered to guide him to safety, first to Craig's ranch and later to The Dalles, Oregon.

Even though deserted by their missionary, the Nez Perces continued to practice their faith as the months passed by, with a few devout souls like Timothy conducting the services. But Tu-eka-kas had cause to ponder the invincibility of the Book.

After the Whitman Massacre, renegade Nez Perces, among them some from the camp of Tu-eka-kas, looted the Spalding home at Lapwai. This brought on a strained feeling between the chief and the Reverend Henry Spalding when he finally returned to the mission for a brief visit months later. It may be the reason why the chief refused to go into the first council of 1863 until Perrin Whitman arrived to interpret, although Spalding was ready and willing to do so. It probably explains, also, why Tu-eka-kas left the vicinity of Lapwai and returned to the Wallowa Valley.

Another contributing cause to his departure from Lapwai, undoubtedly, was the unfriendly attitude of Chief Big Thunder,[7] who, freed from Spalding's restraining

---

[7] J. P. Dunn, Jr., *Massacres of the Mountains*, p. 631. Both Drury and Haines give the name of this chief as Old James.

influence, ordered Tu-eka-kas and his band to leave the valley in which they were encamped, as it belonged to him and his tribe.

After much dissension, the chief led his people back to their old home and never again practiced the white man's religion. But the message of peace and friendship with the whites, implanted by Lewis and Clark, was still cherished in the hearts of the people of Tu-eka-kas, and nurtured there by the teachings of the missionary.

Soon after the Whitman Massacre regular troops and several companies of volunteers were sent to campaign against the Cayuses in revenge for the murder of the whites. When guilty members of the Cayuse tribe fled into the hills, some of the volunteers suspected the Nez Perces of abetting their escape and favored an attack upon the latter. For a while it seemed that the innocent Nez Perces would be involved in the trouble. With the arrival of Colonel Gilliam and his regulars at Waiilatpu, a council was arranged through the efforts of William Craig, who acted in behalf of the Nez Perces.

This meeting took place in March, 1848, and was attended by two hundred and fifty warriors led by Tu-eka-kas, who approached the council grounds under an American flag and carried a New Testament in his hand as proof of his good faith toward the Americans.[8]

General Palmer, Indian agent for Oregon, was favorably impressed by the attitude of the Nez Perces, and told them to return to their homes for the spring planting, and to continue their peaceful relations with the whites.[9]

---

[8] Victor, *Early Indian Wars of Oregon*, pp. 180-84.

[9] *Ibid.*

CHAPTER III

Thunder-rolling-in-the-mountains

TAKEN from Lapwai before he received more than a primary education in Spalding's school, little Joseph's knowledge came from lessons taught him by the experiences of his daily life. Under his father's guidance he learned how to hunt the creatures of the forest and to fish the streams for salmon, and how to ride a pony without saddle or bridle. He could imitate the calls of birds and animals, and he acquired an intimate knowledge of their habits. He learned to fashion spears and knives, arrows and quivers, and other weapons of war. From the red fir he made a spear with barbed stone points to be used for hunting the buffalo when he grew older and stronger. He learned to watch for the roots of plants that provided food and medicine. This training developed his senses to a keen alertness, and fitted him for a life of economic self-sufficiency.

Nor was his spiritual development overlooked. From the tribal myths and legends (akin to the moral lessons of Aesop's Fables), little Joseph learned that selfishness and greed were great sins. Under the gentle teaching of his father, he learned to share his food, even to his last morsel, with the poor, and never wantonly to destroy animals nor plants, but to kill only when in need. His father taught him respect for the wisdom of his elders, and always to be thankful for the bounteous gifts of the Great Spirit.

After he had grown to manhood, Young Joseph said regarding his spiritual training:

Our fathers gave us many laws, which they had learned from their fathers. These laws were good. They told us to treat all men as they treated us; that we should never be the first to break a bargain; that it was a disgrace to tell a lie; that we should speak only the truth; that it was a shame for one man to take from another his wife, or his property without paying for it. We were taught to believe that the Great Spirit sees and hears everything, and that he never forgets; that hereafter he will give every man a spirit-home according to his deserts: if he has been a good man, he will have a good home; if he has been a bad man, he will have a bad home. This I believe, and all my people believe the same.[1]

In this statement of his creed we may recognize the golden-rule philosophy of Christian precept, and the influence on Young Joseph's father of the Reverend Henry Spalding's missionary teaching.

As the years rolled on there were new additions to the family of Young Joseph. Tu-eka-kas returned to the polygamous beliefs of his people, and in addition to his first wife, Arenoth, he married Walla Walla Woman, Cayuse Woman, and Ip-as-ship-ap-la-chon-my. In time the lodge resounded to the laughter of the seven children of his wives.

Before the Whitman Massacre in 1847 diplomats in Washington and London were making decisions regarding the future of the Pacific Northwest, which were vitally to affect the destiny of the Nez Perce Indians. All that region then known as the Oregon country, and now comprising the states of Washington and Oregon, Idaho, western Montana and Wyoming was claimed by the United States by right of discovery, the Lewis and Clark explorations, and settlement by American emigrants. This vast territory had hitherto been shared with the British through the joint-occupation treaty of 1818. Mutual dissatisfaction with this agreement arose, and "Fifty-four Forty or Fight" became the ominous slogan of the American people. But a pacifistic English parliament and the United States government, occupied in a war with Mexico, averted armed hostilities by arbitra-

[1] "An Indian's Views of Indian Affairs," *North American Review*, April, 1879, p. 415.

tion. The dispute was amicably settled by the compromise treaty of June 15, 1846, which placed the international boundary along the forty-ninth parallel. And so the Nez Perces became wards of the white chief at Washington instead of subjects of the king.

Two years later, in 1848, the Territory of Oregon was established, with the new governor being inaugurated on March 3, 1849. The lands of Tu-eka-kas' band were, without the old chief's consent, embraced in this territory, and his people were made subject to the jurisdiction of the federal government.

More important to Young Joseph at this time than these epochal events was the ceremony of the sacred vigil, the most momentous experience in a Nez Perce's life. Every child eagerly looked forward to the time when he could earn his name by divine revelation. Should he, a future warrior, fail to earn it through the rites of the sacred vigil, the men would give him a derisive name and he would thus become the object of the tribe's ridicule. The stigma of such a disgrace could only be removed by a heroic deed of war. So boys and girls between nine and ten years of age awaited a propitious day when their fathers should send them to hold a tryst with the Great Spirit.

When little Joseph reached the proper age, his father sent for him. Here again documentary evidence is lacking, but certain it is that Young Joseph performed the ceremony of the sacred vigil, since it was obligatory for every Nez Perce child to do so. With grave earnestness the chief impressed upon his son the importance of the vigil. Tu-eka-kas cautioned him of danger from wild animals. The boy did not fear them, since he knew that all Nature was the handiwork of the Great Spirit. Flowers, trees, birds, and animals were His children, so surely one need have no fear of the cougar, the wolf, or the bear.

In obedience to his father's instructions, the lad stripped himself of his clothes, and without weapons, set out from the lodge early in the morning. Leaving the comfort and safety of the village behind, Young Joseph first journeyed across meadowland where he passed flowers in full bloom, ripening berries, and cool streams. Then he began to climb a steep ridge through a forest of pine, fir, and cedar. After several hours he came out on the summit. Here, on a rocky ledge near a clump of evergreens, he prepared to hold communion with the Great Spirit. If he had a good heart, his prayers would be answered. Perhaps the revelation would win him a place in the Wolf clan, whose members enjoyed special hunting favors from the Spirit Father.

He made a rude bed of fir boughs and sat cross-legged upon them to begin his vigil. Far below him lay the gleam of winding waters, sparkling in the sunlight. On the banks of one river he could see the buffalo-hide lodges of his father's village. He closed his eyes, the better to concentrate in prayer to Tah-Mah-Ne-Wes, the Spirit Chief.

As darkness came on and the mountain air grew chill, Young Joseph made a small fire, although he was forbidden to eat or drink during the ceremony. In the forest around him deer grazed on the grassy slopes, and during the night hours mountain lions slunk among the trees, stalking their prey. Stout of heart and with patience the little watcher sat facing the flames. Except occasionally to place fresh wood on the fire, he remained as motionless as the stones around him. At intervals from the shadows of the forest the low, weird "hoo, hoo" of an owl came to him. Once in a while he heard the crackling of leaves and the brittle sound of dead branches being snapped as deer climbed the ridge to feed in the moonlight. But these sounds did not disturb the boy's concentration.

Finally the night hours passed, and the sun god mounted high into the heavens. Still Young Joseph sat, resisting sleep as long as possible, while his tongue grew parched and his stomach craved food, yet he prayed more fervently. The fast slowly weakened him, until he could no longer resist Nature's demand for sleep. He fell into troubled slumbers and dreamed his big medicine dream.

Three Eagles, an educated Nez Perce, gives a description of what Young Joseph probably saw in his vision as he dreamed that thunder appeared to him:

> He sees a man coming, and goes to him. He appears to be a man wrapped in a yellow blanket, and he gives the boy whatever he may be carrying. The little boy, if he could be seen now, would be found lying as if dead. When he awakens he may think, "I met a man." That is all he would remember.[2]

Joseph awoke, feeling somewhat refreshed, and started back to his father's lodge, having been absent several days. A great peace filled his soul, and joy lightened his heart. Never again would he know that peace which comes to one who has communed with his God, bringing with it an ethereal calmness after a great emotional experience. The boy repeated the words of the sacred song which the Great Spirit had taught him while he slept. When the proper time came, he would chant the mystic words to his people, so that they might know the name the Spirit Father had bestowed on him. The full dream, though, would remain forever unrevealed, since it represented the most sacred experience of his life.[3]

When he arrived at his father's lodge, Young Joseph took a purifying bath and then ate sparingly of food. Afterwards he dropped into untroubled sleep, knowing he had successfully passed his tribe's test of its youth.

Young Joseph kept the words of the mystic song a secret throughout the summer and fall months. On a winter's day when the Wal-lam-wat-kins were encamped in the Imnaha Valley, the voice of the herald rang out through the village: "People, lay everything aside, for now we are going to have a dance of the Guardian Spirit." This ritual was held to bring Nature, people, and animals into close friendly relations, to promote better hunts, and to bring warm weather.

---

[2] Curtis, *The North American Indian,* VIII, 64. A man in a yellow blanket is the Nez Perce symbol for thunder.

[3] The description of the sacred vigil is taken from the account by Spinden, "The Nez Percé Indians," *Memoirs of the American Anthropological Society,* Vol. II.

For hours the Indians busied themselves in preparing their finest clothes for the religious rites. In the evening they gathered in the dance tent, a huge lodge sixty feet long and fifty feet wide. Two fires, with smoke curling up thirty feet to the ridgepole, warmed the tent for the ceremonies of Wee' kwetset.[4]

After the people had taken their places, a warrior started his dance and song without the accompaniment of a drum. Soon the others joined him in singing the words. They slowly shuffled their feet, keeping rhythmic time with their voices. As he chanted and crouched, partly covered by a wolfskin, the brave imitated the fierce growls of the wolf, and by the movements of his body faithfully mimicked the actions of that animal whose name he bore. Soon the dancer worked himself into a state of ecstasy, half religious and half hypnotic. In the flickering light from the flames, the scene took on a weird, barbaric, and dramatic reality.

When Young Joseph's turn came, he stepped forward within the circle of his tribespeople and sang the mystic words that the Spirit Chief had taught him. His studied movements revealed that Tah-Mah-Ne-Wes had blessed him with the name of Hin-mut-too-yah-lat-kekht, meaning "Thunder-rolling-in-the-mountains."[5] That was an auspicious name, for it offered the protection of Nature, so necessary to one who would become a chieftain. But the full dream would remain locked in Joseph's soul for all time.

---

[4] Spinden, *op. cit.*, p. 262.

[5] Joseph's Indian name and its translation as inscribed on the monument at his grave in Nespelem, Washington.

PART II
Treaty History

CHAPTER IV

The Council Smoke of 1855

THERE were enough settlers in the Northwest by 1853 to warrant an additional territorial government, and so Congress created the Territory of Washington out of the Old Oregon country. It embraced all the land from the forty-second parallel northward to the forty-ninth parallel, and westward from the crest of the Rockies to the Pacific Ocean. The confines of the new territory excluded the present state boundaries of Oregon, and any land which in the future might be set aside through treaties as Indian reservations. Washington thus comprised the land north from the Columbia River to the Canadian border, and from the Pacific Ocean to what is now the northern strip of Idaho south to the Snake River, and the western part of Montana to the summit of the Rockies just east of Butte.

Major Isaac I. Stevens of the U. S. Army, then thirty-four years of age, was appointed the first governor of the new territory. His duties included the superintendency of Indian affairs. What a task faced the new executive! Congress, by the Donation Acts, urged American settlers to take up any piece of land they desired, regardless of whether it was claimed by the Indians. The governor immediately organized the Indian Service and appointed agents for the tribes east and west of the Cascade Mountains.

Meanwhile, the ford of the Grande Ronde River in the valley of that name, which was fifteen or twenty miles west of Wallowa Valley, had become the favorite trading place of the Nez Perces and the emigrants traveling the Oregon Trail. By the time the latter had reached this point on their transcontinental journey, their cattle and horses were worn out. Knowing that fresh ones were desired by the whites, Tu-eka-kas and his people traded their animals for the larger and heavier stock of the emigrants. An Indian pony in good condition commanded in exchange several jaded horses, or a good gun with ammunition. To their discomfiture the settlers learned that the Nez Perces could outsmart a Yankee when it came to horse trading.

The travel-worn animals thus procured by Tu-eka-kas and other chiefs were left to rest for months before being offered in trade to later emigrants. These horses from the East and stallions of Arabian descent, which had been captured in raids upon the Spanish settlements of California,[1] were much sought after by the pioneers. Consequently, they brought more in exchange than ordinary Indian ponies. The Nez Perces used the better grade of American stock to improve the blood lines of their herds, which increased with much rapidity both in numbers and in quality. Some of the chiefs boasted of owning two thousand or more horses, in addition to their herds of of cattle. Among other tribes and among white settlers the Nez Perces became noted for their numerous well-bred horses—a possession that counted heavily in their favor during the war of 1877.[2]

Chief Tu-eka-kas at first welcomed American emigrants to his country, for he believed they would teach his people the good things of civilization. Only a few remained to settle in the Wallowa region though, as most of them were bound for the rich coastal valleys of western Oregon and Washington. The cupidity and greed exhibited by those who stayed soon aroused the old chief's distrust.

Despite his early faith in the white man, Tu-eka-kas had a canny insight into human nature. Says his son:

My father was the first to see through the schemes of the white men, and he warned his tribe to be careful about

[1] Haines, *Red Eagles of the Northwest*, p. 23.

[2] *Ibid.*, p. 22 ff.

trading with them. He had suspicion of men who seemed so anxious to make money. I was a boy then, but I remember well my father's caution. He had sharper eyes than the rest of our people.[3]

It was inevitable that friction should occur between the Indians and the pioneers who were pouring into the Columbia Basin. Governor Stevens, foreseeing grave trouble in the future, asked Congress for appropriations to negotiate treaties with all the tribes of the Northwest, for the purpose of placing the Indians on certain defined reservations. In spite of discouraging delays the governor, by his vigorous efforts, finally convinced Congress of the necessity for such action.

Stevens believed that a treaty to segregate the two races would prevent any ruptures in the peaceful relations between the Nez Perces and the Americans. Prior to this time they had ever been friendly to white men. But serious complications threatened if the Nez Perces, the largest and most powerful nation in the Northwest, should become hostile as were the Cayuse and Klickitat and Yakima tribes. The governor hoped to pacify these belligerent Indians and to hold the friendship of the Nez Perces by a treaty that would be fair to both races, before any dangerous uprisings should occur.

With the thought of peace uppermost in his mind, Stevens sent James Doty to all the representative Columbia River chiefs, asking them to meet the governor's party for a big powwow in the latter part of May, 1855. Chief Kamiakin of the Yakimas chose Walla Walla, the ancient council ground of the tribes, as the meeting place.

Tu-eka-kas accepted the invitation and with a large delegation from his band set out for the council. The two boys, Joseph, then around fifteen, and his brother Alokut, doubtless accompanied their father and mother. The Nez Perces arrived at the conference more promptly than any other tribe. At that, they did not reach Walla Walla until

---

[3] "An Indian's Views of Indian Affairs," *North American Review*, April, 1879, p. 146.

May 24, four days after the time appointed by Governor Stevens.

Next to arrive, after several days' delay, were the Cayuses; then came the Walla Wallas, the Umatillas, and the Yakimas. All tribes but the Palouses were represented. Five thousand Indians and a mere handful of white officials, attended by a military escort of forty-seven dragoons under Lieutenant Archibald Gracie, were present at the council. It was probably the greatest peace gathering of Indians ever held in the West.

Besides Governor Stevens there were present his thirteen-year-old son, Hazard, General Joel Palmer, secretaries James Doty and William C. McKay, Agents R. R. Thompson, R. B. Metcalfe, R. H. Crosby, N. Olney, and R. H. Lansdale, Packmaster C. P. Higgins, the army escort, and interpreters William Craig, N. Raymond, Matthew Danpher, and John Flette. Additional interpreters appointed by the government included A. D. Pambrun, John Whitford, James Coxie, and Patrick McKensie. Two Catholic missionaries, Fathers Chirause and Pandosy, attended the council. The whites—military, aides, and settlers—numbered about one hundred.

The council ground was pleasantly situated on the right bank of Mill Creek, about six miles above the Whitman mission, in the fertile Walla Walla Valley, surrounded by rolling hills covered with grass and sage. As the different tribes arrived, their lodges were raised on the plain, until a veritable city of tepees stood along the creek.

To impress the white officials, the Nez Perces spent hours painting themselves and their ponies with streaks of yellow, white, and crimson before they approached the council ground. Gaily bedecked then with bright beads, plumes, and warbonnets, and resplendent in gaudy paint, the Nez Perces, twenty-five hundred strong, presented an impressive sight when they came in view.

The magnificent cavalcade of more than a thousand braves, naked except for breechclout, their brown bodies striped in garish colors, thundered across the prairie on sleek ponies. As they galloped two abreast toward the mound where the governor's party stood in review, the column suddenly halted and formed a long line across the plain. Again they charged forward. With considerable trepidation Stevens and his aides observed that the warriors were armed with shields, lances, knives, and guns.

Lieutenant Kip, who was a guest of the escort, vividly describes the scene:

When about a mile distant they halted, and half a dozen chiefs [including Lawyer] rode forward and were introduced to Governor Stevens and General Palmer, in order of their rank. Then on came the rest of the wild horsemen in single file, clashing their shields, singing and beating their drums as they marched past us. Then they formed a circle and dashed around us, while our little group stood there, the center of their wild evolutions. They would gallop up as if about to make a charge, then wheel round and round, sounding their loud whoops until they had apparently worked themselves up into an intense excitement.[4]

It was merely a friendly demonstration though, for twenty-five more Nez Perce chiefs went through the same ceremony of introductions. They then dismounted and took a position behind the governor's party, after which the warriors, taking their place behind the chiefs, entertained the commissioners with songs and dances, accompanied by the beating of drums.

Following this program, the braves retired to their campground. The chiefs solemnly and with grave ceremony smoked the pipe of peace with Stevens' party at the tents of the whites, and then withdrew to their lodges.

By May 29 the other tribes of Cayuses, Walla Wallas, Yakimas, and Umatillas had arrived, and Stevens spent the day in the preliminaries of swearing in the interpreters and generally arranging the formalities necessary before the treaty discussions could begin.

The next day, May 30, the Indians were invited to assemble for the first conference. About a thousand at-

[4] Col. Lawrence Kip, *The Indian Council at Walla Walla, 1855*, pp. 10-11.

tended. They sat on the ground before the governor's tent in a semicircle forty rows deep, and consumed a half-hour smoking the peace pipe. General Joel Palmer, Superintendent of Indian Affairs for Oregon, who was one of the commissioners, opened the council with a short address. Governor Stevens then arose and made a lengthy speech in which he outlined the object of the conference. The commissioners spent the following two days explaining in detail the conditions of the treaty and the prices offered by the government for Indian lands. At first two reservations were proposed—one in the country of the Nez Perces and the other in Yakima territory.

These meetings were marked by fierce disputes and sly intrigues. The long-drawn-out negotiations furnished opportunity for the young men to have dances, to compete in footraces, to gamble on horse races, and to seek prospective brides.

Young Chief of the Cayuses asked that the third day be set aside for a holiday, but the Indians remained in their respective camps while the chiefs deliberated among themselves on the proposals of the commissioners. On the fourth day Stevens and Palmer asked the Indians to express their views. Several of the chiefs spoke opposing the recommendations. Peu-peu-mox-mox of the Walla Wallas made a sarcastic speech openly expressing distrust of the whites.

That night Lawyer went alone to the tent of Governor Stevens and informed him that the Cayuse chiefs were plotting treachery against the commissioners. Their plans had not been divulged to the Nez Perces. Lawyer, though, had become suspicious and, through his spies in the Cayuse camp, had learned of the plot to murder the white officials. This massacre would mark the beginning of a war of extermination against the settlers. The Cayuses planned to capture the nearest army post—the garrison at The Dalles.

"I will come with my family," Lawyer told Governor Stevens, "and pitch my lodge in the midst of your camp, that the Cay-uses may see that you and your party are under the protection of the head chief of the Nez Perces."[5]

Although the hour was then past midnight, Lawyer moved his lodge beside the governor's tent. Other Nez Perces followed the chief's lead. His action was a pledge guaranteeing the safety of the whites.

The governor, in turn, quietly told his two most trusted men, Secretary Doty and Packmaster Higgins, of the threatened massacre. Without telling the rest of his party the reason, Stevens ordered them to make their arms ready for instant use. The commissioners, however, continued to maintain an outward show of calmness during the remainder of the conference.

Foiled by this *coup d'état,* the Cayuses and their allies did not dare attack, well knowing that a move against Lawyer, or his friends, the Americans, would bring reprisals from the entire Nez Perce nation.

Stevens asserted that Lawyer in moving his lodge averted the massacre, but A. J. Splawn, who lived among the Yakimas for fifty years and talked with many of them who had been present, says that all denied the existence of any plot. Splawn accuses Lawyer of "playing politics" for the purpose of currying favor with Stevens and so getting a larger reservation for his tribe. General Joel Palmer also contradicts the account given in the *Life of Isaac I. Stevens* by his son Hazard. In a letter written November 21, 1855, to Major General John Wool, Commander of the Department of the Pacific, Palmer says:

> The reported combination of all these tribes with intent to wage a war of extermination against the whites, is, I apprehend, but a phantom conjured up in the brains of alarmists . . . and the plot said to have been nearly consummated of cutting off those engaged in the negotiations last June, I regard as of the same character.[6]

---

[5] A. J. Splawn, *Ka-mi-akin: the Last Hero of the Yakimas*, p. 28.

[6] *House Executive Documents, Vol. XI, No. 93, 34th Congress, 1st Session*, p. 115. McWhorter, too, rejects the existence of a plot and quotes from an educated Nez Perce who likewise scoffed at the story, declaring that Lawyer became scared and moved to the white camp "to save his hide." McWhorter, *Hear Me, My Chiefs!*, p. 95.

But the uprising of most of the Columbia River bands in 1856-58 gives the lie to his letter. Also, it was known at the time that Kamiakin was the leading spirit in an attempt to organize a confederacy of all tribes in the Northwest for the purpose of driving out the whites. His plans were flatly opposed by the Nez Perce chiefs who foresaw the futility of waging war against the Americans.

Lieutenant Lawrence Kip credits Lawyer's tale of an intended massacre. "Some of the friendly Indians," he writes, "afterwards disclosed to the traders that, during the whole meeting of the Council, active negotiations were on foot to cut off the whites. This plot originated with the Cayuses, in their indignation at the prospect of being deprived of their lands."[7] In view of the Indian troubles which followed, the weight of evidence would indicate that a plot was brewing at the time of the council.

At the next meeting of the conference Lawyer, who had been appointed by Stevens as spokesman for the Nez Perces, expressed hearty approval of the treaty, only asking that the whites act toward the Indians in good faith. Young Chief and Five Crows of the Cayuses, the latter a half-brother of Tu-eka-kas, vigorously opposed it. The Indians, Young Chief objected, had no right to sell land given them by the Great Spirit and they feared to do so. He made a long and eloquent speech in which he said in part: "I wonder if the ground has anything to say? I wonder if the ground is listening to what is said?"[8]

Most of the chiefs reiterated that they did not clearly understand what was proposed by the treaty. Some of the tribes, they claimed, were not sufficiently represented, and they wanted another meeting to be held before deciding whether to accept the treaty provisions. All except

---

Yet this claim fails to hold water in view of the fact that of the 5,000 Indians present, 2,500 were Nez Perces, and the 100 whites could scarcely defend Lawyer against 2,500 non-Nez Perces.

[7] Kip, *op. cit.*, p. 24.

[8] George Fuller, *A History of the Pacific Northwest*, p. 221.

the Nez Perces asked for the council to be postponed. As later events proved the other tribes had just cause.

That evening great confusion was manifest in the Indian camps. The Nez Perces alone appeared satisfied with the government's proposals, and spent the night in festivity.

On June 8, to satisfy the disaffected tribes, the commissioners agreed to place the Umatillas, Cayuses, and Walla Wallas on a reservation in their own country. All the chiefs then consented to the treaty as modified, except Kamiakin, who had maintained a sullen silence throughout the conference.

Just as Stevens thought he had the Indians of one mind, a new difficulty arose. A small party of armed Nez Perces approached the assembled council, singing a war song and waving a fresh scalp at the end of a pole. The whites discovered the leader to be old War Chief Looking Glass,[9] who had just returned from a three years' buffalo hunt among the Blackfeet. His greeting to the other chiefs was anything but effusive. From the saddle he delivered a fierce speech.

"My people," said he, "what have you done? While I was gone, you have sold my country. I have come home, and there is not left me a place on which to pitch my lodge. Go home to your lodges. I will talk to you."[10]

The council adjourned immediately.

At the meeting next day the old man's influence was manifested in the attitude of the other Nez Perce chiefs. The Cayuses also supported him, even to his contention that he was head chief. Lawyer retired to his lodge in apparent anger. The conference again dissolved, and the Nez Perces powwowed among themselves. By vote of the majority, Lawyer's claims to head chieftainship were up-

---

[9] This was the father of the Looking Glass who became Joseph's confederate in the Nez Perce War of 1877. Young Looking Glass was about twenty-three years old at this time.

[10] Hazard Stevens, *Life of Isaac I. Stevens*, II, 54.

held, while Looking Glass was conceded to be second in authority.

Then, on June 11, Stevens called the chiefs of all tribes to assemble for a final meeting. When he addressed the Nez Perces, the governor said:

"We meet for the last time. Your words are pledged to sign the treaty. The tribes have spoken through their head chiefs, Joseph [Tu-eka-kas], Red Wolf, the Eagle, Ip-se-male-con, all declaring Lawyer was the head chief. I call upon Lawyer to sign first." Lawyer then signed the treaty. "I now call Joseph [Tu-eka-kas] and the Looking Glass." Looking Glass signed, then Joseph.[11]

Both Tu-eka-kas and Looking Glass were reluctant to do so, but were obviously under pressure from other members of their tribe.[12]

Young Joseph, however, always affirmed that his father did not sign this treaty. In his own words his understanding of it is as follows:

My father, who represented his band, refused to have anything to do with the council, because he wished to be a free man. He claimed that no man owned any part of the earth, and a man could not sell what he did not own.

Mr. Spaulding took hold of my father's arm and said, "Come and sign the treaty." My father pushed him away, and said: "Why do you ask me to sign away my country? It is your business to talk to us about spirit matters, and not to talk to us about parting with our land." Governor Stevens urged my father to sign his treaty, but he refused. "I will not sign your paper," he said; "you go where you please, so do I; you are not a child, I am no child; I can think for myself. No man can think for me. I have no other home than this. I will not give it up to any man. My people would have no home. Take away your paper. I will not touch it with my hand."

My father left the council. Some of the chiefs of the other bands of the Nez Perces signed the treaty, and then Governor Stevens gave them presents of blankets. My father cautioned his people to take no presents, for "after

---

[11] *Ibid.*, p. 58.

[12] H. Clay Wood, *Joseph and His Land Claims or Status of Young Joseph and His Band of Nez Percé Indians*, p. 42.

awhile," he said, "they will claim that you have accepted pay for your country." Since that time four bands of the Nez Perces have received annuities from the United States. My father was invited to many councils, and they tried hard to make him sign the treaty, but he was firm as the rock, and would not sign away his home. His refusal caused a difference among the Nez Perces.[13]

Tu-eka-kas' mark, however, does appear on the treaty.[14] So there are two possible explanations of Young Joseph's contentions which were made in 1878: Either he misunderstood his father, believing that he could not have signed the treaty because he did not cede the Wallowa Valley,[15] or Young Joseph confused the Treaty of 1855 with the one of 1863. The latter supposition appears the more probable because Spalding, apparently, was not present as an interpreter in 1855, although he was in 1863. Besides, Young Joseph's description agrees with the accepted historic account of the 1863 treaty which his father refused to sign.

Three treaties were completed on June 11; one with the Walla Walla, Cayuse, and Umatilla tribes; a second with the Yakima nation signed by Kamiakin; and the third with the Nez Perces, who received the largest reservation, to which their greater numbers entitled them. In return for the lands ceded outside of the reservations, the government pledged annuities such as schools, teachers, agents, sawmills and gristmills, shops, and mechanics. In addition the Indians were to receive about $650,000, out of which the Nez Perces and Yakimas received $200,000 each in the form of annuities, with salaries for head

[13] "An Indian's Views . . . ," *op. cit.*, p. 417.

[14] In a letter to the author dated January 20, 1939, P. M. Hamer, Chief of the Division of Reference of the National Archives in Washington, writes: "The usual cross mark appears with Chief Joseph's [Tu-eka-kas'] name on the original of the treaty. However, it is impossible for us to determine whether the mark was made by Chief Joseph or by someone else. The ink appears to be the same as that used for the marks of the other Indian signatories of the treaty."

[15] This treaty of 1855 guaranteed perpetual ownership of the Wallowa Valley to the band of Tu-eka-kas.

chiefs of $500 a year for twenty years. The Cayuses, Walla Wallas, and Umatillas received compensation of $150,000.

The most important provisions of the amended treaty guaranteed to the Nez Perces the exemption of their lands from settlement by whites, and the preservation of their grazing, fishing, and hunting rights on the reservation. Article III specifically stated these rights as follows:

> The exclusive right of taking fish in all streams where running through or bordering said reservation is further secured to said Indians [the Nez Perces], as also the right of taking fish at all usual and accustomed places in common with citizens of the Territory, and of erecting temporary buildings for curing, together with the privilege of hunting, gathering roots and berries and pasturing their horses and cattle upon open and unclaimed land.[16]

Article II defined the ample boundaries of the Nez Perce Reservation in these terms:

> There is, however, reserved from the lands above ceded [by the Nez Perces to the United States] for the use and occupation of said tribe, and as a general reservation for other friendly tribes and bands of Indians . . . the tract of land included within the following boundaries, to wit: Commencing where the Moh-ha-na-she or southern tributary of the Palouse River flows from the spurs of the Bitter Root Mountains, thence down said tributary to the mouth of the Ti-nat-pan-up Creek; thence southerly to the crossing of the Snake River, ten miles below the mouth of the Al-po-wa-wi River; thence to the source of the Al-po-wa-wi River in the Blue Mountains; thence to the crossing of the Grande Ronde River, midway along the divide between the waters of the Woll-low-how and Powder Rivers; thence to the Salmon River above the crossing, thence by the spurs of the Bitter Root Mountains to the place of beginning.[17]

Roughly, the Nez Perce Reservation included the present counties of Asotin in Washington, Wallowa in

---

[16] *Senate Executive Documents, Vol. XXX, No. 97, 62nd Congress, 1st Session*, p. 7.

[17] *Ibid.*, p. 6.

Oregon, and Lewis, Nez Perce, and the western half of Idaho County in Idaho. The language of the treaty was clear enough to prevent any doubt as to its meaning, although at a later date its provisions were wilfully disregarded by white squatters.

The Indians were not required to move onto their reservations until a year after Congress had ratified the treaties. The treaties were designed to open the country to white settlement in a peaceful manner, and to save, if possible, a costly Indian war. As a result of the treaty signed by the Nez Perces, their disintegration as an independent people began, for the chiefs by being signatories first agreed to sacrifice their aboriginal way of life.

Lawyer hoped that the treaty would lead to an amicable settlement of all the difficulties between the Northwest Indians and the settlers. He was determined that no act of his, or of his people, should show a breach of faith on the Nez Perces' part. Governor Stevens, too, was satisfied with the outcome of the council. He felt that honest administration of the treaties' provisions would win the confidence of the Cayuses and Yakimas, and also hold the friendship of the Nez Perces. It now remained for the United States Senate to ratify the documents.

After the treaties were signed on June 11, presents were distributed among the various chiefs, and the conference disbanded. All the chiefs, except Lawyer and his following, felt disgruntled and resentful and more restless at heart than ever. Upon receiving their gifts the various tribes began packing up and started for their home valleys.

Governor Stevens continued across the Bitterroot Mountains to make a treaty with the Flatheads, Kootenai, and Upper Pend d'Oreilles in western Montana. Old Chief Looking Glass accompanied the governor's party to Fort Benton to attend the great council with the warlike Blackfeet, the hereditary enemies of the Nez Perces.

As the years passed, Tu-eka-kas appears to have regretted signing the treaty of 1855 with increasing dissatisfaction, although he continued to maintain a peaceful attitude toward the whites.

CHAPTER V

War in the Columbia Basin—1856-58

PEACE lasted between the Indians and whites for a few months after the Council of 1855. But a sullen discontent had been brewing for several years, principally among the Cayuse tribesmen of the Walla Walla Valley. This feeling was shared by the Yakimas, farther to the west. Hordes of miners, many of whom were disreputable, were flocking into Washington. They perpetrated numerous outrages against the Indians, which provided one of the underlying causes for the conflict. Then, land-hungry settlers quite literally coveted their neighbors' lands, and the red owners naturally resented it. Dissatisfaction with the Treaty of 1855 was another contributing cause of war. Finally, white depredations and murders in western Washington led to Indian reprisals around Puget Sound. Soon the disaffection spread. In 1856 it flamed into a general uprising when most of the tribes from Spokane to the coast went on the warpath. The insurrection became known as the Yakima War.

The Nez Perces at first were divided in opinion, partly because of the propaganda spread by Chief Kamiakin of the Yakimas, who sent agents to all the tribes of the Northwest in an effort to form an Indian confederacy. This chief warned the whites not to cross the country claimed by his nation. When miners from the coast persisted in rushing across Yakima territory on their way to the Colville gold fields, Kamiakin's young men ambushed and massacred various prospecting parties.

The opening act of the war, however, was caused by the murder of A. J. Bolon, special agent for the Yakimas.

Bolon was traveling to The Dalles after holding a conference with Kamiakin, when he was overtaken by three Indians on September 23, 1855, and treacherously killed by them. His body and that of his horse were then burned. Dr. Edmond Meany in his *History of the State of Washington* places the blame for Bolon's death on Qualchan, son of Chief Owhi, a half brother to Kamiakin. But A. J. Splawn, who again bases his testimony on Indian sources, states that Bolon was murdered by Me-cheil, son of Ice, also a brother of Kamiakin.

Be that as it may, the subagent's death aroused the settlers to organize a volunteer force. Meanwhile, Major G. O. Haller was dispatched from The Dalles with eighty-four men to invade the Yakima country. He was forced to retreat after a surprise attack by the Indians. On October 30, Major Rains took the field with a force of 700 regulars and volunteers. But his campaign consisted only of "scattered skirmishing" with that faction of the Yakimas led by Kamiakin. Another detachment from Fort Steilacoom on the coast was prevented from joining Rains because of heavy snows in the mountains. So the major returned to The Dalles, and thus the campaign ended, having accomplished nothing.

In December a company of Oregon volunteers held Chief Peu-peu-mox-mox of the Walla Wallas, and six of his warriors as hostages when they approached the militia under a flag of truce. A few days later the volunteers were attacked in the Walla Walla Valley, the prisoners tried to escape, and all were killed by the guard. There followed several days of skirmishing, which became known as the battle of Frenchtown.

Governor Stevens returned from Montana in December after making treaties with the tribes in that area, and immediately raised two small regiments of state militia. Sixty-nine Nez Perces were organized as riflemen under Spotted Eagle as captain, while thirty others acted as horse guards. They supplied their own mounts and equipment. At first Stevens suspected Looking Glass of being hostile, but the old chief, on learning that Lawyer and his followers would remain friendly to the whites, apparently had a change of heart and threw in his lot with his people. The governor planned to wage a vigorous campaign against the disaffected Indians, but his efforts were hampered by the intense cold. He was forced to return to Olympia, after disbanding his Nez Perce auxiliaries.

A few sharp skirmishes occurred at the Cascades in Oregon in March of 1856. The arrival of regulars under Lieutenant Phil Sheridan dispersed the siege of the blockhouses. He managed to arrest thirteen Cascade Indians, but their Yakima allies escaped. After a military trial, Colonel George Wright had nine of them hanged. The colonel then set out on an expedition into the Yakima country, but instead of fighting he parleyed with the chiefs for peace. An armed truce resulted.

There is no evidence that Tu-eka-kas shared Looking Glass's open hostility of Governor Stevens, although he did repent of having signed the treaty. Distrustful and dissatisfied, he yet remained strictly neutral toward the Americans during the war, and gave aid neither to the Indians nor to the whites.[1]

His policy of neutrality may have been induced in part by the outcome of the battle that took place in the Grande Ronde Valley on July 17. Lieutenant Colonel Shaw's volunteer force, assisted by William Craig, the agent from Lapwai, and sixty Nez Perces under Spotted Eagle, defeated the hostile Cayuses and Walla Wallas with disastrous loss. This decisive victory of the Americans quelled for a time further outbreaks from the Yakimas, Spokanes, and Coeur d'Alenes. There were other Nez Perces besides Tu-eka-kas who seem to have been wavering in allegiance; but this Indian defeat convinced them of the wisdom of a neutral policy.

---

[1] Haines in *Red Eagles of the Northwest*, p. 143, states that a troop of cavalry under Stevens was composed entirely of Nez Perces, among them being Tu-eka-kas (Old Joseph), and that seventy other warriors served as scouts under Craig. Neither the name Old Joseph nor Tu-eka-kas, however, appears in the official muster rolls. See Stevens, *Life of Isaac I. Stevens*, p. 169.

The warring tribes had been receiving aid from an unexpected quarter, for the Mormons of Utah abetted the uprising. One of the volunteer officers discovered muskets and balls with Mormon brands on them among the hostiles. A. J. Splawn states that a member of the Bannock tribe who visited Kamiakin's camp claimed he had been sent by the Mormons "to arouse the Indians against the whites. . . . He said they wanted the Indians to kill all the whites in their land, and that they would furnish arms and ammunition."[2]

Corroboration of this statement is found in the Report to the Secretary of War for 1858-59.[3] The Mormons, according to this source, promised to furnish arms, ammunition, and civilian troops to the Nez Perces and Columbia River tribes, if the Indians would join them in a war of extermination against the territorial citizens. The negotiations were carried on secretly, the settlers little realizing how completely their fate hinged on the action of the Nez Perces.

Fortunately, Lawyer and Tu-eka-kas and the majority of the chiefs decided upon a peaceful policy, realizing that a war against the United States would be long, bloody—and futile. Besides, the Americans living around Lapwai instructed the Indians in agriculture, engaged in the mutually profitable fur trade, or taught them "spirit law," all of which redounded to their benefit. Lawyer was astute enough to realize, too, that, if the government should keep its word concerning the treaty, the Nez Perces would reap the harvest of schools, mills, and annuities.

The Mormons, unsuccessful in their attempts to arouse the Nez Perces, well understood that the refusal of this nation, the most powerful in the Northwest, to join the proposed alliance would render the Mormon-Indian entente abortive. They therefore finally withdrew their

---

[2] Splawn, *Ka-mi-akin: the Last Hero of the Yakimas,* p. 43.

[3] *Report of Secretary of War,* 1858-59, Vol. I, Part 2, Doc. 1, pp. 335, 338, 339.

proffered support and confined their activities to Utah and southern Idaho.

To prevent the Yakimas from stirring up a general uprising, Stevens established Fort Walla Walla with Lieutenant Colonel Steptoe in command. By July of 1856 there were eighteen hundred regular troops in Washington and Oregon. The governor then called another council with the Nez Perces, and invited the chiefs of hostile tribes to attend in an effort to "confirm the friendship of the Nez Perces and restrain the doubtful and wavering from active hostility."[4] This conference has become known as the second Walla Walla council. Steptoe, with four companies from the new post, acted as an escort to Stevens on this occasion.

The council opened on September 11, 1856, although the Yakima chiefs refused to attend, as did the Spokane chiefs and Looking Glass of the Nez Perces. Many other Nez Perces, however, including Tu-eka-kas, and the Cayuses and Walla Wallas were present. Kamiakin's band bivouacked on the fringe of the encampment and proved a constant menace. The meetings continued until September 17, although the whites daily feared an attack. This was no doubt prevented by the faithful Nez Perces who closely guarded the governor's party, as Steptoe's troops were encamped several miles away. At this council Tu-eka-kas and other chiefs denied that they had understood the treaty of the year before, and they asked for it to be annulled. But the governor would not heed their pleas.

Stevens could make no headway toward peace as all the Indians, except one half of the Nez Perces, remained intractable. Thus the council failed of its purpose, partly owing to the propaganda of Kamiakin, who had spread the idea that the government did not have sufficient military power to whip the Indians.

After the governor's party departed for The Dalles, they had a brush with the hostiles in which some of the

---

[4] Stevens, *op. cit.*, II, 203.

young Nez Perce braves participated. The Indians also attacked Steptoe's command, burning the grass and leaving the dragoon horses without fodder. When the two forces reunited, the hostiles were driven off. Losses on both sides were slight. Following Stevens' attempts at a peaceful solution of the Indian troubles, General Wool, through Lieutenant Colonel Steptoe, issued a proclamation closing the Walla Walla Valley to white settlement. The order remained in effect for two years.

The Indian rebellion was not completely suppressed until 1858, partly because of the lack of cooperation of General Wool, the Commander of the Department of the Pacific, who seems to have borne an old grudge against Governor Stevens. In the autumn of that year, Colonel George Wright set out from Fort Walla Walla on a punitive expedition after Steptoe's command had been cut to pieces north of there on the Snake River by a force of Yakimas and their allies. The harsh measures of Wright's campaign in the Spokane country against the Indians who had become sullen and defiant, brought about peace before the year was out.

In order to retain the friendship of the Nez Perces, Colonel Wright, with the approval of General N. S. Clarke, negotiated an offensive-defensive alliance in 1858 with minor chiefs. It guaranteed mutual support to both parties in case either was attacked by hostile Indians. The agreement provided, furthermore, that the army would supply arms and ammunition in return for the services of warriors, and if any trouble arose between the allies, they would resort to arbitration.[5] The names of Tu-eka-kas and Looking Glass are missing from the list of thirty-eight signatories, which does not necessarily mean that they opposed the alliance, although they may not have favored taking sides.

A company of thirty Nez Perces was organized by Lawyer and placed in charge of Lieutenant Mullan. The

[5] *Report of Secretary of War*, 1858-59, pp. 370, 389. Also in H. Clay Wood, *Joseph and His Land Claims or Status of Young Joseph and His Band of Nez Percé Indians*, pp. 23-24.

warriors were outfitted in regulation blue uniforms, complete to the last detail, to distinguish them from the hostiles. They rendered invaluable service to Colonel Wright on his campaign.

Largely because of the personal animosity between General Wool and Governor Stevens, the Indian treaties of 1855 were not ratified for four years. Wool held a long and an honorable service record, although he was finally relieved of his Pacific post on charges of incompetency. "When a man with such a record," Dr. Meany comments, "took up the cudgels against Governor Stevens and his Indian treaties, it is not surprising that a majority of the U. S. Senate hesitated a long time before consenting to the ratification of those treaties."[6]

The delayed ratification produced a harmful effect on the Indian signatories. It even led to a breach between one faction of the Nez Perces and the government. Their dissatisfaction, growing out of their distrust of the treaty provisions, was intensified by the Senate's reluctance to ratify the agreement. The methods of a government that commissioned an official to make a treaty, and then refused to honor his promises, aroused suspicion in the minds of the Indians. They suspected a weakness in the government's power to enforce the treaty provisions. Then the inrush of miners to Colville strengthened their fears that the whites really intended to steal the tribal lands. Their fears proved well founded when gold was discovered on the Nez Perce Reservation in 1860.

One of the wives of Chief Tu-eka-kas was a Cayuse. Naturally, his relationship with that tribe caused him to share their doubts of the white men. The contradictory statements made by military and civil officials to the Nez Perces added to his confusion of mind. In May, 1857, J. Ross Browne, a special agent of the Treasury Department, was sent by the Indian Bureau to investigate the causes of the war in Oregon and Washington. He told Lawyer that the Treaty of 1855 would be ratified by

---

[6] Meany, *History of the State of Washington*, p. 217.

the Senate. But Lieutenant Colonel Steptoe and other army officers informed their Indian friends that they had no way of knowing whether the treaty would ever be signed.[7]

Browne's statement was in contradiction to the specific instructions of James W. Nesmith, who had been appointed Indian superintendent for Oregon and Washington in 1857. Nesmith ordered the agents to impress upon the Indians that treaties negotiated with them in 1855 would be void and inoperative until the Senate should act favorably and the President proclaim the action.[8] At the same time he recommended that Congress ratify the treaties without further delay.

Young Joseph's later criticism of the government illustrates the Indians' attitude toward the ambiguities existing under a bureaucratic form of government:

> The white people have too many chiefs. They do not understand each other. They do not all talk alike.... I can not understand why so many chiefs are allowed to talk so many different ways, and promise so many different things.[9]

Governor Stevens' constant prodding finally moved the Senate to ratify the 1855 treaties on March 8, 1859. When, on April 29, President James Buchanan proclaimed their ratification, several things were established: The title of the tribes to their ancestral country was confirmed; certain specified lands were to be bought for definite sums by the government; and reservations were established, within the boundaries of which no settlers could live. The Wallowa Valley, beloved by Tu-eka-kas and his son, Joseph, was included in one of these reservation areas.

The patience of the loyal Nez Perces was most remarkable and commendable during the four years between the signing and ratifying of the document. However, the

---

[7] *Report of Secretary of War, 1858-59*, p. 332. Colonel Steptoe's report of October 19, 1857.

[8] *Op. cit.*, p. 333. Letter of J. W. Nesmith of October 18, 1857.

[9] "An Indian's Views of Indian Affairs," *North American Review*, April, 1879, p. 431.

damage had already been done, for the government's procrastination had bred distrust and suspicion among a certain faction of the tribal leaders, notably Tu-eka-kas, Looking Glass, Eagle-from-the-light, Red Heart, and White Bird.

Just prior to the ratification, Congress had admitted Oregon into the Union as a state. The Snake River marked its eastern boundary, so the lands of Tu-eka-kas were included in the new state. Because of the pending ratification of the treaty, however, jurisdiction remained jointly under the federal government and the Nez Perces, and thus completely free from Oregon authority.

Agent A. J. Cain notified Chiefs Tu-eka-kas, Looking Glass, and White Bird of Buchanan's proclamation at the tribal council ground on Weippe prairie in Idaho. Tu-eka-kas told the agent he was pleased that the treaty had been ratified, not for himself, but because it ensured a home for his children and their children's children.[10] The chiefs naïvely believed their homes were secure from white squatters. However, the band of Tu-eka-kas, known as the "Lower" Nez Perces, refused to accept any of the annuities sent to them after the ratification of the treaty.

Although the Indian agent promised by the treaty was on hand to direct the Nez Perces' welfare at Lapwai, none of the pledged annuities arrived. Only part of them came in the following year of 1860. In his report to the Commissioner of Indian Affairs concerning the behavior of certain Nez Perces, Edward R. Geary, the superintendent for Oregon, accuses a faction within the tribe at Lapwai of not exhibiting cordial approval of the cession of their lands. He further complains that this faction had "evinced a spirit of insubordination and sullen opposition to the wishes of the agent, and made vigorous efforts to spread disaffection through the tribe . . ."[11] because of

[10] *Report of Commissioner of Indians Affairs*, 1859, pp. 420-21. Report of Agent Cain.

[11] Report of Secretary of Interior, 1859-60, *House Executive Documents, No. 1, 36th Congress, 2nd Session*, p. 403. Report of Edward R. Geary of October 1, 1860.

the long delay which attended the ratification of the treaty. Geary also adds that the degrading vice of intemperance had extended among the Indians at Lapwai, although the government expressly promised to prevent the sale of liquor to them. More concerned than the superintendent by the spread of intoxication were the chiefs, who did everything in their power to suppress this traffic in spirits.

The lack of cordial approval by a faction of the "Upper" Nez Perces, as those on the Lapwai Reservation were known, was no doubt due to the fact that the government had not furnished the promised supplies. Besides, groups of prospectors were roaming their reserve in north Idaho. One party found large quantities of gold along Orofino Creek, a tributary of the Clearwater River. The word flashed across the Northwest, and hordes of miners rushed to the new bonanza. Five to ten thousand of them, according to estimates, had stampeded there by the fall of 1861. The eastern part of the reservation soon had more whites than the total population of the Nez Perce nation. Driven by the mad lust that knows no restraint, the miners disregarded every article of the 1855 treaty which interfered with their pursuit of treasure.

The pleas of the Indians to the government to drive out the whites went unheeded for two years. The agent wrote: "I could fill page after page in portraying the number and nature of the outrages the Indians and their families were subjected to."[12] Indeed, he did fill several pages regarding the abuses suffered by the Nez Perces at the hands of the miners.

B. F. Kendall, superintendent of Indian Affairs for Washington Territory, frankly stated that he was powerless to control the situation. "To attempt to restrain miners would be, to my mind, like attempting to restrain the whirlwind,"[13] he admitted.

---

[12] Wood, *op. cit.*, p. 24.

[13] Report of Secretary of Interior, 1861-62, *House Executive Documents, No. 1, 37th Congress, 3rd Session*, p. 448. Report of B. F. Kendall in 1862.

Thus the fears of the Indians "that their country was about to be occupied by the whites without their receiving the consideration agreed upon"[14] were justified. The lands reserved for tepee villages were covered by mushroom mining towns.

Although the encroachment of miners was probably first in the list of grievances against the government, the Upper Nez Perces had many reasons to protest the administration of tribal affairs in 1860. Geary even added his complaint to that of the Indians about the supplies they received, which were "damaged in transportation. Had one half of the amount laid out in these purchases been expended in opening farms on the reservations, and the buying of stock cattle and sheep, it would have inured vastly to the benefit of the Indians."[15]

In addition, the management of reservation affairs by the Indian agent was anything but satisfactory. Superintendent Kendall's report of 1862 concisely stated conditions:

> Not far from sixty thousand dollars have been expended by the agent heretofore in charge of this tribe [the Nez Perces], and I regret to say that the visible results of this liberal expenditure are meagre indeed.
>
> The buildings erected by Mr. Cain for the agency and employés were mere shells, hardly fit for human habitations, and the want of comfort displayed can only be accounted for on the ground that the agent did not make the reservation his headquarters, and consequently felt little, if any, interest in the matter.
>
> ... I sought in vain to find the first foot of land fenced or broken by him or his employés; and the only product of the agricultural department that I could discover consisted of some three tons of oats in the straw, piled up within a rude, uncovered enclosure of rails, to raise which must have cost the government more than seven thousand dollars. Even this property was barely saved by the present agent from the hands of the departing employés, who claimed it as the result of their private labor.

[14] Report of Secretary of Interior, 1859-60, p. 395. Edward R. Geary's report to the Commissioner of Indian Affairs.

[15] Report of Secretary of Interior, 1859-60, p. 410. Report of Edward R. Geary.

As I witnessed the withdrawal from this meagre pile of the rations for my horse, I could hardly fail to sigh to think that every movement of his jaws devoured at least a dollar's worth of governmental bounty.[16]

The promised supplies reached the long-suffering Nez Perces in 1861, but the next year they were cut off again because of the Civil War. The government's resources were consumed in that terrific struggle to preserve the Union. The Indians demanded that the treaty obligations be fulfilled. When they learned of the great conflict, however, they realized the government's inability to keep its promises that year.

The deplorable mismanagement of reservation affairs at Lapwai caused Chief Tu-eka-kas and his twenty-one-year-old son, Joseph, rapidly to lose faith in the government. The old man's distrust was justified, and he began to manifest an attitude of passive hostility toward the whites. To salve his discontent, Tu-eka-kas led his people to the plains of central Montana to hunt the buffalo. Other disaffected chiefs did the same.

The prospects of the journey must have thrilled the heart of Young Joseph, savoring as it did of raids and battles with the Sioux, as well as the dangers of the chase.[17] Preceding such an expedition, the Nez Perces never celebrated any "medicine" ceremonies.[18] When all preparations of packing, and food-gathering were completed, the tribe followed their ancient trail across the Bitterroot Mountains and down the Lolo Canyon. They

[16] Report of Secretary of Interior, 1861-62, *op. cit.*, p. 447. Report of B. F. Kendall.

[17] Joseph's familiarity with the buffalo country is conjectural. Documentary evidence records but one visit, that in the spring of 1874 or 1875 along the Yellowstone River; this is indicated in Monteith's letter to Smith, dated March 1, 1875, preserved in the Lapwai files. It is quite possible, however, that Joseph may have accompanied his father on previous visits, although it is unlikely that they made as frequent visits as did the bands of Chiefs Looking Glass and White Bird.

[18] This information is based on the account of the Nez Perces' hunting habits found in Curtis, *The North American Indian*, Vol. VIII.

made a leisurely trek, pausing to visit friends and relatives among the Flatheads. After they crossed the main divide of the Rocky Mountains, their route led to the Judith Basin, favored by the Nez Perces for their buffalo-hunting grounds.

Since they were crowding the territory claimed by the fierce Blackfeet, sentinels kept a sharp watch to prevent a surprise attack. Every day the herald rode through the village, crying his morning and evening speech:

People, remember that when we come to the Buffalo country, we are in danger of war at all times. Our young men must be alert and guard well the camp. Do not let the enemy get the best of you! All young persons, post yourselves and keep watch! Post yourselves on high peaks, and keep watch on the ravines! Now, we shall all be on guard; so if the enemy are seen, we shall be ready for battle. We are liable to be put to death at any minute, so we must keep good watch. Our women and children are liable to be killed at any minute, so all of you must try to guard them.[19]

While sentinels watched the countryside for signs of enemy tribesmen, scouts searched the plains for traces of the huge, shaggy buffalo. Upon locating the herd the riders galloped madly back to the village to report. At the news warriors leaped upon the bare backs of their hunting ponies, and were followed by the women on foot. Whenever possible, the scouts stampeded the animals in the direction of the hunting party. If this could not be done, the warriors followed the trail until they could charge the buffalo. Then a mad race ensued, and we can well imagine that the athletic Young Joseph would not be the last in the chase.

As they closed in, the hunters shot their arrows with true aim to the vital spot behind the shoulders, killing as many of the beasts as the tribe would need. Then the women came along on foot, noting the arrows to learn what warrior had killed which buffalo.[20] The markings

---

[19] Boas, *Folk-Tales of Salishan and Sahaptin Tribes*, p. 201.

[20] When the tribe was badly in need of meat, they tried to

on the arrows revealed the identity of the successful hunter. Because the use of arrows enabled the women to recognize the identities of the hunters, and because ammunition was expensive, they did not use guns to kill the shaggy animals.

The women skinned the carcasses, tanned the hides for robes or lodge coverings, and cut the meat into long strips. These strips of flesh were preserved by drying on racks in the sun. When mixed with marrow, the compound—called pemmican—furnished food for the winter months. The Nez Perces did not use dried berries in their preparation of pemmican, as was the custom among various other aborigines.

Upon the return of the tribe to the Nez Perce country, the band celebrated the successful hunt by giving feasts to their friends who had remained at home. The large number of hides owned by Joseph testified to his prowess as a hunter of buffalo.

---

stampede the buffalo over a precipice so as to kill them *en masse*. Failing this, they resorted to the use of spears; and in this case it was not considered necessary for the women to identify the particular hunter who killed each animal. Spinden, "The Nez Percé Indians," *Memoirs of the American Anthropological Society*, Vol. II.

CHAPTER VI

The Treaty of 1863

FOLLOWING the ratification of the 1855 treaty in 1859, the government, as mentioned in the preceding chapter, disregarded its treaty obligations to the Upper Nez Perces. Indian agents and supertendents, as already shown, made bitter complaints in their annual reports to the Commissioner of Indian Affairs. Mills and buildings promised by the treaty, they pointed out, had not been constructed; Lawyer's salary as head chief was in arrears; work done on the required church was not paid for, nor were the several thousand dollars' worth of horses furnished by the Nez Perces for the Yakima War of 1856-58. These conditions continued year after year, the agents complained, while settlers were constantly encroaching on Nez Perce territory. The Indian lands were overrun by miners, traders, farmers, and stockmen who disregarded reservation boundaries and the rights of the red men. White men took Indian women to live with, then deserted them and left their half-breed children as a burden on the tribe.

To the number of chiefs already angry over the broken pledges, there were now added others who were emboldened to hostility by the rumors set afloat by Southern sympathizers among the miners, who declared that the federal government was bound to collapse. Together, these discontented chiefs had a following of about twelve hundred. It required strenuous efforts on Lawyer's part to keep his faction loyal to the government.

The government, being unable to supply annuities because of the Civil War, appointed a commission to negotiate a new treaty in 1863, and to adjust these matters.

The commissioners included Calvin H. Hale, superintendent of Indian Affairs for Washington Territory; Agents Charles Hutchins and S. D. Howe; and Robert Newell, a friend of the Indians and later agent at Lapwai.

Again Lawyer represented about two thousand of the Nez Perces in the council called at Lapwai for May 15. Tu-eka-kas, Eagle-from-the-light, Three Feathers, Big Thunder, and Coolcoolselina were present to protect the interests of their disaffected bands. The conference was halted at its very beginning, because the Indians demanded Perrin Whitman, whom they trusted and who was then in the Willamette Valley, as interpreter. There was a delay of two weeks before his arrival.

Fort Lapwai—which had been established in the autumn of 1862—was garrisoned for the council with four companies of the First Oregon Cavalry. About four miles from the fort the government furnished a tent city for over three thousand delegates of the Nez Perce nation, at the site of the original Lapwai mission station.

Upon Whitman's arrival the meetings were resumed. The commissioners asked the Indians to cede more land to the government. The proposed cession comprised about 10,000 square miles and included mines and rich agricultural land in Oregon and Washington, and large areas in Idaho. This would have reduced the reservation to five or six hundred square miles in the vicinity of the South Fork of the Clearwater. The Indians were to receive the usual annuities in goods and implements. As one voice the nation objected to having its reservation so drastically cut, so the commission agreed to double the size first proposed.

Tu-eka-kas remained absent for a few days, but sat in the council after Lawyer adroitly expressed his views. The lands to be ceded included Joseph's beloved Wallowa Valley, the summer home of Tu-eka-kas' band in the state of Oregon. Because of the spreading influence among the disaffected chiefs of the Earth-Mother, or Dreamer,[1]

[1] The Dreamer religion will be discussed in the next chapter.

religion, the Nez Perces were more fondly attached to the land than the average tribe. Unlike the Plains Indians, the Nez Perces were but seminomadic, and love of the homeland of their fathers was deeply cherished in their hearts.

Differing views over the reservation question between the Upper and Lower Nez Perces caused a rift in the friendly relations of the various bands, so the commissioners withdrew from the council. This changed Lawyer's attitude, which at first had been one of confidence in his ability to bargain shrewdly for his own ends. He suggested a counterproposition of his own to the commissioners. On June 3 Hale again called a grand council with all the chiefs present, except Eagle-from-the-light, who, however, was represented by a deputation of his warriors.

The meetings continued for several days, and once more it became evident that the dissenters were growing defiant. Commissioner Hutchins told them "that their sullen and unfriendly manner was the occasion of the disagreements among the Nez Perces, and that although they might persist in refusing to accept their annuities, as they had done heretofore, such action would not release them from the obligations of the treaty they had signed in 1855." Naïvely, Agent Hutchins neglected to mention that since the government had repeatedly violated its treaty obligations in past years, such violation constituted an abrogation, and therefore any of the Nez Perces were within their legal rights to renounce the document.

The dissenting chiefs did not alter "their attitude of passive hostility" toward the commission. Instead, they withdrew from the council. Matters now became threatening, and the commissioners feared the defection of the entire nation. Becoming apprehensive for their own safety, they dispatched a message to the fort requesting a guard. A detachment of cavalry under Captain Curry immediately responded, arriving at the council ground shortly after midnight. The soldiers found everything quiet, although at one of the principal lodges fifty-three chiefs and headmen had assembled to hold earnest debate. The arguments revolved around the question of whether to accept or reject the proposed treaty. Being still unable to reach an agreement by daybreak, the head chiefs on each side dissolved their confederacy "in a solemn but not unfriendly manner." After shaking hands all around they separated. The seceders were Tu-eka-kas, Eagle-from-the-light, Big Thunder, Coolcoolselina, and their headmen.[2]

Thus ended on June 7, 1863, the federation of the Nez Perce nation. With its termination the authority of Chief Lawyer no longer extended to the four seceded bands. The dissenters did not consider any subsequent promises made by Lawyer as binding upon themselves. Henceforth, Tu-eka-kas and the other seceders recognized the terms of the Treaty of 1855 alone. This splitting up of the bands had an unfortunate effect on the Nez Perce nation. Since they could no longer count on the support of the entire confederation, they were weakened in any future bargaining with the government. Consequently their claims no longer carried as much weight as before.

The commissioners learned what had taken place between the different factions. They continued negotiations with Lawyer and his followers and concluded a new treaty on June 9. Its provisions reduced the reservation to one sixth of its former size and included the cession of the Wallowa Valley. The Indians were to receive $260,000 for the lands ceded, in addition to the annuities already due them.[3] Lawyer and Big Thunder signed the treaty, since their homes at Kamiah and Lapwai, respectively, were reserved to them.

That one word "home" caused the Nez Perce nation to split. H. Clay Wood has analyzed the sacred meaning of

---

[2] Much of the foregoing is drawn from the *Works of H. H. Bancroft*, XXXI, 487-88. Bancroft states that although Big Thunder seceded from the confederacy of the Nez Perce nation, he did sign the revised treaty of 1863 because its provisions preserved his home at Lapwai.

[3] Charles J. Kappler, *Indian Affairs, Laws and Treaties*, pp. 843-48.

that word to the followers of Tu-eka-kas and other non-treaty chiefs:

To the parties of the treaty, it brought no loss, no change; to the non-treaties it revealed new homes, new scenes; it left behind deserted firesides; homes abandoned and desolate; casting a shadow upon their wounded and sorrowing hearts to darken and embitter their future existence. In this God-given sentiment—the love of home—is to be found the true cause of the Nez Perce division.[4]

Young Joseph, in his own words, explains the attitude of his father regarding this treaty:

My father was not there. He said to me: "When you go into council with the white man, always remember your country. Do not give it away. The white man will cheat you out of your home. I have taken no pay from the United States. I have never sold our land." In this treaty Lawyer acted without authority from our band. He had no right to sell the Wallowa (winding water) country. That had always belonged to my father's own people, and the other bands had never disputed our right to it. No other Indians ever claimed Wallowa.[5]

Although Lawyer and his headmen may have been justified in selling to the government Asotin Valley in Washington and considerable territory in Idaho, they were without legal right in disposing of Wallowa Valley in Oregon. In the form of an allegory illustrating the injustice of Lawyer's act, Young Joseph offers an irrefutable argument:

If we ever owned the land we own it still, for we never sold it. In the treaty councils the commissioners have claimed that our country had been sold to the Government. Suppose a white man should come to me and say, "Joseph, I like your horses, and I want to buy them." I say to him, "No, my horses suit me, I will not sell them." Then he goes to my neighbor, and says to him: "Joseph has some

[4] Wood, *Joseph and His Land Claims or Status of Young Joseph and His Band of Nez Percé Indians*, p. 41.

[5] "An Indian's Views of Indian Affairs," *North American Review*, April, 1879, pp. 417-18.

good horses. I want to buy them, but he refuses to sell." My neighbor answers, "Pay me the money, and I will sell you Joseph's horses." The white man returns to me, and says, "Joseph, I have bought your horses, and you must let me have them." If we sold our lands to the Government, this is the way they were bought.[6]

After the Lapwai council of 1863 the two factions of the Nez Perces went their separate ways. Thereafter they became known as the treaty and nontreaty Indians. Chief Lawyer upheld the government and tried to keep his people loyal; Chief Tu-eka-kas and his Wallowa band of nontreaties continued to refuse their annuities. Nor did they confine themselves to reservation boundaries. Instead they pursued their seminomadic habits and preserved their "rugged individualism" in the best of American traditions. The people of Tu-eka-kas spent their winters in the Imnaha Valley and the summers in Wallowa, as their ancestors had been accustomed to do for generations. However, the two factions at first maintained neutral relations and exchanged visits, and the young people intermarried.

Tu-eka-kas returned to Wallowa after the council and planted poles around the valley he claimed, which was about fifty miles wide. "Inside," he declared, "is the home of my people—the white man may take the land outside. Inside this boundary all our people were born. It circles around the graves of our fathers, and we will never give up these graves to any man."[7]

On April 20, 1867, President Andrew Johnson proclaimed the ratification of the 1863 treaty. In the mean-

---

[6] *Ibid.*, pp. 419-20.

[7] *Ibid.*, p. 418. Although Young Joseph himself is authority for the statement that his father planted poles around the valley he claimed, J. H. Horner is more specific. He states: "Old Joseph built a rock monument around poles in two different places on each side of the trail on top of the Wallowa Hill to show his lines to his Wallowa country, which whites later called 'Joseph's Dead Line.' Different early settlers told me of stopping on their way to the valley and examining them. There were a few monuments of rocks built besides, but only two with poles." Letter to author, December 17, 1945.

time, the government had still neglected to fulfill the provisions of the first document of 1855.

Neither the treaty nor nontreaty Indians needed keen eyesight to see that no school was maintained at Lapwai from 1864 to 1868; that annuities were not being paid; and that agency affairs were handled in such an inefficient way that even the most loyal Nez Perces became disgusted.[8]

Even government investigators were appalled by these conditions, which were due to the negligence and incompetency of Caleb Lyon, governor of Idaho and ex-officio superintendent of Indian Affairs during 1867, who had been absent from his office in Boise since early in the spring. His inefficiency drew severe criticism from J. W. Nesmith, who stated in his report to the Commissioner at Washington: "When present, he [Lyon] conducted them [Indian affairs] with an ignorance unparalleled, and a disregard of the rights and wants of the Indians, and of the laws regulating intercourse with them, deserving the severest rebuke."[9]

The nontreaty Indians denounced the government for its repeated violation of promises, and ridiculed the child-like faith of their Lapwai brethren. Their words aroused a number of treaty Nez Perces, who complained of their grievances to Agent O'Neill. Not receiving the satisfaction they expected, their protests turned into open threats. They were urged on by the nontreaties.

O'Neill called a council with the reservation chiefs. His report to the Commissioner of Indian Affairs describes the seriousness of the disaffection then prevailing among the treaty faction:

The most of the other leading chiefs declined saying anything, leaving it for "Lawyer" to do. "Lawyer" of

[8] Report of Secretary of Interior, 1862-63, *House Executive Documents, No. 1, 38th Congress, 1st Session*, pp. 556-57. Report of Superintendent C. H. Hale, dated September 1, 1863, Olympia, Washington Territory.

[9] *Condition of the Indian Tribes*, Report of the Joint Special Committee, Congressional Report, Appendix, 1867, p. 10. Report of J. W. Nesmith.

course, in obedience to the commands of his chiefs, was compelled to speak in a manner foreign to his feelings; and I can here say truly that had not "Lawyer" spoken as he did, had he shown in his speech the least inclination towards favoring the government in their non-payment of the annuities due his people, had he urged his people, as in times past, to live up to this treaty as they had former ones, and to keep the laws as the Nez Perces ever had, *he would not have lived forty-eight hours after:* I know this to be true; I know that some of his own people would have killed him. As "Little Dog," one of the chiefs of the Blackfeet was killed for *his* friendship to the whites, so "Lawyer" would have been sacrificed. Since the above was written I can see the disaffection growing. They want to know if some "big war will not be again commenced to put off matters for a few years." I can truthfully say that these Indians will not be put off with promises any longer, some of the leading chiefs (Lawyer's chiefs too) will fight if they do not see something done for them soon. The non-treaty side use these arguments (these promises and non-payments) to urge them on to committing some act, which when commenced will be hard for them to back out of.[10]

Still the Indian Bureau procrastinated. In the following year Lieutenant J. W. Wham, appointed agent at Lapwai, regretfully reported that the Nez Perces no longer had faith in the government's pledged word. Since the 1863 treaty was unsatisfactory, Chiefs Lawyer, Utsemilicum, Timothy, and Jason traveled to Washington, D. C., to make a supplemental treaty on August 13, 1868.[11] The government agreed to reimburse the tribe for twenty thousand dollars, which Governor Caleb Lyon claimed had been stolen while in his possession. This loss had necessitated the closing of the school from 1864-68.

The Interior Department renewed its promises to sur-

[10] Report of Secretary of Interior, 1865-66, *House Executive Documents*, p. 250. Italics are those of the agent. Perhaps the leading instigator of war propaganda among the nontreaties was White Bird (a confederate of Joseph in the war of 1877). In his report O'Neill refers to him as a subchief; he was really a chief. White Bird went to Montana after the council of 1863, but voluntarily returned to the reservation in November, 1865.

[11] Kappler, *op. cit.*, pp. 1024-25.

vey the land, so that Indians and whites should know exactly their respective boundaries. But this, too, proved as delusive as the other governmental pledges. The surveyors, with the least possible exertion, marked off the land as suited their fancy, and made no attempt to lay out farm boundaries in the manner provided by the treaties. Regarding this, Colonel De L. Floyd Jones, superintendent of Indian Affairs for Idaho, wrote in his report to the Commissioner, General E. S. Parker: "As now surveyed . . . the work is entirely useless, and the expenditures will be for the benefit of the contractor rather than the Indians. Both the Agent, Captain D. M. Sells, and myself protested against the survey as now going on, but without avail; it is clearly not within the intent or wording of the treaty."[12] An investigating committee frankly admitted: "It was a most scandalous fraud. . . . The Government cannot be a party to such frauds on the people who intrust it with their property."[13]

In the light of all the evidence, the remarkable feature of these relations between the government and the treaty Nez Perces during the fifteen years from 1855 to 1870 is the amazing restraint that was exercised by the chiefs in keeping their people from resorting to guns to exact justice. Certainly the government would not have tolerated any breaches of faith on the Indians' part such as its own officials had been guilty of toward the Nez Perces.

From 1868 the Secretary of the Interior instructed the Lapwai agents to inform Chief Tu-eka-kas that his nontreaty faction was expected to vacate the Wallowa Valley and move onto the greatly reduced reservation. Officials of the Indian Bureau maintained that since Lawyer had signed the Treaty of 1863 as head chief of the Nez Perces, all bands of that nation, whether they were individually signatories or not, were subject to the

[12] Report of Secretary of Interior, 1869-70, *House Executive Documents, No. 1, Part 1, 41st Congress, 3rd Session*, p. 646. Report of Colonel De L. Floyd Jones.

[13] Report of Secretary of Interior, 1872-73, p. 159. Report of Special Commission.

provisions of that document. Government officials applied the parliamentary bible, *Robert's Rules of Order*, to a race that had never heard of such procedure. Evidently the commissioners had no knowledge of Nez Perce character or customs. Among these Indians, as pointed out previously, although a majority might agree to a particular course of action, the minority were at liberty to do as they saw fit. This custom even extended to the warpath—no Indian was forced to fight an enemy if he had no hatred of the foe, or if his "medicine" prophesied disaster.

Because of the treatment accorded the reservation Indians by the government, Tu-eka-kas ignored the orders of the constantly changing agents. He refused to place his welfare in the hands of men who either failed through their own dishonesty, to perform the work they were paid to do, or who were unable to do so because of the lack of cooperation of the federal government, which failed to help those agents who conscientiously tried to fulfill their duties. Upon learning that the Indian Bureau's committee had decided Lawyer's act in signing the treaty was binding upon all the Nez Perce bands, Tu-eka-kas, it is said, tore up a copy of the 1863 treaty and destroyed his New Testament.[14] Thus he definitely broke his friendly relations with the whites.

Young Joseph shared the views of his father. He had reached manhood's estate, for when the council of 1863 was held, he was twenty-three years old. At full growth he possessed an athletic figure and a handsome, intelligent face. He stood six feet two inches in his moccasins, weighed two hundred pounds, and was broad of shoulder and deep of chest. With a square chin, finely shaped features, and black piercing eyes he was an Indian Apollo. He had a dignified and quiet demeanor, and he clung to the aboriginal habit of wearing his hair in two long braids over his shoulders.

That Joseph accompanied his father to the council of

---

[14] Letter from Monteith to Walker, August 27, 1872, in Lapwai Agency files.

1863 and there met his future first wife may perhaps be deduced from the fact that his first child, a baby girl later known as Sarah Moses, was born in 1865. The mother was a daughter of Chief Whisk-tasket of the treaty Nez Perces at Lapwai.[15] In accord with their tribal courtship customs, the lovers told their parents that they intended to marry. Young Joseph then went to the chosen maiden's father and asked for his consent to the match. If he had not been the son of a great chief, his parents would have had to obtain permission for him from the parents of the girl. Then his father would have had to arrange the time of marriage and offer Whisk-tasket gifts of blankets or horses. But being a desirable suitor, Joseph himself could approach his prospective father-in-law with his request. Whisk-tasket gave his consent and waived the presents.

There is no record to indicate whether Young Joseph utilized his privilege of taking his girl-bride to his lodge at once, or whether he waited an interval of several days. He probably left that to the wishes of his heart's desire. In any event, the young couple spent a honeymoon lasting two or three weeks. Then the bride informed her parents that she would come home on a certain day.

In Whisk-tasket's lodge the women made great preparations for the nuptial feast. The chief killed a variety of game, while his wives and daughters picked gallons of berries. When the appointed day arrived, the bride, accompanied by her husband's family, went to the lodge of her parents. She was gaily dressed for the occasion in her finest garments. Joseph's people brought presents with them, and in return for these gifts they would receive others of equal value. Nearly everyone in the village partook of the feast which the bride's relatives had prepared, and all shared in the distribution of presents. The young wife got her start for housekeeping by receiving the horn spoons used at the feast.

Perhaps a month or so later, Joseph's family would give a feast in honor of the bridal couple. These repasts would

[15] *Report of Secretary of War*, 1877, I, 115.

not be repeated when Joseph took another wife, as they were held only for the first marriage.[16]

The non-Christian Nez Perces commonly practiced polygamy, and so it is not surprising that Joseph, like his father, married four times during his life. His various wives were Wa-win-te-pi-ksat, I-a-tu-ton-my,[17] Aye-at-wai-at-naime[18] (Good Woman), and one other whose name has been lost to history. In these unions Joseph became the father of nine children—five girls and four boys. All except two girls died in infancy. Of these, one apparently died in her youth, and the other, Sarah Moses, lived to maturity and married, but passed on without leaving issue.[19]

Regarding the first two wives named above, Inspector McLaughlin says:

> . . . When [Looking Glass] was killed, Joseph honored his memory by taking to wife his two widows—they were with the old chief at Nespelim, on the Colville Reservation, when I visited there, [which was in June and July, 1900].[20]

Although Joseph ruled the men, he did not always have the final say in his household, if we can judge by his statement: "When you can get the last word with an echo, you may have the last word with your wife."[21]

---

[16] The information regarding marriage customs is based on Spinden, "The Nez Percé Indians," *Memoirs of the American Anthropological Society*, II, 250-51.

[17] Meany, "Chief Joseph, the Nez Perce," Master of Letters thesis. Dr. Meany's investigations corroborate McLaughlin's statement that these two wives were with Joseph at Nespelem, Washington. One of the widows of Looking Glass married Joseph in the Indian Territory.

[18] This name was furnished by Baptiste Parris, Flathead Reservation, Montana, to Judge William I. Lippincott, in an interview conducted for Howard and McGrath. However, Samuel Tilden, of Arlee, Montana, a Nez Perce child survivor of the war of 1877, states in a letter to the author that this name is "Iatowinnai," meaning "Woman Walking."

[19] This information relating to Joseph's family is based on the source investigations of Dr. Edmond S. Meany, and recorded in his Master of Letters thesis. One of Joseph's children, Dr. Meany reports, "died since living at Nespilem, two died in Indian Territory and the rest died in Idaho."

[20] James McLaughlin, *My Friend the Indian*, p. 349.

[21] From an article on the death of Joseph, New York *Sun*, September 25, 1904.

CHAPTER VII

The Tah-mah-ne-wes Beckons

As TU-EKA-KAS began to grow blind and feeble, he relied more and more on Young Joseph to assume his duties as chief of the Wal-lam-wat-kin band in the Wallowa Valley. This business of being a chief was no easy task, since the young men were incensed at the encroachments of stockmen whose herds occupied their grazing lands. Settlers had moved into the territory marked off by Tu-eka-kas, and they refused to leave when ordered off by the old chief and his son. Disputes frequently arose concerning the ownership of cattle claimed by both whites and Indians.

Relations with the treaty Nez Perces had also become strained. The nontreaty group taunted the treaty Indians for their loyalty to an unreliable government. Young Joseph's diplomatic powers were severely taxed to maintain peace with the treaty faction of his tribespeople and to prevent his men from precipitating bloodshed with the settlers.

To add to the young chieftain's troubles, the agent at Lapwai began insisting in 1868 that the Wallowa band should move onto the reservation. But Tu-eka-kas and Joseph had witnessed too much dissatisfaction with agency administration among the treaty Indians to accept Lapwai for a home. Consistently, father and son turned a deaf ear to all removal orders.

The nontreaty group, numbering about five hundred in Young Joseph's band at this time, found in their religious beliefs further justification for their refusal to move. Among the Nez Perces a new faith had arisen, preached by the prophet, Smohalla (Shmoquala). He was, in a sense, a forerunner of Freud, as he asserted that divine revelation came from dreams. Those who professed his cult thus became known as "Dreamers." Being subject to catalepsy, he capitalized his misfortune by declaring these spells were the visible evidence of his communication with the Tah-Mah-Ne-Wes, or Great Spirit. Joseph's tribesmen all became followers of this "Dreamer" religion.[1]

It was an auspicious moment for an Indian Moses to arise. James Mooney has clearly expressed this need in his study of the Ghost Dance religion:

> From time to time in every great tribe and at every important crisis of Indian history we find certain men rising above the position of ordinary doctor, soothsayer, or ritual priest, to take upon themselves an apostleship of reform and return to the uncorrupted ancestral beliefs and customs as the necessary means to save their people from impending destruction by decay or conquest.[2]

Smohalla's religion offered a panacea to the distraught people. The prophet was a member of a band of two hundred Indians closely related to Joseph's Wal-lam-wat-kins; and to them he was both medicine man and chief. General Howard, who met him on several occasions, thus describes Smohalla: "He is a large-headed, hump-shouldered, odd little wizard of an Indian, and exhibits a strange mixture of timidity and daring, of superstition and intelligence."[3] William McLeod, another authority on Indian religious beliefs, says of him:

> About 1850, when he was about thirty years old, he began teaching a millennial doctrine, his ideas or revelations apparently having evolved independently of influences from the messianism of the eastern tribes.[4]

After the Indian uprising of 1856-58, sometimes called the Yakima War, Smohalla left his tribe and his people

---

[1] William C. McLeod, *American Indian Frontier*, p. 500.

[2] James Mooney, "The Ghost Dance Religion," *Fourteenth Annual Report, Bureau of American Ethnology*, Part I, p. 309.

[3] Howard, *Chief Joseph: His Pursuit and Capture*, p. 40.

[4] McLeod, *op. cit.*, p. 522.

and wandered from band to band. When he returned to the Nez Perces he began to preach his gospel of passive resistance to white civilization. He condemned his tribesmen for adopting agriculture and stock raising, basing his philosophy on the widespread conception among Indians that the earth was their mother. He declared to his people, reports James Mooney, that

> . . . the Sa' ghalee Tyee [Tah-Mah-Ne-Wes], the Great Spirit Chief Above, was angry at their apostasy, and commanded them through him to return to their primitive manners, as their present miserable condition in the presence of the intrusive race was due to their having abandoned their own religion and violated the laws of nature and the precepts of their ancestors.[5]

The prophet promised his people an Indian would rise up to drive out every white person and would raise to life all the dead Indians. This latter idea had been current among the various tribes for many years. Wily Smohalla undoubtedly incorporated it into his teachings so as to appease the subconscious desires of his people.

The prophet had a persuasive manner of speaking, at times attaining oratorical eloquence, and so impressive was his speech that he held the Indians spellbound. Even white men who could not understand a word spoken were entranced by the tonal beauty of his impassioned discourse. He won hundreds of converts, although his religious philosophy never spread beyond a limited area in the Northwest. Yet the Dreamer religion still exists and is practiced by many highly educated Indians.

Smohalla's religion is described by Mooney as a system "based on the primitive aboriginal mythology and usage, with an elaborate ritual which combined with the genuine Indian features much of what he [Smohalla] had seen and remembered of Catholic ceremonial and military

---

[5] Mooney, *op. cit.*, p. 719. The term given by Mooney, "Sa' ghalee Tyee," is the Chinook word for the Great Spirit. Nipo Strongheart, a Yakima Indian chief and an ethnologist of repute, stated to Howard and McGrath in 1934 that the Nez Perce word is Tah-Mah-Ne-Wes."

parades, with perhaps also some additions from Mormon forms."[6] To this might be appended the essentials of spiritualism.

Smohalla, to render more impressive his public religious ceremonies, used a heraldic flag and the ringing of bells. The mystic numeral seven was an essential feature in the arrangement of the congregation, as the men knelt in rows of seven behind the prophet, who was flanked by six altar boys dressed in white. Along the walls of the lodge-church the women, also, were arranged in groups of seven. Bell ringers started and ended each song with a certain number of rings, and tinkled the bells while the people sang. Loud testimonials, familiar to religious revivals in much more civilized sects, provided the personal touch.

That the prophet's philosophy of the Earth-Mother made an especial appeal to the warriors may be understood from the nature of some of Smohalla's doctrines:

> My young men shall never work. Men who work cannot dream; and wisdom comes to us in dreams. . . . You ask me to plow the ground. Shall I take a knife and tear my mother's bosom? You ask me to dig for stone. Shall I dig under her skin for her bones? You ask me to cut grass and make hay and sell it and be rich like white men. But how dare I cut off my mother's hair?[7]

A knowledge of this deeply engrained religious belief is important for an understanding of Nez Perce history, because in the War of 1877 the nontreaty Indians were fighting not merely for the homeland of their fathers, but for that same land made sacred to them by their religion. Hence, when the crisis came, the war advocates had a powerful argument: the tenets of the Dreamer faith were irreconcilable with the land-tenure system as practiced by the whites. One or the other must go; and this was the reasoning by which the *tewats,* or medicine men, swayed the disaffected chiefs in the decisive war councils.

---

[6] *Ibid.*

[7] *Ibid.,* p. 716.

The differences in religion between the nontreaty group, many of whom were "Dreamers," and the treaty Indians, most of whom were "Christians," added to intertribal friction. The reservation or treaty Indians, however, were even more divided among themselves as to the respective saving graces of the Catholic and Protestant faiths. One of the most vexing problems facing the administration of Indian affairs in the Northwest was the missionary question. In order to put an end to the duplication of missionary work on the reservations by the various rival religious denominations, the government finally apportioned the reservations so that each sect would have an exclusive sphere of influence over one or more tribal reservations. At the time of this allotment the Presbyterians were given the monopoly of carrying salvation to the Nez Perces. The Indians, however, were permitted to continue the practice of the faith of their choice without interference.

In the midst of controversies between white settlers and Indians, between Christian treaty and Dreamer nontreaty tribesmen, Young Joseph successfully maintained a peaceful policy without jeopardizing his freedom from reservation control. His father's increasing infirmities had necessitated transferring the responsibilities of chieftainship upon his broad shoulders before he was thirty.

Then tragedy came to Joseph in 1871.[8] Tu-eka-kas, old and sightless, lay dying in his lodge; he knew the Great Spirit was preparing his spirit home for him. Chief Joseph, with touching sentiment and restraint, has described the death of his father:

---

[8] Some historians assert that Tu-eka-kas died in 1873. This claim is apparently based on a letter written by Agent John Monteith to H. Clay Wood, and dated May 15, 1876, in which Monteith states: "Old Joseph died either on December 1872 or in Jany 1873. I think it was in Jany. 1873." However, Assistant Adjutant General Wood in his report, also written in 1876 after a meeting with Chief Joseph concerning the latter's land claims, says the old chief died in 1871 and was buried in Wallowa Valley. This statement carried the most weight as it comes directly from Young Joseph. Tu-eka-kas, besides his name of Joseph, was also known as "Wal-lam-mute-kint," according to Wood. Indians often change their names due to events in their lives. See p. 48 of Wood's *Status of Young Joseph*.

Photo taken by the author, August, 1940

Monument to Tu-eka-kas, Chief Joseph's father, at Lake Wallowa, Oregon.

. . . my father sent for me. I saw he was dying. I took his hand in mine. He said: "My son, my body is returning to my mother earth, and my spirit is going very soon to see the Great Spirit Chief. When I am gone, think of your country. You are the chief of these people. They look to you to guide them. Always remember that your father never sold his country. You must stop your ears whenever you are asked to sign a treaty selling your home. A few years more, and white men will be all around you. They have their eyes on this land. My son, never forget my dying words. This country holds your father's body. Never sell the bones of your father and your mother." I pressed my father's hand and told him I would protect his grave with my life. My father smiled and passed away to the spirit-land.

I buried him in that beautiful valley of winding waters. I love that land more than all the rest of the world. A man who would not love his father's grave is worse than a wild animal.[9]

For a time the body of the old chief lay in state, dressed in fine clothes and decorated with ornaments and necklaces. Probably his face was painted, in accordance with an ancient custom of his tribe.[10] The widows of Tu-eka-kas, dressed in soiled and tattered clothing, mourned their departed spouse. They cut off their long braids of hair and threw them into the fire.

After an interval of two days the chief's body was tightly wrapped in deerskin and laid upon poles. This rude bier was then carried on the shoulders of four warriors to where a grave had been dug. Tu-eka-kas' sorrowing relations and friends followed his remains, the women voicing their grief in loud wails.

The warriors lowered the corpse into the grave with the head to the east.[11] Beside the opening a shaman, or medi-

---

[9] "An Indian's Views of Indian Affairs," *North American Review*, April, 1879, p. 419.

[10] The old custom of painting the corpse was abandoned at some undetermined period, probably only gradually with the passing of years. Curtis, *The North American Indian*, VIII, 160, indicates that it was no longer done in the 1870's.

[11] An old Indian woman told J. H. Horner, historian of Wallowa Valley, that Old Joseph died in August and was buried on the south slope of the forks of Wallowa and Lostine rivers. Another

cine man, spoke a few words in praise of the deeds of Tu-eka-kas. Then the grave was covered with split cedar staves, on top of which stones were heaped. As a final protection against prowling coyotes, numerous upright cedar pickets were thrust between the stones. The wives and four daughters of Tu-eka-kas, and Joseph and Alokut probably, threw many trinkets into the grave. Then the Earth-Mother was spread over the corpse of her son. In the old days the favorite horse was killed and left near by. Possibly because of the influence of white civilization, the Nez Perces adopted a new custom of laying a stuffed effigy of a horse over the grave.[12] Thus Chief Tu-eka-kas was buried in the valley of winding waters in accordance with the customs of his tribe.

The sad family and friends returned slowly to the village. To prevent the ghost of the dead from bringing madness to the living, the lodge was moved to another location at once. The medicine man then performed the Pasapukitse ("his blowing the ghost away") ceremony of blowing smoke from a pipe in all corners to disperse the ghost spirit before the family entered their home. Those who had touched the corpse had to spend a week in the sweat lodge in order to purify their blood.[13]

Indian woman claims Old Joseph died in October in his sleep. Three white settlers took part in the burial ceremony. Eventually the old chief's remains were removed to the hill at the foot of Wallowa Lake, where a monument was dedicated to him on September 26, 1926.

[12] Early white settlers in Wallowa Valley told Mr. Horner that one horse was killed and a stake run through its body to hold it upright over the grave. Another horse was also killed and laid beside it. Apparently this was done to show greater honor and respect to the influential old chief.

In a letter, October 20, 1941, Mr. Horner further amplifies Nez Perce burial customs. "The Indians," he writes, "killed a good horse every year for several years. The Indians told the settlers it was for the purpose of Joseph having a fresh horse in the happy hunting grounds. The one you mentioned [i.e., the first horse referred to in this footnote] was told me by Aaron Wade who came here [Wallowa Valley] in the seventies. He said this horse dried up and when the wind blew the hide and bones would rattle."

[13] The information regarding burial customs is based on Spinden, "The Nez Percé Indians," *Memoirs of the American Anthropological Society*, II, 251-54.

Mr. Horner, however, implies that these traditional customs were

A month later the family gave a great feast, to which all the friends of the late chief were invited. Many of the personal belongings of Tu-eka-kas were given to the guests. So ended the burial ceremonies.

Joseph's people continued their peaceful occupation of the Wallowa Valley, despite the increasing number of settlers. In filial obedience to his father's wishes the young chief refused all annuities for his band. The Nez Perce agent, John B. Monteith, reported in August of 1872: "... the non-treaty portion, with a very few exceptions, reside on the outside of the reserve, along the Snake River and its tributaries. They never ask for assistance, and take nothing from me, except, perhaps, a little tobacco."[14]

About this time the reorganized Indian Bureau granted to the various sects the privilege of choosing someone from their own denomination as reservation agent. In 1871 the Presbyterian Church selected John B. Monteith, and his appointment was ratified by the government. Of course, the Catholic Nez Perces objected to this choice and accused Monteith of "sectarianism." Yet he probably managed reservation affairs to the best of his ability and tried to perform his duties conscientiously. Such efforts were in marked contrast to the work of a few of his predecessors. He died August 7, 1879, and was buried at Spalding, Idaho.

---

not strictly followed. In a letter to the author, December 17, 1945, he writes that Old Joseph "took sick on north side of the Wallowa River and was immediately moved to the south side at their large camp in forks of Wallowa and Lostine Rivers. Died in night and was buried the next day on the top of the ridge. And that night his remains were moved down the ridge and buried again—where I dug up the remains in September, 1926, and buried them under the Monument at the foot of Wallowa Lake. The grave [i.e., the original grave] was fenced with Balm poles as there is very little Cedar in this county. There were two posts set at each corner and boughs woven in between each two posts, and brush and poles laid on top, then stone. This was told me by A. V. McAlexander whose father homesteaded the land in 1875 and this pen was still there. I have seen Indians buried on Imnaha and that was the way they built their pen around a grave."

[14] Report of Secretary of Interior, 1871-72, *House Executive Documents, Vol. I, 42nd Congress, 3rd Session,* p. 655.

In 1873 the government made a determined attempt to persuade Joseph to move onto the reservation, as both stockmen and Indians in the Wallowa Valley were growing restless and dissatisfied with the presence of the other. T. B. Odeneal, superintendent of Indian Affairs for Oregon, acting under instructions of the Secretary of the Interior, held a council at Lapwai on March 27 with the young chief and the agent. This was the first conference in which Joseph, then thirty-three years old, represented his people. With shrewd logic he well acquitted himself.

They had orders, the commissioners informed him, from the Great White Chief at Washington for the Nez Perces to go upon the Lapwai Reservation. If he obeyed, the government would help his people in many ways, but first he would have to move to the agency. To these arguments Joseph replied:

> I did not want to come to this council, but I came hoping that we could save blood. The white man has no right to come here and take our country. We have never accepted any presents from the Government. Neither Lawyer nor any other chief had authority to sell this land. It has always belonged to my people. It came unclouded to them from our fathers, and we will defend this land as long as a drop of Indian blood warms the hearts of our men.[15]

When Odeneal and Monteith insisted that he *must* move to Lapwai, Joseph answered:

> I will not. I do not need your help; we have plenty, and we are contented and happy if the white man will let us alone. The reservation is too small for so many people with all their stock. You can keep your presents; we can go to your towns and pay for all we need; we have plenty of horses and cattle to sell, and we won't have any help from you; we are free now; we can go where we please. Our fathers were born here. Here they lived, here they died, here are their graves. We will never leave them.[16]

The commissioners, favorably impressed with the char-

---

[15] "An Indian's Views . . . ," *op. cit.*, p. 418.
[16] *Ibid.*, pp. 418-19.

acter of Chief Joseph as well as the logic of his arguments, discussed with him the possibility of making the Wallowa Valley into a reservation. They offered the usual government annuities as an inducement for the tribe to become civilized. Their offer, however, was rejected by the chief for various surprising reasons. Odeneal relates the following conversation in his report to the Secretary of the Interior:

Joseph was asked: "Do you want schools or school houses on the Wallowa Reservation?"

The chief answered: "No, we do not want schools or school houses on the Wallowa Reservation."

Commissioner: "Why do you not want schools?"

Chief Joseph: "They will teach us to have churches."

Commissioner: "Do you not want churches?"

Chief Joseph: "No, we do not want churches."

Commissioner: "Why do you not want churches?"

Chief Joseph: "They will teach us to quarrel about God, as the Catholics and Protestants do on the Nez Perce Reservation and at other places. We do not want to learn that. We may quarrel with men sometimes about things on this earth, but we never quarrel about God. We do not want to learn that."[17]

Joseph won his first verbal battle with the government by convincing Commissioners Odeneal and Monteith that he was in the right, and that it would be impracticable to remove his people. Upon their recommendation President Grant issued an executive order on June 16, 1873, withdrawing Wallowa Valley from settlement as public domain.[18] However, the tract did not include all the land claimed by Joseph, nor all the area which the commissioners had recommended. It excluded the headwaters of the Wallowa and Imnaha rivers, Wallowa Lake, and the territory adjacent to the left bank of the Grande Ronde River.[19]

---

[17] Helen Hunt Jackson, *A Century of Dishonor*, p. 127. Requoted from the Report of Secretary of Interior, 1872-73.

[18] Wood, *Joseph and His Land Claims or Status of Young Joseph and His Band of Nez Percé Indians*, p. 33.

[19] *Ibid.*, pp. 31-32.

Monteith tried to induce Joseph's band to settle permanently near Wallowa Lake. Joseph, though, asked the agent's permission to visit Washington during the fall of 1873, for the purpose of taking the matter up with the President. For some reason Agent Monteith refused the chief's request.[20]

In September, Monteith reported: "Joseph and band have spent the greater part of the summer in the Wallowa Valley and will remain there until snow falls."[21] It was the habit of Joseph's people to spend the winters in the Imnaha Valley, which was closer to the Snake River gorge and which, being sheltered, had a milder climate. This valley was recognized by other Indians as belonging to the Wal-lam-wat-kins. In the summer the Wallowa was shared with visiting tribes of Nez Perces, but Joseph's band alone asserted their claim to ownership. Neither the nontreaty nor treaty Indians disputed Joseph's sole claim.

In Monteith's report quoted above, he protested to the Commissioner of Indian Affairs the nomadic life of Looking Glass's nontreaty band:

> Some measures ought to be adopted whereby the Indians can be prevented from going to the buffalo country. A party has just come in with great stories of how they whipped a party of Sioux and captured mules, horses, etc., creating quite a desire on the part of many to go back next spring and try their hand at it.[22]

Such expeditions, sometimes lasting one or two years, seriously interfered with the agent's efforts to civilize the reservation Indians.

Upon pressure brought by white settlers, Governor L. F. Grover of Oregon wrote to the Secretary of the Interior

---

[20] Letter from Monteith to Walker, November 22, 1873, in the Lapwai files.

[21] Report of Secretary of Interior, 1872-73, *House Executive Documents, Vol. I, 43rd Congress, 1st Session,* p. 613. Report of John B. Monteith.

[22] *Ibid.,* p. 614. Monteith was referring, of course, to young Chief Looking Glass, about forty-one years old at this time.

on July 21, 1873, protesting Grant's revocation order. The Wallowa Road and Bridge Company and the Prairie Creek Ditch Company owned improvements in the valley which, together with those of stockmen, amounted to $67,-860, according to the assessment made by the Department of the Interior. These interests, apparently, were behind the move to oust the Indians.

The following excerpts are taken from Grover's letter:

By this amendatory treaty (1863) the Nez Perces tribe relinquished to the United States all the territory embraced in the reservation created by the treaty of 1855, which lay within the boundaries of the state of Oregon, including the said Wallowa valley; so that on and after said 9th day of June, 1863, the Nez Perces tribe did not lawfully hold or occupy any land within the state of Oregon. . . .

I learn that young Joseph does not object to going on the reservation at this time, but that certain leading spirits of his band do object, for the reason that by so doing they would have to abandon some of their nomadic habits and haunts. The very objection which they make is a strong reason why they should be required to do so; for no beneficial influence can be exerted by agents and missionaries among the Indians while they maintain their aboriginal habits. . . .

JOSEPH'S BAND DO NOT DESIRE WALLOWA VALLEY FOR A RESERVATION AND FOR A HOME. I understand that they will not accept it on condition that they shall occupy it as such. . . . This small band wish the possession of this large section of Oregon simply for room to gratify a wild, roaming disposition and not for a home.[23]

While Grover advances seemingly strong arguments for the removal of Joseph's band, a study of his statements reveals numerous fallacies here, as in the rest of the letter. In the first place, his contention that the Nez Perces did not own the Wallowa Valley after June 9, 1863, is patently incorrect. After careful consideration

[23] *History of North Idaho*, pp. 46-47. The full text of Governor Grover's letter is quoted therein. The italicized capitals are supposedly Grover's.

of all the facts, Major Henry Clay Wood, the Assistant Adjutant General to the Commander of the Department of the Pacific, made an official report on the matter directly contrary to Grover's assertion. Wood states:

> The non-treaty Nez-Perces cannot in law be regarded as bound by the treaty of 1863; and in so far as it attempts to deprive them of a right to occupancy of any land its provisions are null and void. The extinguishment of their title of occupancy contemplated by this treaty is imperfect and incomplete . . . this title of occupancy is "as sacred as the fee simple, absolute title of the whites."[24]

If failure of one party to fulfill treaty provisions nullifies a document, then the government had already abrogated its treaties with the Nez Perces. On this point Wood further states: "The Nez Perces, undoubtedly, were at liberty to renounce the treaty of 1855 (and probably the treaty of 1863), the Government having violated the treaty obligations."[25]

Again the governor's statement asserting Joseph's willingness to move onto a reservation is diametrically the opposite of all government reports, which show Joseph to be emphatically opposed to reservations. Naturally the Indians desired to maintain their "nomadic habits," for freedom of movement is a human urge in practically every race. Had the governor given due consideration to the matter, he would have realized that these same nomadic habits in the white race had been responsible for populating his own state of Oregon, with the thousands of pioneers who crossed the plains in covered wagons. Assuredly, he must have known the whites were not "indigenous to Oregon."

As to the "beneficial influence" exerted by "agents and missionaries," that is a moot question. It must be remembered that the aboriginal morals of the Nez Perces were very high. Their agent remarked that the tribe "in general avoids its [civilization's] vices to a greater extent than

---

[24] Wood, *op. cit.*, p. 45; second part of quotation from p. 7.

[25] *Ibid.*, p. 44.

is usual among Indians."[26] Certainly, the actions of those agents who diverted the Nez Perce funds could exert no exemplary influence on such a tribe. Nor were all the missionaries of the high caliber of Dr. Marcus Whitman and Father Pierre Jean De Smet, although it may be granted that, as a whole, they were actuated by spiritual motives.

It is true that Joseph's band did not want Wallowa Valley for a "reservation," as his people were definitely opposed to any form of reservation control. But Grover made a grossly incorrect statement when he declared that Joseph and his people did not desire the Wallowa "for a home." Never did the chief renounce his claims to Wallowa as the home of the Wal-lam-wat-kins. On the contrary, Joseph's desire to remain at home in that beloved valley of winding waters became the wellspring of his life.

Grover's letter further revealed that the disputed territory was nearly as large as the state of Massachusetts. The governor emphasized that such an extensive area should not be granted to the Indians, as the few hundred natives would interfere with the growth of settlements in the region. At the time approximately eighty families were settled in Wallowa Valley proper, so the argument about overcrowding was ridiculous. Even today the valley has few towns of any consequence. The largest place, Enterprise, has less than fifteen hundred population, while Imnaha Valley is practically a wilderness roamed by sheepherders with their flocks. And yet the fallacious and ridiculous arguments of Governor Grover were accepted by the Commission of 1876. Acting on its recommendation, the government forced the removal of Joseph's band from Wallowa.

[26] Report of Secretary of Interior, *House Executive Documents, No. 4, Special Session*, 1867, p. 13.

CHAPTER VIII

The Earth-mother Drinks Blood

IN THE winter of 1872-73 news of the Modoc Indian uprising in western Oregon and northern California reached the Nez Perces. This rebellion stirred all the tribes throughout the Northwest as well as the white settlers. Nontreaty bands of Nez Perces assembled in Paradise Valley, near where the Grande Ronde River flows from Oregon into Washington, to discuss their future course if the insurrection should become general. They supplemented their councils by digging roots and gathering berries. However, the agitation of the malcontents among the nontreaties wore away in talk, and no hostile action resulted.

The following year (1874), the Nez Perces held another meeting at the Weippe prairie in Idaho near the start of the Lolo Trail to Montana. The nontreaties used to gather there annually to engage in trading, gambling, collecting the camas roots, and horse racing. But this time they met for a "long talk."

Agent Monteith suspected that trouble might eventuate from the gathering, and so he attended the conference, escorted by a company of cavalry from Fort Lapwai under Captain David Perry. Starting on July 4, the meetings lasted several days, but the appearance of troops probably intimidated the malcontents among the chiefs and the parleys abruptly ended.

Brief though it was, this council is important for revealing the dissatisfaction in White Bird's band. It also indicates that he had been active for several years in spreading war propaganda among the nontreaty Indians. As to the subjects discussed at this powwow, we have the account of Grizzly Bear Ferocious, who relates:

Three years before the council with General Howard in 1877, while I was down on Snake river, word came that there was to be a dead feast at Tipahliwam, and I was wanted there. The word came from ... Rainbow, and ... Shot Five Times, both brave and well-known warriors like myself. We three were to speak before the council of the chiefs. I did not know what it was about. The house of the feasting was of nine fires. When the Kamiahpu, who were church Indians, heard that there was to be a feast, they came, but although they were not refused admission to the feast, when it was time for the council guards were posted around the council-house, that none of them might spy on us and hear what was said. Jim Lawyer, son of the old Lawyer, was their chief.

... Before this council and feast, White Bird had been going to the country of Joseph and Alokut and discussing with them the possibilities of successful war with the white people. Others had gone to Waiilatpu, and others even to the Shoshoni, our old enemies. After the council with General Howard, nobody had any intention to fight. Joseph, Alokut, White Bird—all had made up their minds to go to the reservation.

The council was held at night. White Bird, Tuhulhutsut, Joseph, Alokut, Looking Glass, and others were there. Joseph, son of the Joseph who signed the treaty of 1855, was chief of the bands on upper Snake river, and particularly of the Inantoinnu [Wal-lam-wat-kins], who were at the mouth of the Grande Ronde. Alokut was his younger brother. White Bird was chief of the Lamtama, on White-bird creek, and was the most influential man among the Salmon River bands. Tuhulhutsut was a tiwat and chief of the Pikunanmu, on Snake river above the mouth of the Imnaha, and Looking Glass, son of the Looking Glass who was present at the council of 1855, was chief at Hasotoin [Asotin]. After the chiefs had assembled, we three warriors were called before them. White Bird sat at the end. This did not signify that he was of any more importance than the others. Looking Glass said: "Brothers, you have been called to hear our plans. The question is, if the Waiilatpu [Cayuses, Umatillas, and Walla Wallas], the people of Moses [Sinkiuses], and ourselves shall fight with the white people. This plan is before the council-house today. We have called you to come and speak."[1]

[1] Curtis, *The North American Indian*, VIII, 13-14.

When White Bird requested that he express his views, Grizzly Bear Ferocious spoke in favor of peace. White Bird then asked several other chiefs to speak. Finally Looking Glass said: "*Aa*, brothers, I do not like to fight the white man." Another old chief voiced this same opinion. No one else spoke, and the council terminated.

Fate, or the unknown power that guides the destiny of a people, relentlessly entangled Joseph's hapless band in a web of unfortunate circumstances. In the first place the combined efforts of Governor Grover and the Oregon congressman, in behalf of their constituents, changed the attitude of President Grant and the Secretary of the Interior toward Wallowa. The Interior Department recommended a revocation of the executive order of 1873. The President, on June 10, 1875, issued a new proclamation throwing open the Wallowa Valley to white settlement, and once again took away from Joseph's people their exclusive right to it. The valley of winding waters became known as Union County, from which Wallowa County, embracing the valley of that name, was carved in 1887. Henry Clay Wood said of the President's action: "If *not* a crime, it *was* a blunder. In intercourse with the Indian, it is not wise to speak with a forked tongue."[2]

The summary revocation order perplexed and angered the Nez Perces. However, the presence of Major John Green's two troops of cavalry averted trouble in the valley when Joseph's band made their summer visit to Wallowa for purposes of fishing and grazing their ponies. After a short stay the detachment returned to its post. According to Captain Whipple, when Joseph learned of Grant's decision,

> . . . he looked disappointed, and after a short silence he said he hoped I could tell something of a possible doubt of their being obliged to relinquish this valley to the settlers. I told him the case was decided against the Indians by higher authority than that of any army officer. This

---

[2] Wood, *Joseph and His Land Claims or Status of Young Joseph and his Band of Nez Percé Indians*, p. 34.

declaration did not make the countenances of the Indians more cheerful.[3]

In 1875 General Oliver O. Howard,[4] the new Commander of the Department of the Columbia with headquarters at Fort Vancouver, for the first time met Joseph, against whom in two short years he was to be aligned in the hardest-fought campaign known to Indian warfare. Howard was on a tour of inspection of the military posts of the Northwest. Joseph and ten warriors were visiting Young Chief at the Umatilla Agency in northeastern Oregon, and requested an interview with the new "long-knife chief," thinking that the latter, perhaps, could shed some light on the President's contradictory order. The general writes that the Nez Perces were

. . . carefully dressed in Indian costume. . . . At the time I was out of doors with the agent, looking at his buildings. The Indians first approached in single file, Young Joseph ahead. One after another took the agent's hand, and then mine, in the most solemn manner. Joseph put his large black eyes on my face, and maintained a fixed look for some time. It did not appear to me as an audacious stare; but I thought he was trying to open the windows of his heart to me, and at the same time endeavoring to read my disposition and character. . . . I think that Joseph and I became then quite good friends. There was at the time little appearance of that distrust and deceit which some

---

[3] J. P. Dunn, Jr., *Massacres of the Mountains*, p. 637.

[4] Oliver Otis Howard was born at Leeds, Maine, November 8, 1830, and died at Burlington, Vermont, October 26, 1909. He entered West Point in 1850 and was graduated fourth in his class, in 1854. He participated in the first battle of Bull Run in Virginia. At Fair Oaks he lost his right arm. He took part in the action at Second Bull Run, South Mountain, Antietam, Fredericksburg, Chancellorsville, Chattanooga, and Gettysburg. During Sherman's march through Georgia, Howard commanded the right wing. He was promoted to brigadier general in the regular army in 1864, with brevet rank of major general.

In 1874 he was placed in command of the Department of the Columbia. He became Superintendent of West Point in 1880. He was promoted to major general in 1886 and placed in command of the Division of the East, a post he held until his retirement in 1894.

The author is no known relation of General Howard's. On the contrary, her paternal grandfather, Adolphus Howard, served with General Lee's Army of Virginia.

time afterward very strongly marked his face, especially while listening to white men in council.[5]

After a short chat, the Indians took their leave. Following this visit, Howard wrote in his first report to the Secretary of War:

The troubles at Lapwai, and at Wallowa Valley, have not thus far resulted in bloodshed; but it has been prevented by great carefulness on the part of government agents. . . . I think it a great mistake to take from Joseph and his band of Nez Perces Indians that valley. The white people really do not want it. They wished to be bought out. . . . Possibly congress can be induced to let these really peaceable Indians have this poor valley for their own.[6]

But these "peaceable Indians" continued to have their own difficulties in remaining so. Agent Monteith writes of an erroneous report sent out by the settlers of the Wallowa Valley in February of 1876. They had telegraphed the governor of Oregon that Joseph's band was driving off and killing stock and threatening the citizens. General Howard had responded by dispatching two troops of cavalry to the valley. Upon investigating the rumors Monteith found them to be even more than the opposite of the truth. In his report to the Commissioner of Indian Affairs, he states:

Joseph and most of his band have been spending Xmas and New Years in the vicinity of the Agency attending feasts and having a good time generally, and at no time have they been more than twenty miles from the Agency, and were here at the time that the trouble was said to have taken place in the Wallowa Valley, in connection with them.[7]

The Indians, Monteith further explained, had driven cattle back into the hills that had come along with herds of Indian ponies. Foreseeing future troubles, the agent

---

[5] Howard, *Chief Joseph, His Pursuit and Capture*, p. 29.

[6] *Ibid.*, p. 31.

[7] Original letters of John B. Monteith, in Idaho State Historical Library, Boise, Idaho.

again urged the Military Department of the Columbia to force the nontreaties to move onto the reservation in order to prevent more friction with stockmen.

Another link in the chain of unfortunate incidents was forged when two settlers in the Wallowa Valley, A. B. Findley and Wells McNall,[8] believed their horses had been stolen by Indians of Joseph's band. The whites took their rifles and set out to search for the animals on June 23, 1876. On reaching the Indian village they met several warriors, among them, We-lot-yah, who objected to their accusation that Nez Perces had stolen their horses. A bitter argument ensued and the unarmed We-lot-yah attempted to wrest the gun from McNall when he threatened the Indians. McNall called to Findley to help him. Findley fired, and We-lot-yah fell dead. The two men then made a hasty escape from the village.

McNall was a quarrelsome, quick-tempered man, and it is significant that the Indians blamed him for the murder. The missing horses were found quietly grazing near the Findley ranch.

In a letter to General Howard, dated July 3, 1876, Agent Monteith reported the trouble and stated that the attack had been entirely unprovoked by the Indians. It was, he wrote, a case "of willful, deliberate murder." He asked Howard for troops "to protect the Indians while fishing."[9] It would appear that certain settlers in the Wallowa Valley deliberately tried to provoke the Nez Perces to committing some act of reprisal, hoping thus to obtain an excuse for the Indians' forcible removal. In speaking of these troubled times, Joseph says:

> They [white men] stole a great many horses from us, and we could not get them back because we were Indians. The white men told lies for each other. They drove off a great many of our cattle. Some white men branded our young cattle so they could claim them. We had no friend who would plead our cause before the law councils. It

[8] *Report of Secretary of War,* 1877, I, 7, 579. Report of General of the Army. Mr. J. H. Horner, in a letter, August 28, 1941, gives the date of the killing as June 6.

[9] Monteith, original letters.

seemed to me that some of the white men in Wallowa were doing these things on purpose to get up a war. They knew that we were not strong enough to fight them. I labored hard to avoid trouble and bloodshed. . . . When the white men were few and we were strong we could have killed them all off, but the Nez Perces wished to live at peace.

We have had a few good friends among white men, and they have always advised my people to bear these taunts without fighting. Our young men were quick-tempered, and I have had great trouble in keeping them from doing rash things. I have carried a heavy load on my back ever since I was a boy.[10]

In the meanwhile the Wal-lam-wat-kins held a council. Young warriors demanded revenge—a life for a life. Pleas by Joseph and the old men for a peaceful settlement met deaf and malicious resistance on the part of the young men. How could they expect justice from the white man's tribunals? Had not thefts of cattle and land clearly showed the rapacious greed of the whites, and were the evil-doing settlers not supported by the government chiefs? These impassioned orators, standing in the light of the campfire, aroused other hot-tempered young men to a feverish pitch of excitement.

As the harangue grew more clamorous the slight figure of a woman quietly rose and moved to the center of the assembly. She, the daughter of the murdered We-lot-yah, raised her hand to speak. Simply, her voice saddened by her recent tragedy, she pleaded, "My friends, we do not wish other people or our other friends to be killed for the killing of one person, so let us drop the matter."[11] It was a brave, unselfish gesture, and no doubt had the calming effect of oil on raging waters.

---

[10] "An Indian's Views of Indian Affairs," *North American Review*, April, 1879, pp. 419-20.

[11] Report of Secretary of Interior, 1911, *Executive Documents, No. 97, 62nd Congress, 1st Session*, p. 112, "Memorial of the Nez Percés Indians." From the notarized statement of Stot-Ka-i (also spelled Stot-Ka-Yai) made on July 10, 1911. He also spoke of another murder of an Indian over a dispute concerning land and improvements made by this Indian. Stot-Ka-i, however, was in error in respect to the settlement of the argument over the death of We-lot-yah, as Joseph went ahead and made his ultimatum.

Nevertheless, Chief Joseph sent an ultimatum to the whites in the valley demanding surrender of the guilty men. If, within a week's time, this demand was not complied with, he threatened to destroy the farms of the settlers. As the deadline drew near the ranchers prepared for war and appealed to the army post at Walla Walla to come to their rescue. Forty whites collected at McNall's ranch, ready to resist an Indian attack.

Lieutenant Albert G. Forse with forty-eight regulars of Company E, First Cavalry, arrived on the day of retribution set by Joseph. Forse left his troops at a ranch five miles from Joseph's camp, which was located at the foot of Wallowa Lake. The lieutenant took two men, Jim Davis and Thomas H. Veasey, with him and rode on to the Indian village. Davis would act as interpreter. They met the chief and his men, all of whom were "mounted and posted on a long, flat bluff, which now overlooks the town of Joseph."[12] All the Indians except Joseph were stripped to the waist and daubed with war paint.[13]

Accompanied by Davis and Veasey, Forse advanced to meet the chief for a parley between the lines. After considerable discussion Joseph willingly agreed to withdraw his threats and to keep his men on the south side of Hurricane Creek, if the whites would stay on their north bank of the stream. Forse was favorably impressed with Joseph and the justice of his case. The lieutenant promised to use his influence to bring the accused men to trial before civil authorities.

Having reached an amicable agreement, the troops went into camp, while the Nez Perces washed off their war paint. The military continued peacefully to occupy the valley until the last of September, when they returned to Fort Walla Walla.

The truce, though, did not lessen the resentful feeling among the Indians. So tense did the situation become that Major, later Colonel, Henry Clay Wood—ac-

[12] J. H. Horner and Grace Butterfield, "The Nez Perce-Findley Affair," *Oregon Historical Quarterly*, March, 1939, p. 49.

[13] *Ibid.*, p. 46.

companied by Captain David Perry, First Cavalry, commanding officer at Fort Lapwai; Assistant Surgeon Jenkins A. Fitzgerald; and Lieutenant (Brevet Colonel) William R. Parnell, First Cavalry—held a conference with Joseph at Umatilla on July 23, 1876. The chief frankly stated his case to the officers, declaring that

> ...it was true one of his brothers had been killed by whites in Wallowa Valley; that the Indian who was killed was much respected by the tribe, and was always considered a quiet, peaceable, well-disposed man; that the whites who killed him were bad, quarrelsome men, and the aggressive party; that the whites in the valley were instigated by those in authority, and others in Grande Ronde Valley, to assault and injure the Indians while fishing and hunting in that section of country; that he wished the white man who killed the Indian brought to the agency to be there confronted with his accusers.
>
> Joseph said that among the Indians the chiefs controlled the members of their band, and had power to prevent bad Indians doing wicked things; and he reasoned that those in authority over the whites had, or should have, the same control over white men, and hence the white authorities in the vicinity of Wallowa Valley and elsewhere were directly responsible for the killing of his brother; that his brother's life was of great value; that it was worth more than the Wallowa Valley; that it was worth more than this country; that it was worth more than all the world; that the value of his life could not be estimated; nevertheless, that now, since the murder had been done, since his brother's life had been taken in Wallowa Valley, his body buried there, and the earth had drunk up his blood, that the valley was more sacred to him than ever before, and he would and did claim it for the life taken; that he should hold it for himself and his people from this time forward, forever; and that all the whites must be removed from the valley.[14]

This council drew forth censure from Agent Monteith, who maintained that Joseph had at first not seemed much concerned over his tribesman's death, and had

[14] *Report of Secretary of War*, 1877, I, 7-8. Report of General of the Army.

decided to press his advantage and become demanding only because of the importance given the affair.

It became evident to the Department of the Interior that Joseph was determined to assert his rights to the valley, and that he would hold the United States and Oregon officials responsible for any future murders or depredations committed by the settlers. Major Wood was able to adjust matters to some extent by telling Joseph that the white men would be tried in that vicinity, and that Indians would be summoned as witnesses.

The accused murderers were eventually brought to trial at Union (Oregon), where a jury of ranchers acquitted them. The Indians, it is said, refused to testify against Findley, who was a peaceable man and a friend of Joseph's.[15] This verdict, however, aroused other Nez Perces to demand that the men be surrendered to them and tried according to tribal law. Of course, the settlers refused to comply, and the feeling of resentment and unrest persisted. It led to a second council in November of 1876. Howard asked that another commission be appointed to "settle the whole matter before war is even thought of."[16]

On this occasion the Interior Department appointed a commission consisting of D. H. Jerome, of Saginaw, Michigan, as chairman; Brigadier General O. O. Howard; Major H. Clay Wood; William Stickney, of Washington, D. C.; and A. C. Barstow, of Providence, Rhode Island, "to visit these Indians, with a view to secure their permanent settlement on the reservation, their early entrance on a civilized life, and to adjust the difficulties then existing between them and the settlers."[17]

The council was held in the mission church at Lapwai. Joseph and his brother, Alokut, with several headmen and *tewats,* or medicine men, attended the conference. The commissioners said of Joseph: "An alertness and

---

[15] Horner and Butterfield, *op. cit.*, p. 50.

[16] Howard, *Chief Joseph, His Pursuit and Capture*, p. 32.

[17] Helen Hunt Jackson ("H H"), *A Century of Dishonor*, p. 125.

dexterity in intellectual fencing was exhibited by him that was quite remarkable."[18]

Several times during the protracted meetings Joseph and Alokut seemed willing to agree to the proposals of the committee. But the powerful influence of the belligerent *tewats* overcame their hope for compromise and they refused to relinquish their claims to Wallowa. This put the commission in a dilemma, because as history amply testifies, it is dangerous to try to modify or influence the religious beliefs of a subject people. However, the committee investigated the teachings of Smohalla and made a recommendation concerning the Dreamers.

The commissioners explained as follows the government's reasons for requesting Joseph's band to move onto the Lapwai Reservation:

> Owing to the coldness of the climate, it is not a suitable location for an Indian reservation.... It is embraced within the limits of the State of Oregon.... The State of Oregon could not probably be induced to cede the jurisdiction of the valley to the United States for an Indian reservation.... In the conflicts which might arise in the future, as in the past, between him and the whites, the President might not be able to justify or defend him.... A part of the valley had already been surveyed and opened to settlement... if by some arrangement, the white settlers in the valley could be induced to leave it, others would come.[19]

To all these statements Joseph replied that

> ... the Creative Power, when he made the earth, made no marks, no lines of division or separation on it, and that it should be allowed to remain as then made. The earth was his mother. He was made of the earth and grew up on its bosom. The earth, as his mother and nurse, was sacred to his affections, too sacred to be valued by or sold for silver and gold. He could not consent to sever his affections from the land that bore him. He asked nothing of the President. He was able to take care of himself. He

---

[18] Dunn, *op. cit.*, p. 638.

[19] *Ibid.* Requoted from Report of Secretary of Interior, Commission reports, Bureau of Indian Affairs, 1875, I, 762. *Ibid.*, 1876, I, 449.

did not desire Wallowa Valley as a reservation, for that would subject him and his band to the will of and dependence on another, and to laws not of their own making. He was disposed to live peaceably. He and his band had suffered wrong rather than do wrong. One of their number was wickedly slain by a white man during the last summer, but he would not avenge his death.[20]

"The serious feeling and manner in which he uttered these sentiments was impressive," the commissioners wrote. To the chief's arguments they lamely replied that the President "was not disposed to deprive him of any just right or govern him by his individual will, but merely subject him [Joseph] to the same just and equal laws by which he himself [the President] as well as all his people were ruled."[21]

Young Joseph might well have asked the commissioners whether they thought the climate too cold for the settlers to thrive in Wallowa. He could have pointed out that Nez Perces for generations had survived the rigorous climate of Oregon without complaint, and now white men found it suitable for farming and stock raising.

As for the alleged fact that the land was within the state of Oregon, Major Wood exploded this theory in his official report. He would not grant Joseph sole right to claim the valley over all other Nez Perces, but he stated all bands should have equal rights there. He frankly admitted, though, that "the extinguishment of their title of occupancy [of Wallowa Valley] . . . is imperfect and incomplete."[22] If Joseph's contention, supported by Wood's report, that Lawyer had no legal right to sell Wallowa, was correct, then the state of Oregon had no basis for claiming it.

That the President might not be able to "justify or defend" the Indians in future conflicts which might arise between the two races, Joseph knew only too well; the inrush of ten thousand miners and settlers to the Lapwai

---

[20] Dunn, *op. cit.*, pp. 638-39.

[21] Report of Secretary of Interior, 1876, I, 449.

[22] Wood, *op. cit.*, p. 45.

country in complete disregard of treaty stipulations had proved the government's inability to cope with the situation. Nor had the Interior Department ever carried out the Treaty of 1855 in respect to the survey of farms for the Indians. Seemingly, it never occurred to the committee to make a recommendation for the land to be surveyed at such a late date, and so adjust one of the main conflicts between the Nez Percés and the settlers. Some of the Indians, hoping to settle disputes with the whites, had fenced off the areas they claimed for farming and grazing.

The most amusing argument advanced by the commissioners was their assertion of Joseph's being "subject to the same just and equal laws" by which the President "as well as all his people were ruled." The commission failed to mention that Indians were wards of the government and, as such, under existing reservation laws, they were subject to the orders of the agents, who could control the Nez Perces' freedom of movement. To a man of Joseph's strength of character and independence, arbitrary rules were obnoxious. No doubt he felt the same as Sitting Bull, who once declared: "God made me an Indian, but not a reservation Indian."

The committee's weak arguments failed to convince Joseph, who refused to agree to the demands of the government and quit the council. Doubtless three factors influenced his action: He firmly believed his people owned the land in question; his native spirit of independence rebelled at any plan which would subject him or his people to the will or whims of an alien state; and he distrusted the government's faith in keeping a promise. Moreover, he had no assurance that the land would be permanently secured to his people if he did consent to move to Lapwai. Twice the reservation's size had been reduced since the Treaty of 1855. If he came to Lapwai, the treaty faction could sell his land there, just as they had sold the Wallowa Valley in 1863. Furthermore, Joseph had learned that the white man's phrase, *permanent home*, had two interpretations—one for theory, and one for expediency. Believing he had won another round with the government, Joseph returned to Wallowa.

In its report to the Secretary of the Interior, the commission accepted the tenets of Grover's letter and upon these as precedent recommended four things: that the Dreamer medicine men be confined to their agencies, since their influence on the nontreaty Indians was pernicious; that a military post be established in Wallowa Valley at once; thirdly, that "unless in a reasonable time Joseph consented to be removed, he should be forcibly taken with his people and given lands on the reservation";[23] and finally, that if members of his band overran property belonging to whites, or committed depredations, or disturbed the peace by threats of hostility, then sufficient force should be employed to bring them into subjection. Major H. Clay Wood made a minority report recommending that "until Joseph commits some overt act of hostility, force should not be used to put him upon any reservation."[24]

In January, 1877, the Department of the Interior, promptly acting upon the commission's report, decided to move Joseph onto the reserve—by compulsion, if necessary—and issued orders to Agent Monteith to that effect. Early in February the latter sent a delegation of treaty Nez Perces to ask Joseph to move of his own free will, lest the government be obliged to resort to force.

Reuben, head chief and Joseph's brother-in-law; his son, James Reuben; Whisk-tasket, Joseph's father-in-law; and Captain John, a Nez Perce scout, were the delegates who visited Wallowa. James Reuben, acting as spokesman, explained to Joseph and his headmen the nature of the visit on the first night of the group's arrival. He repeated the orders of the Indian Bureau and outlined the advantages of reservation life. The government, he affirmed, wanted all the Indians to lead a peaceful existence, unhampered by white men. It could not offer protec-

[23] *Works of H. H. Bancroft*, XXXI, 499.

[24] Dunn, *op. cit.*, p. 646.

tion to roving bands, nor could it give them material assistance to establish homes and farms if they persisted in remaining off the reservation. The delegates urged the chief and his people to choose farms before the other non-treaty Indians settled on the choicest of vacant lands.

Joseph listened quietly and attentively to his nephew's plea, but refused to give any indication of his feelings that night. The next morning, after hours of meditation, he addressed the treaty delegation in the council lodge:

> I have been talking to the whites many years about the land in question, and it is strange they cannot understand me. The country they claim belonged to my father, and when he died it was given to me and my people, and I will not leave it until I am compelled to.[25]

Supporting the decision of their chief, the headmen expressed their determination to remain in the Wallowa Valley. After a short stay, the treaty Nez Perces returned to Lapwai and reported the outcome of their interview to the agent. Monteith then wrote to the Commissioner of Indian Affairs:

> I think, from Joseph's actions, he will not come on the reserve until compelled to. He has said so much to the Indians who have moved on the reserve, calling them cowards, etc., that he would be lowering himself in his own estimation, as well as in that of his immediate followers, did he not make some show of resistance. By making such resistance, he could say to the other Indians, "I was overpowered, and did not come of my own choice," in case he is forced on the reserve.[26]

However, Monteith wisely recommended that Joseph's band be permitted to spend four or six weeks annually at Imnaha in order to fish, since there were no settlers in the region and only trails leading into it. The Imnaha Valley was a "great salmon-fishing resort of the Indians." Acting under orders of the Indian Bureau, the agent

[25] *Report of Secretary of War,* 1877, p. 115. Report of John B. Monteith.

[26] *Ibid.*

notified Joseph that he would be given until April 1, 1877, "to come on the reserve peaceably."[27]

Upon receiving Monteith's order and being told of the findings of the committee of 1876 in respect to the Wallowa Valley, Joseph would not believe that his case could have been truthfully presented by the interpreters, without having been decided in his favor. So he sent a message through his friend, Young Chief, head of the Umatillas, to Cornoyer, the Umatilla agent, asking for an interview with General Howard. The agent, visiting the general at Portland in March, informed him of Joseph's request.

At this time Joseph appears to have favored going on the Umatilla reserve rather than the Nez Perce one at Lapwai. The Indian historian L. V. WcWhorter gives as reasons for this preference: the Umatillas shared the same religious views as the Dreamer Nez Perces, in addition to blood ties through intermarriage.

The following month Howard sent his aide-de-camp, Lieutenant Boyle, who had much experience with Indians, to conduct the negotiations. The lieutenant returned to Umatilla with the agent and there met Alokut, who represented his brother, as Joseph was ill and could not be present. Alokut produced maps of the Wallowa, Grande Ronde, and Imnaha Valleys, to which the Wal-lam-wat-kins now laid claim. He had prepared these maps himself—an unusual accomplishment for an Indian. Dotted marks, Boyle found upon close inspection, represented the open hoof tracks of horses, thus marking the trails of the country. Those figures which represented people and fish were depicted in the Egyptian method of drawing. The lieutenant and Agent Cornoyer attempted to obtain a copy of these unique pictographic efforts, but Alokut refused to part with them.

Upon Lieutenant Boyle's return to Walla Walla he telegraphed Howard that Joseph expected to have another interview with him.

---

[27] *Ibid.*

Based upon the statements of a volunteer officer in the Bannock War of 1878, a Captain W. C. Painter, McWhorter described the meeting between Alokut and Boyle as a stormy one. Alokut apparently believed General Howard had promised that Joseph's people could remove to the Umatilla Reservation, whereupon the lieutenant abruptly stated that the general had ordered them to move at once to Lapwai.[28] Alokut resented Boyle's manner.

Howard made the trip by steamer up the Columbia River. From the head of navigation at Wallula, he went by train to Fort Walla Walla and arrived on April 18.

Late the next afternoon Alokut, followed by Young Chief and five other headmen, paid his respects to the general and tendered Joseph's regrets that he could not be present, as he was ill yet. The Indians arranged a meeting with Howard for the next day. At that time Alokut explained that neither he nor the other delegates could make any promises, and requested another conference with all the disaffected chiefs present. He declared for his brother that the interpreter at Lapwai could not have spoken the truth to the committee, and for that reason Joseph desired a second council. Apparently the chief hoped once more to talk the Indian Bureau out of removing his people to Lapwai.

Although no hint of the alleged misunderstanding between Alokut and Lieutenant William Boyle appears in Howard's report to the Secretary of War, he does refer to the Wallowa Nez Perces' desire to join the Umatillas. In reporting the Walla Walla council the general stated:

"I explained the requirement of the government; that the Indians would be required to go on the reservation—some reservation. . . . The Indians seemed at first to wish to join the Umatillas, then it appears there was a project (probably originating with white men) to combine the reservation Indians of Umatilla with the non-treaty Nez Perces, and ask for them thus joined the Wallowa and Imnaha country giving up the Umatilla reserve. But I replied that the instructions are definite; that I should

[28] McWhorter, *Hear Me, My Chiefs!*, pp. 152 ff.

send troops very soon to occupy the Wallowa, and proceed to Lapwai as soon as possible in execution of my instructions.

"Ollicut [Alokut], who manifested a good disposition, was evidently afraid to promise anything, and I was aware that some representative of the Indian Bureau should take the initiative in dealing with these Indians, so that I was glad to have him ask to gather the Indians, all the non-treaties, to meet me at Fort Lapwai during my coming visit."[29]

Howard then agreed to meet Joseph and other nontreaty chiefs at Lapwai twelve days later. He hoped to settle matters at that time with all Nez Perces not living on the reservation. The Indians accordingly dispatched runners to notify Chiefs Looking Glass, White Bird, Hush-hush-cute, and Tuhulhutsut of the coming council. All these were leaders of disaffected bands.

Looking Glass's people lived on Clear Creek, a tributary of the Middle Fork of the Clearwater River. His band's village, third in size and numbering about forty warriors, was usually located above the town of Kamiah on the eastern side of the Lapwai Reservation. This chief, son of old Chief Looking Glass who signed the Treaty of 1855, was "almost six feet tall, well proportioned, with features denoting strength and tenacity of purpose,"[30] and was nearly forty-five years of age. In the center of his forehead, tied to his scalp lock, hung a round mirror; from this he received his name in English. To the Nez Perces he was known as A-push-wa-hite. Looking Glass had just returned from a buffalo hunt in Montana where his band spent most of the time. Among the whites he was known as a diplomat and a leader for peace.

White Bird, also known as Joe Hale, whose Nez Perce name was Pen-pen-hi-hi (meaning, literally, "White Pelican"), was the oldest of the nontreaty chiefs. He was a heavyset man of mild countenance, which deceptively masked his shrewd trading ability. Howard describes

[29] Howard, in *Report of Secretary of War*, 1877, I, 590.

[30] McWhorter, *op. cit.*, p. 182.

him as being "a demure-looking Indian, about five feet, eight inches tall. His face assumed the condition of impassibility, or rigid fixedness, while in council; and . . . he kept his immense ceremonial hat on, and placed a large eagle's wing in front of his eyes and nose."[31] This aging chief's band, second in size, when not in Montana hunting buffalo, roamed among the steep mountains along the Salmon River which lay to the south of the reservation. Indian testimony disagrees as to White Bird's stand on war, but some Nez Perces claim he and his fifty braves were willing to fight the whites any time the other nontreaty bands would rally to his support.

Hush-hush-cute lived in the Asotin country of southeastern Washington on the west bank of the Snake River. A subleader of a small Palouse band, including about sixteen warriors under Chief Hahtalekin, he was a renowned orator. He was about Joseph's age, close to thirty-six at the time, and his manner of extreme cunning inspired distrust in those whites who dealt with him in councils.

Tuhulhutsut, already past middle age, was still a powerfully strong man of five feet ten, broad-shouldered, deep-chested and thick of neck. Howard describes him as one of the leading *tewats,* or medicine men, of the Dreamer faith, but McWhorter's Indian informants flatly denied this. He was a Dreamer, they affirmed, but not a *tewat*. Grizzly Bear Ferocious, though, did call him a *"tiwat"* in describing him to Edward S. Curtis. McWhorter himself, in *Yellow Wolf: His Own Story,* page 36, note 3, referred to "Toohoolhoolzote" (Tuhulhutsut) as a "Dreamer prophet and medicine man." Although his band on the Snake River numbered only about 183 people, of whom 30 were fighting men, he did exert great influence on the followers of Smohalla's religion as his oratory was passionate and vindictive. Like the prophet, this old chief could drop his querulous manner and speak smoothly and convincingly.

[31] Howard, *Chief Joseph, His Pursuit and Capture,* p. 58.

Photo courtesy of Baker & Taylor Co.

Major General O. O. Howard. Taken upon his retirement, November 4, 1894.

Joseph and Alokut, leaders of the largest band of nearly five hundred persons, of whom fifty-five were warriors, presented the finest appearance of the invited chiefs. Alokut, the younger of the two, was even taller than his brother, as graceful and supple as a cougar. Carefree and full of youthful enthusiasm, his happy disposition attracted whites and Indians alike. Clearly, he was the idol and leader of the young men.[32]

Lieutenant C. E. S. Wood, Howard's aide-de-camp, thus describes the chief:

> Joseph at this time must have been about thirty-seven or thirty-eight [he was thirty-seven] years old. He is tall, straight and handsome, with a mouth and chin not unlike that of Napoleon I. He was in council, at first probably not so influential as White Bird and the group of chiefs that sustained him, but from first to last he was preeminently their "war chief." Such was the testimony of his followers after his surrender, and such seems to be the evidence of the campaign itself.[33]

These chiefs, together with Young Chief of the Umatillas who wished to observe the conference, were the different types of Indians who met in council with the dignified and handsome Howard, a full-bearded, broad-shouldered man with a straight military carriage. Sergeant Martin L. Brown, Twenty-first Infantry, one of Howard's soldiers, described his commanding officer as follows:

> He was a soldierly figure, a little below average height, and he had but one arm, the other being shot off in a cavalry charge during the Civil war. He wore the con-

[32] According to Indian testimony, Alokut was not present at this council. Yellow Serpent, a Walla Walla chief, says: "Alokut was at Nihyawi [Umatilla River]. . . . General Howard made the first speech. He said: '. . . I see all of you to-day are before me. Only Alokut is absent.'" (Curtis, *op. cit.*, VIII, 20.) Three Eagles, a Nez Perce and a friend of Joseph's corroborates Yellow Serpent's statement: "Alokut was not at this council; he was at Umatilla. He joined his brother [Joseph] at Lapwai after the council." (*Ibid.*, p. 23.)

[33] Quoted by Brady, *Northwestern Fights and Fighters*, pp. 6-7, from Col. C. E. S. Wood's *Century* article.

ventional whiskers of that day. I remember him most for his ever-friendly speech, and his quiet manner. I don't believe I ever saw or heard of his being in a controversy.

He took a personal interest in me, though I was just a sergeant, and he used to come down to the basement [at Vancouver Barracks] to chat with me. I was 19 at the time, so he would ask me where my home was, when I enlisted, what I had seen, and so on.

Yes, Brigadier-General Howard was always as courteous to a corporal or a sergeant as he was to a major or a colonel, and those under him liked and respected him for it. Always kind and thoughtful, he was everything a man and an officer could be.[34]

Howard's deeply religious nature was reflected in his face, and he appeared not unlike the Jewish prophets of the Old Testament. By those who knew him (and the testimony is unanimous) he was said to be honest, kindly, fair-minded, and always willing to believe the best of anyone. His right sleeve hung empty at his side because he had lost his arm at Fair Oaks, and so he became known to the Indians as the "one-armed soldier-chief."

---

[34] From a feature article by Addison Howard in the *Daily Missoulian*, Missoula, Montana, June 14, 1925.

CHAPTER IX

The Council at Fort Lapwai—1877

ABOUT fifty of Joseph's people encamped on May 2 in a secluded spot up the Lapwai Valley not far from the fort, and just above the garrison gardens. That afternoon and evening the Indians prepared their clothes for the meeting by rubbing them with chalk, which gave a gleamy white appearance to their buckskin garments. Their faces and their ponies they painted and streaked with red. Although he came from the greatest distance, Joseph and his band was the first to reach the council ground.

In the morning, bright with May sunshine, the warriors and their women rode many-colored horses down to the garrison. The men's hair had been carefully braided and tied with gaudy strings. Wrapped around their bodies were gay blankets of various colors, and their legs and feet were encased in beaded buckskin leggings and moccasins. The women vied with their men by wearing bright shawls or blankets, skirts to the ankle, and high-top moccasins.

Chanting a weird tune, pitched low and plaintive, or at times high and fierce, this picturesque cavalcade rode completely around Fort Lapwai, and paused for a review by the soldiers on the parade ground. The notes of the chant reechoed among the log buildings, which "broke the refrain into irregular bubblings of sound till the ceremony was completed."[1]

Then the head chiefs dismounted. Led by Joseph, they walked behind Captain Perry's quarters and filed through

[1] Howard, *Chief Joseph, His Pursuit and Capture,* p. 53.

the transverse hall to the hospital tent, which had been prepared for the council immediately south of the guardhouse. According to Yellow Serpent, Howard

> placed the head chiefs in the front circle. I sat on one side and Joseph was on my right. On his right were Looking Glass, Tuhulhutsut, Hushush-keut.... This council sat in front of one of the buildings at Fort Lapwai.[2]

Two of Howard's aides, Lieutenants Wilkinson and Boyle, sat behind him. All the chiefs shook hands with the military, Agent Monteith, and the interpreters, and then everybody sat down. Young Chief of the Umatillas accompanied Joseph. Eager to behold the council, also, were several wives of the officers. The presence of white women lent a friendly air to the meeting.

Massed outside the tent (the sides of which were raised) were the treaty Indians. Fearful lest trouble should break out, they stood or crouched around the group assembled in conference and observed proceedings with a wary attitude. They knew the resentful feeling of their nontreaty brethren toward the governmental order requiring them to move onto the reservation. Howard, though, had prepared for any emergency by having the soldiers of the garrison remain in their barracks, and had ordered other troops to close in from various directions.

Before the discussions began, the venerable Catholic missionary, Father Cataldo, whose mission was in a valley of Craig Mountain, eight miles from Lapwai, opened the meeting with a prayer in the Nez Perce tongue. Perrin Whitman, a nephew of Dr. Marcus Whitman, and James Reuben, Joseph's nephew, acted as interpreters. The Reverend Henry Spalding was not present.

The general addressed Joseph, with Whitman interpreting: "I heard from your brother Ollicut [Alokut], twelve days ago, at Walla-Walla, that you wished to see me. I am here to listen to what you have to say."[3]

Joseph, knowing that White Bird and his followers

---

[2] Curtis, *The North American Indian,* VIII, 20.

[3] Howard, *Chief Joseph, His Pursuit and Capture,* p. 53.

would not arrive until the morrow, asked that the council be delayed until then.

To this Howard replied, "Mr. Monteith's instructions and mine are directly to YOUR people; if you decide at once to comply with the wishes of the government, you can have the first pick of vacant land. We will not wait for White Bird; instructions to him are the same; he can take his turn."[4]

Howard then informed the assembled Nez Perces that

> . . . they must know in the outset, that in any event [regardless of how long the council lasted], they were to obey the orders of the Government of the United States. As it was evident that the Indians were more curious to get something from us, and more disposed to parley and waste time than to communicate anything to us, or make any request, I asked the agent, Monteith, if he had not better read his instructions from Washington to the Indians. This he then did.[5]

John Monteith was a tall, well-built man of thirty-five. As he read, Perrin Whitman interpreted the message to the chiefs.

Two old medicine men protested the government's order to move onto the reservation. They reiterated that they wanted a long talk of several days about their land. One *tewat* sharply demanded of the interpreters to speak the truth in making the translations.

When the medicine men had finished speaking, Howard sternly told them in turn to give good advice to the Indians. Then the general addressed Joseph, again offering him first choice of the vacant lands if he would agree to move onto the reservation at once. The chief, though, declared he would wait until White Bird arrived before speaking his mind. With nothing accomplished, the council adjourned until the following day.

On Friday, joined by White Bird's band, the Indians again went through the same formalities of display, and

---

[4] *Report of Secretary of War*, 1877, I, 593. Report of Brigadier General Howard.

[5] *Ibid.*

for the effect waited some time before coming to the tent. This day Joseph, with his hair shining and carefully braided, "and his face slightly rouged, sat on a low bench."[6] Alpowa Jim, a treaty Nez Perce, opened the second day's meeting with a brief prayer in his native tongue. The agent then reread his instructions, and Howard recapitulated his orders from Washington.

Following these preliminaries, Joseph introduced his ally to the general: "This is White Bird. I spoke to you of him; this is the first time he has seen you, and you him. I want him and his Indians to understand what has been said to us."[7]

The red man and the white man shook hands, and then White Bird with his followers squatted on the grass behind Joseph.

By previous arrangement, no doubt, the Indians put forth Tuhulhutsut as their principal speaker and advocate. He told of the religious beliefs of the Dreamers regarding the ownership of the earth. As he spoke, the words fell from his lips like arrows shot from a warrior's bow. There was nothing in those beliefs, he asserted, which taught that white men could dictate where each race should live—that was the sole right of the Spirit Chief.

His words aroused the Indians, who apparently wished to learn if this fiery orator would inspire reverential fear in the white officials, and possibly get some concession from them. The treaty Nez Perces fully expected serious trouble. They broke out with murmurings of "*Aa,*" at the chief's defiant assertions. White Bird, his face partly hidden behind a big eagle feather, symbol of his *tewat* status, kept silent. Joseph covertly watched the reactions of the military to the speech. If the general and his staff gave any sign of fear, then Joseph and the other chiefs would know whether or not to adopt an attitude of defiance, because, he explained, "an Indian respects a brave

---

[6] Howard, *Chief Joseph, His Pursuit and Capture*, p. 58.
[7] *Ibid.*

man, but he despises a coward. He loves a straight tongue, but he hates a forked tongue."[8] He closely observed to see if their eyes would "tell what the tongue would hide."[9]

Instead of showing fear, Howard retained an aspect of self-possession, although he realized the possibility of the council's ending in violence. In order to gain time so that the troops, already on the march in Wallowa, could get closer, the general heartily granted Joseph's request to defer the next meeting. Howard suggested the following Monday as the day on which to resume the conference. This would give the Indians time over the week end "to talk among themselves." Apparently the arrangement pleased the chiefs, for with a friendly handshake all around, they dissolved the meeting.

To be ready for any emergency, the general had ordered Captain Trimble's company from Fort Walla Walla to Lewiston. Captain Stephen G. Whipple's cavalry he had advised to cross the Wallowa Valley to the confluence of the Grande Ronde and Snake Rivers, where they could be reached easily in case they were wanted. Howard had also directed two more companies to move from Vancouver Barracks and encamp near Wallula to be convenient if needed. The presence of troops in the valley of winding waters would be a warning to Joseph's people who had remained behind. With the soldiers near by they would not be so likely to foment trouble. However, the Indians kept the peace in Wallowa.

During the intermission on Saturday the nontreaties held a council among themselves. The treaty Indians showed evidence of fear as young braves made boastful, warlike speeches about the encampment. This gossip was circulated by the women, who retailed it to the servants of the officers as threats made by Chief White Bird. For their part the soldiers, too, were fearful, and

---

[8] "An Indian's Views of Indian Affairs," *North American Review*, April, 1879, p. 416.

[9] New York *Sun*, September 25, 1904. From a news account on the death of Chief Joseph.

distrusted the nontreaty Nez Perces because the Modoc massacre was still fresh in their memory.

On Sunday, Joseph and a number of his followers held their Dreamer rites, accompanied by loud drumming. The rest of the nontreaties attended the Christian services in the agency chapel. Their cheerful attitude reassured the reservation Indians and the whites of the Lapwai garrison.

When the council reopened on Monday, May 7, however, some of the nontreaties came armed. Hush-hush-cute and Looking Glass are mentioned in the official reports for the first time, although it is likely that Looking Glass had been present at the Friday meeting. Monteith told the Indians that he had forgotten to tell them one thing: the government would not interfere in their religious beliefs, except when the medicine men disturbed the peace. The nontreaties had evidently heard rumors that their Dreamer rites were to be prohibited, which put them in rather an ugly mood.

In his own story Joseph says he rose to speak this time and thus addressed the assemblage:

> I am ready to talk to-day. I have been in a great many councils, but I am no wiser. We are all sprung from a woman, although we are unlike in many things. We can not be made over again. You are as you were made, and as you were made you can remain. We are just as we were made by the Great Spirit, and you can not change us; then why should children of one mother and one father quarrel—why should one try to cheat the other? I do not believe that the Great Spirit Chief gave one kind of men the right to tell another kind of men what they must do.[10]

According to Joseph, Howard replied, "You deny my authority, do you? You want to dictate to me, do you?"[11]

---

[10] "An Indian's Views . . . ," *op. cit.*, p. 421.

[11] *Ibid.* However, the general, in an article republished in C. T. Brady's *Northwestern Fights and Fighters*, p. 85, denies making this remark, and denies that Joseph made the speech quoted above. Undoubtedly, the fact that every word spoken had to be interpreted gave rise to much misunderstanding.

Again Tuhulhutsut voiced the arguments of the chiefs, repeating the Dreamer beliefs in a loud, harsh tone. His speech as reported by Joseph is: "The Great Spirit Chief made the world as it is, and as he wanted it, and he made a part of it for us to live upon. I do not see where you get your authority to say that we shall not live where he placed us."[12]

The general warned Tuhulhutsut that his words were inciting the Indians, and threatened to have him placed in the guardhouse if he persisted in so speaking. To this the old man retorted:

Who are you that you ask us to talk, and then tell me I shan't talk? Are you the Great Spirit? Did you make the world? Did you make the sun? Did you make the rivers to run for us to drink? Did you make the grass to grow? Did you make all these things, that you talk to us as though we were boys? If you did, then you have the right to talk as you do.[13]

The agent explained in a conciliatory tone that the law, made in Washington, required the Indians to live upon the reservation. Howard added that the reserve was created to protect and to give prosperity to the Nez Perces.

Unconvinced, Tuhulhutsut continued his inflammatory oration, and then finally concluded, "What person pretended to divide the land, and put me on it?"[14]

Howard, thinking that boldness would carry the day,

---

[12] *Ibid.* In his reply to Joseph's article, Howard denies that Tuhulhutsut spoke as the chief said he did. Yet in his book, *Chief Joseph, His Pursuit and Capture,* chap. X, the general credits Tuhulhutsut with speaking in much the same vein as Joseph declares. Howard denies, further, that he lost his temper, but in his official "Report of Brigadier General Howard to the Secretary of War," *Report of Secretary of War,* 1877, Vol. I, he states that Tuhulhutsut did speak at great length on the philosophy of the Dreamer teachings, and that he (Howard) spoke sharply in reply and said that the *tewat's* words were causing disaffection among the other chiefs. No doubt the fact that the speeches had to be translated caused misunderstanding. Howard's command to the old chief to change his tone was probably misinterpreted by the translator to "shut up," just as Joseph claims in his version published in the *North American Review.*

[13] "An Indian's Views . . . ," *op. cit.,* p. 421.

[14] *Report of Secretary of War,* 1877, p. 594.

emphatically replied: "I am the man. I stand here for the President, and there is no spirit, good or bad, that will hinder me. My orders are plain, and will be executed. I hoped the Indians had good sense enough to make me their friend, and not their enemy."[15]

This heated argument inflamed the Indians and they stirred uneasily. The general asked for the views of Looking Glass and White Bird, but he received no assurance from either. Looking Glass replied evasively, and White Bird quietly endorsed the spokesman. Joseph remained silent. Howard grasped the import of the situation—a display of weakness might precipitate another Modoc massacre.

He turned again to the surly chief and asked, "Our old friend does not seem to understand that the question is, will the Indians come peaceably on the reservation, or do they want me to put them there by force?"[16]

In a vehement tone Tuhulhutsut denied the authority of the government to take away his land, and asseverated, "The Indians can do what they like, but I am NOT going on the reservation."[17]

The general rebuked him, and then addressed the other chiefs, "Will Joseph and White Bird and Looking Glass go with me to look after the land? The old man shall not go; he must stay with Captain Perry."[18]

Tuhulhutsut muttered, "Do you want to scare me with reference to my body?"[19]

"I will leave your body with Captain Perry," Howard answered.[20]

Unable to conciliate Tuhulhutsut, the general had determined to remove him by force from the council. His aide being absent at the moment, Howard, with Perry's

---

[15] *Ibid.*

[16] *Ibid.*

[17] *Ibid.*

[18] *Ibid.*, p. 595.

[19] *Ibid.*

[20] Howard, *Chief Joseph, His Pursuit and Capture*, p. 66.

assistance, took the unresisting arm of the old Dreamer and started to lead him from the tent.

Before he was taken out, the old chief voiced his feelings: "Is that your order? I do not care. I have expressed my heart to you. I have nothing to take back. I have spoken for my country. You can arrest me, but you can not change me or make me take back what I have said."[21]

The general then placed Tuhulhutsut in the guardhouse, with orders for him to be confined there until the council was concluded.

In defending this unfortunate act, Howard explained:

> My conduct was summary, it is true, but I knew it was hopeless to get the Indians to agree to anything so long as they could keep this old Dreamer on the lead, and defy the agents of the government; and I believed that the Modoc massacre would very soon be repeated, if I gave time for concert of action.[22]

The arrest of the Indians' speaker did have a temporary restraining effect, but in the long run the action caused serious trouble. Within thirty-five days the reckless young bloods were to use this incident as an excuse to incite the older men to war.

Angered by the general's peremptory act, the Indians covertly fingered the knives hidden beneath their blankets. Joseph reports:

> My men whispered among themselves, whether they should let this thing be done. I counseled them to submit. I knew if we resisted that all the white men present, including General Howard would be killed in a moment, and we [the chiefs] would be blamed. If I had said nothing, General Howard would never have given another unjust order against my men. I saw the danger, and, while they dragged Too-hool-hool-suit to prison, I arose and said: "*I am going to talk now.* I don't care whether you arrest me or not." I turned to my people and said: "The arrest of Too-hool-hool-suit was wrong, but we will not resent

[21] "An Indian's Views . . . ," *op. cit.*, p. 422.

[22] Howard, *Chief Joseph, His Pursuit and Capture*, p. 67.

the insult. We were invited to this council to express our hearts, and we have done so."[23]

The Indians now realized that they would either have to move to the reservation or fight. Again the chiefs, obedient to Joseph's wishes, decided in favor of peace and manifested an air of friendliness, but rancor blazed in their hearts.

Before the council adjourned, Joseph, Looking Glass, and White Bird expressed to Howard their willingness to ride to Kamiah for the purpose of looking over the land they wanted for their farms when they moved to the Lapwai Reservation.

In the early hours of May 8 rain delayed the start of the party, composed of Chiefs Joseph, White Bird, and Looking Glass, and General Howard, his aide, Lieutenant Wilkinson, Joe Roboses, interpreter, and Jonah, a subchief and treaty Nez Perce. After ten o'clock, though, the sky cleared and they started on a reconnaissance of the reservation. The chiefs were dressed in their best clothes, and had their faces painted "with a line of red running back along the parting of the hair over the head." They were all well mounted on good-sized horses with gay blankets "dropped from the shoulders to the saddle. . . . They appeared hearty and cheerful," Howard wrote, "chatting with us and with each other as we rode along."[24] White Bird, on a compact roan, even challenged Lieutenant Wilkinson to a race!

The group rode up the valley of Lapwai toward the mouth of Sweetwater Creek and on past the agency farm. High, steep-sided hills with rounded summits, practically barren of trees, flanked the valley. Looking Glass pleaded with the general to release Tuhulhutsut, and promised he and White Bird would be responsible to Howard with their lives for the Dreamer's good behavior. But the general told them the old man would be confined to the

[23] "An Indian's Views . . . ," *op. cit.*, p. 422.
[24] Howard, *Chief Joseph, His Pursuit and Capture*, p. 68.

guardhouse until the land matters were settled. Joseph reports:

As we rode along, we came to some good land that was already occupied by Indians and white people. General Howard, pointing to this land, said: "If you will come on to the reservation, I will give you these lands and move these people off."

I replied: "No. It would be wrong to disturb these people. I have no right to take their homes. I have never taken what did not belong to me. I will not now."[25]

The party was passing the well-cultivated farms of two white settlers, Finney and Caldwell. The ordered neatness of the places seemed to impress the Indians. Howard told Joseph he understood that the chief "preferred a canvas house."

To which Joseph answered, "When I come on the reservation I want a good frame house."[26]

Howard continues in his report to the Secretary of War: "He [Joseph] looked through Mr. Caldwell's house with great interest when we stopped there, and were kindly received by the ladies of Mr. Caldwell's family."[27]

During the afternoon they inspected the grazing lands past the "extensive upland agency farm," and then returned to Fort Lapwai for the night.

On the ride the chiefs again begged the general to free their chosen leader from the guardhouse. Howard permitted them to have an interview with Tuhulhutsut, but still refused to order his release as yet.

Agent Monteith, Captain Perry, and six cavalrymen joined the escort the next day. A bright, cloudless morning greeted them for an early start. Red men and white were in good spirits as they rode through lush grass and past the fresh green of trees along the stream courses. Joseph soon decided on land in the Lapwai Valley near the agency. However, his choice did not altogether please

---

[25] "An Indian's Views . . . ," *op. cit.*, p. 422.

[26] *Report of Secretary of War,* 1877, p. 595.

[27] *Ibid.*

him, since it was the location of the farms of Finney and Caldwell.

The party rode over the foothills to Craig Mountain and Kamiah, and across extensive prairie lands to the Clearwater Valley, covering between sixty and seventy miles. Alokut, who had joined his brother, thoroughly enjoyed the trip and proved an amusing companion to the officers.

During the day Joseph asked Howard, "If we come and live here, what will you give us . . . schools, teachers, houses, churches, and gardens?"

"Yes," agreed the general.

"Well, those are just the things we do not want. The Earth is our Mother, and do you think we want to dig and break it? No, indeed! We want to hunt buffalo and fish for salmon, not plow and use the hoe. We do not plant; we harvest only the grain and berries that Mother Earth willingly gives us."

"Yours is a strange answer," the general remarked.[28]

That night the group stopped at Mr. Fee's boarding school at the subagency. The next day, May 10, the party recrossed the Clearwater and rode eighteen miles farther into the mountainous country of that region. In the vicinity of Kamiah, White Bird selected land which he felt would make a good home for his people. Looking Glass chose to live farther down the Clearwater Valley.

On Friday, May 11, the party started back to Fort Lapwai. The Indians rode alone as Howard wished to see Finney and Caldwell about the purchase of their holdings in the area preferred by Joseph. That evening the two groups reunited at a prearranged campsite. The combined party returned to Fort Lapwai on Saturday evening, May 12.

There they met Captain Trimble, who had arrived at the post from Fort Walla Walla with his troop of the First Cavalry. Howard received a dispatch notifying him that

---

[28] Howard, "Famous Indian Chiefs," *St. Nicholas Magazine*, June, 1908, p. 697. Also found in the book of the same title on p. 193.

Captains Whipple and Winters had entered the Grande Ronde Valley with their cavalry companies.

Early Sunday morning Joseph received the same intelligence by runner that these troops had reached the vicinity of Wallowa Valley. The chief thought the military had been sent to "drive us out upon our return home." He hurried to the tent of Lieutenant Wilkinson and asked that his village be protected against the soldiers. The officer reassured Joseph as to the peaceful intentions of the troops.

Howard had received orders from the War Department advising him: "You are to occupy Wallowa Valley *in the interest of peace.* You are to comply with the request of the Department of the Interior as set forth in the papers sent you, to the extent only of *merely protecting and aiding them* [Joseph's band] in the execution of their instructions."[29]

On May 15 a final meeting was held at which Agent Monteith explained where each band was to locate. According to Howard, when Joseph was offered his protection paper, "he said that he had *decided* to go *above Kamiah,* on the Clearwater, for he wished to be with his *friends.*"[30]

After a few moments of consultation, the agent and the general agreed to the change, for it relieved them of any arbitrary decision regarding the titles to the farms of Finney and Caldwell.

White Bird received his paper bearing Howard's signature as department commander. It read:

> White Bird to-day has *agreed* to come on the Nez Perces reservation, and I believe he means to keep his word, and do right; do the best he can for himself and his people. Wherever he appears with proper pass from the agent of the reservation and with good behavior he should be treated with kindness.[31]

---

[29] *Report of Secretary of War,* 1877, p. 117.

[30] *Ibid.,* p. 596.

[31] *Ibid.*

The chief accepted this paper with the understanding that he had thirty days to collect his stock and come onto the reservation. Since the settlers had protested against the wild and reckless young men of his band, he explained to Howard that when Indians or whites drank whiskey they both "acted with folly." He counseled his people against using liquor, but he found it difficult to control some of them, and he might not be able "to make them come to Kamiah." The general advised him to call on Captain Perry "when he had done his best."[32]

Howard granted the Indians only thirty days to move onto the reserve.[33] Joseph, whose band lived farther away than the others, had protested the shortness of the time and declared that it would be impossible to round up all the stock and swim them across the turbulent Snake River, swollen as it was with the spring rains. The general refused to extend the period, as he believed any further delay would aggravate the hostility between the settlers and the Nez Perces in the Wallowa Valley. The Indians grumbled, but realized they could do nothing about it. As it turned out, Howard's command proved too severe, for the presence of the military in the valley served to antagonize the Nez Perces, in addition to the general's threat to drive them onto the reservation by force if necessary.

Howard did not trust Hush-hush-cute, and so withheld his protection paper, leaving it with Monteith to keep until the chief complied with the terms of the agreement.

Before leaving for Portland on May 19, the general ordered the release of Tuhulhutsut from the guardhouse. Instead of causing repentance, the chief's short imprisonment inflamed his heart to be revenged on the whites.

Upon hearing the outcome of the council, one Columbia River renegade Indian left his wife and lodge, threatened Howard's life, and roamed over the country, vowing that

---

[32] *Ibid.*

[33] According to Yellow Serpent, Howard had said in the council: "I am to give you thirty days to come in. This is the order I received from Washington." Curtis, *op. cit.*, p. 20.

no man could force him to live on a reservation. His act symbolized the spirit of rebellion that began to seethe in the hearts of the Nez Perces, and white settlers in Idaho would have done well to heed this omen.

CHAPTER X

Chief White Bird's Murders

THE NEZ PERCE chiefs returned to their respective bands after the council at Fort Lapwai to carry out the government's orders. It has been charged that the chiefs agreed to obey Howard's command only in order to give them time to prepare for war. That may have been true in Tuhulhutsut's and White Bird's case, but the subsequent actions of Joseph, Hush-hush-cute, and Looking Glass indisputably disprove such a charge against them, as will be shown. Joseph says:

> When I returned to Wallowa, I found my people very much excited upon discovering that the soldiers were already in the Wallowa Valley. We held a council, and decided to move immediately, to avoid bloodshed.
>
> Too-hool-hool-suit, who felt outraged by his imprisonment, talked for war, and made many of my young men willing to fight rather than be driven like dogs from the land where they were born. He declared that blood alone would wash out the disgrace General Howard had put upon him. It required a strong heart to stand up against such talk, but I urged my people to be quiet, and not to begin a war.
>
> I said in my heart that, rather than have war, I would give up my country. I would give up my father's grave. I would give up everything rather than have the blood of white men upon the hands of my people.[1]

Joseph ordered preparations made for an immediate exodus to avert trouble. Herdsmen went out to round up the horses and cattle that had wandered into the hills.

[1] "An Indian's Views of Indian Affairs," *North American Review,* April, 1879, p. 423.

The ill feeling among his people became so great that a few of the young men flatly refused to leave the valley of winding waters. At this defiance of his authority, Joseph —armed with pistols, it is asserted[2]—rode through the village and threatened to shoot the first person who disobeyed the government's command to move.

With grieving hearts the Wal-lam-wat-kin band began their trek—a trek that was to take them many weary, bloody miles, and would become a famous epoch in the annals of American Indian history. As Joseph rode away from his beloved valley of winding waters, did he feel in his heart that it would be the last time but one his eyes would ever gaze upon Wallowa, and those scenes familiar to him since babyhood?

When the band reached the Snake River, the women and children and the family possessions were ferried on buffalo-hide rafts to the Idaho shore. Mounted by warriors, four ponies, one to each corner of the raft, swam the people across the quarter mile of treacherous whirlpools in the swift-flowing current.

With the old and the young safely on the other side, the herdsmen drove part of the stock into the swirling waters. A sudden and fierce cloudburst beat down on the river. The maelstrom of waters swept an alarming number of ponies and cattle to a quick death.[3] Fearful that hundreds more would be drowned, Joseph advised his men to keep part of the herd on the Oregon side until the river had subsided. While they were doing so, a party of white men attacked the guards and ran off the cattle.[4]

Although Joseph's order was in contravention of Howard's instructions, the chief felt that the general would realize the need for the delay when apprised of the circumstances. The government required the Indians to move, but it did not require them to lose their only source of wealth in doing so.

---

[2] Helen Hunt Jackson, *A Century of Dishonor*, p. 131.

[3] "An Indian's Views . . . ," *op. cit.*, p. 423.

[4] *Fourteenth Annual Report, Bureau of American Ethnology*, Part II, pp. 713-14.

Joseph's band crossed another ford upon arrival at the Salmon River, a tributary of the Snake, but they effected this without loss. A few miles from there they joined the camp of White Bird's band in Rocky Canyon. This defile was one of the eastern branches of the Salmon River Canyon, lying eight miles west of Grangeville. Eleven days remained before their time limit was up, but the bands were near the southwest boundary of the Lapwai Reservation. Tuhulhutsut's people had already encamped with those of White Bird and Joseph. So the Indians killed their beef cattle, jerked the meat, and cached their food supplies in a cave. They were evidently preparing for trouble.

Here, in Rocky Canyon, the Indians held a ten-day grand council in which everyone who had a grievance against the white race told of the wrongs he had suffered. Many of them demanded vengeance. Tuhulhutsut inflamed the hearts of the young men with his oratorical appeals for bloodshed to wipe out the stigma of his arrest. Youth, stung with personal and tribal resentment and visualizing only the supposed glories of battle, clamored for war. These hotheaded young men were blind to the disastrous consequences of war, to the women and children who would be widowed and orphaned, and to the useless destruction of property. While the conclave was being held, sentinels warned those assembled in secret conference of the approach of any white settlers who came to visit the encampment.

Joseph had steadfastly maintained an almost inhuman self-control in the face of repeated acts of aggression by white men in Wallowa. Now, against the inflamed feelings of his own people, he once more pleaded for peace and pointed out the folly of taking the warpath. Looking Glass concurred with his sentiments. But the powerful Dreamer medicine men taunted Joseph with accusations of cowardice. Reciting the horde of injustices and insults heaped for years upon the peace-loving Nez Perces by the white race, the *tewats* made impassioned orations for war. This martial spirit was heartily echoed by Tuhulhutsut and doubtless, too, by White Bird. Stout of heart, Joseph was not swayed by natural anger and steadfastly refused to yield to the almost unanimous desire to fight.

Some of the Indians frankly expected trouble with the military if they did not hurry onto the reservation. Others suggested to the council that settlers be warned by their Nez Perce friends they would not be harmed if they remained neutral during hostilities. But the chiefs voted down that suggestion.

On the tenth day of the meetings one young man, Walaitits, left the council in disgust after boldly threatening to take revenge on the whites. His father had been murdered by a settler in an unprovoked quarrel over land. This settler was Larry Ott, who had killed an Indian on March 1, 1875.[5] As in the case of We-lot-yah, the white man was not punished for his crime.

Joseph spoke at great length in answer to the youth's demand for blood. Apparently convinced, then, that he had won over the conclave to his viewpoint, the chief left the conference to butcher his cattle for his family. Especially in need of beef at this time was one of his wives who soon expected to become a mother. Joseph did not know then that many of the young men were obtaining whiskey from settlers, the fiery effect of which on their brains would drive them to acts of madness.[6] If the chief had anticipated any trouble at this time, as has often been charged against him, he would have followed the Indian custom of sending the women and children to a place of safety, instead of exposing them.

The young brave who had quitted the council secured his share of the dangerous firewater and rode through the camp, shouting defiance of white men. According to

---

[5] J. P. Dunn, Jr., *Massacres of the Mountains*, p. 636. Also Howard, *Chief Joseph, His Pursuit and Capture*, pp. 92-93, 101. Haines, in *Red Eagles of the Northwest*, p. 241, gives a somewhat different version based on the pamphlet by Will Cave, whose account was written many years after the events occurred. The account of Walaitits in this text is based on Yellow Bull's own testimony.

[6] Curtis, *The North American Indian*, VIII, 23. This account is corroborated by Yellow Bull, p. 164, also by Joseph, "An Indian's Views . . . ," *op. cit.*, p. 424.

the Indian testimony, an old man ridiculed him, saying, "If you are so brave, why do you not avenge the murder of your father by killing the man who did it?"[7] Goaded by the taunt, the youth's anger flared into action.

Two other intoxicated young men, Isapsis-ilpilp (Red Moccasin-top) and Um-til-ilp-cown, joined Walaitits, a cousin of the former, and the three started for Slate Creek, their blood ignited with a burning lust to kill. It is significant that all were members of White Bird's band, and must have felt sure of their warlike chief's moral support for whatever acts they might commit. Red Moccasin-top was the son of Yellow Bull, a subchief of the same band. The latter pursued his boy and tried to persuade the youth to return to the village with him. But Isapsis-ilpilp refused to heed his father's advice and rode along with the others.

McWhorter gives a somewhat different version, stating the young men, Wahlitits (Walaitits) included, were staging a war parade through the camp when his horse stepped "on a spread canvas covered with *kouse* roots drying in the sun." Thereupon Heyoom Moxmox (Yellow Grizzly Bear) chided Wahlitits for spoiling his wife's "hardworked food" and taunted him for "playing brave," but failing to avenge his father's murder. After brooding over the matter overnight, Wahlitits determined to seek revenge, and took along his cousin Red Moccasin-top and his seventeen-year-old nephew Swan Necklace (Um-til-ilp-cown) as horse holder. None of the young warriors was intoxicated at this time, according to McWhorter's Indian sources.[8]

Slate Creek was a tributary of the Salmon River, about one hundred miles, Howard estimated, from Fort Lapwai. Here, on the afternoon of June 13, the three young Indians failed to find Larry Ott, who had fled to

[7] Curtis, *op. cit.*, VIII, 23.

[8] McWhorter, *Hear Me, My Chiefs!*, pp. 189 ff. E. S. Curtis' informant, Yellow Bull, claims the three young men were drunk. (Curtis, *op. cit.*, VIII, 164.) Two Moons corroborated this fact to McWhorter, but other Indian sources denied it.

the Florence mines and disguised himself as a Chinaman. Instead they murdered Richard Divine, an old, retired English sailor who lived alone, but who, Yellow Wolf declares, "had badly treated the Indians." Early the next day they killed Robert Bland, Henry Elfers, a member of the council of arbitration,[9] and Henry Beckroge, taking the settlers' guns and ammunition. The youths then mounted the horses of the murdered men and rode down the Salmon River. Soon they met and fired upon Samuel Benedict, painfully wounding him. He had killed a drunken Indian in 1875, and was accused of having sold liquor to the Nez Perces. Benedict managed to escape to his cabin.

Exulting in their sanguinary deeds, the young braves rode back to White Bird's camp on the morning of June 14. Aflame with reckless courage, they exhibited the horses and guns they had taken from the murdered whites.

Big Dawn, a brother of Yellow Bull and the uncle of Red Moccasin-top, leaped on one of the captured horses and rode through the village, shouting, "Now you will have to go to war! See! Walaitits has killed men and stolen horses! Now the soldiers will be after us! Prepare for war! Prepare for war!"[10]

At Big Dawn's words a near panic seized the camp. For a time shock paralyzed everyone, and then all the pent-up emotions of the last few years burst forth like the fury of lions at the kill. Here, as elsewhere, the Indian testimony is contradictory. McWhorter's informants declared Two Moons rode through the camp urging further forays. But Two Moons himself did not mention it in giving his own story to McWhorter. On the contrary, Two Moons declared he left camp in the morning upon arising to seek Joseph and inform him of the kill-

[9] Elfers had rendered a legal decision in the Mason case unfavorable to the Indians. For a further discussion see p. 155 of this volume. For additional Indian testimony see McWhorter, *Yellow Wolf: His Own Story*, pp. 44-45, and note 11, p. 45.

[10] Curtis, *op. cit.*, VIII, 164.

ings. Curtis' Nez Perce sources, though, state that White Bird, who had been favoring war for years, mounted his horse and rode around the village, calling for all warriors to join the killers. The young men and the *tewats,* in hearty accord, cheered him on.

These revengeful acts, perpetrated by reckless youths, would precipitate the bloody, costly, and tragic Nez Perce War. While the Indians affirmed that it was the settlers who brought on the conflict by their numerous acts of injustice and aggression, many other causes were responsible, and the settlers' acts furnished a contributory factor. As already shown, the roots of other causes of the war reached back into the years. One remote cause was found in Dr. Elijah White's proposal of 1842 that the Nez Perce nation elect a head chief over all the bands. Again, Stevens' arbitrary recognition of Lawyer as head chief at the council of 1855 first strained the relationship between the United States government and the Indians, and hostility was increased by the Nez Perces' dissatisfaction with the treaty of that year. Then the government's dilatory action in not ratifying either the Treaty of 1855 or the one of 1863 for four years after signing intensified the disaffection among the chiefs. The government's failure to keep faith with the Nez Perces by violating treaty obligations further aggravated them. Finally, the action taken by the commission of 1863 in holding all bands of the Nez Perces bound to a rule by majority became an inciting cause, when the government accepted Lawyer's sale of the Wallowa Valley as binding and legal.

Immediate causes of the war included the white settlers' unlawful preëmption of Indian lands, and their mistreatment of the Nez Perces; the favoritism shown white men in the frontier courts; the decision of the committee of 1876 to accept Governor Grover's declaration that Joseph's band had no legal right to Wallowa after 1863; and the government's command to the Wal-lam-wat-kins to quit the valley of winding waters—a land made sacred to Joseph's people by their Dreamer religious beliefs. All these were inciting causes of the conflict, touched off by the bloodthirsty acts of the three young braves.

Tuhulhutsut, boiling with mortification over his imprisonment, is said to have organized another raiding party of seventeen warriors. They, along with Yellow Bull, joined the three murderers and rode back to the valleys and steep slopes of the Salmon River mountains to spread the carnage. The war party hunted down the wounded Benedict and killed him as he tried to escape.

Unsuspecting whites found themselves in the midst of the frontier's worst scourge—an Indian war. James Baker and a Frenchman, August Bacon, were the next victims of the raiders, who then ransacked and burned their cabins to the ground and drove off the cattle. The postmaster of White Bird, John J. Manuel, and his little daughter, Maggie, although both badly wounded, managed to escape with their lives into the brush.

Meanwhile, the more conservative element in the Indian village took down their lodges and moved to Cottonwood Creek, leaving at the old site one double and one single tepee. Apart from the others stood the confinement lodge where Joseph's wife was giving birth to a baby girl. A number of treaty Indians fled to the Lapwai Reservation.

The nontreaties from Tuhulhutsut's and White Bird's bands joined Looking Glass, who was encamped on Cottonwood Creek. But this chief, not wishing to be involved in the trouble, promptly packed up and hurried to his own territory on the Clearwater. Hush-hush-cute did the same, but set up his new village above Stites and also on the Clearwater. Many of Joseph's band likewise took the hint to depart from the troubled zone.

When the three young murderers had returned to camp, Two Moons rode out on the morning of June 14 to inform Joseph of what had happened. He met the chief, Alokut, Half Moon, John Wilson, Three Eagles, Welweyas (described by Alokut's wife as "a half-man-and-half-woman, who dressed like a woman"), Joseph's daughter Sound of Running Feet, and Alokut's wife

Wetatonmi all coming home to Joseph's lodge after butchering the cattle. Just at this time, according to Three Eagles, Big Dawn was riding around the village, inciting the people to fight. While he was talking, the Indians caught up their ponies and began to move away.

Two Moons relates that Joseph and Alokut made no reply to his news of the killings, but rode silently and swiftly to camp, leaving the women to bring on the twelve packhorses loaded with beef. The brothers found most of the lodges already down. They tried to halt the panicked exodus to Cottonwood but failed. Wetatonmi recounts how Joseph and Alokut rode among the people, exhorting them, "Let us stay here till the army comes! We will then make some kind of peace with them."[11]

But the rest hurried after their families, leaving five men in the two lodges. However, Yellow Wolf declared, "All left but Joseph and his band and about thirty-five other men. These stayed to guard against any enemy surprise, but some were afraid Joseph and Ollokot [Alokut] might desert the other Indians."[12] Alokut's wife confirmed this latter point to McWhorter, but stated only the brothers' tepees remained and "three men were with them." If fighting started, apparently Joseph's fifty-five warriors would be badly needed and the hostiles would tolerate no defection by their Wallowa brethren.

Three Eagles relates:

Joseph's brother-in-law told him: "We must go back to Lapwai. There is no reason why we should have trouble. We were not here when the white men were killed, and we need not go with them."[13]

Three Eagles agreed to this, but Joseph, who apparently had second thoughts, answered:

---

[11] McWhorter, *Hear Me, My Chiefs!*, p. 196.

[12] McWhorter, *Yellow Wolf: His Own Story*, p. 45. Yellow Wolf's reference to "thirty-five other men" who remained in camp with Joseph and Alokut may be a misprint as other Indian witnesses all mentioned only five men as staying.

[13] Curtis, *op. cit.*, VIII, 24-25. From the account by Three Eagles.

"I can hardly go back. The white people will blame me, telling me that my young men have killed the white men, and the blame will come on me." Alokut said nothing. The young men who had killed the white men did not belong to Joseph's band, but to the Lamtama [White Bird's band]. . . . So we packed up [June 15] and moved to the camp at Sapatsash [Cottonwood Creek].[14]

The next day (June 16) all of the Indians went on to White Bird Canyon.

Analyzing the situation later, Joseph said:

I was deeply grieved. . . . I knew that their acts would involve all my people. I saw that the war could not then be prevented. The time had passed. I counseled peace from the beginning. I knew that we were too weak to fight the United States. We had many grievances, but I knew that war would bring more. . . . I would have given my own life if I could have undone the killing of white men by my people.

I know that my young men did a great wrong, but I ask, Who was first to blame? They had been insulted a thousand times; their fathers and brothers had been killed; their mothers and wives had been disgraced; they had been driven to madness by the whisky sold to them by white men; they had been told by General Howard that all their horses and cattle which they had been unable to drive out of Wallowa were to fall into the hands of white men; and, added to all this, they were homeless and desperate.

I blame my young men and I blame the white men. I blame General Howard for not giving my people time to get their stock away from Wallowa. I do not acknowledge that he had the right to order me to leave Wallowa at any time. I deny that either my father or myself ever sold that land. . . . It may never again be our home, but my father sleeps there, and I love it as I love my mother. I left there, hoping to avoid bloodshed.[15]

When Joseph learned the young men had been secretly buying large quantities of ammunition and food in the neighboring towns, he realized that all his hopes and ef-

---

[14] *Ibid.*, p. 50.

[15] "An Indian's Views . . . ," *op. cit.*, pp. 424-25.

forts for peace were futile. His somber thoughts must then have turned to his wife and the new baby—born at Tepahlewam, near Tolo Lake, the place called Rocky Canyon by the whites. They, together with the other women and children, would suffer most from war. Yet, as chief of his people, his first duty was to look after their welfare and safety.

"I knew I must lead them in fight," said the chief, "for the whites would not believe my story."[16]

Ever since the war of 1877 there had been a controversy as to whether the nontreaties had a war chief during the retreat, and whether Joseph or Looking Glass was entitled to that honor. Most documentary evidence available when the author and her assistant, Dan McGrath, did their original research in 1933-34 indicated there was, in truth, a war chief, and Joseph was the most likely candidate. All the army officers—Perry, Parnell, C. E. S. Wood, Whipple, and Forse; and Generals Sherman, Howard, Gibbon, Sturgis, and Miles—credited Joseph with the real leadership, as did Commissioner of Indian Affairs Hayt. George W. Fuller, former librarian of the Spokane Public Library and historian of repute, also corroborated the premise that Joseph was the war chief. Fuller's *History of the Pacific Northwest* was one of the most scholarly works on the history of that region written to 1934.

Indian sources contacted by Howard and McGrath also supported the foregoing thesis. Samuel Tilden, former member of the Flathead Indian Reservation police, and one of the few Nez Perce survivors of the war, declared Joseph to be the real leader. This was likewise the understanding of Joseph Blackeagle, grand-nephew of the chief, who, as a boy, often heard the older members of his tribe discuss the Nez Perce War.

In addition, settlers in the region of hostilities believed Joseph to be the war chieftain. Dan McGrath's mother,

---

[16] *Ibid.* This statement is substantiated by Mr. Samuel Tilden, Nez Perce of Arlee, Montana, in a letter to the author dated November 10, 1934. Tilden was a member of the hostile bands.

living in Missoula at the time, vividly remembered seeking refuge at the Higgins and Worden store. Her mother, Mrs. Peter Deery, was nursing Captain Rawn's wife during the summer, and knew Joseph personally. Mrs. McGrath spoke the Nez Perce tongue and often played with the Indian children. The Nez Perces frequently camped near her father's homestead while on their way to and from the buffalo hunt and visited with the family. Both Mrs. McGrath and her mother stated that Chief Joseph led the fighting forces, while Looking Glass acted the part of diplomat. This statement was based on conversations with the old men and women who were captured in the Bitterroot Valley. They received medical treatment from Mrs. Deery, and for hours would sit in the farmhouse telling her their story of woes and injustice. All protested that the white men had driven them into war—also they declared Joseph to be the war chief. None of the Nez Perces, they averred, had any intentions of harming the people of Montana, for they considered them their friends.

An early dissenter to this viewpoint was Duncan MacDonald, half Scot and half Nez Perce, and a relative of White Bird. He interviewed that chief in 1877-78 during his exile in Canada, and published the Nez Perce account of the war in the *New Northwest* of Deer Lodge during 1878-79. MacDonald stated that White Bird called Looking Glass the war chief. Judge William I. Lippincott, of Butte, made a special trip to the Flathead Indian Reservation at Arlee in 1934 to inquire about this and other information for Howard and McGrath, but Duncan MacDonald was unable to enlighten the judge about the matter. No doubt, the element of time had caused MacDonald to forget many details at this late date.

Also Will Cave, historian of Missoula, Montana, and volunteer in the Nez Perce War, supported MacDonald's claim. However, Cave's contention that everyone in Missoula spoke only of Looking Glass is disproved by quotations from letters written at the time and reprinted in Chapter XVI of this volume. Looking Glass, however, was better known in Missoula than Joseph, and had, in fact, passed through the town shortly before the Lapwai council in May.

Another dissenter, Edward S. Curtis, photographer and historian, who researched Nez Perce sources in the early 1900's, concluded Joseph was "no more responsible for the success or failure [of the campaign] than were several other chiefs, and far less so than Looking Glass, and at no time, with the possible exception of the first battle, was he either in executive or active command of the Indian forces; that his voice in council during that period was no greater than that of any other individual among the head-men; and that Looking Glass—after he had joined the hostile forces—was in fact their leader, and was, so far as such is possible in Indian wars, their commander."[17] Curtis considered Looking Glass "the ablest of all the chiefs."

Recent Nez Perce testimony coincides with the above. Josiah Red Wolf, who went through the war as a child of five, in an interview in the *Spokesman-Review Inland Empire Magazine,* November 17, 1963, declared: "Joseph was not a war chief. He was not the main leader nor was he the great leader of the war. . . . We (children and old people) were taken care of by Joseph and kept away from the fights. . . . Joseph was a good man, but he was not the battle leader. Looking Glass was the leader with battle experience (gained helping the Crows fight the Sioux in 1874). Looking Glass spoke for all the bands."

The late L. V. McWhorter, who made the most exhaustive study of the subject among Indian sources of any investigator, believed Joseph was too inexperienced in fighting in the intertribal wars during buffalo hunting expeditions to be a battle leader. He was also the youngest chief of the five warring bands, and the only one who made but a single known journey to the buffalo country. Besides, "In the more than two dozen narratives [of Nez Perce sources] recorded by McWhorter, Joseph never

[17] Curtis, *op. cit.*, VIII, 22.

once emerges as war chief or as a leading warrior."[18] Philip Williams, a Nez Perce, explains "that leadership on the battlefield was never assumed by any of the chiefs."[19] McWhorter concludes: "Apparently none of the chiefs participated very actively in the fighting until the last battle, the final defense of the tribe in the fight for survival."[20]

It is perhaps highly significant that a nephew of Chief Joseph, Yellow Wolf, a warrior and scout throughout the war, scarcely mentions his uncle in his account of the fighting in *His Own Story,* as recorded by McWhorter, until the last battle. Had Joseph been an active participant in the battles it is inconceivable Yellow Wolf would have ignored all reference to his relative, particularly since he lived in Joseph's lodge and was therefore on friendly terms. Nor does Chief Joseph himself in his own story relate his personal exploits in any battle except the final one at Bearpaw. Presumably, this was not due to extreme modesty on the chief's part, but to a lack of fighting activities. Thus, confronted by this formidable array of Indian testimony, the modern historian must reevaluate Chief Joseph's role in the war as a peace leader, a guardian of the noncombatants, and as a most reluctant warrior.

But Joseph has long become identified in the public mind as symbolic of the fighting prowess of the warring Nez Perces and he may long remain so, despite the Indian evidence to the contrary. The whites have invested him with the title of military genius, a quality shared, the Indians avow, by many warriors and chiefs of the five bands.

---

[18] McWhorter, *Hear Me, My Chiefs!*, p. 505.

[19] *Ibid.*, p. 506.

[20] *Ibid.*

PART III
The Military Campaign of 1877

CHAPTER XI

The Settlers Prepare for War

ALARMED by the belligerent attitude of the Indians prior to the first murderous outbreak, the settlers of Mount Idaho had erected barricades. Farmers abandoned their crops, ranchers let their stock go astray, and all fled with their wives and children to the protection of the settlements.

Arthur I. Chapman, reputedly a friend of Joseph, had been warned on June 13 by Tucallacasena, a "handsome and stalwart" brother of Looking Glass, that the Nez Perces were practically on the warpath. The chief's brother also notified M. H. Rice to be on his guard. Chapman was married to a Nez Perce woman and fluently spoke the language of his wife's tribe. He would later be retained by General Howard as official interpreter. But in the latter part of June he organized a company of volunteers and was elected captain.

Some of the treaty Nez Perces who had been engaging in the sports and contests held in Rocky Canyon became fearful of trouble after the first murders, and, as mentioned in the preceding chapter, left the main camp in haste. They warned their white friends to go into town and wait until all danger had passed.

Letters and telegrams poured into the Boise office of Mason Brayman, governor of Idaho Territory. The citizens[1] were afraid that trouble might spread to the Weiser and Paiute Indians, who might burn their crops and

[1] Even by the military the term "citizens," rather than "civilians," was customarily applied to the white settlers, whether they lived on farms or in the towns. The two terms, however, will be used interchangeably in this volume.

buildings. In answer to these urgent pleas the governor dispensed arms and ammunition to the settlers of north and west central Idaho. Offers of assistance from adventure-loving spirits who wanted to join the volunteers came to Governor Brayman from as far away as Utah, Oregon, and California.

Volunteer companies sprang into being in all the affected areas. Edward McConville became captain of one group which he organized at Lewiston. In July, D. B. Randall mustered a company of eighty mounted men in addition to Chapman's volunteers at Mount Idaho, since that town was in the center of the Indian troubles. Randall was elected captain, James L. Cearley, first lieutenant, and Lew P. Wilmot, second lieutenant.

Before fear had reached the point of a general hysteria, L. P. Brown, secretary of the volunteers at Mount Idaho, sent a letter to Captain David Perry, the commanding officer at Fort Lapwai. On the evening of June 14 (the second day of the massacres), the messenger arrived with the note, which stated that the Indians were insolent, and the citizens feared trouble.

Part of the message ran:

> Yesterday they [the Nez Perces] had a grand parade. About a hundred were mounted, and well armed, and went through the manoeuvres of a fight—were thus engaged for about two hours. . . . A good many were in town to-day, and were trying to obtain powder and other ammunition.[2]

This referred to White Bird's band, as the chief boasted that the Indians would not go on the reservation. The communication further suggested that Captain Perry send a force to hurry the Nez Perces onto the reserve should they resist.

Since many of the military operations took place in this area, the region will be briefly described. Mount Idaho was situated at the farther edge of a large camas prairie near mountain spurs that lay between the Salmon and

[2] Howard, *Chief Joseph, His Pursuit and Capture*, p. 91.

From collection of J. W. Redington. Photo courtesy of the Misses Brady

Chief Joseph

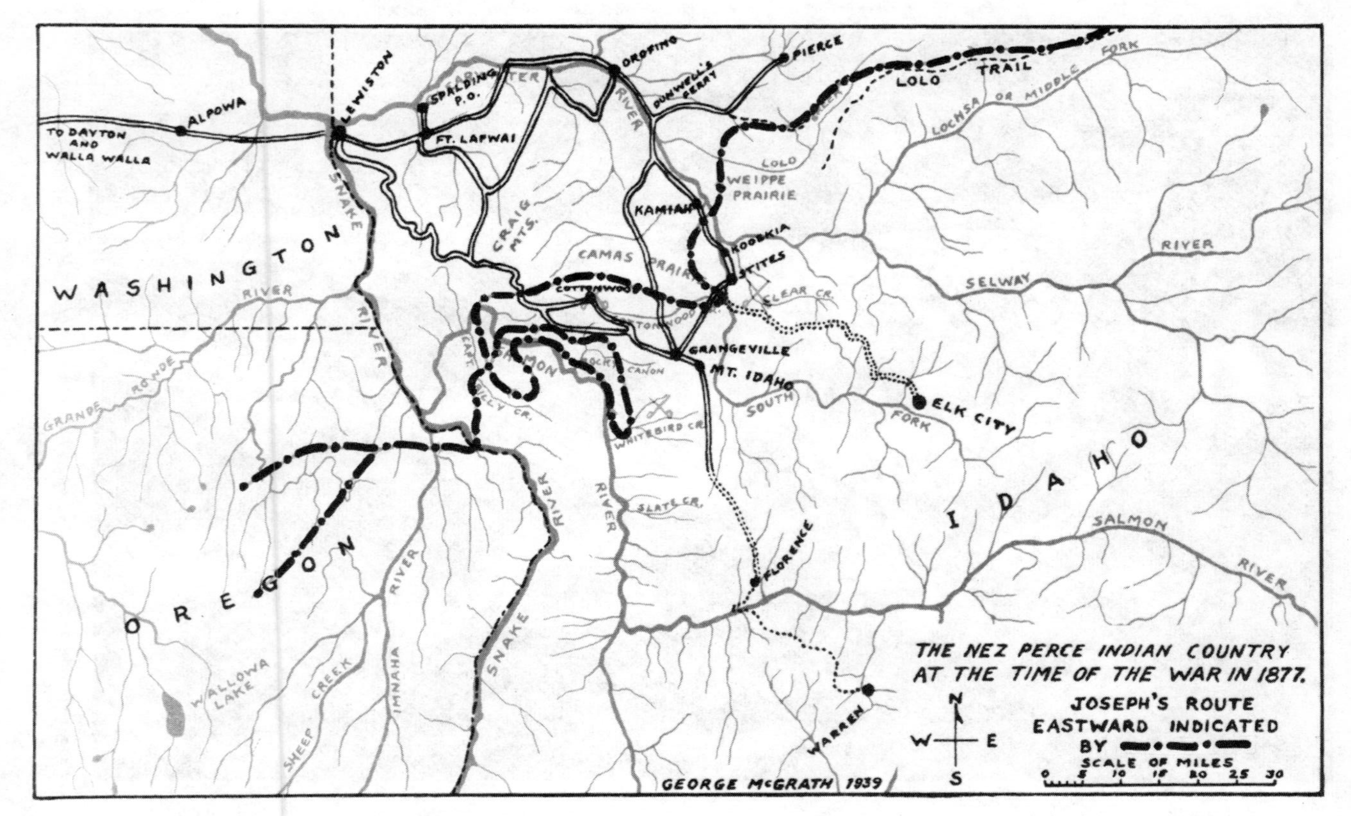
THE NEZ PERCE INDIAN COUNTRY AT THE TIME OF THE WAR IN 1877.
JOSEPH'S ROUTE EASTWARD INDICATED BY
SCALE OF MILES
0 5 10 15 20 25 30
N
W E
S
GEORGE McGRATH 1939
WASHINGTON
OREGON
IDAHO
TO DAYTON AND WALLA WALLA
ALPOWA
LEWISTON
SPALDING P.O.
FT. LAPWAI
OROFINO
DUNWELL'S FERRY
PIERCE
LOLO TRAIL
LOLO
WEIPPE PRAIRIE
KAMIAH
KOOSKIA
STITES
CRAIG MTS.
CAMAS PRAIRIE
COTTONWOOD
CLEAR CR.
GRANGEVILLE
MT. IDAHO
ELK CITY
SOUTH FORK
WHITEBIRD CR.
SLATE CR.
FLORENCE
WARREN
LOCHSA OR MIDDLE FORK
SELWAY
RIVER
SALMON
SNAKE
RIVER
GRANDE RONDE
IMNAHA
SHEEP CREEK
WALLOWA LAKE

Clearwater rivers, sixty miles southeast of Fort Lapwai. Rocky Canyon, where the bands of both White Bird and Joseph were then encamped, was the same distance from the post, but nearer the Salmon River. Slate Creek was forty miles beyond Mount Idaho. This settlement lay three miles southeast of Grangeville.

General Howard had returned to Fort Lapwai on June 14, accompanied by Colonel Watkins, Inspector of Indian Affairs, to see if the bands were moving in accordance with his orders.

At dawn on June 15, Captain Perry sent a detachment of troops to reconnoiter toward Mount Idaho. Joe Roboses went with them as interpreter. Near Craig Mountain the soldiers met two excited Indians, one a lad of fourteen, who told the details of the Slate Creek murders. The detachment returned to Fort Lapwai at noon and reported to Howard, who thereupon investigated the rumor of the massacres. He established that they were committed by a few Indians in private revenge.

But as everything seemed to indicate trouble, Howard and Watkins, acting upon the advice of Agent Monteith and Perrin Whitman, the interpreter, sent Subchief Jonah and Joseph's father-in-law, Whisk-tasket, to the group of malcontents said to be gathered at Chapman's ranch. Old Whisk-tasket, the father of Joseph's first wife, had volunteered to go and stoutly affirmed that his son-in-law would not fight. On the way, these emissaries encountered Looking Glass's brother and a half-breed citizen named West. They were bringing to Perry more letters from Mount Idaho, giving detailed accounts of the killings. Together, the four Nez Perces hurried back to the fort. Brown's communication said, in part: "One thing is certain, we are in the midst of an Indian war."[3]

In the face of that General Howard immediately detailed ninety-nine men from Troops F and H of the First Cavalry, commanded by Captain David Perry, for the relief of the Grangeville and Mount Idaho citizens. Cap-

[3] *Report of Secretary of War*, 1877, I, 601. Report of Brigadier General Howard.

tain Joel G. Trimble, a brevet major of Company C, and Lieutenants William R. Parnell and Edward R. Theller, the latter loaned from the Twenty-first Infantry, were ordered to assist Perry. This officer, a brevet colonel of Company F, was "a little over six feet in height, and very erect," according to Howard. "He shows a clear Saxon eye, and usually wears a pleasant smile—pleasant, but with a reserve in it."[4]

All the officers—Perry, Trimble, Theller, and Parnell—were married. Mrs. Trimble and her children and Mrs. Parnell had remained at Fort Walla Walla. Mrs. Perry had gone by boat to Portland shortly before Howard issued the order to leave on the campaign. Mrs. Theller was the only officer's wife at Fort Lapwai when the command left. Literally holding down the fort with her were twenty soldiers to act as a guard, commanded by Captain Boyle, Howard's former aide-de-camp.

At this time the general thought all the nontreaty bands were involved. If he had known that actually only White Bird's young men were guilty, this history might never have been written. Howard remained at Fort Lapwai to direct the operations in the field. He sent dispatches to Walla Walla for reenforcements, and ordered Captain Whipple's command from the Grande Ronde Valley to the post.

The women at the agency, three miles from Fort Lapwai, were escorted to Lewiston, although a few remained to give aid to settlers who had sought safety there. At Kamiah the hostiles ransacked the subagency after the employees had left it. The Indians took food, bedding, and cooking utensils. Wild rumors added to the confusion as treaty and nontreaty Nez Perces, full of tales of expected massacres, took refuge at the fort.

A group of thirty settlers, including many women and children from Salmon River, found protection in a barricade on Slate Creek.[5] The men formed a volunteer com-

---

[4] Howard, *op. cit.*, p. 88.

[5] Harry W. Cone reports that White Bird's young men who murdered the settlers in cold blood told him in the Nez Perce tongue

pany, although they had only shotguns and revolvers with which to defend themselves.

Marauding bands of hostiles raided the prairies to the very limits of Grangeville and Mount Idaho. Many settlers who had not heeded the first warnings of their Nez Perce friends now attempted flight, only to fall into the hands of Indians turned savage fiends by overindulgence in whiskey. On June 15 raiders wounded and abducted Mrs. John J. Manuel, and killed William Osborne and Harry Mason. The latter had whipped two Indians in the spring. A council of arbitration had decided in favor of the white man, and so another cankering sore was added to the Nez Perces' lacerated feelings against American injustice.

Like a modern Paul Revere, Lew Day volunteered to ride from Mount Idaho to Fort Lapwai to secure military aid. He galloped over the countryside, warning the white people to flee to the towns, for the redskins were on a rampage of murder and rapine. Being fired upon and wounded by the Indians, he stopped at Cottonwood House, a ranch and stage station owned by B. B. Norton. Day assisted a party of whites there to escape on the evening of June 14. With the men, women, and children in a wagon, escorted by two of the men on horseback, the ten people left Norton's ranch after dark in a desperate attempt to reach Mount Idaho, eighteen miles away.

They had not traveled far before a war party overtook them about midnight. In the running fight that ensued the men attempted to hold off the superior force of Indians. But every gun flash attracted the bullets of the attackers and the team horses were quickly shot down, bringing the wagon to a halt. In the confusion Miss

---

that the Indians were on the warpath, and they warned the friendly whites to stay home. Cone spread the alarm, and the surviving ranchers barricaded themselves on Slate Creek. Cone also recounts the story of Tolo, a friendly Nez Perce woman, who brought reenforcements to the settlers from the mining town of Florence. Cone, "The White Bird Battle," MS. in Idaho State Historical Library, Boise.

Bowers and little Hill Norton jumped out and escaped into the brush.

John Chamberlain, his wife, and two children tried to escape from the wagon in the darkness, but their progress through the bushes was soon discovered by the war party. During the hand-to-hand combat Chamberlain was fatally shot. While he lay dying the terrifying shrieks of his wife rang in his ears as the marauders repeatedly attacked her and inflicted severe injuries. One Indian cruelly cut off a piece of the daughter's tongue, and in so doing stabbed her in the neck; another placed the little boy's head beneath his knees and crushed the youngster to death. This is the only record of deliberate atrocities perpetrated by the Nez Perces. Naturally such acts were not sanctioned by the chiefs, but appear to have been committed by bloodthirsty young braves.

The remainder of the party protected themselves behind the dead horses and fought off the desultory fire of the Indians until daylight. Lew Day and Joseph Moore fell mortally wounded. Day survived until the morning, and Moore lingered on for six weeks. During the night one of the raider's bullets killed Norton. His wife was shot through both legs, but later, like Mrs. Chamberlain and her daughter, recovered.

Miss Bowers managed to reach Mount Idaho by a tortuous route and gave the alarm to the citizens. Forty of them rushed out to the rescue and brought the wounded into town the next day.

Patrick Brice, a husky miner from Florence, was traveling northward when he found a little girl, Maggie Manuel,[6] hiding from the Indians in the bushes. She had been badly wounded by an arrow. Brice carried the child

[6] Maggie Manuel was the daughter of Mrs. John J. Manuel. She is now Mrs. Maggie Bowman, and was residing in Butte, Montana, in 1934. At the time of the Salmon River massacres she was seven years old. Mrs. Bowman testifies under oath that she saw Chief Joseph drive a knife into her mother's breast while she was nursing her baby in their cabin home. She claims their house was set on fire that day and her mother and the infant cremated. Later she recovered the charred remains of her mother's earrings.

But James Conley, who saw service in the Nez Perce War, says he

to her home on White Bird Creek, where he constructed a rude chair from the burned remains of the house. He strapped the improvised litter to his back and started to carry the girl to Mount Idaho by a devious route of fifty miles. For two nights he hiked, and he hid himself and the wounded child in the brush during the day.

A highly dramatized account of this incident, written by Charles S. Moody, narrates that Brice met a raiding

---

went to the Manuel home, accompanied by other men, and although they raked over the ashes they failed to find any human bones.

Harry Cone, who speaks the Nez Perce language and was also in the war, says that Yellow Bull was in command of the Salmon River group of Chief Joseph's tribe and encamped near his home on Slate Creek. Yellow Bull, Mr. Cone reports, boasted that he had Mrs. Manuel with him. (Yellow Bull, however, was a member of White Bird's—not Joseph's—band.)

C. T. Stranahan of Lewiston, former Nez Perce Indian agent, testifies that later an Indian in Yellow Bull's band told him under a pledge of secrecy that the story then circulating about Mrs. Manuel's murder by Chief Joseph and her subsequent cremation was untrue. Two members of Joseph's band told this Indian that the chief took no part in the massacre. Instead he "stayed for some time by her side and made his men leave her alone."

Mr. Stranahan further reports General Howard told him personally that Joseph did not harm Mrs. Manuel, but instead did everything to protect her.

In 1900 Mr. Stranahan cornered Yellow Bull about the mystery of Mrs. Manuel. He promised the chief not to reveal the information until after his death, which occurred July 20, 1919. Yellow Bull told Mr. Stranahan that Mrs. Manuel was taken captive. After the Indians crossed the divide into Montana, her captor and another warrior had a fight over her. One or the other killed her and dragged her into the brush, but Yellow Bull refused to reveal the name of the murderer. Reported in Robert G. Bailey, *River of No Return*, p. 189.

McWhorter's Indian informants told him Red Wolf tried to abduct Mrs. Manuel on horseback "when she snatched the knife from his belt and attempted to kill him. He struck her, felling her to the ground, and she died from the fall." Presumably she was carried back to her home and the house then set afire. (McWhorter, *Hear Me, My Chiefs!*, pp. 215-16.)

This Indian statement is probably the most factual of all and agrees in essentials with Charles Moody's account which appeared in the *Century Magazine*, March, 1911. He relates that both Manuel and his wife, mounted on a horse apiece, the father with Maggie riding double, and Mrs. Manuel holding the baby, tried to escape the Indians. They were overtaken by the raiders and fired upon. The same arrow wounded both Maggie and her father but both were able to hide in the brush. The Indians then captured the mother and baby, with the results already described by McWhorter.

The circumstances surrounding the disappearance of Mrs. Manuel are the most hopelessly confused of any incident connected with the war. It appears more reasonable for the charge of murdering her, though, to be placed against Tuhulhutsut and Yellow Bull (Chuslum Moxmox) than Chief Joseph. Only one member of the party whose leader, Mox Mox, proposed to kill him and the girl. He overawed the Indians by displaying a blood-red cross tattooed on his breast. They permitted him to go on, but threatened reprisal against all inhabitants of Mount Idaho if he didn't return in "two sleeps."

Brice continued on his way and carried the child safely into Mount Idaho. After a day's rest, he went back to the Indian camp where he presented himself as a hostage, supposedly to Chief Joseph, who magnanimously sent him on his way unharmed.[7]

---

latter's band, Philip Williams (Lahpeealoot), joined in the second Salmon River raid and did accidentally wound Maggie Manuel with an arrow. See McWhorter, *op. cit.*, p. 199; pp. 213-14. But both Tuhulhutsut and Yellow Bull are mentioned as being with the sixteen or seventeen other warriors on the foray, along with the latter's son, Red Moccasin-top. Tuhulhutsut is described as the strongest man in the Nez Perce tribe and was very active in battle despite his age. As an example of his great strength the Indians affirm he got drunk on one occasion and became so troublesome in his village that eight of his own men tried to subdue and tie him up. But so powerful was he they were forced to let him go. See McWhorter, *op. cit.*, p. 184. The Indians admit the raiders taking part in the second foray were intoxicated when the Manuel home was pillaged. Yet Chief Joseph was known among both whites and Indians as a teetotaler. See Kate McBeth, *The Nez Percés Since Lewis and Clark*, p. 98. Besides, the day of Mrs. Manuel's disappearance, June 15, Two Moons, Wetatonmi, Alokut's wife, and Yellow Wolf all affirm Joseph and his brother were busy moving their camp from Tolo Lake to Cottonwood, while warriors kept Joseph under surveillance to prevent his escape to Kamiah or Lapwai! McWhorter accuses Arthur "Ad" Chapman of hatching and circulating the vicious story implicating Joseph.

Furthermore, despite Maggie Manuel Bowman's sworn testimony to the contrary, Patrick Brice is known to have rescued her from the bushes in a wounded condition and carried her to her home, which was already "only a heap of smoldering ashes. Among the embers lay the charred body of a woman and her infant. The Indians had taken Mrs. Manuel and her baby back to the house, killed them, and then fired the house." See Charles S. Moody, "The Bravest Deed I Ever Knew," *Century Magazine*, March, 1911, p. 783.

Out of all the contradictions, one fact is indisputably clear: Mrs. Manuel disappeared as a result of drunken Indians plundering her home during the second marauding expedition. But the charge of murder against Joseph, in the light of all present evidence, does seem preposterous and wholly without foundation.

[7] Charles Stuart Moody, "The Bravest Deed I Ever Knew," *Century Magazine*, March, 1911, pp. 783-84. It is very unlikely that Brice spoke to Chief Joseph. The chief could not speak English, although he understood it a little. Besides, during these confused days from June 14 to June 17, when the White Bird battle took place, the Indians moved their village each day to a new site and it would have been difficult, if not impossible, to locate Joseph's camp.

The Indian version of this episode is far less dramatic. In September, 1931, Black Feather (Black Eagle), who was one of the principals in the incident, gave McWhorter this account: Black Feather was approaching three Nez Perce warriors, who were smoking near the banks of White Bird Creek, when he heard a noise in the bushes and soon saw a white man (Patrick Brice) carrying a child on his left arm.

The white man nodded and asked, "Will you kill me?"

"No," said Black Feather, who then walked over to the three Indians. One of them, startled, attempted to shoot the white man. The other two objected because of the child. Black Feather motioned Brice to the bushes.

"When he reached the thicket," Black Feather continued, "he turned again and nodded to me, then disappeared in the brush. I saw him no more."[8]

Not knowing how many more settlers might be killed in the Salmon River mountains and fearing the worst, Mount Idaho citizens armed themselves with pitchforks, butcher knives, guns, and other weapons with lethal potentialities. The wildest excitement prevailed there and in the neighboring town of Grangeville until the troops arrived on the evening of June 16.

After leaving Fort Lapwai at 8:00 P.M. on the fifteenth, Perry's force marched all night. But finding the Indians had left Cottonwood Creek, the soldiers proceeded to Grangeville. The townsmen, certain the redskins could be given a thorough whipping, urged Perry to attack the Indian village at once. The officers, too, fully believed that these Indians, like all others in their experience, would scamper away from a show of military force. But as yet, the fighting mettle of the peaceful Nez Perces had never been tested against the whites; and later events proved that Perry's command was inadequate for offensive action.

Perry rested his men for an hour while he held a consultation with his officers and the citizens. The latter

---

[8] McWhorter, *op. cit.*, pp. 216-17.

declared they had seen the Indians going in force to White Bird Canyon with the likely intention of crossing the Salmon River at that point. From there the Nez Perces could go south to the Little Salmon, take the buffalo trail eastward, and so escape from the country. Fearing the Indians might do just that, Perry decided to attack them at White Bird Canyon before they could effect the river crossing.

Fully confident of victory, the cavalry, the Indian scouts, and eleven volunteers under George Shearer, an ex-Confederate major, started at ten o'clock that night for the Indian camp, sixteen miles from Grangeville. Advancing under cover of darkness, Perry hoped to make a surprise attack at dawn.

Wearied by the loss of two nights' sleep after a forced march of seventy miles, few of the men cared to talk as they rode across the rolling prairie. One trooper, though, struck a match to light his pipe. Instantly, from the hillside came the howl of a coyote that ended unnaturally on a high note.[9] However, none of the soldiers took particular notice of it.

Perry halted his command on the edge of the plateau near the head of White Bird Canyon, about four miles from the Indian encampment. Before the troops stopped to rest, a white woman with a babe in her arms, followed by a girl of six, had emerged from her place of concealment among the willows in a nearby gulch. The soldiers quickly emptied the food from their haversacks for the refugees who had lain three days in hiding. The mother was Mrs. Samuel Benedict. Her older girl's head had been badly crushed. Escorted by two volunteers, the woman and children finally reached Mount Idaho in safety.[10]

The troops caught only fitful snatches of sleep during what remained of the hours of darkness. At dawn of

---

[9] Major W. R. Parnell, "The Battle of White Bird Cañon," in Brady, *Northwestern Fights and Fighters*, p. 100.

[10] Howard, *Life and Experiences among Our Hostile Indians*, p. 284.

June 17 the bugle called boots and saddles, and soon the fatigued soldiers, keyed up now by the anticipation of forthcoming battle with the Indians, rode down the trail into the canyon still darkened by the shadows of night.

CHAPTER XII

The Battle of White Bird Canyon

AT FIRST there were only about thirty lodges in the camp of the hostiles on Cottonwood Creek. Most of the people were members of Tuhulhutsut's band, with some of Joseph's and White Bird's. Tuhulhutsut anticipated an attack by the soldiers, and the next day (June 15) he urged his tribesmen to move their village into the timber where they would find better protection. The Indians took his advice, and so he led them westward to a hill on the eastern side of the Salmon River.

The following day scouts kept the Nez Perces warned of the approach of Perry's force. To gain a more strategic location, the hostiles moved their camp to White Bird Creek, pitching their lodges in a small valley at the mouth of the stream where it debouched from the gorge. Behind the village lay the Salmon River. The rough, rocky, and precipitous slopes of White Bird Canyon concealed the encampment from Perry's sight.

Each hour of the day and night brought fresh news to the village. Lone horsemen posted on ridges and knolls secretly watched the roads leading from Fort Lapwai and Mount Idaho. Sentinels fired strawstacks on abandoned ranches, and the columns of smoke revealed to the Nez Perces the movements of the enemy.[1] Then the unnatural coyote call warned scouts posted on ridges above the village that the army was on the plateau and approaching the camp that night.

In a lodge apart from the village, Joseph's wife lay

[1] David Perry, "The Battle of White Bird Cañon," in Brady, *Northwestern Fights and Fighters*, p. 113.

resting after giving birth to a baby girl. Yellow Wolf[2] recalled that the event took place before the move to White Bird Canyon. The chief, anticipating battle at dawn, must have thought often of his wife and newborn daughter. Perhaps dark thoughts of death for himself on this new day dwelled in his mind. He could do nothing but wait—wait and hope and pray to the Spirit Chief to protect his life for the sake of the woman and helpless infant who needed him.

Joseph now knew nothing could prevent the inevitable conflict. Probably he discussed plans for the expected attack with the other chiefs, his brother Alokut, White Bird, and Tuhulhutsut.

On the morning of June 17, the brothers—Joseph and Alokut—watched from behind a pile of boulders that flanked the village the coming of dawn as it shed increasing light between shadowed canyon walls. Every able-bodied man, young and old, the Indians declared, who had not imbibed too freely of firewater the night before and so still lay in drunken stupor in the camp, was concealed by rock ridges or brush behind buttes near the base of the hillslopes. Soon scouts alerted the warriors with cries of "Soldiers coming! Soldiers coming this way!"

According to the Indian testimony the chiefs still hoped to avert trouble. The Nez Perces sent out a peace commission, some say of six, others two, carrying a white flag to meet the advancing soldiers, among whom were Arthur Chapman, Jonah Hayes, and his treaty Indians. Alokut had advised the warriors not to fire the first shot if fighting should ensue. He and the ruling chiefs wanted to learn the troops' intentions. All Indian sources interviewed by McWhorter state that Chapman, interpreter for Perry, fired at the truce party. An answering shot came from a Nez Perce warrior.

Meanwhile, before hostilities began, according to Gen-

[2] McWhorter, *Hear Me, My Chiefs!*, p. 197.

eral Howard's statement, Joseph had sent Alokut to borrow the spyglass from the Indian herder, Old Blackfoot.

Three Eagles, who was present, gives the following version of events:

> In the morning the Indians heard the bugle and Joseph said, "Maybe there are some Nez Perces with them, and they will tell us if the soldiers are coming with good hearts." Alokut looked through field-glasses to see if there were any Indians with the soldiers, and then passed the glasses to Joseph. Two of our men started riding up the hill. We saw a man [Chapman] shoot at them. Then the two Nez Perces shot. Jonah Hayes was with the soldiers, and came with the intention of talking to Joseph to see if he could not bring him back in peace. If Chapman had not fired, Jonah Hayes would have come and talked with Joseph, and the whole war would have been avoided.[3]

This account by Three Eagles is not mentioned by Howard or Perry or Joseph, but it is corroborated by other Nez Perce sources, notably Yellow Wolf, who states that five Indians under John Boyd constituted the truce party. It also indicates that Joseph hoped to the last to avert war.

Perry's men filed over the crest of the first slope of the canyon and started down into the shadows of the ravine. Mox Mox and another Indian dashed from their outpost near the plateau a mile away to confirm the report of the presence of troops to Joseph. Everyone in the village had been aroused from sleep. Most of the lodges had been taken down and loaded on ponies. Joseph ordered the women, under Mox Mox, to take charge of the spare horse herd and drive them down the river behind the bluffs.

---

[3] Curtis, *The North American Indian*, VIII, 26. According to Brady, *op. cit.*, p. 113, Jonah Hayes and Reuben, treaty Nez Perces friendly to the whites, were scouts who had been sent to watch "on the distant and commanding hill nearer the Salmon River."

Yellow Wolf, a youth of twenty-one years at the time of the battle and a member of Joseph's band, relates substantially the same account as Three Eagles. See McWhorter, *Yellow Wolf: His Own Story*, pp. 55-56.

The warriors divided into two main groups. Some went to line the buttes commanding the valley where White Bird Canyon debouched into the flat ground. Another squad of braves took cover behind a ridge to the left of the camp. Nez Perce testimony disagrees as to the activities of the chiefs. According to Three Eagles,[4] Joseph took "charge at one end of the line and Alokut at the other," the brothers commanding the center and right flanks, respectively. But Yellow Bull states: "In the fighting that followed, Joseph and Tuhulhutsut fought just like any other warriors, while the active arrangement of forces was made by . . . [Pile-Of-Clouds] of Hasotoin. . . . Three Nez Perces were wounded, but none killed." John Miles, another Indian, declares that none of the chiefs, "Joseph, White Bird, or Toohoolhoolzote [Tuhulhutsut], were in the charging fight [when the Indians charged the soldiers' left flank]. Joseph did some fighting but he was not with either bunch of the charging warriors. He did no leading."

Three Eagles states that only fifty men had guns at the beginning of the fight, the others being armed only with bows and arrows.

While camp was breaking up, women and children shouted and screamed in the excitement. Mox Mox placed the pony herd in a safe position behind a protecting butte, from where the women were prepared to bring fresh mounts to the warriors. The braves and their war ponies hurried to their positions in the line of battle, where the animals patiently stood beside their riders with ropes dragging on the ground. After the first flurries of excitement, everything became hushed. The warriors, completely hidden behind the rocks and knolls, quietly awaited the coming of the long knives. It was to be the first battle ever fought by the Nez Perces against the whites.

For four miles the trail of the cavalry wound down

---

[4] Three Eagles' account is quoted in Curtis, *op. cit.*, p. 26; Yellow Bull's statement is found in *ibid.*, p. 165; and John Miles' testimony appears in McWhorter, *Hear Me, My Chiefs!*, p. 249.

into the bottom of the narrow ravine, "now and again crossing a dry creek bed with here and there a heavy growth of willows and underbrush," Lieutenant Parnell writes. When the canyon widened farther on, the column changed from single file to four abreast again. Down the steep incline the horses slid and skirted boulders and willow brush.

The troops were now following a defile flanked by two ridges, and at a lower elevation rounded knolls appeared on their left. White Bird Creek lay over the more distant butte and emptied into the Salmon beyond the mouth of the canyon. A high ridge paralleled the trail on the right, lifting a sheer barrier. Still farther down, the canyon swung around to the east and opened into a valley four or five hundred yards wide between high bluffs.

As the cavalry in column of fours, with carbines ready, approached the buttes that concealed the Indian camp, Lieutenant Theller and eight men rode a hundred yards in advance of the main force. They had been ordered by Perry to act as advance guard. Next came Captain Perry and his Troop F with the citizen volunteers. Trimble's company brought up the rear, the ranks being separated by an interval of forty or fifty yards. Theller had been instructed to deploy and halt as soon as he saw the Indians, and to relay the information to his commanding officer.

Perry, having discovered the stir at the Indian camp, thought the Nez Perces were hurrying to cross the Salmon.

Lieutenant Theller, on the farther ridge to the left in the direction of White Bird Creek, perhaps still a hundred yards ahead of the other troops, halted and deployed his advance guard as rifle bullets began whizzing about him. Rushing word back to Perry, "The Indians are in sight!" he opened fire.

Indeed, the warriors had appeared suddenly in skirmish order, "stretched out in an irregular line." Their heads were bobbing from behind boulders, out of gulches and

From the L. V. McWhorter Manuscript Collection, Washington State University Library, 133

Alokut, Joseph's brother, was killed in the Battle of the Bearpaw Mountains. The photograph was taken at Walla Walla, Washington, in June, 1877, according to W. C. Painter, who saw the picture made.

ravines, and from behind the brush. Two Moons' flanking party of sixteen mounted braves was galloping well to the left, in the two-hundred-yard space between the butte and the creek. They charged toward the approaching column, yelling and firing. Three young men wearing "full length red blanket coats," Two Moons recalls, and two mounted on gray horses, rode side by side leading the Indian ranks. Two of them, Walaitits and Red Moccasin-top, were the reckless hotbloods who started hostilities. Strong Eagle was the third warrior. This trio afterwards became known as the "Three Red Coats."

Perry directed the nine civilians to hold the knoll on the left, and with Troop F charged to the front at a trot to support Theller. Trimble with Company H, fifty yards in Perry's rear, advanced to the right of the captain—a tactical error, as no reserves were left to protect the charging cavalry in event of a retreat. Nor did the men dismount, and so present a smaller target to the enemy. The volunteers, under Shearer, took their position on the rocky knolls to the left, which commanded all approaches from that direction.

Joseph and Alokut, on the center and right of the Indian lines, blocked the advance of the troops. But Theller's men, fighting grimly, checked the Nez Perces also, while the soldiers retreated to Perry who had halted on a ridge. On this elevated position the captain had dismounted, deployed his men, and sent his horses into the valley behind the lines. Perry had discovered that the level ground in front of him and behind the buttes was filled with Indians, and so he had prudently halted his charge.

The canyon soon filled with smoke. The shouts of soldiers and the war whoops of braves rang out above the din of rifles cracking. Both sides made thrusts to gain advantageous positions on higher ground to the right of the whole line.

Trimble's men were forced to dismount hurriedly, for their horses, unused to such tumult, became unmanageable. A few of the troopers had already been shot from their saddles. The animals' frantic attempts to break free and stampede required the attention of numerous horse holders. This unavoidable splitting of men weakened the force engaged on the firing line.

Two Moons' warriors soon reached their position around the two knolls and charged the citizens on the left one. Under the deadly fire of the Indian marksmen using Winchester magazine rifles, two whites fell wounded, and the remaining seven volunteers broke and fled. With hoarse shouts of victory the Indians swept over the knoll and immediately opened a cross fire on Perry's troops below. This strategy proved the turning point of the battle.

Trimble, unaware of the disaster to the volunteers' left line, repulsed Alokut's flanking movement to the right. Here the ground lifted gently upward from the canyon for perhaps two hundred yards, and then reared steeply to a plateau.

The Indians, concealing "some sixty or seventy warriors" among a large herd of loose ponies, drove them through the soldiers' lines. The braves opened fire from the rear, demoralizing the already confused troops, many of whom were recruits. Lieutenant Parnell's account is the only one that tells of this stratagem. Since he was the only officer to retreat directly up the canyon, he was the only one who could have observed this incident.[5]

Perry had lost his trumpet and so was unable to sound orders in the noise and confusion of battle. He started toward Captain Trimble. "When about three-fourths of the way to Trimble's position," he wrote, "I became aware of something wrong, and saw that the citizens had been driven off the knoll and were in full retreat and that

[5] Parnell received a brevet of colonel and a medal of honor for his gallant conduct in this battle. He apparently overestimated the number of warriors in this particular maneuver, for the testimony indicated that there was scarcely a total of seventy Indians engaged.

Yellow Wolf, however, denied this stratagem in McWhorter, *Yellow Wolf: His Own Story*, p. 57. He does state that the Nez Perces used the time-honored Indian custom of hanging on the sides of their ponies. This may have been the ruse referred to by Parnell.

the Indians were occupying their places, thus enabling them to enfilade my line and control the first ridge. The line of the left was already giving away under the galling fire."[6]

Although Perry was too far away to retake the hill by a charge, he realized his only alternative "was to fall back to the second ridge." Unable to blow recall without a bugle, he rode at a run to his center line and shouted at his men, directing them to pass his orders along to the command to fall back on the first ridge in their rear. As the men began obeying, he spurred again to Trimble and found that officer had lost his trumpet, also. Trimble occupied a high point on the right of the ridge. For the moment, his position was more tenable than Perry's.

Perry now noticed a commotion among his led horses, and saw that the left of his line had broken, and the men were "in a mad scramble for their horses." Realizing that many of the recruits were under fire for the first time and could not be depended upon in the stress of battle, Perry just had time to order Trimble to retreat toward higher and more defensible ground if he could not hold his position. The captain then dashed for the left to head off the men who had got mounted, and to attempt the formation of a new line.

The Indians sensed victory and charged up the hillside to cut off Trimble's men. Theller's troops, seeing the volunteers fleeing on the left and Trimble's force retreating on the right, became seized with the general panic and broke ranks, too. "Then the whole right of the line," Perry writes, "seeing the mad rush for horses on the left, also gave way and the panic became general."[7]

The officers—Perry, Trimble, Parnell, and Theller—each ordered, and then desperately pleaded with, their recruits to reform and retreat in a semblance of order, but even Trimble's veteran Company H, seeing the fear-crazed men below, lost all sense of organization and raced

[6] Perry, *op. cit.*, p. 115.

[7] *Ibid.*, p. 116.

for the plateau above. Perry and Trimble, bearing to the left, again and again managed to halt briefly first one squad and then another, "facing them about and holding the position until flanked out. In this way," Perry writes, "we retreated up the low ground to the right of the road,"[8] and thence up the canyon.

The captain then saw a trail to his rear leading up a bluff across the road. On the summit a group of soldiers were making a stand. Perry thought he could successfully defend the point for a time and turned his horse up the trail. But the leg-weary animal would not respond. Jumping off, the captain asked one of his men to carry him behind the saddle, which the trooper did. Perry directed a sergeant of Company H to hold a point near by with his squad, until he could place more men on the trail "to command there our position."

Fired upon from front and rear, though, the main body of soldiers broke their partially formed ranks again and fled, heedless of the officer's entreaties to form squads and protect their flight.

Lieutenant Parnell, with exceptional coolness and bravery, collected thirteen or fourteen mounted men and retreated up the main canyon in the direction from which the troops had come. For two hours this group doggedly fought and retreated from knoll to knoll before the Indians, who were swarming and firing from the hillsides and ravine. The soldiers paused to tighten up their saddle girths, and then continued to repulse attack after attack as braves finally charged within pistol range. Even after Parnell discharged his last cartridge, the bullet hitting one warrior in the thigh, his squad with admirable courage refused to be routed as they battled their way for four miles to the plateau.

Lieutenant Theller and eighteen men, acting as a rear guard, sought escape up one of the lateral ravines, hoping to overtake Perry's main force. Too late they discovered they had dashed into a cul-de-sac and were cut off from

---

[8] *Ibid.*

their comrades, now in mad flight to the highest ridges. With Indians on all sides and facing a blind canyon wall, Theller and his men gave shot for shot until the last soldier fell dead, surrounded by a pile of empty cartridges.

Perry's fourteen men and Trimble's squad made their way up the ridge, "keeping under cover as much as possible. . . . The Indians were all the time pressing us hard, but were a little more wary," Perry relates, "as our ascending position gave us a little better command of the lower position. . . . I saw Trimble some distance away, too far to make myself heard, but motioned him toward the road which we went down, and up which I believed Parnell and Theller to be working their way, but evidently was misunderstood. I then turned to the right (late left) with the few men I had, and made my way to the head of the cañon just as Parnell emerged with about a dozen men."[9]

Captains Perry and Trimble met Parnell's squad as the latter reached the plain. The two captains' forces had fallen back in a line nearly parallel to Parnell's and on the ridge above him.

Perry caught a loose horse and, mounted again, ordered the united command and the citizens to continue their fighting retreat toward Mount Idaho, eighteen miles away. The officers, with the greatest difficulty, saved the men this time from utter rout.

Directly to their rear was a deep ravine which had to be crossed. Parnell, at Perry's request, fought off repeated Indian sallies from the ridge while the captain crossed the gulch. He, in turn, was to cover the lieutenant's retreat. But on gaining the opposite ridge the frightened troops broke from Perry and scampered off. Parnell's cavalry made the other side, though, at a mad gallop. Again he halted his men to fire at the warriors. Then began a running battle until they reached Johnson's abandoned ranch, two or three miles away. Time and

[9] *Ibid.*, pp. 117-18.

again the command halted until the stragglers caught up with the main force.

At the ranch the cavalrymen dismounted, tied their horses to a rail fence, and took cover among the rocks. The house and barn appeared a short distance to their left with a small creek between. Of a sudden, bullets came whizzing from the front and right flank over their heads. The warriors had taken possession of higher ground among the rocks, and so commanded the troops' position.

Parnell then discovered Indians sneaking along the fence "that ran from the house up the hill perpendicular to our front," with intent to disable the horses. He reported this move to Perry, who realized their only hope of safety lay in reaching the town. The captain upon first reaching the ranch had decided to hold the place until dark and then fall back.

Parnell, amazed, stared at his superior officer.

"Do you know," he cried, "that it is seven o'clock in the morning—not evening—that we have been fighting nearly four hours and have but a few rounds per man left?"[10] Each soldier had started with forty rounds of ammunition.

Apparently, Perry was confused by the unexpected turn of the battle, and the Nez Perces' surprisingly efficient resistance. He asked Parnell to hold the position until he could get his men mounted.

The lieutenant did so, and then discovered his own horse missing and that the command was a hundred yards away. He shouted, but no one heard him. He thus continues:

> The Indians were now gaining on me, and shots kept whizzing past me from every direction in rear. I looked around for a hiding-place, but nothing presented itself that would secure me from observation. I fully made up my mind that I would not be taken prisoner, and determined to use my hunting-knife or a small derringer pistol I always carried in my vest-pocket.[11]

[10] William Parnell, "The Battle of White Bird Cañon," in Brady, *Northwestern Fights and Fighters*, p. 106.

[11] *Ibid.*, pp. 106-7.

Meanwhile, Parnell kept running after the troops. Some of his own men missed him, and, glancing back, saw him and reported to Perry. The captain halted the troops, and had Parnell's horse caught and led back to him. Perry then asked the lieutenant to reorganize the command. Parnell writes:

> I did so quickly, for there was little to organize, and requesting Perry to support me at a distance not greater than one hundred yards, I stated that I would take charge of the skirmish-line. The line was deployed at unusually great intervals, so as to cover as much front as possible and then, after a few words of caution and instructions, we waited the coming of the Indians, who at a distance had been closely watching us.[12]

With a yell the Nez Perces soon dashed up to the troops. Parnell waited until they were a hundred yards away, and then gave the order to commence firing. This fusillade brought down several warriors and ponies. The troops retreated at a walk and halted to fire again. Once more their volley checked the Indians' charge. These tactics of retreat, halt, fire, retreat another eighty or ninety yards was repeated by the troops for miles until they came close to Mount Idaho.

One warrior, presumed by Parnell to be White Bird, led repeated flanking movements in an attempt to force the soldiers off the plateau into Rocky Canyon on the right. Well-directed volleys by Perry repulsed the attacks and saved the command from being driven to certain annihilation.

While the troops were sloshing through a marsh, Parnell noticed the head of a man. He appeared to be stumbling through the swamp's long grass about halfway between the soldiers and the Indians. Parnell rallied his men and advanced toward the lone trooper, firing at the enemy as he did so. The man proved to be a private of Company H whose horse had been shot. Another cavalryman pulled him onto his own mount, and the soldiers con-

---

[12] *Ibid.*

tinued their retreat. Not until they were within four miles of Mount Idaho and citizen reinforcements had come to their aid, did the Indians give up the pursuit.

Unlike the usual procedure in Indian warfare the Nez Perces followed through, sustaining their attack to a definite goal. Then the victors hurried back to the canyon to share in the spoils of battle. The bodies of the fallen troops were stripped of their clothing, pistols, rifles, and ammunition.

Thirty-three soldiers, one third of Companies F and H, and one officer had been killed in this brief and decisive battle. The Indian casualties were never determined officially. Three Eagles, however, is authority for the statement that the Nez Perces had two wounded, but none killed. Both Yellow Bull and Yellow Wolf give the number as three wounded. In the Lewiston (Idaho) *Teller* for June 23, 1877, four Indians were reported wounded. It is possible that the Nez Perces' casualties may have been somewhat higher, since it is an Indian characteristic to minimize losses in battle.

In speaking of the White Bird fight, Joseph told Inspector McLaughlin in 1900:

I had two hundred and forty fighting men at first... but Looking Glass came in afterwards with more. [This would be after the Cottonwood skirmish.] I knew that there would be much fighting, and I had talked to my people, and it was settled that we would go to the buffalo country over to the east. I told my people that they must not fight with settlers, but wait for the soldiers, and our scouts told us that the soldiers would soon come after us. They didn't think that the Nez Perces would stand against the troops. I found that our young men had been making ready for the trouble, and so had the other chiefs, and we had many guns and much ammunition—we had more before the fight was over.... Until the first fight had been fought and the victory had been given to the Nez Perces, I did not think that we would go farther than the buffalo grounds. After the fight, I knew that I would have to lead my people to the country where Sitting Bull had found a refuge when pursued.[13]

However, in an interview given in 1878, Joseph said, "We numbered in that battle sixty men, and the soldiers a hundred." The chief probably meant the figure of 240 to include the disaffected Indians from other bands who joined him after the fight at White Bird Creek, and in time for the Cottonwood skirmish.

After the battle Joseph's first thoughts turned to his family. He hastened back to his lodge to see how his wife and infant daughter were getting along.

That night the Nez Perces, nearly delirious with joy, celebrated with victory dances before the blazing campfires. The canyon walls reverberated with the wild war whoops of young men and the excited screams of women and children mingling with the pulse-maddening drumming of the *tewats*. Painted bodies, made weirdly grotesque by the flickering firelight, swayed, gyrated, and leaped to the barbaric rhythm of the tomtoms.

From Mount Idaho, Captain Perry immediately sent off a dispatch to General Howard at Fort Lapwai, informing him of the army's overwhelming defeat. His message concluded with: "Please break the news of her husband's death to Mrs. Theller."[14]

But six hours *before* the battle took place, the general had been apprised of the disastrous outcome by a Nez Perce woman. Regarding this strange prophecy, Howard wrote:

I was awakened by loud talking in front of the porch at Lapwai, and went out. Jonah's wife, a large sized Indian woman, sat upon her horse. She was accompanied by another woman, the one that, as I understood, had just come from the hostiles. One of the half-breeds interpreted. She spoke so emphatically and so excitedly that she awakened everybody, and she declared:

---

[13] McLaughlin, *My Friend the Indian*, p. 351. Yellow Wolf claims that of the "fewer than seventy warriors" engaged in the battle, three were wounded and none killed. McWhorter, *op. cit.*, p. 60.

[14] Howard, *Chief Joseph, His Pursuit and Capture*, p. 118.

"The Indians had fixed a trap. All our troops had run straight into it. They [the hostiles] had come up on every side, and killed all the soldiers and all the scouts, including the friendly Indians."[15]

Perry, however, had not taken the Nez Perce scouts into the canyon, for they were unarmed. Thus, they had escaped danger. Nor had all the troops been killed. Otherwise, the woman's story veraciously depicted the events in White Bird Canyon.

The general realized the Indians' victory would not only give them confidence to engage the soldiers in another battle, but that very likely a number of malcontents from other bands would rush to the hostile ranks—as indeed they did. The fighting courage of the Nez Perces had been tested and proved on the field of combat, and the overconfidence of the whites changed to wholesome respect for the prowess of the enemy. This White Bird battle was the second most disastrous defeat ever suffered by the United States Army at the hands of Indians, being surpassed only by the Custer Massacre in 1876.

It was plain to the officers now that they had a foe worthy of their mettle, and one practiced in military tactics. General Shanks reports that

> ... Joseph's party was thoroughly disciplined; that they rode at full gallop along the mountain side in a steady formation by fours; formed twos, at a given signal, with perfect precision, to cross a narrow bridge; then galloped into line, reined in to a sudden halt, and dismounted with as much system as regulars.[16]

As a result of the fight, the Nez Perces not only replenished their supply of ammunition and rifles from the bodies of the soldiers, but they held the upper hand. Howard dared not attempt another battle with demoralized troops, and he would have to wait for reenforcements. He had already sent couriers to Walla Walla, 120

---

[15] *Ibid.*, p. 122.

[16] Norman B. Wood, *Lives of Famous Indian Chiefs*, p. 507.

miles distant, to telegraph General McDowell in San Francisco for aid. Troops on the way from Alaska to California were rerouted to Idaho. The general also appealed to Governor Brayman of Idaho Territory to lend what assistance he could, and to Major Green, commanding Fort Boise, to bring his cavalry from that region.

Before attempting another display of force, Howard waited for the troops and volunteers to arrive from Walla Walla, and for Whipple's and Winters' commands to come from the Wallowa Valley. Captains Miller and Miles brought several companies of the Fourth Artillery and Twenty-first Infantry to Fort Lapwai to join the concentration of troops for a major campaign. Miners and their packtrains of mules came to the post for the same purpose.

The citizens and the press clamored for action, but the general chose the wiser course of avoiding an engagement until he was thoroughly prepared. He declined to march immediately to Mount Idaho with what forces were then available, for that would leave Lapwai and Lewiston unguarded. Besides, he felt that Perry could defend Mount Idaho against any attack for a few days. Every citizen had a plan which he believed was the best one for conducting the campaign, and many besieged Howard with their ideas. The general was obliged not only to try to calm the fears of settlers, but also to appease the demands of volunteers who resented the authority and slow tactics of the military.

Finally, at noon of June 22, five days after Perry's battle, Howard's column of cavalry, infantry, and artillery, under command of Captain Marcus P. Miller, was ready to leave Fort Lapwai. Miller, a graduate of West Point and an officer in the Civil War, had also seen service in the Modoc uprising. He was a man of "middling height, well knit for toughness, with light beard and lightish hair, handsome forehead, blue eyes, and a pleasant face."[17] At this time the general's force numbered 227 men and was later joined by other troops, bringing the total to four hundred in the field.

---

[17] Howard, *op. cit.*, p. 133.

CHAPTER XIII

The Skirmish at Cottonwood

AFTER the first victory Joseph brought the young men under control.[1] He, with White Bird, Alokut, Tuhulhutsut, Yellow Bull, and others planned their next move while in the White Bird camp. Although Joseph was considered the "dominant leader by every officer and civilian who reported the progress of the campaign," as Professor Beal points out,[2] the Indian testimony does not confirm this view. The Nez Perces themselves declare plans were discussed at a council of the chiefs and older warriors.

Since the scouts kept the chiefs informed of the general's movements after leaving Lapwai, they knew that Howard would follow them, and they waited until the command had almost reached the Salmon River Valley. Then, on June 19, two days after the battle, the chiefs moved down the river a few miles, crossed at Horseshoe Bend, and took an admirably strong position in the mountains on the other side, using superb generalship in doing so. The warriors now held strategic command of the countryside. The only way in which they could be dislodged was for Howard to cross the Salmon and attack

---

[1] Lieutenant Forse, a graduate of West Point and the same officer who powwowed with Joseph in the Wallowa Valley incident in 1876, says that Joseph sent his brother, Alokut, to White Bird "to tell him that during the campaign he did not want to hear of any of White Bird's band injuring a woman or child; that if he did they would hear from him." Forse does not state his source of information, but the fact remains that the Nez Perces committed no more atrocities in Idaho, so that the statement carries some weight. Albert G. Forse, "Chief Joseph as a Commander," *Winners of the West*, November, 1936, p. 5.

[2] Merrill D. Beal, *"I Will Fight No More Forever": Chief Joseph and the Nez Perce War*, p. 63.

them in their rocky wilderness, which would give the Nez Perces a chance for a counterstroke. They could recross the river to the north, pass the troops' flank, and cut off Howard's communications and supplies from Fort Lapwai.

Besides, this strategic move in crossing to the south bank of the Salmon left the Indians three possible routes of escape: they could turn south and hide in the Seven Devils country, an extremely rough and inaccessible mountain region where they could resist superior numbers for an indefinite period; or, farther south, they could take flight across the Little Salmon and head for the buffalo trail eastward; or, immediately to their rear, they could recross the Snake River into Oregon where Joseph could fight on his own land in Wallowa. At the same time the enemy had, as Howard recognized, "a wonderful natural barrier between him and us in the Salmon, a river that delights itself in its furious flow."[3]

On June 23, the day after leaving Fort Lapwai, Howard's command reached Norton's ranch, Cottonwood House, which had been pillaged by the Indians and was now a shambles. The roadhouse and corrals were situated on the extensive and rolling Camas Prairie. The general laid over on Sunday, the twenty-fourth, and the press accused him of halting in order to preach to his men and distribute Bibles! In reality, he was awaiting the scout's report to determine the exact location of the hostiles, and was also waiting for reenforcements from Lewiston. He dispatched Captain Trimble to Slate Creek to protect the barricaded settlers there. The general hoped this company would check the Indians in that direction by occupying their attention, thus preventing further massacres in the vicinity, and giving the main force time to move on the hostiles directly.

On the twenty-fifth Howard moved his column by two routes to Johnson's ranch, about four miles from the head of White Bird Canyon. The general himself led his cav-

[3] Quoted in Brady, *Northwestern Fights and Fighters*, p. 14. Reprinted from Howard, *Chief Joseph, His Pursuit and Capture.*

alry to Grangeville, being joined there by the remnants of Perry's defeated command. The citizens of Mount Idaho, three miles away, demanded action, and Howard grimly promised them plenty of it as soon as he could find the enemy.

With his force reunited on June 26, the general made a reconnaissance into that part of the canyon which had so lately been Perry's battlefield. The troops found the bodies of their comrades which had lain there stripped of clothing for over a week. However, the corpses had not been mutilated, as most victorious Indians would have treated them.

It has been charged that the Nez Perces scalped the troops after the White Bird fight. Lieutenant Albert G. Forse, First U.S. Cavalry, conclusively refutes this:

> The dead had been lying for about 12 days before General Howard's command came to bury them. By that time, through the effects of heat, sun, and rain, they were in such a state that when a body was lifted up or rolled over into his grave, his hair and whiskers would adhere to the ground, tearing off the scalp and skin, which gave to the uninitiated the appearance of their being scalped and caused the circulation of the rumor. I did not see all the dead, but from inquiries made at the time I failed to find any one who had seen a body that had been scalped or mutilated in any way.[4]

In one transverse canyon the command found the mute evidence of the gallant stand of Edward Theller and his men, the large number of empty cartridges around the bodies proving how valiantly they had resisted. Howard's troops buried the corpses where they fell, except the brave lieutenant's remains, which were shrouded and sent under escort to Fort Lapwai.[5] The sight of their fallen

---

[4] Forse, *op. cit.*, p. 5. Forse's testimony is corroborated by Private Frederick Mayer, of Troop L, First U.S. Cavalry. "Nez Perce War Diary of Private Frederick Mayer," *Seventeenth Biennial Report*, Idaho State Historical Society, December, 1939-40.

[5] Lieutenant Theller's body was later reinterred in San Francisco, while the remains of the enlisted men were removed to the cemetery at Fort Walla Walla.

comrades aroused the soldiers of the First Cavalry, and they swore vengeance against the hostiles.

While the troops were burying the dead, Captain Paige and twenty volunteers from Walla Walla, who had joined the command at Lapwai, scouted along the crest of a ridge to the right of White Bird Canyon until they could get a view of the country beyond the Salmon. They saw the hostiles in force, and hastened back to report to the general.

Since the Indians had crossed the river and turned south, Howard ordered immediate pursuit before the Nez Perces could escape, as it was feared Joseph's band would return to Wallowa. On June 27 and 28 the troops marched toward the crossing of the Salmon about one and one-half miles above the mouth of White Bird Creek. Here the expected reenforcements joined Howard's column, bringing his command to four hundred men.

In the afternoon of the twenty-eighth, as the soldiers approached the mouth of the creek where it empties into the Salmon River, Indian snipers rushed down from the ridges on the other bank and taunted the long knives to come after them. The warriors tried to pick off any troops who ventured too near. However, when the command opened fire with long-range rifles, the Indians scrambled for the cover of the trees on the heights beyond. A sergeant and several of Paige's Walla Walla volunteers managed to swim the river and crawl to the top of the bluffs, but to their amazement not an Indian could they see!

However, the Nez Perce snipers had remained long enough to accomplish their mission. They had been sent to occupy the troops' attention, and so prevent them from learning that the Indians were recrossing to the north bank of the Salmon at Craig's Ferry, fifteen or twenty miles away. This ruse placed the hostiles in Howard's rear and isolated the general from Fort Lapwai for a few days. Joseph had hoped the general would follow them by crossing the river. "He did follow us," the chief said, "and we got . . . between him and his supplies, and cut him off for three days."[6]

Unsuspicious of the trick as yet, Howard decided to ferry his command to the south shore. However, as the troops did not know how to float their equipment across such a swift-flowing torrent, that objective was reached only after considerable delay. The Salmon River was running high, carrying a full flood of water from snows melting in the mountains. After careful mathematical calculations, Lieutenant H. G. Otis, an engineer of the Fourth Artillery, declared that a rope made of the cavalrymen's lariats would be strong enough to hold a raft against a current of seven miles an hour. So the troops constructed a raft of rough-hewn twelve-inch logs, thirty or forty feet long. One end of the rope they tied to a tree, and the raft was then launched into the river to test its strength. Swift eddies caught it and swung it downstream, the terrific strain broke the rope, and the raft disappeared far down the Salmon. Undoubtedly, Otis received much chaffing from his comrades.

An Indian scout with Howard's command had watched the experiment in amusement. He now demonstrated to the military technicians how four Indians, mounted on horses, one at each corner of the raft, could ferry it across to the opposite bank, 250 feet away. Attempts to imitate the Indian were partially successful, but the greater part of the troops and equipment were ferried over on boats by means of a cable,[7] fastened to trees on the opposite shore. The soldiers had carried a cable as part of their equipment.

During this time Howard received reports from friendly Indians that some of Looking Glass's young men had slipped away to join the hostiles, and the settlers feared his whole band might enter the war. To thwart this, the general dispatched a company of cavalry and a small party of volunteers under Captain Stephen G.

[6] "An Indian's Views of Indian Affairs," *North American Review*, April, 1879, p. 425.

[7] Howard, *op. cit.*, p. 147.

Whipple to Looking Glass's camp with orders to surprise and capture the chief and "all that belonged to him," and to "turn all prisoners over, for safe-keeping, to the volunteer organization at Mount Idaho."[8]

Howard had great confidence in this officer whom he describes as: "Dark-browed, strongly built, apparently forty years of age.... Whipple... Captain of Company L, First Cavalry, was a reliable man."[9]

Although Yellow Wolf denies the hostiles received any reenforcements from Looking Glass's village, Josiah Red Wolf, a member of the band, affirmed in an interview in the *Spokesman-Review Inland Empire Magazine* (November 17, 1963): "A few of our men had been in White Bird's fight."

Looking Glass was then peacefully encamped in his own territory on the banks of Clear Creek, a tributary of the Clearwater, where his people had gardens planted. Here he had taken refuge after the hostiles had joined him at Cottonwood Creek following the massacres by White Bird's young men. Looking Glass's village was four miles from the town of Kooskia and northeast of Mount Idaho. Although a few of his braves had joined the insurgent ranks, the chief had committed no overt act that might implicate him in the war. Indeed, some of the citizens declared that "thus far Looking Glass had maintained . . . a perfectly neutral attitude, if anything leaning toward the cause of the whites, although there were doubtless many would-be hostiles among the younger element."[10]

However, a different version of Looking Glass's guilt, based on Indian testimony, appeared in the Lewiston *Teller* extra for June 27, 1877:

Baird reports that the Clearwater Indians under Lookingglass had turned loose and plundered George Dempster's place between the Middle and South forks of Clearwater and driven off all the stock of the settlers found

[8] *Ibid.*, p. 149.
[9] *Ibid.*, p. 120.
[10] *History of North Idaho*, p. 62.

between these forks and had it at their camp about six miles above Kamia. This confirms Jim Lawyer's [head chief of the Kamiah treaty faction] statement made in the Indian Council yesterday at Lapwai as to the purposes of Lookingglass and his forty men. Baird says these Indians told two Chinamen near them on Clearwater that they had declared war against the whites and would commence their raids upon the inhabitants within two days. When this news reached Mt. Idaho a force of 20 volunteers started immediately for the Clearwater. No news from them when Baird left. General Howard was notified and said that he would send a detachment of regulars to scour the country in that direction this morning.

It was also rumored, contrariwise, that Looking Glass sent word to the agent after Whipple's fight that he wanted to come on the reservation and not fight. The agent sent for him, but nothing came of it. In the light of all the evidence, it would appear that Looking Glass sincerely desired peace.

By making a night ride Whipple's command arrived at the camp about dawn of July 1. Since the distance was ten miles farther than he supposed, the captain was unable to make the approach of his force a complete surprise, or to attack before dawn.

The Indians were unaware of the troops until the "shrill notes of the bugle rang out across the canyon and were caught and echoed back by the surrounding hills and bluffs. In an instant the camp was astir, and by the hazy light of approaching dawn the Indians could be seen running back and forth."[11]

Whipple arranged to parley, and Looking Glass, according to Indian testimony, sent a warrior, Peopeo Tholekt, forward to meet Whipple, and Randall, a captain of the Mount Idaho volunteers. But the white interpreter demanded Looking Glass. Instead of appearing the chief sent an old man to join Peopeo, with instructions to tell the whites to go away and leave them alone. However, historian Brosnan declares the chief did discuss the mat-

[11] *Ibid.*

ter of surrender, but explained that he had not been involved in the troubles, and, since his band was already upon the reservation, he did not think his people should be made prisoners of war. He asked for time to talk with his tribesmen. Looking Glass may have been afraid to surrender, because he had guaranteed to Howard the good conduct of Tuhulhutsut while the latter had been a prisoner at Fort Lapwai during the council in May. Looking Glass is reported to have said after the outbreak of murders, "General Howard will surely hang us."

While the parley was being held Washington Holmes, a volunteer, took it upon himself, in apparent revenge, to fire into the Indian camp.[12] Negotiations were immediately broken off, and fighting began.

Mr. Redfield, an employee at the Nez Perce subagency, corroborates this:

> I have talked with several Indians who were present at the time who explained to me all the details. They were friendly Indians who had met with the hostiles and had induced them to surrender the guilty parties, which was agreed upon, but when the troops arrived and an Indian went forward with a white cloth on a stick, in token of surrender, they were fired upon by some volunteers, who were with the command. Of course a fight ensued.[13]

Mr. Redfield's description is somewhat in error, since the volunteer fired during the parley.

The Indians fled eastward to the mountains, abandoning their possessions, their lodges, and over seven hundred ponies. One child was killed by the soldiers, the only casualty of the skirmish according to one account. But McWhorter's Indian sources declare Peopeo Tholekt, Red Heart, and Tahkoopen were wounded in addition to a seventeen-year-old boy killed.[14] Whipple, disappointed

---

[12] *Ibid.* McWhorter states that "Dutch" Holmes fired at an Indian against whom he held a grudge. McWhorter, *Hear Me, My Chiefs!*, pp. 272-73 and note 13. A detailed Indian account of this incident is given pp. 265-70.

[13] "Redfield's Reminiscences," *Pacific Northwest Quarterly*, January, 1936, p. 72.

[14] McWhorter, *op. cit.*, p. 267. Haines, *Red Eagles of the North-*

that he had been unable to make the chief and his band prisoners, destroyed the camp and drove the horses to Mount Idaho. Looking Glass with his main force hid in the Clearwater Mountains while awaiting an opportunity to join the hostiles. This unfortunate move on Howard's part drove Looking Glass to the side of Joseph, where he and his forty braves supplied reenforcements to the warring chiefs.

At Mount Idaho, Captain Whipple received information from Howard that Perry would arrive at Norton's Cottonwood Ranch with an ammunition train. Whipple was instructed to hurry in that direction with his cavalry so as to arrive before Joseph, who, it was thought probable, would recross the Salmon again to effect a junction with Looking Glass.

From spies the chiefs learned Whipple's position and that of Perry's supply train coming from Fort Lapwai. If the chiefs were to join forces with Looking Glass in the Clearwater Mountains, they would have to move their people across the route taken by Perry, and at the same time prevent Whipple from attacking the caravan of men, women, and children when they reached the open Camas Prairie. With that intention the hostiles moved from Craig's Ferry to the north of Cottonwood Ranch, thus placing themselves between the commands of the two officers.

This ranch, generally known as Cottonwood House, was situated on high and easily defensible prairie land between wooded foothills on the road connecting Lewiston with Mount Idaho. Whipple reached this point July 2 and waited for Perry and the twenty men bringing the expected supply train of ammunition. On the morning of July 3, Whipple sent two citizen scouts, Blewett and Foster, to reconnoiter the vicinity of Craig's Ferry where the Nez Perces had swum the Salmon River, in order to determine the number and exact location of the hostiles.

Foster returned toward evening on a lathered horse

---

west, p. 257, states that a woman and her baby were drowned while escaping from the soldiers.

with the information that he had been fired at, and the Indians, about twelve miles away, were heading for Craig Mountain nearby. Blewett, he reported, had probably been killed, as they had become separated and he had not seen the scout since the attack.

Whipple, realizing Perry's danger, directed Second Lieutenant Sevier M. Rains and ten picked men, accompanied by Scout Foster, "to proceed at once toward the point where the Indians had been seen, for the purpose of ascertaining the strength of the enemy, and to aid young Blewett. I particularly cautioned Rains not to precede the command too far, to keep on high ground, and to report the first sign of the Indians."[15] Whipple put his force in motion soon afterward and followed the direction taken by Rains's detail.

The Indians anticipated an attack and had concealed a large force of warriors led by Five Wounds, Rainbow,

[15] Howard, *op. cit.*, p. 151. For an Indian account of this attack, see McWhorter, *Yellow Wolf: His Own Story*, pp. 71-74. Private Frederick Mayer, *op. cit.*, pp. 28-29, gives a somewhat different eyewitness version to Captain Whipple's report related in this text, which may be explained by the fact that the officer saw an over-all picture of the skirmish, whereas the private had a necessarily limited view. In any event, it is interesting to note that Private Mayer supports his captain's good judgment in the action. Mayer states: "... (The advance guard were act. Sergt. Major Lambman, Privates Roach, Ryan, Burke and Quinn of 'E' Troop, Privates Richter, Moody, Carroll, Denteman and Meyer, and Lt. Rains of L Troop. The command left about 5 minutes later, during the time that the scout reported and the time of our getting ready to start out, the Indians came within 1½ miles of our camp intending to surprise us, but seeing our advance guard coming they lay'd in a ravine at the foot of Craigs Mountain, Idaho, and allowed our guard to ride into the ambush prepared for them, and killed them all. (Lt. Rains, Troop 'L,' and Pvt. Ryan, Troop 'E,' almost succeeded in making theyr escape by clearing their way through the Indians again towards us, but there were too many for those brave men.) We heard rapid firing for a few minutes, but seen nothing more of our guard. On our approach the Indians rallied on the Mountain, but they outnumbered us (three or four to One). Besides, it being after sundown, and only about 56 men in Skirmish line, (after No. 4's were taken out to hold horses). We had two good reasons not to give battle, so we formed a square around the horses, and retreated in good order (as they call it) to Cottonwood Rancho, some of the men growling because we did not attack the Indians, or look for our advance guard, but the more sensible ones guessed that either the guard were all killed or cut they'r way through to Fort Lapaway. Anyway what was done, was right."

and Two Moons on both sides of the road two miles north of Cottonwood.[16] When Rains's detachment, a few minutes in advance of Whipple, entered a shallow ravine the Indians sprang the trap, pouring a hail of bullets on the cavalrymen. Rains dismounted his men and dashed for a boulder in an open clearing to escape the withering fire of the enemy.

Whipple's troops, in the act of mounting, heard the sound of firing and charged forward at a gallop. After covering about two miles they saw the hostiles a half mile away in force and well entrenched. The captain realized his few men would suffer a disastrous loss if he charged the Indians' fortified position, and so he had to witness the fearful sight of Rains's doomed cavalrymen being picked off one by one until the last of them fell dead.

It was a serious blow to Captain Whipple. With his scouts, Blewett and Foster, killed and the Rains detail massacred, he dared not risk more lives until he knew more definitely the enemy's strength. Yet, if he retreated to Mount Idaho he would expose Perry to the same fate as Rains, besides losing the valuable supply train. Whipple decided to continue a short distance onward from the spot where the massacre had taken place and he halted in a more defensible position on open ground. He dismounted on the east side of a ravine, deployed his men in two long lines, and placed his mountain guns in the center in readiness for any attack. The Indians were on the west side of the canyon, but too far away for effective action. The combatants, one thousand yards apart, continued to menace each other for two hours until dusk, when the Indians withdrew and Whipple encamped for the night. In the morning (July 4) he started out again to meet Perry.

---

[16] Felix Warren, a dispatch carrier, claims White Bird led the party which ambushed Lieutenant Rains. Bailey, *River of No Return*, pp. 195 ff. But Two Moons, an eyewitness, states Five Wounds led the attack on the right, supported by his friend, Rainbow, on the left, while Two Moons himself headed the center charge. White Bird was past seventy and too old for active fighting. Two Moons' detailed account appears in McWhorter, *Hear Me, My Chiefs!*, pp. 282-83.

That officer, coming from Fort Lapwai with the pack train, was unaware of any danger, for the last reports he had received stated that the hostiles were in the Salmon River Mountains, where Howard was even then chasing them. Riding over the brow of a hill, he looked down in amazement to see Whipple's troops, several miles from Cottonwood, stretched out in battle formation. He rushed his detail of twenty men forward and gained the lines without being fired upon. Perry, as senior officer, then assumed command, and the united force marched back to Whipple's former position at Cottonwood. Here Perry received instructions from Howard to wait for further orders from him.

During the interim the volunteer forces had been doing their bit in scouting duty. McConville's company, acting under orders from Howard, had joined Trimble at Slate Creek on June 30. A short time later the volunteers crossed the Salmon River at Horseshoe Bend and made connections with the general's command to reconnoiter the country in advance of the troops. The citizens soon found the Indians' trail and bivouacked at the intersection of Canoe Encampment and Rocky Canyon trails. Here, about an hour later, a dispatch arrived from Whipple, informing Howard of the Nez Perces' attack on him and the massacre of Lieutenant Rains's detachment.

Hunter's Dayton, Washington, volunteers and McConville's own Lewiston company set out to reinforce Whipple. While riding along Rocky Canyon the citizens narrowly evaded an ambush and a fate like Rains's, when McConville, becoming suspicious of several Indians who ran away as they advanced into the canyon, ordered his men to take a different trail. Later, they learned these Nez Perces were decoys to lure the citizens deeper into the rocky defile where a larger squad lay hidden.[17]

At noon on the Fourth of July the Indians collected in force at Norton's and completely surrounded the camp

---

[17] "Nez Perce War Letters to Governor Mason Brayman," *Fifteenth Biennial Report, Idaho State Historical Society*, December, 1936, p. 64.

of the soldiers, where, Whipple reports, "for hours they made the most frantic efforts to dislodge us. Every man of the command was kept on the lines this afternoon (rifle-pits having been dug at a little distance from the Cottonwood house) until about sundown, when the enemy withdrew for the night."[18]

The Nez Perces appeared at Cottonwood again in the morning (July 5), after sending up from a butte three signal smokes into a clear sky to signify their readiness to fight. Henry C. Johnson, a volunteer, reports in his manuscript[19] that the Nez Perces were "camped on a high plateau about three miles in a westerly direction from Cottonwood. . . ."

For hours the soldiers of Perry's command waited, anticipating an attack as they watched the rapidly growing ranks of the foe. Whipple's men were busy constructing some defenses east of Norton's. Suddenly two mounted men, pursued by warriors, galloped madly from the direction of Johnson's ranch. These were messengers sent to Howard who was still beyond the Salmon. They safely reached the soldiers' lines. Other couriers dared not leave the fortifications, and the troops, believing themselves outnumbered by nearly three to one, wisely refrained from making any sorties.

About noon the expected attack began when the warriors charged all exposed positions at the same time. Braves crawled stealthily through the tall grass until they were discovered when within fifty feet of the soldiers. From their elevated position the troops repulsed every charge until the main body of Indians finally withdrew, although desultory firing continued for a long time.

The citizens of Mount Idaho had not heard from Whipple for two days. Then on July 5, Captain Randall received word that the Indians were in force at Cottonwood and had attacked Whipple's and Perry's commands.

[18] Howard, *op. cit.*, p. 152.

[19] Henry C. Johnson, "Volunteer Survivor Recalls Battle with Indians East of Cottonwood," MS. in Idaho State Historical Library, Boise.

Randall's detail of seventeen men immediately left to relieve the troops.

Within two miles of the soldiers' position, the seventeen volunteers were promptly attacked by a band of warriors, estimated at 125, who left the main body, then engaged in driving the herds across the prairie. Randall ordered a charge through the Indians' lines, apparently hoping it would carry his force through to the troops. They had almost gained their objective when Randall and B. F. Evans fell mortally wounded. The volunteers dismounted on an eminence and hoped to hold their position until help should come from the regulars.

A short time after the couriers had arrived from Howard, Whipple was standing on the hill where the defenses were being built, when he noticed a commotion on the summit where a few of the volunteers had gathered. Captain Perry came walking toward him, and Whipple asked the cause of the excitement.

Perry replied, "Some citizens, a couple of miles away on the Mount Idaho road, are surrounded by Indians, and are being all cut to pieces, and nothing can be done to help them!"

"Why not?"

"It is too late!"[20]

Perry delayed sending help, fearing that if he left his barricade the ammunition would fall into the hands of the hostiles, and that if he divided his force of one hundred, neither division could resist an attack by what he believed to be 250 or 300 warriors, let alone saving the citizens from massacre. In all probability, too, he had learned respect for the fighting abilities of the Nez Perces after his defeat at White Bird Canyon. His delay in aiding the civilians was in all likelihood prompted by caution.

Whipple pleaded with his senior officer to risk the ammunition and save the lives of the fighting volunteers. The soldiers and citizens within the defenses impatiently watched the skirmish while Perry deliberated. Unable to

[20] Howard, *op. cit.*, p. 153.

restrain themselves, about twenty-five volunteers dashed from their safe position to join the battle. They were led by Sergeant Simpson, who cried, "If your officers won't lead you, I will!"[21] Their daring act at last caused Perry to move, and he sent to the rescue a cavalry detachment under Captain Whipple. Only after the civilians had stood off 132 Indians for a full hour—according to an item in the Lewiston *Teller* extra for July 6, 1877—did the Nez Perces retire before the onslaught of Whipple's cavalry.

Then the united force of soldiers and citizens retreated to the ammunition train at Norton's before a counter-attack could be launched, although firing continued for an hour and a half. McConville's volunteers arrived, but too late to render any assistance to the ill-fated Randall.

Later, Perry was tried before a court-martial, and accused of not making any effort to save the civilian party. After considering the captain's reasons for not acting promptly, the court-martial exonerated him. Lew Wilmot, a second lieutenant under Randall, declared that the volunteers were between the Indians and Perry's force after the first charge. The only mention made of this controversial incident in the first report to Governor Brayman by L. P. Brown, of Mount Idaho, was:

> After the Battle had nearly ceased the troops came on the field with two gattling Guns but no effort was made by them to continue the fight or pursue them [the Indians] and [the troops] soon returned to their quarters at Cottonwood, with our [the volunteers'] dead and wounded.[22]

There is no mention here that Perry was at fault. The charge made against him was apparently an afterthought, possibly fostered by the newspapers of the region. The incident caused further dissension between the military and their civilian allies.

---

[21] Simpson was arrested for insubordination, but the charge against him was withdrawn after he had been seriously wounded in the Clearwater fight.

[22] "Nez Perce War Letters," p. 57.

While the warriors had been engaging the attention of the troops, the main body of Indians had prepared their stock and families for a dash across the prairie from the timbered slopes of Craig Mountain. By feigning a sustained attack, the Nez Perces kept the soldiers and scouts inside the barricades at Cottonwood and prevented them from learning the chiefs' plans until late in the afternoon. Then, six or eight miles away, the troops saw the herds of ponies and cattle, accompanied by the women and children, dash from the woods and gallop over the prairie in the direction of the Clearwater. Since the officers, Perry and Whipple, estimated that the tribe was guarded by 250 warriors, they did not consider it discreet to pursue them with but a hundred soldiers and citizens. Besides, it would expose their supply of ammunition. So the troops contented themselves by watching the flight of Joseph's, Tuhulhutsut's, and White Bird's bands to join Looking Glass.

After learning how the chiefs had eluded him at the Salmon River and temporarily cut him off from Fort Lapwai, Howard at once turned about and by night marching reached Grangeville on July 9. There he reunited with Perry's command for the purpose of running the Nez Perces to earth and forcing them into a decisive battle, since they threatened to burn ranch buildings and the crops, as soon as the dry season would permit.

The Indians' circular movement from the White Bird battlefield was a master stroke, as it left Howard and Perry in the hostiles' rear, and avoided the danger of running into Major Green's three companies of cavalry and twenty Bannock scouts en route from Fort Boise. Besides, it gave the chiefs an open road to Looking Glass's band in the Clearwater Mountains. Thus, although the attack on Randall's party had cost the Nez Perces the lives of nine warriors—according to the volunteer testimony—these unschooled Indians had, for nearly a month, succeeded in outwitting West Point's skilled tacticians without losing an engagement—part of the time by playing hide-and-seek with them!

Yellow Wolf credits the two greatest warriors in the Nez Perces' fighting forces, Five Wounds (Pahkatos Owyeen) and Rainbow (Wahchumyus), as counseling the trick of turning back by recrossing the Salmon so as to elude the soldiers. They planned this strategic maneuver, he states, "while in Lahmotta [White Bird] camp."[23] Rainbow and Five Wounds had joined the hostiles here upon their return from a buffalo hunt in Montana the day after the White Bird battle.

The Indians admitted only two casualties—one killed and one wounded—in the Randall fight, not nine as claimed by the volunteers.[24]

But this cheap victory for the red men would soon prove their undoing on the Clearwater because of their overconfidence.

---

[23] McWhorter, "*Yellow Wolf: His Own Story*, p. 69.

[24] *Ibid.*, p. 77.

CHAPTER XIV

The Battle of the Clearwater

NEWS of the Indian victories spread throughout the Northwest. There were, at the time, about twelve thousand Indians residing in that part of eastern Washington and northern Idaho now called the Inland Empire.[1] However, only a score of treaty Nez Perces and a few Coeur d'Alenes threw in their lot with the warring bands. The majority of those who favored war against the whites decided to await further developments before they started a general uprising. Others who were unfriendly to the Americans preferred to let the hostiles do the fighting. If they should meet Howard in pitched battle and score a decisive victory, the number of malcontents probably would swell to thousands. Such a victory might even precipitate outbreaks among all tribes in the Columbia River Basin.

The warring chiefs were not concerned with the plans of other tribes, their first interest being to effect the coalition of their forces with those of Looking Glass. This they accomplished after leaving Craig Mountain and Cottonwood ranch by retreating rapidly toward the northeast until they reached their ally's camp a few miles from Grangeville. Together the hostiles encamped near the mouth of Cottonwood Creek where it debouched into the South Fork of the Clearwater River. The foothills and prairies in that region provided excellent forage for the tired ponies and the large herds of cattle, while the streams offered good fishing. To the east rose the Bitter-

[1] Dr. H. L. Talkington, Manuscript, "History of the Nez Perce Reservation," State Historical Library, Boise, Idaho.

root Mountains, on the timbered slopes of which numerous deer, elk, cougar, and bear could be hunted.

Knowing Howard's troops to be several days behind, the Nez Perces rested, repaired their camp equipment, grazed their thousands of animals, and hunted for game. Small parties raided nearby farms of reservation Indians and settlers, stealing cattle and horses.

In the meantime, having learned from two friendly Nez Perce scouts that the hostiles had cut him off from his supply base at Fort Lapwai and were devastating the countryside, General Howard ordered the troops to retrace their line of march through the Salmon River Mountains. But after their departure from Brown's ranch at the head of Sink Creek on July 3, fog, rain, and snow added to the difficulties of the march. It required two days (July 3 and 4) to haul the heavy artillery guns and supplies up steep and muddy ridges. Several mules, unable to gain a footing in the mud on precipitous hills, slipped over the edge and crashed to their deaths in the canyon two thousand feet below. On the way the troops found and destroyed several caches of the Indians' provisions at Canoe Encampment, about eight miles below Pittsburg Landing on Snake River. They recrossed the Salmon at Billy's Crossing.

Cold and drenched to the skin, the cavalrymen suffered from exposure, as they were without bedding or food until noon of the following day (July 4) when the supply train caught up with them. With their clothes steaming from the rays of the sun, the cavalry pushed on to White Bird Canyon, leaving Captain Miles's infantry to follow later. Upon their arrival at the battleground, the troops found that the heavy rainfall of the past few days had washed away many of the grave mounds, leaving the corpses exposed. The cavalrymen paused to rebury their dead comrades and then resumed the march toward Craig Mountain.[2]

[2] The bodies were later reinterred at Fort Walla Walla. The monument erected in honor of the dead of the White Bird battle was purchased by funds contributed by comrades of the regiment,

Howard's column made rapid progress across the rolling prairie where the wide trail left by the Indians plainly showed their line of retreat from Cottonwood. The general by forced marches reached Grangeville the night of July 9. He replenished his stores of food and ammunition from the supplies which the Cottonwood defenders had saved in that skirmish. Here Perry's and Whipple's cavalry reenforced his command, and Miles's infantry arrived later that night.

During the interim the volunteer companies under command of Edward McConville, James Cearley, who had been elected captain in Randall's place, and Hunter were in the field again engaged in scouting duty for Howard's regulars. The citizens discovered the main camp of the Nez Perces on the night of July 9, and learned from a friendly Indian of Kamiah that the red forces could muster 313 warriors. They were having a war dance and powwow. Being on the same side of the river as the Indians, the volunteers at once entrenched themselves in rifle pits on top of a hill about a mile from the Clearwater. A brief skirmish followed. McConville sent a message to Howard informing him of the discovery of the hostiles and requesting him to aid the citizens.

The next night the volunteers, still holding their position, were again attacked, but the Indians withdrew at daybreak after capturing forty-three head of the citizens' horses. The civilians were ten miles from Howard, who was on the opposite side of the Clearwater River.[3]

Later in the day a band of thirty Nez Perces attempted to cut off a small party of Mount Idaho volunteers, led by Major George Shearer, who were coming to McConville's assistance. But twenty men commanded by Captain Cearley and Lieutenant Wilmot, acting under McConville's orders, managed to check the Indians and bring in

through the efforts of First Sergeant Michael McCarthy, one of the survivors of the fight.

[3] "Nez Perce War Letters to Governor Mason Brayman," *Fifteenth Biennial Report, Idaho State Historical Society*, December, 1936, pp. 65-66.

the citizens without losing a man. Howard had sent Shearer's party to inform McConville that the regulars had crossed the South Fork of the Clearwater at Jackson's Bridge.

The next day, receiving no reenforcements from Howard, the volunteers left their fortifications and marched on foot to Three Mile Creek, about six miles from Mount Idaho, where they encamped to protect the town against a possible attack.

On the morning of July 11, Howard ordered the command to march on to the Clearwater. Guided by the citizens, Troop E of the First Cavalry under Captain Winters led the column, followed by Perry's F troop, Whipple's L troop, and Trimble's H troop. Captain David Perry commanded the cavalry battalion which preceded four companies of infantry under Captain Evan Miles. Four artillery companies led by Captain (Brevet Colonel) Marcus Miller came next in line with two Gatling guns. Their complement of cannoneers brought up the rear.

The column had proceeded four miles through woods and gullies and along the ridges between the forks of the river, when Trimble's advance troopers "reported the presence of two Indian herders driving stock over the bluffs down the Clearwater river."[4] The troops took their position on the east side of the South Fork of the Clearwater, while the volunteers were on the west side of the same stream. Thus the Nez Perce camp was between these two forces in a deep ravine near the mouth of Cottonwood Creek. Guided by Lieutenant Fletcher, who had discovered the village at noon, Howard's command suddenly appeared on the right ridge above the river. They could see the ponies, guarded by herdsmen, grazing in the canyons. The general writes:

Trimble's troop . . . was sent forward to watch, toward the front and right, while I rode to the bluff at the left, where Fletcher was, and saw plainly the hostiles, who, judging from their motions, had just discovered our ap-

[4] Major J. G. Trimble, "The Battle of Clearwater," in Brady, *Northwestern Fights and Fighters*, p. 141.

proach. By one o'clock a howitzer and two gatling guns, manned by a detachment under Lieutenant Otis, Fourth Artillery, were firing towards the masses of Indians below.[5]

Howitzer shells bursting over their heads sent the Nez Perces with their herds scurrying up the canyon on both banks of the river and around a bend out of range. But knowing the soldiers had to travel another mile before they could descend from the ridge and make an attack, the Indians, after driving the herds out of danger, crossed the Clearwater and built rock barricades.

Aroused by the thundering reports of the artillery echoing and reechoing from the canyon walls, the chiefs and warriors in the village seized their weapons and dashed out to support the herdsmen.

To reach the next bluff, Howard had to cross a steep, rocky ravine. He ordered the howitzer battery, supported by Winters' cavalry, to hasten forward and take a position on the ridge. But the troops had to pass for a mile around the head of the canyon, and so they found the warriors dismounted and in position to receive the soldiers when they reached their objective.

Meanwhile a party of mounted Indians had galloped beyond range to strike the left flank of the soldiers' advancing line. Other warriors opened fire on the right, putting the troops on the defensive and in a perilous situation. Caught between the cross fire, the soldiers desperately held their ground until Major Mason with Burton's infantry company came from the rear, and, deploying to the right, forced back the flankers. More warriors, emerging from two ravines, charged the main line. Winters, with his dismounted cavalry, was able to repulse the assaults on the left. The four hundred soldiers then maneuvered into a line two and a half miles in extent,[6] cavalry to the left, infantry and artillery battalions

[5] Howard, *Chief Joseph, His Pursuit and Capture*, p. 158. For the Indian account, see McWhorter, *Yellow Wolf: His Own Story*, pp. 85 ff.

[6] *Report of Secretary of War*, 1877, I, 122. Report of Brigadier General Howard.

to the right. All pushed forward until they enveloped the bluff and commanded the heights in that vicinity.

Undaunted by the raking fire of the Gatling guns and howitzer, the braves shouted taunts at the soldiers. From an exposed position on the rocky hillside one warrior enacted the motions of a dance, leaping up and down with arms outstretched and swinging his red blanket in defiance. Cheered and goaded by their leaders, whom the soldiers believed to be Joseph and White Bird, the Indians charged to the bayonet points of the troops.

That Joseph inspired his men by his daring courage is attested by Howard's aide-de-camp, Lieutenant C. E. S. Wood, who recounts:

> Joseph, White Bird and Too-hul-hul-suit, all seemed to be in command, but—and as one of Joseph's band told the writer—Joseph was after this fight called "the war-chief." He was everywhere along the line; running from point to point, he directed the flanking movements and the charges. It was his long fierce calls which sometimes we heard loudly in front of us, and sometimes faintly resounding from the distant rocks.[7]

However, recent Indian testimony denies Joseph's part as war leader. Alokut's wife declared that the middle-aged Chief Tuhulhutsut led the first charge to meet the soldiers, which Yellow Wolf confirmed. The preeminent warrior, Rainbow, led another group of young braves. Although Five Wounds was said to be the recognized battle leader, McWhorter also states "each of the five separate bands was under its own recognized chief with the exception of the Wallowa, Joseph's band, which was led by Chief Ollokot [Alokut]. . . . While it is known that Chief Looking Glass joined the patriots early at their camp on the Clearwater, no mention of his taking any part in the battle was made by any of the Nez Perces."[8]

---

[7] Lieutenant C. E. S. Wood, "Chief Joseph, the Nez Percé," *Century Magazine*, May, 1884, p. 137.

[8] McWhorter, *Hear Me, My Chiefs!*, pp. 318-19. Yellow Bull's statement is quoted in Curtis, *The North American Indian*, VIII, 166.

But Yellow Bull declared to Curtis that "Joseph was there [at the Clearwater] and fought like anybody else." Although not one of the main leaders, apparently Joseph did act as a fighting warrior.

The first packtrain to bring up supplies of ammunition and food safely entered Howard's lines. It had left Kamiah escorted by Captain Rodney's company several hours after the main force. Then a smaller one appeared on the road nearer the troops than the Indians. Forty or fifty mounted warriors espied it and made a wild charge. In a swift flanking movement they killed two packers and disabled two mules loaded with howitzer ammunition. Harassed by the attackers, the supply train raced forward to Howard's position, guided by Lieutenant Wilkinson. Trimble's men dashed from their rifle pits to the rescue of their comrades. Rodney's artillerymen with Perry's and Whipple's cavalry directed their fire to cover the packtrain until it reached the lines. This train, Captain Trimble explains, was

> . . . moved to the high ground in the rear of the location where the principal fighting was going on, and Rodney's and my company forming a line in the rear, the whole position was thus defended.
>
> The other troops of cavalry were, or had been, dismounted, the horses assembled on the plateau on which the train was halted, and the men became engaged beside the infantry in what was now a defensive fight. Assaults were made on the Indian position which was established in the woods on the edge of the bluff, but each one was repulsed by the hostiles, who finally only engaged the troops at long range, although there was some fierce fighting at times and a dozen or more men were killed with a proportion of wounded. . . .
>
> The lines were separated about eight hundred yards and extended about half the circle inclosed, though a defense was maintained around the whole. . . . The cavalry horses and pack animals to the number of about three hundred were collected and held in the center of the circumference, and suffered much from want of water. For thirty hours or more they were thus confined.[9]

---

[9] Trimble, *op. cit.*, pp. 143-44.

Beyond the Clearwater, five miles in a straight line to the north, was a high, round hill where the volunteers were located. Farther away loomed Craig Mountain, from the slopes of which Cottonwood Canyon traced a crooked course toward the troops to vanish behind their bank of the Clearwater. Steep, high bluffs and numerous side ravines flanked the river's course. The Indian village, with its pony herd of hundreds in nearby gulches, was across the Clearwater. Some of the canyons near the battlefield contained slopes grown with trees and open bottomland strewn with boulders.

From these hillsides and ravines Indians thrust themselves into view, took quick aim, fired, and then dropped behind the rocks. Lieutenant Wood relates: "...their brown naked bodies were seen flying from shelter to shelter. Their yells were incessant as they cheered each other on or signalled a successful shot." Such tactics as rock entrenchments, and the besieging of superior numbers of troops, were never known before in Indian warfare.

The red men also commanded the only source of water in the vicinity—a spring. Deprived of that precious liquid, the troops suffered from the burning rays of the July sun. As the long hours of the hot afternoon wore on, they became parched with thirst and fought desperately to gain control of the coveted spring.

The Indians made sallies on foot and horseback to attack the flanks of the troops' position, but were stoutly repulsed. Late in the afternoon Captain Miles's infantry battalion led a vicious countercharge on the right down into a ravine where Nez Perce sharpshooters were entrenched too close for comfort. Captain Bancroft, Fourth Artillery, and Lieutenants Williams and Farrow, Twenty-first Infantry, were seriously wounded. But the sortie forced the Indians to leave their dead and withdraw from the canyon. Thus the disputed ravine was cleared of all the enemy within close range. Time and again the troops drove snipers from behind the stumps and boulders, only to retreat in their turn before the main body of Indians.

A gap in the army's lines permitted braves to sneak up the river bluff and enfilade the soldiers. General Howard ordered Captain Miller to hurry his men to that point near the center. While hostile bullets were flying through the air all about him, Miller nonchalantly smoked a short-stem pipe as he executed this movement. He so placed his artillery troops that their backs were toward Company B of the Twenty-first Infantry. In the excitement of battle, Miller's artillerymen mistook the infantrymen in their rear for Indians. Then occurred one of those episodes in combat which are tragicomic. In a moment Company B and the artillery unit started firing at each other. Fortunately, high grass obscured the aim of each.

The incident is best described by Major (then Lieutenant) H. L. Bailey, one of the participants:

It was while I was back at the center [headquarters] for cartridges and hospital men that his men [Miller's] took the men of my company [infantrymen] for Indians, all being in the prone position in rocky grassy ground, and as I was returning the artillery company and the infantry company were bobbing up and down firing at each other at a lively rate.

Lieut. Peter Leary, Fourth Artillery, commissary officer, rushed out with a carbine flourishing in the air, shouting: "Packers to the rescue, packers and scouts to the rescue." I saw and knew the situation at a glance, as I had seen Captain Miller lead his men out, and I passed Leary, rushing between the two lines, yelling: "Cease firing, you're firing into your own men."

The trouble was quickly ended, though at least one poor man (Winters of my company [not Captain Winters]) always believed his dreadful hip wound was by a friendly bullet. This was during the first day of the battle. It was Captain Jocelyn (now Colonel General Staff, and I hope soon the next Brigadier-General) who got General Howard to send Captain Miller out to that vital part of our lines.[10]

---

[10] Major H. L. Bailey, "Letter Regarding the Battle of the Clearwater," in Brady, *Northwestern Fights and Fighters*, p. 163. Stephen P. Jocelyn states in *Mostly Alkali*, a comprehensive biography of Western military life, that his father, General Jocelyn was brevetted for "conspicuous gallantry in action" at the Clearwater, and, twenty-three years later, "of the four-hundred-odd

The acute water shortage caused Howard to order Perry's and Whipple's dismounted cavalry and Morris' artillery to countercharge on the left and drive back the Indians who held the spring. On the right Lieutenant Wilkinson led a charge by using the artillery, infantry, and every man of the cavalry, including horse holders, orderlies, and extra-duty men. Lieutenant Fletcher directed the howitzer fire inside the Nez Perces' rock barricades.

At three-thirty in the afternoon the troops stormed the canyon, while additional charges were being made on the center. Miller's onslaught gained the ridge in front and captured the ravine near Winters' position. The Indians gave way before the assault and then counterattacked.

Although unsuccessful in retaking the canyon, Nez Perce snipers still commanded the spring and prevented the soldiers from obtaining more than a meager supply of water during the afternoon and night.

Handicapped by lack of water, and unable to light campfires lest the flames should draw the bullets of the sharpshooters, the troops suffered from the heavy dew and chill mountain air after sundown. Working in shifts, the men built additional rock barricades and dug more rifle pits.

Captain Trimble sums up the situation at dark on July 11 at the end of the first day's battle:

> The troops were in the circle on the defensive, the Indians in similar manner, though upon a line or nearly so at the edge of the bluff and in the timber. . . . I should think the area absolutely commanded by the hostiles was about twenty miles in every direction; that is, it would be unsafe for any one to venture out of our lines or immediate vicinity. When night fell there was almost complete cessation of shooting. . . . [11]

The night being clear and still, the troops could discern smoke from the Indian village across the Clearwater

---

brevets which had been conferred for bravery on officers of the active list, only three were for *conspicuous* gallantry. . . . " (p. 230.)

[11] Trimble, *op. cit.*, p. 144.

River. From the blood-chilling yells that rent the air, the soldiers knew the braves were whirling madly in the war dance. Lieutenant Wood vividly describes the scene:

> All through the night, from the vast Indian camp in the river-bottom, rose the wail of the death-song and the dull drumming of the tooats [*tewats*]. The dirge of the widows drifted to us through the summer night—now plaintive and faint, now suddenly bursting into shrieks, as if their very heart-strings had snapped. But mingling with these unpleasant sounds came the rapid movement of the scalp chant, *hum, hum, hum,* hurrying to the climax of fierce war-whoops.[12]

The troops heard, too, the thunderous voices, presumably, of Joseph, Alokut, and White Bird firing the hearts of the warriors with courage for the morrow, or reprimanding others. Dissension was splitting the Indian ranks. Some braves had quit the battle, arguing there was no use fighting when soldiers were not attacking their village.

During the hours of darkness, soldiers and Indians alike heard the scraping sounds of rocks as both sides strengthened their defenses.

As the gray light of dawn dissolved the black shadows of night, the troops under Miller and Perry charged the Indian barricades around the spring, the swiftness of their assault driving off the snipers. The precious water was then fortified by riflemen against counterattacks and flanking movements by the Nez Perces. After their successful charge the famished troops refilled their empty canteens and gulped down a scanty breakfast of hardtack, bacon, and hot coffee at headquarters camp in the center of their lines. Refreshed, the soldiers then renewed the attack. Captain Trimble writes:

> About sunrise several of the hostiles essayed to discover if any reinforcements were on the way for us. They would shoot out from the timber and at top speed gain the trail. This fact required exposure, as each attempt was made a target for the long range rifle of our infantry.

[12] Wood, *op. cit.*, p. 138.

I saw one horse shot, but it was astonishing to see the swiftness of their ponies and the savage maneuvers performed by those expert horsemen.[13]

Acrid smoke from the guns, wild yells of Indians, fierce shouts of soldiers, dust from charging Indian cavalry, zinging of bullets, and burning rays of the sun all combined to make the battlefield an inferno on the second day, July 12.

Howard, who had helped to plan the Union strategy at the battle of Gettysburg, now found that he had met worthy tacticians in the Nez Perces. He had to exercise, by his own admission, the most thorough generalship of his career to avert defeat. Although his lines were already thin, he left their defense to the infantry and cavalry, and withdrew the artillery battalion to act as a reserve force in case of an offensive movement by the Indians.

Joseph, White Bird, Looking Glass, Alokut, Yellow Bull, and Tuhulhutsut, the military declared, were everywhere directing their forces. "Joseph," writes Lieutenant Wood, "unlike his men, did not strip off his clothes for battle, as is the Indian custom, but wore his shirt, breechclout, and moccasins; and though (as I was told by one of his men) he was wholly reckless of himself in directing the various fights, he did not receive a wound."[14] Apparently Joseph was determined to live down before his tribesmen the accusation of cowardice hurled at him in the ten-day council in Rocky Canyon, when he had pleaded for peace just prior to the outbreak of hostilities.

Time and again the soldiers supposedly aimed their fire at Joseph, but it was probably at his brother Alokut that they shot as he fearlessly led the charges of Indian cavalry against the troops. But historian Brady claims Joseph had several horses killed under him. Miraculously, not a bullet scratched him.[15]

---

[13] Trimble, *op. cit.*, p. 145.

[14] Wood, *op. cit.*, p. 138.

[15] Brady, *op. cit.*, pp. 16-17.

On the other hand, McWhorter's Indian sources deny Joseph's active role in the battle. He was undoubtedly an observer of the conflict, though, because McWhorter, in *Hear Me, My Chiefs!*, credits Joseph with warning the camp to be struck for hasty flight when he foresaw defeat for his tribesmen. The disagreement between Indian and white testimony about Joseph may be reconciled by the possibility that the soldiers mistook Alokut for his brother. All Indians consulted by McWhorter agreed Alokut (sometimes also called Young Joseph) was the chief fighting warrior in his brother's band, and also "spoke highly of Ollokot's [Alokut] bravery and warrior ability."[16] Indeed, mistaken identity may largely explain why the army men considered Joseph the war chief, whereas the military honors throughout the campaign really belonged to Alokut who, in Joseph's own words, "led the young men."

Both sides gained temporary advantages during the morning hours by brief skirmishes. In the afternoon Howard decided to use a spearhead attack to break the stubborn line of the Nez Perces. He ordered Captain Miller to take a company of infantry through the troops' left flank, strike the left center of the Indian line, cross the Nez Perces' entrenched ravine, then suddenly face right and charge the enemy "so as to strike the Indian position in reverse."

Just as the captain prepared to execute the command, the supply train expected from Fort Lapwai appeared in the distance from the south enveloped in a dust cloud. It was escorted by Captain Jackson's troop of cavalry. Seeing Indian skirmishers mounted on fleet ponies swooping down on the packtrain, Miller changed his plans and swerved to rescue it, thereby anticipating Howard's revised order. He "marched his company between the coming train and the position occupied by the enemy, a very pretty movement as we watched it from our greater elevation," relates Captain Trimble.[17]

---

[16] McWhorter, *Hear Me, My Chiefs!*, p. 320 and p. 181.

[17] Trimble, *op. cit.*, p. 146.

The attention of the embattled forces switched to the race for life between the train and the attackers. Through swirling clouds of dust the pack mules rushed across the plain. The Indian skirmishers retreated before Miller's determined assault. His quick action saved the ammunition and supplies.

An hour later the hoarse, exultant cries of the soldiers rent the air as Miller escorted the train almost to Howard's position. Then, suddenly, before either the Indians or his comrades could guess his move, Miller, riding parallel to the line of battle, swung his column left and "moved quickly in line for nearly a mile across our front," Howard writes, and repeatedly charged to the left of the Indians' center. "This manner of striking at an angle," Howard explains, "and following up the break, is called 'rolling up the enemy's line.' "[18]

Immediately the Nez Perces attempted to turn Miller's left flank. The captain's onslaught stopped at the barricades, but Rodney's company, acting as a reserve in his rear, deployed quickly and "flanked the flankers." The soldiers' line paused at the stubborn resistance of the Nez Perces, but charged forward again and broke through the ranks of the Indians. The artillerymen faced to the right then and effectively rolled up the line. That surprise movement, successfully executed, turned the tide of battle in favor of the army.

Howard then ordered a full charge of all troops. Blue-clothed men rushed forward in skirmish order, firing by volley. Since the Nez Perces' position had become untenable, they fled "through the ravines into the deep canyon, thence to the river, over rocks, down precipices, and along trails almost too steep and craggy to traverse," the general reports. "The footmen pursued them to the river opposite the Indian camp. The river being too deep and rapid for the men to ford, they here waited for the cavalry under Captain Perry."[19]

---

[18] Howard, in *Report of Secretary of War*, 1877, I, 123.

[19] *Ibid.*

The Nez Perces, their ranks broken and disorganized, fled up the heights to the left of Cottonwood Creek and beyond the Clearwater. The Indians left behind about eighty tepees with food cooking over the fires, supplies of flour and jerked beef, cooking utensils, buffalo robes, clothing, and blankets.

Yellow Wolf recalled that Chief Joseph's wife was left behind during the retreat. When Yellow Wolf reached the abandoned village, he found a woman with an infant in a cradleboard attempting to mount a frantic, plunging horse. He helped her to escape. "This woman," he related, "with the little baby was Toma Alwawinmi [possibly meaning 'Spring of Year', or 'Springtime'], wife of Chief Joseph. Her baby girl was born at Tepahlewam camp a few days before the White Bird Canyon battle, but it died in the hot country [Indian Territory] after the war.

"I did not ask why she was as I found her. Chief Joseph left the battlefield ahead of the retreat. Seeing it coming, he hurried to warn the families. He could not leave his wife had he known. The women were all supposed to be ahead. A bad time—everybody busy getting away."[20]

Sustaining the attack, the cavalry worked its way rapidly on the left down the steep mountainsides to a deep ford, and slowly crossed over to the deserted village. Howard writes:

> At this time (about 5 P. M.), I was following up the movement, descending a steep trail, when about half way down the mountain side I discovered a number of the warriors apparently returning toward their camp from the Cottonwood ravine, at least three miles from us. I warned Captain Perry, and directed him to immediately carry over the foot-men with his horses.
>
> While doing this, time was consumed, and the Indians had turned eastward, crossed the Cottonwood Canon, and under cover of a transverse ravine got well in advance of

[20] McWhorter, *Yellow Wolf: His Own Story*, p. 97. Because of dissension within their fighting forces the Indians claim they decided to retreat before the soldiers charged.

us, so that I concluded to postpone further pursuit until the next morning.[21]

Lieutenant Parnell reports that Perry's movement "was so dilatory and irritating that General Howard became annoyed and countermanding the order directed the cavalry to aid the foot troops in crossing the river."[22] It is Parnell's opinion that had Perry's cavalry vigorously pushed the pursuit of the fleeing Nez Perces on this occasion, "the hostiles would never have crossed the Lolo trail."[23]

The chiefs reorganized their people and retreated slowly and in good order toward Kamiah. The warriors referred to by Howard, forty in number, had become separated from the main body in the retreat from the battlefield. As they were making their way back to their tribesmen, Howard sent McConville's volunteers in pursuit, ordering the citizens to harass the Indians. But the volunteers had difficulty in following the trail and reached the Clearwater after the last of the warriors had crossed it.

Burial parties next day interred thirteen soldiers and fifteen Indian bodies. Later eight more warriors were found on their trail. Two officers and twenty-two men were given first-aid treatment for their wounds and the following day sent to Fort Lapwai under escort. The number of wounded Nez Perces could not be determined as they successfully escaped with the hostiles.

Yellow Wolf, however, denied that twenty-three warriors were killed, as reported by General Howard. He listed the names of four Nez Perces who were fatally wounded: Going Across, Grizzly Bear Blanket, Red Thunder, and Whittling, also six injured who recovered.[24]

Regarding the outcome of this battle, Lieutenant William R. Parnell wrote:

---

[21] Howard, in *Report of Secretary of War*, 1877, I, 123.

[22] William Parnell, "The Salmon River Expedition," in Brady, *Northwestern Fights and Fighters*, p. 132.

[23] *Ibid.*

[24] McWhorter, *Yellow Wolf: His Own Story*, pp. 98-99.

> At the "Clearwater" the opposing forces were about equal. If anything the troops had the advantage in numbers as well as position. And yet, strictly speaking, the Indians were not defeated. Their loss must have been insignificant and their retreat to Kamai was masterly, deliberate and unmolested, leaving us with victory barren of results.[25]

This Clearwater battle, however, had a distinct effect on the Nez Perces, in that it integrated their forces, and the Indians learned that they could effectively cope with the scientific methods of warfare employed by the military. And lastly, they had once more earned their freedom.

Scouting parties of volunteers found food caches belonging to the Nez Perces, consisting mostly of flour, camas root, sugar, tea, axes, knives, cooking utensils, clothing, saddles, and buffalo robes. All was abandoned, probably, during the Indians' flight from the vicinity of the Clearwater. This indicates that the hostiles were preparing for a long siege and had intended to fight on and to hold their own land.

In capitulation Howard agreed that the Nez Perces "had been well led, and well fought," since they had won the pitched battle at White Bird Canyon; had eluded capture; had crossed the army communications at Cottonwood; had kept the cavalry on the defensive there; and had been able to hold out for two days in the Clearwater battle against seasoned veterans, led by the sixth ranking general of the War of Secession. Then, the conflict tied, they had again eluded pursuit with all their women, children, the aged and the wounded, their herds, and most of their belongings. But, Howard consoles himself, the murders in Idaho had been stopped and the surrounding country "freed from their terrible presence." After property damage in burned buildings and ruined crops in north Idaho estimated at $200,000, peace between Indian and white reigned once more in northeastern Oregon and Idaho. However, the long "trail of tears" had begun for Joseph and his tribespeople.

---

[25] Parnell, *op. cit.*, p. 133.

CHAPTER XV

The March Over the Lolo Trail

ON JULY 13, the day after the battle, the hostile forces crossed about a mile above the Kamiah ferry to the east bank of the Clearwater. Some of the supplies which the women had saved from the deserted village were swept off the overloaded rafts into the swirling eddies of the river. At this spot the chiefs decided to give battle again, but before barricades could be erected or rifle pits dug, Howard's cavalry loomed on the bluffs above Kamiah and trotted rapidly down the trail toward the Indians. Captain Trimble reports:

> It was a lovely sight we beheld on arriving at the heights overlooking the Kamai Valley. The fields belonging to the still loyal bands of Nez Perces were green with grain not yet ripe, the hills beyond clad in spring attire, the beautiful river flowing between, and the Agency buildings shining white in the background.[1]

Menaced by the approaching soldiers, the Indians rushed the work of crossing the people and stock. As the last Nez Perce gained the safety of the eastern bank, Captain Jackson's troop of cavalry charged down to the water's edge. Indian marksmen, deployed on the opposite shore, opened fire.

After the artillerymen had discharged several volleys from the Gatling guns, the cavalry "retired in some haste, if not confusion"[2] from their advance position.

Regarding the sudden panic of the mounted troops, General Howard relates:

---

[1] Major J. G. Trimble, "The Battle of the Clearwater," in Brady, *Northwestern Fights and Fighters*, p. 148.

[2] *Ibid.*, p. 149.

As Perry's and Whipple's cavalry were passing a high bluff which was beyond the river, a brisk fire was opened by the enemy for a few minutes, throwing this cavalry into considerable confusion for a time, but without loss.[3]

One enlisted man was slightly wounded in this skirmish at the river. In his book, Howard expands his official report and adds a subtle touch of humor: "... our men jumped from their horses, and ran to the cover of the fences. Little damage resulted, except the shame to us, and a fierce delight to the foe."[4]

The general's prompt pursuit evidently surprised the Nez Perces; and as a result they continued their retreat toward the east, and thus gave up their favorable position at the river.

The chiefs realized that their safety depended on reaching the Lolo Trail in the Bitterroot Mountains. Lest Howard block their escape, they posted scouts to keep them informed of the one-armed general's movements. These sentinels reported on the fifteenth that Howard's battalion of cavalry had left Kamiah and was on the heights to the Indians' rear, presumably going back to Fort Lapwai. However, this ruse did not deceive the chiefs. They grasped the situation at once, divining that Howard intended to feint retreat toward the north, then suddenly to change his direction and cross to the east side of the Clearwater at a point farther downstream, probably at Dunwell's Ferry. From there his cavalry could reach the north fork of the Lolo Trail at the junction fifteen miles beyond the Nez Perce camp, and thus cut off the Indians' escape. At the same time Howard could attack the hostiles' rear by engaging the chiefs from the west with the infantry and artillery battalions.

The Nez Perce camp was then four miles from Kamiah. Promptly packing up, the Indians hastened toward the Lolo Trail. Joseph sent a messenger to Howard under a flag of truce to ask upon what terms he could surrender.

---

[3] Howard, in *Report of Secretary of War*, 1877, I, 124.

[4] Howard, *Chief Joseph, His Pursuit and Capture*, p. 167.

Lieutenant C. E. S. Wood says that he was "told long afterward, by an Indian of that region, that Joseph wished to surrender rather than leave the country or bring further misery on his people, but that, in council, he was overruled by the older chiefs, Ap-push-wa-hite (Looking Glass), White Bird, and Too-hul-hul-suit; and Joseph would not desert the common cause."[5]

In the Lewiston *Teller* extra for July 16, 1877, Joseph is reported to have said that he was "not to blame in this war, that he was forced into it. He did not speak for the rest of the hostiles." A later issue of the *Teller* (August 2) states: "Jim Lawyer says that . . . White Bird and Lookingglass . . . actually prevented Joseph and his men from surrender by an armed force of 40 warriors who threatened to kill them if they attempted to escape and surrender." Josiah Red Wolf confirms Joseph's surrender attempt. He states in the *Inland Empire Magazine (Spokesman-Review,* November 17, 1963): "Not only was Joseph hard to persuade to stay in the fight but he tried to drop out after the end of the Stites (Clearwater) fight."

Howard had already proceeded six miles toward Fort Lapwai when he received word of Joseph's intention to surrender. He hurried back to Kamiah to negotiate, and ordered the cavalry and volunteers to continue twenty miles in a northwesterly direction.

In his report to the Secretary of War the general explains:

The fifteenth I started a column of cavalry with intention of ascending the heights to the rear, as if *en route* to Lapwai, to move 20 miles down the Clearwater to Dunnwell's Ferry, and crossing there, to attempt to gain the trail to the rear of the Indians, as they were encamping in plain sight, not more than 4 miles from Kamiah. I had not proceeded more than 6 miles before the Indians began their retreat in good earnest along the Lolo trail. Therefore, leaving Captain Jackson with his company and a few volunteers who had just returned to me to

[5] C. E. S. Wood, "Chief Joseph, the Nez Percé," *Century Magazine*, May, 1884, p. 138.

watch Dunnwell's Ferry, I returned to Kamiah and prepared at once to move my entire command over the river.

My own return was hastened by a request, said to be sent in from Joseph, asking on what terms he could surrender.[6]

Joseph's peace action delayed Howard in parley with the messenger. The terms of surrender as laid down by Howard were unconditional, and Joseph would be tried by a military court of regular officers. During the negotiations the Indians' rear guard fired a farewell shot at the army pickets. While the cavalry made a forty-mile round trip to the ferry, the hostiles safely reached the start of the famous trail. The Nez Perce messenger, with his wife and two others, afterward surrendered to the general.

When the cavalry and volunteers reached Dunwell's Ferry they found the boat had been cut adrift and had floated a half mile down the river. A scouting party of Nez Perces had anticipated them and even burned all the buildings. The next morning the troops received orders to return to Kamiah.

Forty more Nez Perces—twenty-three warriors and seventeen women and children—were captured by Howard's troops at Weippe on July 16. These captives, according to Yellow Wolf, were members of Red Heart's band and were a part of the reservation Indians who had just returned from a buffalo hunt in Montana. Being caught fraternizing with the hostiles, they were seized as prisoners, although apparently they had no desire to become involved in the war.

The Nez Perces appear to have been divided on their future plans. The chiefs called a council "of momentous consequence" on the Weippe prairie near the start of the Lolo Trail. Before the older tribal leaders Joseph made his last appeal by passionately condemning further retreat from Idaho:

What are we fighting for? Is it for our lives? No. It

[6] Howard, in *Report of Secretary of War*, 1877, I, 124.

is for this land where the bones of our fathers are buried. I do not want to take my women among strangers. I do not want to die in a strange land. Some of you tried to say, once, that I was afraid of the whites. Stay here with me now, and you shall have plenty of fighting. We will put our women behind us in these mountains, and die on our own land fighting for them. I would rather do that than run I know not where.[7]

According to Yellow Bull, a member of White Bird's band, both Joseph and White Bird wanted to cross the mountains to Montana and return to the Salmon River in Idaho among the Shoshone. "Joseph was really the chief," Yellow Bull further testifies, "but he appointed Pile of Clouds [a medicine man] as the war-leader to carry out his directions."[8] Looking Glass, however, insisted on going to the country of the Crow Indians to enlist that tribe's aid. McWhorter declares Looking Glass was aggressive and dominated the councils. He became the war leader at the Weippe powwow.

Overruled by the council, Joseph finally consented to this plan and agreed to lead his people out of this land of bondage and deliver them into freedom. Messengers were sent ahead to Charlot and Michel, chiefs respectively of the Flathead and Pend d'Oreille tribes in western Montana, to ask permission to pass through their country.[9]

On July 17 Howard dispatched the battalion of cavalry under Major Mason, accompanied by McConville's company of volunteers and Indian scouts, to determine wheth-

---

[7] Wood, *op. cit.*, p. 138.

[8] Curtis, *The North American Indian*, VIII, 166. From the account by Yellow Bull.

[9] Chauncey Barbour, editor of the *Weekly Missoulian*, in a letter to Governor Potts of Montana Territory, dated June 29, 1877, states that three young men from the Nez Perce tribe had come from Camas Prairie to the Bitterroot Valley of Montana after the White Bird fight. Two of them came over the Mullan road to the Flathead Reservation to talk to Chiefs Michel and Arlee, probably to induce them to join the hostile Nez Perces. Barbour and Captain C. P. Higgins, organizer of the Missoula Volunteers, could not locate Chief Charlot at the time to ascertain his attitude. (Paul C. Phillips, ed., "The Battle of the Big Hole," *Frontier Magazine*, November, 1929, p. 64.)

er or not the Nez Perces had indeed headed for the Lolo Trail.

However, to forestall pursuit, the chiefs had cunningly prepared an ambush about three miles from Orofino Creek. Here, unaware of the danger that lurked in the silent aisles of this primeval forest, Mason's troops threaded their way in single file around boulders and fallen logs which choked their passageway for seventeen miles. Fresh bloodstains and horsehair on down timber showed where the Nez Perces had jammed their ponies over all obstacles. From this mute testimony the troops knew they were not far behind the enemy. Five Indian scouts preceded the column by several hundred yards.

Concealed nontreaty warriors listened for the sound of the hoofbeats of approaching cavalry. The noise made by hoofs clicking on rocks told them that soldiers were advancing. Silently the braves watched five red men ride along the trail, their rifles lying across their saddles. The hidden Indians let this advance guard come close as they were waiting for the main force to enter the ambuscade.

Shortly the file of Mason's cavalry approached the trap. Suddenly, shots rang out from far up the canyon. McConville and Chapman, heading the column, immediately halted and waited for the troops to close up, the majority being yet outside the dangerous area. Chapman, the interpreter, went ahead to reconnoiter.

An alarming discovery the whites made is best described by Lieutenant William R. Parnell, an eyewitness:

"While we were at a halt, the pawing of the horses removed some leaves and dirt, and exposed a quantity of fresh sawdust. Upon investigation we found considerable of it covered over in a similar manner. We then discovered that many of the trees had been sawed off, here and there, near the trail, at a height of three or four feet from the ground, leaving the trees still standing on their stumps and easily supported by the adjacent trees. The marks of the saw were covered over with dirt and bark, and no doubt would have escaped observation had we not been stopped by the attack on our advance. We overtook them too soon for their purpose, their object evidently being to let us pass until our rear-guard had advanced beyond that point, whereupon some fifty or sixty warriors who were concealed in the timber were to drop the trees across the trail and block our retreat while they would attack us in front and rear from behind the fallen trees, for they had done the same thing some distance ahead."[10]

McConville's volunteers and Captain Winters' Company E of the First Cavalry immediately dismounted and deployed as skirmishers through the dense underbrush and fallen timber. Chapman returned from his reconnoitering, and meanwhile the troops came upon the body of one of their scouts where the sound of gunfire had been heard. Two others of the five had been wounded; and the other two, after killing an Indian of the ambushing party, had surrendered to the Nez Perces.

The troops then rejoined the main command under Major Mason, who ordered immediate retreat before the rear guard of Indians could surround his men and throw them into confusion. His quick action probably saved his force from annihilation.

However, L. V. McWhorter scouts the sawed-through trees as a "myth" as his Indian informants denied any knowledge of the trap. They also disclaimed suffering any casualties. Only five scouts were in the original rear guard, White Cloud told McWhorter. They remained behind to watch for pursuing soldiers. Should any enemies be sighted, "two were to ride ahead with news of the danger, so that the warriors could prepare to hold the troops back on the trail until the families could escape to a place of safety."[11] Walaitits did bring word to the chiefs that soldiers were following after the main band. So Two Moons and another party rode back to join the original five under Rainbow as leader in time for the at-

[10] Parnell, "The Salmon River Expedition," in Brady, *Northwestern Fights and Fighters*, pp. 134-35.

[11] McWhorter, *Hear Me, My Chiefs!*, p. 335.

tempted ambuscade.[12] On hearing the approach of the Army's Nez Perce scouts who were discussing the fresh pony tracks in their native tongue, the hostiles hid in the brush and waited. When the advance guard came in sight, Rainbow, for some unaccountable reason, fired and wounded one. His men then started shooting and routed the army scouts.

Despite statements by McWhorter's Nez Perce informants that they possessed no saws with which to fell trees, it would seem that the telltale signs detected by the military cannot be dismissed so completely as a "myth." Parnell's account is told in matter-of-fact detail, and the Indians employed similar obstructionist tactics during their withdrawal after the Canyon Creek conflict. It is possible the rear-guard scouts only (exclusive of Two Moons' group) endeavored to cut down trees in order to blockade the passage of any pursuing force and were overtaken before they could finish the job. The whites then mistakenly interpreted the Indians' intentions as an attempt to corral them for massacre. The Nez Perces might have been loath through pride or loyalty to their famous leader to admit to McWhorter the failure of their design, which appears to have been due to Rainbow's ill-timed shot. Or the ones interviewed could have been honestly unaware of their comrades' initial preparations for defense.

Since the hostiles' surprise plan had failed and the soldiers were on their guard, the Indians did not attempt to attack the superior numbers. The safety of the families, in McWhorter's words, was "the paramount object in view." The troops hastily retreated toward Kamiah, arriving there the next morning.

Thereafter the volunteer forces remained in Idaho to assist Captain Trimble in scouting duty. Despite the ill feeling between the regulars and the citizen allies, amicable relations and mutual trust existed between the leaders. Proof of this is found in a letter to Governor Bray-

[12] *Ibid.*, pp. 340-41.

man of Idaho. Colonel Edward McConville, in command of the volunteers, wrote:

> I would respectfully call the attention of the Governor to the uniform Kindness shown to my [me] by General Howard and the members of his staff in fact all the officers we came in contact with while in the field.[13]

Before he left Idaho, Howard publicly thanked the volunteers for their valuable services.

The Lolo reconnaissance party revealed to the general that the Nez Perces were definitely on their way toward Missoula, Montana, and that the rough character of the country would make it impossible for cavalry to operate effectively against the hostiles on this trail. Howard was satisfied, though, that his efforts had driven the warring bands from the country and stopped the raids upon the citizens. His Clearwater victory, although not decisive, had ended hostilities in Idaho. The Nez Perce campaign had officially ended in his department, but the general of the army ordered him to pursue and capture, if possible, the hostiles. Thereafter, they became facetiously known to the press as "Howard's Indians."

The general now proposed to divide his command by leaving a small garrison at Kamiah, and proceeding with his main force over the Mullan wagon road through the Coeur d'Alenes to Missoula. Several factors caused Howard to decide upon this plan: He could make a show of force on the northern route and thereby intimidate unfriendly chiefs among the Coeur d'Alene and Spokane tribes; he could give assurance to the settlers of those regions; and he could also block Joseph if he attempted to return to Idaho by that route. Major Green's cavalry from Boise would be left to guard Camas Prairie against any small scouting parties that the hostiles might have left behind.

Howard and his cavalry were halfway to Cold Spring,

---

[13] "Nez Perce War Letters to Governor Mason Brayman," *Fifteenth Biennial Report, Idaho State Historical Society*, December, 1936, p. 72.

where he would be joined by the artillery and infantry, when he received messages from Colonel Watkins, the Indian Bureau inspector, and Agent John B. Monteith, that the Indians were returning to Kamiah. Another message reported the Nez Perces to be burning houses on the North Fork of the Clearwater. Captain Throckmorton, in command at Kamiah, reported his position was threatened by the Indians. James Lawyer, head chief of the Kamiah treaty faction, informed Howard that the hostiles had stolen several hundred ponies from his people.

This alarm had been caused, the general learned later, by a small rear guard which had followed the cavalry on its return from the Lolo Trail. The warriors had seized the opportunity to make a surprise raid on the stock of Indians and whites living around Kooskia. They made off with nearly five hundred horses. Hence, Howard did not deem it advisable to leave the vicinity until the arrival of forces under Green, or those of Colonel Frank Wheaton, whose Second Infantry was being rushed from Georgia. He moved his command to Camas Prairie, the strategical center of the late scene of hostilities. This raiding party detained the general and gave the Nez Perces a favorable head start over the trail.

The delay caused Howard to discard his first plans. He decided now to lead his main command, which would form the army's right column, over the Lolo Pass, and leave Camas Prairie to be guarded by Major John Green's troops from Fort Boise, in case the Nez Perces returned to Idaho by another route while he was in pursuit. Colonel Wheaton's infantry he would send as the left column by the northern route, supported by a battalion of the First Cavalry under Colonel Cuvier Grover and two hundred mounted volunteers from Washington Territory. This column would proceed by way of Coeur d'Alene Mission to Missoula.

Howard's own command consisted of a battalion of the Fourth Artillery, in charge of Captain Marcus P. Miller; a battalion of the Twenty-first Infantry, captained by Evan Miles; and a battalion of four companies of the

First Cavalry, officered by Major George Sanford, which joined Howard at Kamiah.

The general had to wait eight days for Major Green to come from Fort Boise, so that he did not start his entire command over the Lolo Trail until July 26. This delay subjected him to much abusive criticism from the press and the citizens of Idaho. Because of his religious nature, the newspapers accused him of refusing to fight on Sunday. In fact, the national press, without realizing the difficulties he faced, or without giving the Nez Perces credit for their great fighting ability, charged Howard, the sixth ranking general of the Civil War, with being incompetent and dilatory. The truth was that the Bitterroot Mountains presented a barrier of the first magnitude to any military force that attempted to cross them.

As proof of the general's ability, Sergeant Martin L. Brown stated to the writer in an interview:

Howard was a Christian man and a praying man, and I never saw it interfere with either his duty or his bravery.

But those people who were always criticizing him didn't realize that it was quite a feat of generalship on Howard's part to take several hundred men, mules, and horses over some of the roughest, steepest trails anywhere, and keep a good lookout for possible ambuscades. It speaks well for the general that no part of his column was ever ambushed. Although we sometimes marched 40 miles[14] in a day, we went slower than the Indians, as Howard always camped at the best feeding grounds, and where good water could be found. He aimed to save the strength of his men and animals as much as possible, for he never knew when they might be called on for an emergency. Even so, part of the soldiers had to miss their sleep a third of the night to keep a guard on the camp and the animals. Then it was usually hard to find good grazing as the Indians would have been there ahead of us, and so had the advantage.

Yes, all things considered, the only wonder was that

[14] The general stated that the troops seldom traveled more than eighteen miles a day while crossing the mountains, but when marching up the Bitterroot Valley, they made forty miles or better a day.

with a column strung out four or five miles through the densest timber, Howard made as good time as he did.[15]

Further praise of Howard's generalship comes from the historian, Cyrus T. Brady, who writes:

Joseph had enough horses to remount his tribe several times.... The cavalry in pursuit had no remounts. The infantry had to go afoot. That Howard was able to keep so close behind the Indians is marvelous. That the infantry could keep up is even more remarkable.[16]

Meanwhile, the Nez Perces were pushing their way over the steep trail covered with rockslides, choked with fallen timber, and washed out in many places by the freshets of bygone years. At night they camped beside swampy lakes where the ponies grazed on wire grass, the women dug edible roots, and the men fished for salmon in deep pools of the Middle Fork of the Clearwater. The Indians cut temporary lodgepoles of spruce, hemlock, and white-pine trees. Although it was late in July, they kept fires burning all night to temper the chill air of these high altitudes, where rain fell daily and frosts lingered on the mountain slopes.

The Lewiston *Teller* extra of August 5, 1877, made a mysterious reference to Joseph:

The Indians report that White Bird and Joseph with his best warriors and good stock left the LoLo trail and turned through to the South fork of the LoLo of the Bitter Root and made camp at the Warm Springs near the head of that fork from which point he can cross into the Elk City trail without discovery from the other side.

This unexplained comment suggests that Joseph still wanted to remain in Idaho and sustains the Nez Perce's claims that he was neither the war chief nor the main

---

[15] From a feature article by Addison Howard in *Sunday Missoulian,* June 14, 1925, Missoula, Montana. Sergeant Brown, Company B, Second Infantry, was detailed with about fifty others for detached service in the Twenty-first Infantry, which formed a part of Howard's brigade during the pursuit.

[16] Brady, *op. cit.*, p. 22.

leader. Evidently White Bird and the other chiefs again applied coercion against him and his men, for they followed the others across the Bitterroots.

As the Indians climbed toward the pass on the Montana border, the trail became rougher and steeper and wound along the ridges. Trees appeared stunted as compared to the giants growing at a lower elevation. Jagged boulders lacerated the horses' feet. Rains made the narrow trail slippery and dangerous to man and animal. A misplaced step would hurtle a pony or a person over the brink to a quick death in yawning chasms far below.

At Summit Prairie near the Idaho-Montana boundary, the Nez Perces paused to graze their overworked horses. Many animals had been abandoned along the trail because of broken legs or raw backs. The pursuing troops mercifully shot them. On reaching the summit of Lolo Pass the Indians found footprints of white men's boots.

Howard had sent telegraphic messages to Captain Charles C. Rawn, commanding officer at Fort Missoula, to blockade the hostiles in Lolo Canyon until the general's pursuing force could come up, or until Colonel John Gibbon could bring Rawn reenforcements from Fort Shaw on Sun River in northern Montana. In pursuance of these orders, Rawn had sent out a small scouting party. Thus it happened that, three hours before the first Nez Perce reached the pass, Second Lieutenant Francis Woodbridge, with a reconnaissance party of four soldiers from Fort Missoula, had stood there and gazed westward to see if the Indians were coming. The dense timber, however, completely hid from his view the long procession of people and animals winding along the trail. Having scouted the Lolo as far as the Clearwater without seeing any trace of the hostiles, Woodbridge had started back.

On July 21, several days after Woodbridge left the fort, not hearing from him, Captain Rawn detailed First Lieutenant Charles A. Coolidge and a party of volunteers to search for him. The searchers met Woodbridge's detachment in the trail on July 22, and they continued together toward Fort Missoula. Later that same day a half-breed,

John Hill, who had been a prisoner in the Nez Perce camp, overtook Coolidge's party. He gave information as to the whereabouts of the Indians and the route they were traveling. Accompanied by the breed, the soldiers hastened on to report to Captain Rawn.

The descending trail on the east side of the mountains traversed ledges narrower than those on the west side, and the canyons appeared more terrifying. Not far from the summit (on its eastern slope) the Indians had to dismount and lead their horses along a sheer ledge, man and mount pressing against the wall of the cliff lest they should lose their footing on wet rocks and plunge into the gorge. Safely past this dangerous place, they ascended another crest and started down the widened and less rugged path into Lolo Canyon. The chiefs ordered a halt on the banks of a shallow stream (Lolo Creek) winding through a green valley margined by gently sloping and sparsely wooded hills. Hot sulphur springs erupted thin columns of steam into the air. These waters of Lolo Hot Springs, Montana, provided the Indians with natural bathing and washing facilities. In this paradise of the wilderness, the sick and the wounded sought the healing properties of the "medicine" waters.

However, new difficulties confronted the chiefs. Messengers brought information that Charlot awaited an excuse to ally his people with the whites, even though his tribe, like the Nez Perces, were also nontreaty Indians.[17]

---

[17] Chief Charlot, in common with Chief Joseph, had land troubles with the United States. When he refused to sign a treaty and move onto the Flathead Reservation, Commissioner James A. Garfield, later President of the United States, forged Charlot's signature to the document, later excusing the act on the grounds of expediency. Mrs. Peter Ronan, in an interview with Addison Howard, stated that her husband, Major Peter Ronan, Flathead Indian agent, had examined the original agreement in Washington, D.C., and had found Charlot's mark missing. The chief always denied signing it. Only the copy presented by Congressman Garfield to the Senate for ratification bore the forged mark. The commissioners arbitarily recognized Arlee (a Nez Perce adopted into the Flathead tribe) as head chief, despite Charlot's hereditary right to that rank. Arlee signed the agreement in 1872 and moved part of the tribe to the present reservation north of Missoula. Charlot's people were not removed from the Bitterroot Valley until 1891. Unlike Joseph, however, Charlot did not go on the warpath against

This Flathead chief sent a warning to Joseph's warriors not to harm a single hair of any white person in the Bitterroot Valley. If the Nez Perces stole any stock belonging to either settlers or Indians, Charlot would use the act as a pretext to join the soldiers. His belligerent attitude toward his former friends was said to be prompted by his desire to steal the Nez Perces' fine horses.[18]

Nevertheless, the chiefs decided to go south up the Bitterroot Valley and pass through the land owned by Charlot's band of Flatheads. Although Canada—and freedom—lay but 240 miles to the north, the Nez Perces at this time apparently had formed no decision to turn in that direction. They proposed, rather, to reach the country of the Crows, who had promised them a safe passage to the buffalo hunting grounds. Then, too, they hoped to outdistance Howard's pursuing force by keeping to a rough, mountainous region. If they attempted to go directly east through the sixty-mile defile of Hell Gate Canyon, they would have to pass the town of Missoula and they wished to avoid large settlements. Besides, they undoubtedly had warning of Wheaton's command approaching from the west over the Coeur d'Alenes, and thus the direct way north toward Canada was closed to them.

Nez Perce survivors of the campaign told Edward Curtis "that when the passage of Lolo cañon was begun, there was no thought of escaping to Canada, but that later it was decided that if the Apsaroke [Crows] would not help them they would learn from that tribe the route to the 'Old Woman's Country.' "[19]

This southerly route through the Bitterroot meant hundreds of extra miles to travel, but it offered greater safety and a plentiful food supply, which would also provide

---

the whites, but instead maintained the most cordial relations with certain white people, notably Father Ravalli and Major Ronan. A complete documentary account of Charlot's story appears in chap. 8 of Helen Addison Howard's *Northwest Trail Blazers* (Caldwell, Idaho: The Caxton Printers, Ltd., 1963).

[18] Phillips, *op. cit.*, p. 74.

[19] Curtis, *op. cit.*, VIII, 32, note 1.

skins to replace the lodges they had lost at the battle of the Clearwater.

Meanwhile, alarmed by the approaching menace of Joseph's warriors, the citizens of Missoula became active in organizing volunteer companies. Christopher P. Higgins,[20] who had come West with Governor Stevens' expedition in 1853 and was present as Stevens' packmaster at the Walla Walla council in 1855, was elected captain.

With the hostiles almost on the outskirts of the town, Missoula was in tumult. Every new refugee from the country brought more tales of impending doom. One intensely excited woman drove for miles in mad haste to reach the town. Not until she was safely inside Higgins and Worden's store did she realize that her bonnet was on backwards, with the long ribbons hanging over her face.

While the settlers of western Montana had visions of being massacred by the invading Nez Perces, Joseph's people leisurely traveled down the Lolo Canyon until they were stopped by the hasty log fortifications of "Fort Fizzle."

---

[20] Higgins, with his business partner, Francis L. Worden, founded in 1865 the present city of Missoula, Montana.

Retreat of the Nez Perces through Montana

CHAPTER XVI

The Affair at "Fort Fizzle"

THE report of Lieutenant Coolidge convinced many Montanans that the scene of hostilities would shift to the Bitterroot Valley. Wild rumors made the whites fear that their erstwhile friends, the Nez Perces, might attack Missoula. Many citizens there were personally acquainted with White Bird and Looking Glass, who in past years had bartered at the stores and paid social visits at the homes of townspeople.[1] The citizens also expected the Flatheads in racial sympathy to join their red brethren.

This put the members of Charlot's band in a quandary, for they realized that the whites, in their hysteria, would hardly know one Indian from another and might through error shoot them in event of battle.

Missoula was not prepared for an Indian war, which increased the citizens' alarm. Four miles south of the town, Fort Missoula was then in process of construction, and garrisoned with only two reduced companies, A and I, of the Seventh Infantry, commanded by Captain Charles C. Rawn. The post had forty-four soldiers, who, regardless of their bravery, were certainly no match for, possibly, 300 warriors supported by 450 women and children, many of whom could handle a gun as well as the braves.

In response to Rawn's call for volunteers, scores of

---

[1] Among the many ranches often visited bv the Nez Perces was Eliza Deery's homestead, on the south side of the river opposite the town of Missoula. Mrs. Deery, being a practical nurse, gave them first aid from simple remedies for injuries they received when going to or returning from the buffalo hunts. Her stepson was with the Missoula volunteers who accompanied Rawn for seventeen days.

settlers rushed into town, over one hundred men coming from Bitterroot farms. Captain C. P. Higgins recruited another hundred in Missoula. The women and children were crowded into the general merchandise store of Higgins and Worden. Being a stout log building with ample space, it had been converted into a temporary barricade.

With his command increased by two hundred civilian volunteers, Captain Rawn, his five commissioned regular officers, and thirty enlisted men of the Seventh Infantry, marched the twelve miles south to Lolo Canyon on July 25. Eight miles above where the canyon debouched into the Bitterroot Valley, Rawn erected log breastworks three feet high, and had trenches dug. He had chosen a strategic location at the narrowest part of the defile, flanked on either side by steep-sided, sparsely wooded hills. Thus the enemy approaching from the west could not, theoretically, force a way past. Besides, the fortifications gave the defenders a decided advantage over the Indians, who would be placed in an exposed position.

Nez Perce scouts informed the chiefs about the entrenchments barring their progress. The main body of Indians reached the site of "Fort Fizzle" on July 26. They raised their lodges two miles up the canyon, Rawn stated (but McWhorter gives the distance as twelve miles), and settled down to study how they could pass the armed force in front of them without bloodshed.

No doubt the chiefs, with military insight, realized a direct attack would be foolhardy, for, even if their men could successfully assault the barricade, they would suffer fearful losses. The chiefs therefore sent out spies to reconnoiter the region for a passageway around the breastworks. The Nez Perces could not rely upon Charlot's band of Flatheads to attack Rawn's forces from the rear, because scouts brought word that this chief had not changed his stipulations regarding the invasion of his territory by the hostiles. Indeed, about twenty to twenty-five Flathead braves led by Charlot's son, according to Indian Agent Ronan, had joined Rawn.

Apparently the Nez Perces were surprised at the bellicose reception accorded them by the Montana people, who had always been their friends. Since they felt no enmity toward the settlers of the Bitterroot, the chiefs willingly agreed to parley with the military.

In his report to the Secretary of War, Captain Rawn states that he held a council on July 27 with Joseph, White Bird, and Looking Glass.[2] The chiefs protested only friendship for the people of Montana, and proposed, if allowed to pass unmolested, to refrain from any acts of depredation on their march up the Bitterroot Valley. Rawn, however, would agree to give them free passage only on condition that they surrender to him their arms, their ammunition, and their mounts.

This, of course, the chiefs refused to do, for Rawn's ultimatum meant unconditional surrender. Without horses or arms the Nez Perces would be at the mercy of the army, and all their sacrifices of life and property in Idaho would have been in vain.

In order to gain time and to hold the hostiles in check, so that either Howard's or Gibbon's force could arrive with reenforcements, the captain appointed another meeting for the next day. He arranged to talk with Looking Glass and one other Indian.

This arrangement suited the chiefs, for they were planning a means of escape, should the diplomacy of Looking Glass fail to elicit permission from Rawn for a safe passage. Since he was better known in Missoula than the other chiefs, Looking Glass might have more influence with the whites.

Accordingly, the next day, at a spot on the prairie out of range of rifles in the Indian camp, Looking Glass and one of his braves met the captain, who was accompanied by Delaware Jim as interpreter.

---

[2] *Report of Secretary of War*, 1877, I, 501. Report of Captain Rawn.

However, the meeting was not satisfactory to Rawn, for he wrote in his report:

I submitted to him the same conditions as before, to wit, that if they wished to enter the valley they must disarm and dismount, surrendering all stock. Looking-Glass said he would talk to his people, and would tell me what they said at 9 a. m. the next day. Distrusting him, I would not agree to that hour, but proposed 12 m. We separated without agreement. Nothing satisfactory having resulted from the conference, I returned to the breastworks, expecting to be attacked.[3]

Rawn held a consultation with his officers and the civilian allies. When the Bitterroot volunteers learned of the Nez Perces' pledge of peace, they decided that no act of theirs should precipitate destruction to their farms in the valley. One hundred or more, in groups of one to twelve, departed for home at once, "without leave," the captain reports. Rawn immediately posted rear guards to prevent further desertions. The remainder of his force of regulars and Missoula men became excited by the activity in the hostiles' camp and tensely waited for the attack.

The Nez Perces were determined to reach the Bitterroot Valley in spite of Rawn's warlike attitude. The women began preparing everything for a quick march. They pulled down the lodges and loaded them with the supplies on the backs of packhorses after the chiefs had agreed to a plan of action. There is no testimony to indicate who originated the stratagem, but it was probably decided on in the council of the leaders.

By ten o'clock the next morning the Indian cavalcade began moving from the canyon to the hills, ascending the slopes a half mile in front of the right flank of the entrenchments. The Nez Perces' line of march, screened

[3] *Ibid.* The Indian and white testimonies are contradictory as to whether one, two, or more powwows were held with the hostiles and on what dates. McWhorter's Nez Perce informants declared only one meeting took place, whereas several volunteers gave the number as three in as many days. But Rawn's report is the official contemporary record written at the time.

by gullies and trees on the north side of the gorge, led them safely past the flank of the fortifications, and thus into the Bitterroot Valley. The chiefs apparently had made a topographical study of the vicinity, and had seized upon a route of escape which the whites believed to be impossible.

W. R. Logan, who was present at "Fort Fizzle" with his father, Captain William Logan, and Captain Rawn, has written an eyewitness description of the exodus of the Nez Perces:

> About ten o'clock we heard singing, apparently above our heads. Upon looking up we discovered the Indians passing along the side of the cliff, where we thought a goat could not pass, much less an entire tribe of Indians with all their impedimenta. The entire band dropped into the valley beyond us and then proceeded up the Bitter Root. Two civilians and I rode down from our camp and followed with the Indians for a mile or more. They were good-natured, cracked jokes, and seemed very much amused at the way they had fooled Rawn and Logan.[4]

Amazed and completely outwitted by the maneuver, Rawn formed skirmish lines across the canyon with his regulars and the remaining volunteers and advanced toward the Indians. He expected them to attack, but the Nez Perces continued up the valley while the rear guard fired a parting shot over the heads of the troops. Believing that the chiefs intended to keep the peace, all but a dozen or twenty Missoula citizens had deserted. So the captain

---

[4] Curtis, *The North American Indian*, VIII, 33. A hewn log marker, set up in recent years by the people of Montana to designate the site of Fort Fizzle, bears the following inscription: "Here Capt. Charles C. Rawn, 7th Infantry, with four officers and twenty-five enlisted men from Fort Missoula, approximately 150 citizen volunteers and 25 Flathead braves erected and occupied a redoubt from July 25 to 28, 1877, to challenge the passage of the hostile non-treaty Nez Perce Indians under Chief Joseph. On July 28 the Nez Perces evaded the troops by ascending a gulch on the north side of Lolo Creek half a mile above this place and going down Sleeman Creek in the Bitter Root Valley."

According to an item in the *Rocky Mountain Husbandman*, February 26, 1942, "a forest fire on Sept. 30, 1934, destroyed the last visible sector of the old log redoubt, which is now marked by five cement piers."

wisely returned to the fort with his skeleton force, no doubt chagrined by his failure to check the Indians.

One settler, when asked why he had left the command, stated laconically, "We didn't lose any Indians." He was willing to let Idaho solve its own problems. Most of the volunteers were glad to escape a battle, and with droll humor referred to their recent barricade as "Fort Fizzle."

The Nez Perces kept their promise as they moved up the valley, making twelve to fourteen miles a day. There was no need to hurry, for they knew Howard to be many days behind them. Besides, their footsore and gaunt ponies needed the opportunity to rest and graze after their arduous trip over the Lolo Trail. Grass had been scarce, but the meadowlands of the Bitterroot afforded abundant pasturage. The people, too, had been on scanty rations of food.

Evidence of strain showed most clearly in members of Joseph's band, for during the entire two months since leaving the Wallowa Valley, they had been traveling and fighting. Joseph's heart was sick with his troubles, and each mile of retreat from Idaho appeared to depress him the more. Doubtless he thought often of his homeland, the valley of winding waters, where lay the graves of his father and mother. Imbued with the Dreamer's sacred love for the land of his ancestors, Joseph seems to have dreaded most of all that death would claim him and his people in a strange country, far from the graves of forefathers. This Oriental veneration of ancestors made bitter the Indians' fear of racial extinction in alien lands.

After leaving Lolo, Yellow Bull states, the chiefs held another council in which Looking Glass and Joseph again agreed to go to the Crows' country, although they were opposed by Pile of Clouds, who wanted to return to the Salmon River. At this powwow, Yellow Bull reports:

Joseph did not rise, but said: "While we were fighting for our own country, there was reason to fight, but while we are here, I would not have anything to say in favor of fighting, for this is not my country. Since we have left our country, it matters little where we go.[5]

White Bird remained neutral this time, but insisted, "If we go to the Crows, we must all go."[6] This remark of White Bird's would indicate continued dissension among the various bands, and perhaps talk of splitting up, each band to go its own way. However, the Indians stayed together, with Looking Glass as dominant leader to select the campsites and pace the day's march. Joseph continued in the role of guardian of the old people, the women and children. Although Charlot disapproved of the intrusion of his former allies, he passively watched the cavalcade of Nez Perces go through his land.

During the caravan's leisurely trek up the valley most of the white population peeked from barricaded cabins in consternation. That Bitterroot settlers distrusted the peaceful intentions of the Indians is brought out in a letter written by Washington J. McCormick, a prominent attorney of Missoula, to Territorial Governor Potts. He thus describes conditions in the valley:

Their men [warriors] are disciplined their horses are trained, and they are commanded by a man who thoroughly understands his business. There is no longer any doubt but that Joseph with his entire fighting force is here. The Indians have plenty of Gold dust Coin and greenbacks and have been paying exhorbitant prices for flour Coffee sugar and tobacco. They told the merchants of Stevensville (thirty miles up the Bitter Root from Missoula) on Wednesday that they had money to pay for what supplies they wanted and if they did not sell to them they would take them by force. So far as I am advised they have killed no stock and molested no one except to disarm two or three citizens, returning their guns however but keeping their amunition. The people of the Bitter Root with their

---

[5] Curtis, *ibid.*, p. 166.

[6] *Ibid.* McWhorter states that this "meeting was held at the camp of Left Hand, a brother or blood kin to Chief Eagle From the Light. Looking Glass, Five Wounds, and Rainbow, he continues, favored the Crow country. Opposing them were White Bird, Toohoolhoolzote (Tuhulhutsut), Red Owl, Two Moons, and Wottolen who preferred the northern route. Joseph, he claims, had no part in this council. McWhorter, *Hear Me, My Chiefs!*, p. 357.

families are still in their fortifications and propose to remain there until the danger is past. The situation is a most deplorable one their wheat crops are ready for the machine, and no one to harvest them while in many instances stock have broken into their fields and ruined their crops. . . . The people are thoroughly convinced that Capt Rawn acted wisely in not attacking the Indians.[7]

Only one merchant in the valley refused to make money by trading with the Nez Perces. Mr. Young, of Corvallis, angrily ordered them out of his store and barred it shut. His rivals at Stevensville and Hamilton profited by the extra business. With one exception no white man's property was pillaged. This lone case was the Lockwood ranch in Ross Hole. The owner fled when a party of young braves approached his home, and the Indians proceeded to gut the house and take everything that caught their fancy.[8]

Despite the peaceful attitude of the invaders, the people of Deer Lodge, a town eighty miles east of Missoula, fled to the penitentiary and locked themselves in. In their alarm they appealed to the copper-mining town of Butte for volunteers. William A. Clark,[9] later United States Senator from Montana, offered to ride to that settlement to recruit help. He made a remarkable trip on horseback, covering the forty-two miles in three and one-half hours through the scorching heat. Mrs. Al Pearce[10] had thoughtfully placed cabbage leaves in his hat to keep him from getting sunstroke. Later the Butte and Deer Lodge volunteers joined Colonel Gibbon's force.

In the meanwhile, Howard was still toiling over the

---

[7] Phillips, ed., "The Battle of the Big Hole," *Frontier Magazine*, November, 1929, p. 75.

[8] Lockwood joined Gibbon's force and was seriously wounded at the Big Hole battle.

[9] The late W. A. Clark, Jr., noted Los Angeles philanthropist, who was five months old at the time, was among the "temporary convicts" with his mother at the penitentiary. He recounted to Dan McGrath the amusement that his father, the late Senator Clark, had received from the incident.

[10] Mrs. Pearce was, in 1934, a resident of Los Angeles, California. Judge Lippincott, of Butte, told the incident to the author and Dan McGrath.

Lolo Trail.[11] The last of his command had left the Weippe prairie in Idaho for the Bitterroot on July 30. On August 4 a message from Rawn informed him of the Indians' slow movement up the valley, and that Colonel Gibbon was expected to reach Missoula from Fort Shaw immediately. Howard decided to divide his command in the hope of forming a junction with Gibbon earlier than he could with the whole of it. A dispatch from Gibbon himself asking for reenforcements reached the general at Summit Prairie, so he pushed ahead with two hundred picked cavalrymen.

Colonel Wheaton's left column of Howard's brigade, coming by way of Spokane through the Coeur d'Alene Mountains, returned to Lewiston when the Nez Perces turned south up the Bitterroot.

The hostiles' fighting force received reenforcements in the valley from a Nez Perce band of six lodges under Poker Joe (Lean Elk). He and his group had recently arrived in the Bitterroot from a buffalo hunt. Poker Joe, half Indian and half French, is described as an intelligent man whom the Indians considered a great leader and warrior. He was thoroughly familiar with the Montana country and preferred to live away from the Nez Perce Reservation.[12]

The Indians, believing themselves far in advance of Howard's troops, crossed the Continental Divide into the Big Hole Valley, still traveling leisurely to take advantage of the nutritious forage. Looking Glass guided the Nez Perces through the Bitterroot, then the chiefs replaced him with Poker Joe after the disastrous Big Hole battle.

That Joseph sincerely intended to leave a clean trail by a strict adherence to his promise of peace to the Montana people, there can be no doubt. But if he were at-

---

[11] A party of Moscow hunters told Dr. Clifford M. Drury a number of years ago of finding cannon deserted by Howard's command on the Lolo Trail.

[12] Merrill D. Beal, *"I Will Fight No More Forever"; Chief Joseph and the Nez Perce War*, p. 252.

tacked by the "Bostons,"[13] who could blame him for fighting in self-defense? Joseph cherished the hope in his heart that he could yet win back by negotiation his native Wallowa Valley. Failing in that, he thought he might be able to secure a home among Charlot's people in the Bitterroot, known to the Flatheads as "the land of shining mountains."

"We understood that there was to be no war," Joseph said later. "We intended to go peaceably to the buffalo country, and leave the question of returning to our country to be settled afterward."[14]

---

[13] Crawford, *The Nez Percés Since Spalding*, p. 6. Mary M. Crawford, forty-one years a missionary among the Nez Perces at Lapwai, says this term was applied by the Indians. "Everything not Nez Perces was 'Boston'—a hand-down from the old days of the Hudson Bay Company."

[14] "An Indian's Views of Indian Affairs," *North American Review*, April, 1879, p. 426.

CHAPTER XVII

The Battle of the Big Hole

THE Big Hole Valley was a beautiful prairie basin of rolling hills and meadowland, intersected by numerous streams and woods, and encircled by precipitous, forest-clad mountains. In a grassy meadow on the banks of Ruby Creek near its confluence with Trail Creek, the Indians erected their tepee village of some ninety lodges, arranging them in the form of an irregular V with the apex upstream. Here the nutritious grass of the basin afforded excellent forage for their herd of some two thousand ponies. The river and its tributary streams supplied an abundance of fish for the people, while pine thickets on the hillslope west of the village would furnish them with a plenteous supply of lodgepoles. These would be used when they reached the treeless plains of the buffalo country. The young men formed gay parties and roamed far afield to hunt the fleet antelope. Is it any wonder that Chief Looking Glass ordered his people to make a rest camp in such a favored spot? He felt so secure in the friendship of the Montana people that he even refused to scout the back trail.

White Bird, though, haunted by his guilty conscience since he had been the leading spirit to favor war with the whites, opposed this rest halt. He urged haste, well knowing it was the murders committed by three young men of his band which fomented the war.

Already the coming tragic event began to cast its ominous shadow, for, on the eve of the Big Hole battle, one of the medicine men, Pile of Clouds, warned that "death is on our trail!" He asked the chiefs assembled in council:

What are we doing here? While I slept, my medicine told me to move on; that death is approaching us. Chiefs, I only tell you this for the good of our people. If you take my advice you can avoid death, and that advice is to speed through this country. If we do not there will be tears in our eyes.[1]

Of a surety there was to be "tears in their eyes," for instead of heeding the warning, the chiefs ordered a feast and celebrated with a war dance, and then retired to their lodges to fall into the sleep of security.

Samuel Tilden,[2] a Nez Perce formerly employed by the government on the Flathead Reservation in Montana, recalls:

There was a lot of fun going on at night, and there was a stick game and other amusements such as the Indians used to have when they camped long ago—footraces and horseraces.

That last night there was a lot going on, singing until late. Along about twelve or one or two o'clock they quieted down and went to sleep.[3]

How could they know that General Howard had telegraphed Colonel John Gibbon at Fort Shaw, apprising him of the situation? Nor did they suspect that Gibbon had hastily collected 146 men, comprising six companies of the Seventh Infantry, a wagon train, and thirty-four citizen volunteers, and already had started in pursuit several days before from Helena. Gibbon marched the 150 miles from Fort Shaw, just east of the Rocky Mountains, to

---

[1] Shields, *The Battle of the Big Hole*, pp. 78-79. Yellow Wolf states in his *Yellow Wolf: His Own Story*, p. 109, that this prophecy was unknown to him. Lone Bird, "a brave fighter," he further relates, gave the first warning and urged more haste before reaching the Big Hole camp. But Yellow Bull affirms "Pile Of [*sic*] Clouds was a medicine-man and had visions showing the enemy." Curtis, *The North American Indian*, VIII, 166. Because Looking Glass refused to hurry the march or heed the warnings, he was blamed for the disaster which followed. The chiefs then deposed him as leader and appointed Poker Joe (Lean Elk).

[2] Tilden was seventy-one years old in 1934, and he was a boy of nine at the time of Joseph's march.

[3] Ralph R. Wayne, *Sunday Missoulian*, August 5, 1934, Missoula, Montana. From a newspaper article featuring Samuel Tilden.

Missoula in seven days. Here he was reenforced by Rawn's command and additional volunteers from Missoula and the Bitterroot, which brought his total force to 191 men.

Regarding the difficulties of the march from Ross Hole to the Continental Divide, Thomas Sherrill, a volunteer member of Gibbon's command, relates:

> The next morning we started up again at 5 o'clock and started to climb the steep barrier, and the traveling was much more difficult on account of the fallen timber which had to be removed or climbed over, but our wagons were lightly loaded and by doubling our teams and using the men to help drag the wagons, we finally reached the summit, making only two miles in six hours.[4]

Although Gibbon's advance was considerably delayed by the rough, mountainous country he had to cross with his wagons, he was already within a few hours' march of the Nez Perce village that night. So certain of their safety did the Indians feel that they had neglected to post sentinels, or to send out scouts, although that very day Lieutenant James H. Bradley[5] and a small detachment had been sent to reconnoiter their position. Bradley had offered to try and stampede the Indians' herd of ponies. He had pushed forward the night before with a force of sixty men in the hopes of striking the camp before daylight. If he could succeed in doing this and put the Nez Perces on foot, their defeat would be assured. But the village was farther away than he had supposed, and dawn overtook him before he reached it.

About noon of August 8, Corporal Drummond reported to the lieutenant that he had found plenty of fresh signs of Indians. Bradley, the corporal, and Lieutenant J. W. Jacobs, regimental quartermaster of the Seventh Infantry, then set out to determine the exact location of the village. The officers proceeded with stealthy caution and

---

[4] Thomas C. Sherrill, *Battle of the Big Hole in August, 1877*, p. 4.

[5] This is the same Lieutenant Bradley who discovered the bodies of Custer's troops after the battle of the Little Big Horn.

heard at a distance the clear, ringing tones of axes as the Indian women chopped the lodgepole pines. They veered in that direction and soon could hear the choppers' voices very distinctly.

Fearing detection, Lieutenants Bradley and Jacobs climbed a tall tree. From its topmost branches the officers could see hundreds of Indian ponies grazing in a meadow almost beneath them. Small boys on horseback were wandering in and about the herd, while others were lazily stretched on the ground in the shade of nearby trees. Several hundred yards away across the river was the Indian village, partially screened by alder and willow thickets. Many of the lodges were just being set up by the women, others of whom were engaged in carrying more lodgepoles, making the beds, and cooking the midday meal. Scores of warriors lounged about the tepees already pitched.

One glance was sufficient. The officers made their silent way back to their concealed camp, and immediately sent off a dispatch to Gibbon.

When the colonel received it, he gave orders for each man to be supplied with ninety rounds of ammunition and one day's rations, and for twenty men to guard the wagon train, as he intended to push ahead on foot. His command marched forward as rapidly as possible over a terrain choked with fallen timber. The main force reached Bradley's camp at sundown, at approximately the same time, perhaps, as the Nez Perces were feasting.

The soldiers broke ranks in a gulch to eat a scanty supper of hardtack and raw pork, and then lay down to rest without fires or blankets. The colonel himself lay under a pine tree and slept until the officer of the guard awoke him. It was Gibbon's intention to make a surprise attack on the Indian camp at dawn.

Quietly each man was awakened, and orders were whispered to form into a line of march. Guided by Joe Blodgett, citizen scout, and Lieutenant Bradley, the troops, as silently as possible, followed through the tangled underbrush, over rocky ledges, up and down numerous ravines, across washouts, waded waist deep in the icy waters of the stream, and floundered in the oozy mire of the swamps. The starry August night was cold with the chill air of the mountains, but no moon betrayed their presence.

After five miles of marching, the soldiers saw the campfires of the Indian village glowing in the dark. They could hear the barking of dogs answering the howls of coyotes. Now and again a blaze would flare up, disclosing smoky lodges. A few hundred yards from the camp the troops again forded the stream, and upon ascending the bluff ran into a herd of ponies. Some of them neighed and snorted at the strange invasion, but fortunately the animals did not stampede. The soldiers continued to pick their way cautiously through the brush and over rocks to halt at a point overlooking the village, not more than 150 yards from the nearest tepees. It was then two o'clock in the morning. The men lay down beside their rifles to shiver in the chilly air until daylight. They watched the Indians' smoldering campfires flicker occasionally—a scene fantastic and weird in the waning light of the stars.

Bostwick, a half-breed scout, told Colonel Gibbon, "They have no idea of our presence.... After a while you'll see some fires built up if we remain undiscovered."[6]

Within the hour several Indian women emerged from their lodges and threw fresh fuel on the smoldering fires. As the wood flared up the troops could see them turning before the blaze to warm themselves, and could hear them chattering between yawns. Gradually they all drifted back to their beds of buffalo and bear robes. The doomed village slept on. Sam Tilden says:

About three o'clock, a woman went down to get a bucket of water, and she heard a crackling in the bushes—heard something like a gun rattling as it was carried through the brush. She told her man, but he told her she didn't know what it was.[7]

---

[6] Shields, *The Battle of the Big Hole*, p. 46.

[7] Wayne, *op. cit.*

In the weird, gray light of dawn, acting under whispered orders, the troops deployed in line of battle and moved forward in an eerie silence. Ahead went the skirmishers, Captain Sanno's and Comba's companies, stealthily descending the slope to feel their way across the icy river, the water nearly reaching their armpits. The companies of Captains Logan, Williams, and Rawn, and Lieutenant Bradley's men stole quietly forward, the first three going to the extreme right of the camp to attack the Indians' left flank near Ruby Creek. Bradley's platoon with the citizen scouts had been ordered to go left downstream and strike the lower end. A dense growth of willows extended from the slope to the village. Herds of ponies grazed in grassy spaces among the brush. Gibbon reports: "A deep slough with water in places waist-deep wound through this bottom from right to left, and had to be crossed before the stream itself could be reached."[8]

Dawn comes quickly in the mountains, spreading across the eastern sky with a halo of rosy light. As it appeared on that morning of August 9 a mounted Indian rode out of the willows, going toward the pony herd on the slope above. In such silence had the advance of the soldiers been made that the Indian nearly collided with Bradley's men. Before he had time to raise a gun or shout a cry of alarm, both he and his horse were shot down.

That was the signal for the battle to start, for Gibbon's order had been: "When the first shot is fired, charge the camp with the whole line." Instantly a barrage of rifle fire saluted the dawn. With loud yells the line of infantrymen surged forward. Like the terrific rush of a tidal wave they swept into the midst of the slumbering village.

Panic-stricken Indians dashed from their lodges, heavy-lidded from sleep, and ran for the shelter of the riverbank and thickets of alder and willow. Most of the warriors were naked. Almost in an instant the peaceful village became a scene of confusion—women yelling, children screaming, papooses crying, dogs barking, ponies neigh-

[8] *Report of Secretary of War*, 1877, I, 70. Report of Colonel Gibbon.

ing, many of them breaking their tethers and stampeding in fright. A few warriors had had the presence of mind to seize their guns, but at first were too dazed to use them. Others who had madly raced away returned to their lodges under the soldiers' galling fire to get their weapons. The braves then took cover under the river-banks and in the stream bed itself.

Amid this mad scene the troops remained cool and shot to kill. In the first confusion it was inevitable that women and children should be injured. But there is evidence the whites fired on these noncombatants later in the fighting as well. However, instead of fleeing in terror far from the camp, the Indians soon rallied and began to lay down a telling fire on the soldiers.

Lieutenant Bradley and his handful of men were the first to assault the village. His orders from Colonel Gibbon had been to exercise great care in entering the brush, and to keep under cover as much as possible. But his was a fearless soul, and he waved on his men to charge, himself in the lead. He plunged into a thicket to drive out a group of Indians supposedly lurking therein, as a soldier cried out, "Hold on, Lieutenant; don't go in there; it's sure death." With the reckless abandon of fighting courage he dashed in. Suddenly an Indian raised out of the brush and fired, instantly killing the officer. Bradley's men immediately retaliated by riddling the warrior with bullets. With maddened courage then, they too charged into the midst of the Indians, dealing death on all sides in their fury.

Captain Logan's men crossed the stream and came upon the rear of a force of Indians hidden in the willows. The warriors turned on the soldiers, cutting them down with a melting fire. It was here the greatest slaughter took place. The whites claim a powerful brave rushed upon Captain Logan, and that he took deliberate aim with his revolver and killed the Indian. But the Nez Perces declare the warrior was lying in a shallow depression behind a small pine log. The warrior's woman, thought by the troops to be his sister, but who, the Indians affirm, was his pregnant wife, leaped to the side of her fallen mate. She wrenched his smoking rifle from his dead hand and fired it point-blank at Logan's head. The gallant captain fell with a mortal wound.[9]

At the sight Logan's men went mad and riddled the Indian girl with bullets. She collapsed across her young husband's body. Heedless of their own lives, the soldiers ran wildly among the Indians, using the butts of their rifles to club to death all who came within reach. The battle had become "an eye for an eye," with no quarter asked or given on either side.

But the courage of the Indians ran high also, and they fought as savagely as the whites, giving blow for blow. Many a warrior and soldier fell dead or wounded into the river and were carried away together by its blood-reddened current.

Comba's and Sanno's companies struck the camp at the apex of the V and poured their fire at close range into the lodges and the Indians as they emerged from the tepees. It was here, near the upper end of the village, Yellow Wolf recalls, that Chief Joseph's lodge was located.

One brave, Grizzly Bear Youth, worked his way behind the soldiers, firing right and left and exacting heavy toll. Suddenly a huge, ugly-looking rancher, a citizen volunteer, turned around. With an oath he raced toward the Indian, swinging his gun over his head by the barrel. The red man met the charge with the same kind of defense. Each delivered the other a terrific blow at the same time. The white man fell, and the Indian leaped on top, but the volunteer recovered from his daze and grappled with his adversary. Locked in a deadly clinch, they rolled and tossed. The white finally got on top and choked the red into unconsciousness.

---

[9] Regarding this Tilden says, "There was an officer killed by an Indian woman. She stayed with her man, Supsis Elpelp, one of the bravest Nez Perce warriors, when he went out. The officer dying, or someone else near-by killed the woman—anyway she was killed." Yellow Wolf confirms this, identifying the warrior as Wahlitits (Walaitits) and his wife. McWhorter, *Yellow Wolf: His Own Story*, p. 133. Eloosykasit gives a detailed account in *ibid.*, p. 135.

Then along came the son of Red Owl. Thrusting the muzzle of his gun into the white man's side, he pulled the trigger. The ball passed through the volunteer's body, killing him and breaking the arm of Grizzly Bear Youth.

Within twenty minutes the soldiers had captured the village. They had been given orders to destroy it. So, lighting torches, they set the lodges on fire, but the night's heavy dew made them too damp, and the skin tepees would not burn at all.

Seeing their homes and possessions on fire, Chiefs Joseph, White Bird, and Looking Glass rallied their warriors to renewed courage. Their voices could be heard above the noise of battle. Very plainly the troops heard White Bird, his words translated by the friendly Nez Perce scouts, challenging the braves:

Why are we retreating? Since the world was made, brave men have fought for their women and children. Shall we run into the mountains and let these white dogs kill our women and children before our eyes? It is better that we should be killed fighting. Now is our time to fight. These soldiers cannot fight harder than the ones we defeated on Salmon River and White Bird Canon. Fight! Shoot them down! We can shoot as well as any of these soldiers.[10]

The voice of Looking Glass at the other end of the camp could be heard shouting the names of the three Indians who brought on the war by the killing of white settlers:

Wal-lit-ze! Tap-sis-il-pilp! Um-til-ilp-cown! This is battle! These men are not asleep as those you murdered in Idaho. These soldiers mean battle. You tried to break my promise at Lolo. You wanted to fire at the fortified place. Now is the time to show your courage and fight. You can kill right and left. I would rather see you killed than the rest, for you commenced the war. It was you who murdered the settlers in Idaho. Now fight![11]

---

[10] Shields, *The Battle of the Big Hole*, pp. 51-52.

[11] *Ibid.* Although Joseph's words have not been recorded for posterity, J. H. Horner, in a letter, October 20, 1941, writes: "I was well acquainted with one of the volunteer scouts who was at the

These "pep" talks bore psychological fruit, for the Indians made a concerted charge to regain their camp, and fought like demons in hand-to-hand encounters. The force of their savage onslaught lasted but a few minutes, when they again retired to the riverbank. From there they poured a cool, deadly fire into the unprotected troops, for the Nez Perces were the straightest-shooting Indians in North America! Two of the braves named by Looking Glass were soon killed, and the third one was reported by the Nez Perces to have died some time later in a skirmish.[12]

Meanwhile, the onslaught of the troops raged fiercely. They were subjected to a cross fire not only by the sharpshooters in the hills, thickets, and riverbanks, but even by boys and Indian women who exercised a deadly aim. It was at this time that a touching sight attracted Colonel Gibbon's attention. Some of the women, carrying their babies in their arms, waded into deep water to avoid the firing. Upon spying the white soldier-chief they held out their papooses at arm's length, looking "as pleasant and wistful as they could" for his protection.

Soon the colonel's horse was shot under him, and he received a flesh wound in the leg. Then Lieutenant Woodruff's horse went down, and he, too, received a wound. Lieutenant Coolidge was struck by a ball that pierced both thighs. Two brother officers carried him to a sheltered spot near the body of Captain Logan. Gibbon formed his men into a double line, back to back, and repeatedly charged the Indians through the brush in opposite directions, only to have them retreat more deeply into the willows.

---

battle of the Big Hole and he told me he could hear Joseph give his commands above the roar of the guns and cannon. Yes, Joseph was indisputably the War Chief."

[12] The Indians affirmed that these three young men who precipitated the war were killed by the whites, but McWhorter in *Yellow Wolf*, p. 44, states that Swan Necklace, the youngest of the trio, survived the war and successfully kept his identity concealed from the whites until after his death in the late twenties on the Nez Perce Reservation. (For an Indian's personal account of the Big Hole battle, see McWhorter, *op. cit.*, pp. 114 ff.)

A hand-to-hand encounter during the battle of the Big Hole

From original sketch made by Granville Stuart, May 11, 1878. Reproduced by courtesy of W. A. Clark Memorial Library.

Big Hole battlefield, looking north. Point of timber fortified by Gibbon may be seen in middle background

The position of the troops had become untenable, so Colonel Gibbon ordered them to retreat up the hill and take cover among the scanty growth of small pine trees, the only defensive point near by. Valiantly fighting, they withdrew across the river through the clumps of willow, carrying their wounded comrades, being compelled to drive the Indian sharpshooters out of the very timber they wanted as shelter. These warriors took refuge in a shallow washout, their accurate aim decimating the troops. Expert marksmen among the soldiers finally killed or routed all the Nez Perce sharpshooters.

One warrior had piled large rocks about the roots of a pine tree. From a loophole through the stones he was able to shoot five soldiers, although he himself was safe from the bullets of the troops. G. O. Shields reports:

> Finally, however, a soldier, who was an expert marksman and cool as a veteran, took careful aim and sent a bullet into this loophole which struck the rock on one side, glanced and entered the Indian's eye, passing out at the back of his head—a veritable carom shot. This tree was girdled with bullets. . . . [13]

Soon after the battle had started a squad of mounted braves rounded up their hundreds of ponies, and drove them down the river beyond reach of the troops after a sharp skirmish with a party of citizen scouts on foot.

Colonel Gibbon writes in his report to the Secretary of War:

> Just as we took up our position in the timber, two shots from our howitzer on the trail above us were heard, and we afterward learned that the gun and pack-mule with ammunition were, on the road to us, intercepted by Indians.[14]

So desperate had the plight of the soldiers become that the colonel himself was reduced to using his rifle like a

---

[13] Shields, "The Battle of the Big Hole," in Brady, *Northwestern Fights and Fighters*, p. 179.

[14] *Report of Secretary of War*, 1877, I, 70, Report of Colonel Gibbon.

private of the ranks. Ammunition was getting low, and the supply train had not been heard from. Gibbon gave orders for the troops to reserve their fire. As meager protection against the deadly aim of the Indians, the soldiers dug rifle pits with their trowel bayonets and piled up rock defenses. G. O. Shields relates: "A half-breed in the camp, familiar with the Nez Perce tongue, heard White Bird encouraging his men and urging them to charge, assuring them that the white soldiers' ammunition was nearly gone."[15] But they made no concerted assault.

As quickly as the command withdrew from the village the Indians reoccupied it. "Few of us will soon forget," Gibbon wrote later, "the wail of mingled grief, rage, and horror which came from the camp . . . when the Indians returned to it and recognized their slaughtered warriors, women, and children."[16]

The women began pulling down some of the tepees and packed a few of their belongings on ponies. Then they quickly mounted saddle animals and with the children fled down the valley. White historians state that all this was accomplished under a hot fire by the troops who were returning the volleys of the Nez Perce sharpshooters. The Indians paid for their boldness in the loss of some horses and the lives of several people. Those slain at this time, the whites believed, were two of Joseph's wives and a daughter of Looking Glass.[17]

However, Indian survivors deny this. Black Eagle told L. V. McWhorter, "No! The horses were packed without enemy firing. Soldiers were then in the woods entrenching. They could no longer see our camp, what we were doing." Sergeant Noyes (Loynes?) of Captain Rawn's company also confirmed this to McWhorter.[18]

Yellow Wolf likewise corrects the account by historian

---

[15] Shields, in Brady, *op. cit.*, p. 184. White Bird was the oldest of the chiefs, being past seventy, and according to the Indians did no active fighting until the last battle.

[16] Gibbon, "The Battle of the Big Hole," *Harper's Weekly*, 1895, p. 1235.

[17] Shields, *Blanket Indians of the Northwest*, p. 107.

[18] McWhorter, *Yellow Wolf: His Own Story*, p. 157, note 11.

Shields. Only one of Joseph's wives was wounded, and she recovered.[19] A wife of Alokut's he declared, who was wounded in the fighting, died later.[20]

In their hurried retreat the Nez Perces had to abandon many buffalo robes, large quantities of dried meat, and other food and clothing.

Indian marksmen from the cover of the riverbanks and from behind trees and rocks, harassed the troops all day. Lieutenant English received a fatal wound, and Captain Williams was hit a second time.

In the afternoon the wagon train and the howitzer, guarded by twenty men in charge of Hugh Kirkendall, the citizen wagon master, was brought to within five miles of the command. During the night there occurred one of those incidents on the hairsplitting borderline between tragedy and comedy, but which relieves the nervous tension of men in battle. William Woodcuck, Lieutenant Jacob's Negro servant, was on sentry duty, armed with a double-barreled shotgun. Kirkendall went the rounds to see if his guards were on the alert. Near William's post he was commanded to "Halt!" and was almost instantly fired upon. The buckshot tore up the ground at the wagon master's feet, but luckily did not hit him. The next day the too-alert sentry became the butt of the men's jokes, and he was slyly asked, "Who goes there?—Bang!"

At daylight six men started with the howitzer to join Gibbon's command. They halted a half mile from the scene of action when a band of thirty mounted Indians emerged from the timber. As the soldiers placed the lone piece of artillery in a position to fire, the warriors attacked them. Two of the privates became panic-stricken and fled. Nor did they stop until they had put a hundred miles between themselves and the Indians. Such was their terror that they spread exaggerated reports of the fate befallen the command. The other four soldiers stood their

---

[19] McWhorter, *Hear Me, My Chiefs!*, p. 385, note 44.

[20] McWhorter, *Yellow Wolf, His Own Story*, pp. 132, 162. It would appear that Alokut had at least two wives at this time, for another one, Wetatonmi, was not injured. *Ibid.*, pp. 137-38.

ground, firing the gun twice. Then the Indians closed around them, and they resorted to their rifles.

Being unable to defend the howitzer, the soldiers threw it off the trunnion and retreated, but not until Sergeants Daly and Frederics were wounded at their posts and Corporal Sale killed. Private Bennett, the driver, was pinned beneath one of the wounded horses. By feigning death he was able to make his escape after the warriors withdrew, and reached the wagon train ahead of the sergeants. The Indians dismantled the howitzer and captured a pack mule carrying two thousand rounds of ammunition—a serious blow to the troops.

Late in the afternoon Gibbon's men noticed a cloud of smoke approaching them. Someone cried out that the Indians had set fire to the grass. A strong wind was blowing the blaze directly toward the soldiers. Gibbon feared the warriors would assault his men under cover of the smoke screen. Only the year before, Gibbon recalled, Looking Glass's band of Nez Perces had entertained the soldiers and their wives at Fort Shaw by a mimic battle in which similar tactics had been employed. On this occasion they were used in deadly earnest.

He issued orders to his troops, "If the worst comes, my men, if this fire reaches us, we will charge through it, meet the redskins in the open ground, and send them to a hotter place than they have prepared for us."[21]

Anxiously the soldiers watched those leaping, crackling tongues of flame racing uphill toward them. Nearer and nearer they came, the smoke blinding the men and almost suffocating them. When the fire was only a few yards away the wind turned about and blew the flames back over their own blackened embers, where they died for lack of fuel. A wild cheer came from the hoarse throats of the soldiers.

As the hours wore on the troops suffered from hunger, from the heat of the August sun, but mostly from thirst. Not until after dark could a fatigue party dare to crawl

[21] Gibbon, in *Harper's Weekly*, *ibid.*

the few hundred yards to the river for water. For food that night the famished men cut up Lieutenant Woodruff's horse, conveniently killed by the Indians inside the lines. The soldiers devoured it raw, since they were not allowed to make fires. Fearful of a night attack and being without blankets, the men could not sleep, but shivered the cold night away, the second one since the battle began. Occasional shots came from the Indians who feigned several charges nearly to the troops' entrenchments. The soldiers greeted these sallies with businesslike fusillades. Chief Joseph afterward told Gibbon that a night attack was "proposed, and arranged for, but finally abandoned." Just what caused the change of plans, Joseph did not explain. But Yellow Wolf told McWhorter that the Indians did not charge because if they killed one soldier, a thousand would take his place. There was no one, though, to replace the loss of a single warrior.

Since it seemed likely that his command would be indefinitely besieged, Colonel Gibbon dispatched a man to Deer Lodge, one hundred miles away, for medical assistance and supplies. This man, an Englishman, W. H. Edwards, made his way on foot for sixty miles and the remaining forty on horseback.

On the morning of the tenth of August a courier arrived from General Howard with the news that he was bringing up a force of cavalrymen and Indians.

It was a day of good news for Gibbon. Later on a messenger from the wagon train brought information that it was safe. Although white historians claim it had been successfully defended against attack, the Indians deny ever discovering it. By sundown a detachment of twenty-five men under Captain Browning escorted the train into camp, and thankful were the troops to get their blankets and provisions.

Fearful that Edwards might have been killed, Gibbon dispatched another messenger to Deer Lodge. Sergeant Wilson, who had so bravely guarded the wagon train, volunteered for the service. Both men safely reached the settlement by morning.

The last rear guard of the Indians withdrew by eleven o'clock in the night, Gibbon reported, after a farewell salute of bullets. The remainder of the night passed quietly, giving the men a much-needed rest, for they had only slept for two hours out of forty-eight.

When Howard had learned of the Big Hole battle he had rushed ahead to overtake Gibbon on the morning of August 12 with a detachment of twenty men of the First Cavalry under Lieutenant Bacon and seventeen Indian scouts. Across the Continental Divide he met seven citizen volunteers, who, he writes to the Secretary of War, "gave a fearful picture of matters at the front." The general made due allowance for exaggeration, but a growing anxiety hurried him on. The rest of his cavalry, a day's march ahead of the infantry and artillery, followed more slowly up the Bitterroot Valley. Howard's headquarters party saw occasional glimpses of what they presumed to be a Nez Perce scout who kept watch on their movements.

The main force of Nez Perces had retreated as quickly as possible after the attack began, because they learned from a volunteer that Howard was close by with reenforcements. It was most fortunate for Gibbon's command, since the Indians knew that the soldiers were nearly out of ammunition and would have repeated the Custer Massacre, no doubt, had it not been for Howard's timely presence.

The Nez Perces had first learned of Howard's coming through questioning a citizen whom they found wounded on the field of battle, after the troops had retired on the morning of the ninth. When discovered by the warriors the citizen feigned death, but on being picked up by them he tried to run away. Looking Glass ordered the braves not to kill him, but to ask him for information about the soldiers. He told them of Howard's approach, and of the presence of citizen volunteers from Virginia City who would attempt to head off the Indians. A woman who had lost relatives in the battle slapped the citizen in the face.

He retaliated with a vicious kick at her, and the warriors promptly killed him.

The sun shone during the day of August 11 on a peaceful if sad scene, for fatigue parties under Captain Comba were afield burying the bodies of their comrades. Not a man was scalped, as the Nez Perces no longer practiced this barbarous custom. The casualties of the 191 soldiers engaged as given in the *Report of the Secretary of War* for 1877 stood at twenty-nine dead and forty wounded, including the colonel himself. Later two of the wounded died, bringing the final total to thirty-one killed and thirty-eight wounded. Three officers had been killed—Captain Logan and Lieutenants Bradley and English. The soldiers counted eighty-nine dead Indians on the battlefield. Two of these were the foremost warriors—Five Wounds and Rainbow, sometimes called "Looking Glass."

It has been erroneously stated by various historians that Chief Looking Glass[22] died in the Big Hole fight, Howard and Gibbon both reporting that he was buried "under the cut-bank." However, Miles states that he was killed at the Bearpaw battle by a bullet in his forehead, and Joseph himself corroborates the fact of the chief's death in the final battle.[23] There were two Looking Glasses, the confusion arising in the fact that the chief of that name and the warrior, correctly called Rainbow,[24] both wore small mirrors. Rainbow, who was killed in the Big Hole,

---

[22] Jack Conley, a soldier with Miles's command, told Howard and McGrath that the mirror worn on Looking Glass's forehead reflected the sun's rays, which attracted the troops' attention, and they turned the cannon upon him. But the scout, Milan Tripp, is reputedly the sharpshooter who killed Looking Glass as he raised up from a rifle pit. McWhorter, *Hear Me, My Chiefs!*, p. 495 and note 6.

[23] Dr. Edmond S. Meany, "Chief Joseph, the Nez Perce," Master of Letters Thesis, University of Wisconsin, Madison. Professor Edmond Meany in his thesis relates: "On June 25, 1901, while visiting at Nespilem, the writer went with Chief Joseph to the blacksmith shop and . . . the Chief talked of his last battle. With his cane he drew on the earth-floor a rough outline of the field, locating the opposed forces. The spots were indicated where had fallen his brother, Chief Ollicutt, *Chief Looking Glass* and Chief Too-hul-hul-sote—three chiefs lost in the last battle."

[24] McLaughlin, *My Friend the Indian*, p. 365.

was mistaken for the great chief because of his unique adornment.

Lieutenant Albert G. Forse, First Cavalry, talked with several officers who had been in the Big Hole fight. They told him that they estimated "the number of women and children killed at about 70, which would leave but about 19 warriors killed. I do not wish to criticize General Gibbon's report, but it certainly gave the public a wrong impression."[25] In the colonel's report he had stated that eighty-nine Indians lay dead, but he did not specify their sex or age.

Indeed, the ethics of an unprovoked assault upon a peaceful and undefended village has since raised grave moral questions among white Americans about many aspects of the Big Hole combat.

An article in the Anaconda *Standard* for September 25, 1904, states that during the night many of the wounded Indians were strapped onto ponies by the squaws and hidden in the hills surrounding the Big Hole Basin. There for weeks the women nursed them back to health without being discovered by whites. Joseph is reported to have admitted after his capture that 208 of his people died as a result of the Big Hole battle, many of them during the flight. This seems probable, as the pursuing troops observed many fresh graves along his line of march.

The Nez Perces were accused by Lieutenant Van Orsdale, who participated in the battle, of digging up the bodies of the soldiers and scalping them.[26] He returned

[25] Forse, "Chief Joseph as a Commander," *Winners of the West*, November, 1936, p. 4. Regarding the deplorable slaughter of noncombatant women and children, Yellow Wolf and other Nez Perces give eyewitness testimony in McWhorter, *Yellow Wolf: His Own Story*, pp. 132, 136 ff. Judging by all the evidence the whites came off the Big Hole battlefield with anything but a glorious record.

[26] *Report of Secretary of War*, 1877, I, 549. Report of Captain Rawn. Rawn writes: "A detachment of one commissioned officer, Second Lieutenant J. T. Van Orsdale,... and six enlisted men... left the post on September 20 for the battlefield of the Big Hole, with instructions to reinter the bodies of their comrades ... as information was received that several of the graves were opened, and the bodies buried therein dragged to the surface by bears and other animals."

to the battlefield six weeks after the engagement, and found that "both Captain Logan and Lieutenant Bradley, as well as several private soldiers, had been dug up and scalped, presumably by those Indians who had been left behind to care for the wounded hidden in the hills near there."[27] However, in his report to the Secretary of War, Van Orsdale makes no mention of the Nez Perces being guilty of the scalping, although he notes, "the officers had been scalped."

It is more probable that war parties of Bannocks who were roaming through the region at the time did the scalping, or even the Bannock scouts attached to Howard's command, for it is well authenticated that on three different occasions Bannock and white scouts scalped and mutilated the bodies of the Nez Perces.[28] Joseph himself says in his own story:

> We never scalp our enemies, but when General Howard came up and joined General Gibbon, their Indian scouts dug up our dead and scalped them. I have been told that General Howard did not order this great shame to be done.[29]

It is possible, of course, that the officers may have been scalped by vengeful squaws who had lost relatives in the fight, and in retaliation for the disrespect shown their dead by Howard's scouts. Be that as it may, there is no evidence of scalping by the Nez Perces in any other battle. This fact is substantiated by the testimony of Captain Romeyn, and by Sherman's statements (he was then General of the Army) in the Secretary of War's reports, based on the official reports of the commanders who at various times engaged the Nez Perces—Perry, Howard, Gibbon, Sturgis, and Miles.

Upon Howard's arrival at the battlefield at 10:00 A.M. on August 12, he found the wounded Colonel Gibbon

---

[27] Shields, *The Battle of the Big Hole*, p. 87.

[28] Howard, *Chief Joseph, His Pursuit and Capture*, p. 210. Also J. P. Dunn, Jr., *Massacres of the Mountains*, p. 663.

[29] "An Indian's Views of Indian Affairs," *North American Review*, April, 1879, p. 427.

sitting under a roughly constructed shelter of pine boughs, cheerfully awaiting him. In discussing the recent engagement the colonel inquired, wonder still uppermost in his mind, "Who could have believed that those Indians would have rallied after such a surprise, and made such a fight?"[30]

The five chiefs and their warriors were a worthy foe, indeed. Veterans of the Civil War and the Indian campaigns declared "it was the most hotly-contested field they were ever on." The cool and determined fighting by the Indians at such short range was most remarkable, as was also the deadly shooting by red and white alike.

Military authorities[31] say the Nez Perce War would have been settled at the Big Hole had the Seventh Infantry been recruited to its full war strength of six hundred men, instead of being pared down by a thrifty-minded Congress to less than a meager two hundred. The soldiers engaged were outnumbered by nearly two to one, as the Indian women and boys fought as desperately as the warriors.

An example of this was reported by a scout with Lieutenant Bradley, who told of seeing three squaws hiding in a clump of willows. He was tempted to kill them, but since they made no resistance and were apparently unarmed, he did not fire upon them. While out with a burial party two days later he saw the three squaws in their same hiding place, all dead this time. One had a Henry rifle and another a revolver, containing five empty cartridges in the cylinder. He conjectured that they had taken the weapons from dead warriors and joined as combatants in the battle, to be in turn slain by the soldiers.

After being joined by Howard's force, Gibbon's troops left the battlefield. The colonel wrote:

> The following day [the 13th], leaving three officers and fifty men to continue the pursuit with General Howard's command, the balance of my party with the wounded,

---

[30] Howard, *op. cit.*, p. 208.

[31] Shields, *The Battle of the Big Hole*, pp. 88, 89, 92.

started for Deer Lodge, and twelve miles from the battlefield met a large party sent out by the warm-hearted people of Montana to our relief, with every comfort which could be hastily gotten together.[32]

The Big Hole battle had a salutary effect upon the Nez Perces. Before that engagement the Indians had held a contemptuous attitude toward the soldiers; after it they had acquired wholesome respect for the United States Army. They had learned that even the "walking soldiers" of the infantry were a hard-fighting unit.

Despite the Nez Perces' huge losses, though, both in lives and property, the chiefs came off the field with honor.

In regard to Joseph's retreat from the Big Hole battle, General Howard wrote these words in generous praise:

> After Gibbon's battle, Joseph showed his influence over the Indians by rallying them on a height, just beyond the reach of the long-range rifles. He gathered the warriors, recovered lost ground, and recaptured his numerous herd of ponies, which had already been cut off by Gibbon's men, buried the most of his dead, and make good his retreat before the force with me was near enough to harm him. Few military commanders, with good troops, could better have recovered after so fearful a surprise.[33]

Although Howard credits Joseph with being the mastermind, the Indian testimony contradicts this. Joseph himself makes no mention of his battle deeds in his own story. But some of his personal activities right after the surprise attack have been reported by Black Eagle, who states:

---

[32] Gibbon, in *Harper's Weekly*, *op. cit.* A stone monument, sculptured by Alonzo V. Lewis, of Seattle, Washington, has been erected to Joseph on the Big Hole battlefield. In a letter, dated October 5, 1942, L. V. McWhorter writes: "The Chief Joseph Memorial shaft... on the Big Hole field stands on the brink of the bluff and slightly southeast of the Soldier monument. Not far from where Five Wounds was killed." Also, in this connection, under date of September 25, 1942, Mr. McWhorter asks: "I presume that you [i.e., Miss Howard] are aware of the fact that a Bill for erecting a monument to Chief Joseph at Lapwai, Idaho, was fought by the Christian element among the Nez Perces? This was in 1939."

[33] Howard, *op. cit.*, pp. 272-73.

"Chief Joseph's horses with many others were on the open hillside to the west. The herd was back of and above the soldiers when they first charged the camp. I saw Chief Joseph and No Heart, a young man, up the hillside, going afoot after the horses. Both were barefooted, and Joseph had no leggings. Only shirt and blanket. Reaching their own horses, they mounted and drove the herd farther up the hill. Out of sight of soldiers and the fighting. . . . The horses were brought to camp by Joseph and others after the soldiers were driven to the timber flat, where they dug holes for hiding. . . . Chief Joseph and Chief White Bird went with the families"[34] (during the retreat from the battlefield).

This rescue of the horses indicates Joseph's great presence of mind and ability to think and act in an emergency, for, had Gibbon's men captured the herd of Indian ponies, the Nez Perces could have been defeated.

Another warrior, Two Moons, reported he met Joseph during the battle holding his baby girl in his arms because her mother had been wounded (not slain as the whites believed). The chief told his friend he had no gun with which to defend himself. Most of the warriors found themselves in the same predicament in the early part of the assault. Two Moons advised Joseph to "skip for his life" and "save the child."[35]

Joseph heeded his friend's counsel for he and White Bird, who was too old to do much fighting, left with the families, accompanied by an escort of warriors, about noon of the first day's fighting, Joseph "in his usual role of protector of the women and children."[36]

His brother, Alokut, though, remained as leader of the young men acting as a rear guard to keep the soldiers besieged in the trenches after the families and pony herd retreated from the battle scene. Near dawn of the second day, Yellow Wolf relates, Alokut proposed to break off the fighting and rejoin their tribespeople. This they did after giving the troops "two volleys as a 'Goodby!' "

[34] McWhorter, *Yellow Wolf: His Own Story*, pp. 145-46.

[35] McWhorter, *Hear Me, My Chiefs!*, p. 385.

[36] *Ibid.*, p. 394. Yellow Wolf confirms this in McWhorter, *Yellow Wolf: His Own Story*, p. 155.

CHAPTER XVIII

The Camas Meadows Raid

HOWARD'S command again took up pursuit of the Nez Perces, who had retreated in a southeasterly direction. The remainder of the general's force had reached the Big Hole battleground on the night of August 12. The next day with his column reunited, the indefatigable general, reenforced by Captain Browning's fifty men of the Seventh Infantry, continued the chase. Howard hoped to catch the Indians before they left the Big Hole Basin. At the first night's camp Captain Wells and Lieutenant Humphrey's company of infantrymen in wagons joined the command.

The Indians left an easy trail, 150 feet wide, to follow, as the grass had been beaten down by hundreds of pony hoofs and furrowed by dragging travois poles. The troops found the carcasses of many cattle owned by settlers which the Indians had slaughtered for food.

Howard's scouts informed him that the Nez Perces had passed through a gap across a ridge dividing Horse Prairie from the Grasshopper Creek Valley, in which the mining camp of Bannack was located. Farther on the Indians had then turned right out of a ravine called "Bloody Dick" Canyon and marched south through Stevensons Canyon toward its junction with Lemhi Canyon. "Bloody Dick" was the nickname of an English settler.

This route back into Idaho again would indicate the Indians intended to return to, and fight for, the land of their ancestors. White Bird held a council with the Nez Perces' hereditary enemies, the Shoshones, and endeavored to enlist their aid. But that attempt at a coalition failed. Had that tribe agreed to become the ally of the

Nez Perces, it is possible Howard might have been ambushed in the mountains of Idaho.

Upon being turned down by the Shoshones, however, the Nez Perces again headed east, urged on by Poker Joe as leader and guide. They made peace with the fortified settlers at Lemhi and proceeded through that valley after bypassing the whites' barricade.

Reports, meanwhile, had been coming to Howard that the Indians were raiding and pillaging the ranches they passed. Their anger over the deaths of their women and children at the Big Hole battle probably explains their wanton attack, three days later, on eight white men at Horse Prairie Creek. Alexander Cruikshank, a scout engaged by Howard, recounts in his manuscript[1] that a foraging party of Nez Perces surrounded the ranch, and since the whites put up resistance, all were slaughtered. The braves then proceeded to round up the horses and drive them away. Not only did they want remounts for their tribesmen, but they intended to prevent Howard's pursuing force from getting any fresh animals.

After the Indians had crossed back into Idaho and proceeded up the Lemhi Valley, they overtook a party of teamsters hauling supplies for Colonel Shoup and his volunteer company. J. P. Clough, in a manuscript reminiscence,[2] accuses members of White Bird's band, who, he declares, massacred all the freighters. It must be remembered that Indians did not believe in majority rule, and often the reckless young bloods would disobey the orders of their chiefs. Regarding this attack on the freighters, the Nez Perces claim they had no intention of killing them until the whites tried to escape. Besides, the teamsters had given the young braves a keg of whiskey, and many had become intoxicated. Two of the drunken

---

[1] Alexander Cruikshank, "Reminiscences," Manuscript in Idaho State Historical Library, Boise.

[2] J. P. Clough, "Recollections of the Nez Perce Indian War of 1877, and Their Entrance into Lemhi Valley," Manuscript in Idaho State Historical Library, Boise.

Indians, Yellow Wolf recalls, shot at each other; another was stabbed; and a sober warrior was fatally wounded by a "mad drunk" because he deliberately poured whiskey on the ground. This massacre of the freighters took place on the Salmon River, according to Citizen Volunteer Henry C. Johnson,[3] about twenty-five miles from the main camp of the Nez Perces.

Howard hoped to head off the Indians, whom he suspected were moving toward Yellowstone Park, by pushing to their left at "some point along the stage-road from Deer Lodge to Corinne [Utah] or at Henry Lake."[4] Upon learning from the settlers at Lemhi that the Nez Perces had passed them by without harm, the general continued his march toward the stage road, hoping to reach that point first where the Indians were bound to cross it. At Junction Station on August 17, Howard detached Lieutenant George Bacon with forty cavalrymen to intercept the Nez Perces at Tacher's Pass (now called Targhee), the western entrance into Yellowstone, two miles east of Henrys Lake. This force was ordered to blockade the Indians should they attempt to enter the park from that direction.

Captain Calloway's volunteers from Virginia City joined Howard's command at Junction camp, and materially added to his reserves. A company of cavalry under Captain Randolph Norwood also reenforced the general's column at Pleasant Valley. They came from Fort Ellis by way of Virginia City.

The Nez Perces, however, crossed the stage road ahead of the troops at Dry Creek Station beyond Pleasant Valley. When Howard learned of it, he hastened his command thither and pushed on to Camas Meadows, there to rest his exhausted men and horses. He went into camp at "a strong, natural position on the first elevated ground

---

[3] Henry C. Johnson, "Volunteer Survivor Recalls Battle with Indians East of Cottonwood," Manuscript in the Idaho State Historical Library, Boise.

[4] *Report of Secretary of War*, 1877, I, 129. Report of Brigadier General Howard.

which overlooks the meadows toward the west and some lavabeds toward the north and east."[5] It was a beautiful region, abounding in lush grass for the stock, and plenteous shade from cottonwoods and willows along the banks of a clear stream for the tired soldiers. As the waters of the creek fairly teemed with gamy trout, a part of the command spent the time in fishing.

The general had the foresight to post the cavalry in line of battle in order to protect the camp. Captain Wells's forty infantrymen bivouacked near the creek in reserve formation, while Major Edwin Mason, Twenty-first Infantry, posted pickets in every direction. Captain Calloway's volunteers pitched their tents one hundred yards from the headquarters camp located on a knoll across the stream from them. This placed the citizens between two creeks with willow-fringed banks.

Just before dark Howard's scouts saw two or three Nez Perces hovering about the camp, but that was an ordinary occurrence and so caused no comment. At night every horse and mule was brought within the enclosure. The cavalry stock were tied to picket ropes, the team animals to their wagons, and the bell mares belonging to the mule packtrains were hobbled. Howard wrote to the Secretary of War:

> An unusual feeling of security pervaded the camp. My command, with Lieutenant Bacon's detachment absent, did not at this time exceed in effectiveness one hundred cavalry and fifty infantry. This was, however, sufficient for any defensive purpose.[6]

"Well," said Lieutenant C. E. S. Wood, aide-de-camp, as he and the general were preparing for bed, "I'll take off my pants to-night; it is so safe a place." The soldiers, expecting to be attacked at each campsite, had slept in boots and belts for seven nights.

Lieutenant Guy Howard, the general's son and aide-de-camp, laughed and remarked, "I've loaned my pistol to a

[5] *Ibid.*

[6] *Ibid.*, p. 611.

scout for to-night, so think likely the Indians will come back."[7]

The Nez Perces likewise had gone into camp on the Camas Meadows, but they were a day's march of sixteen or eighteen miles ahead of the troops toward Henrys Lake. Wary from the lesson taught them at the Big Hole, the Indians now maintained a vigilant guard. Scouts apprised the chiefs of Bacon's mission and of Howard's layover. Before the lieutenant's return to the command, they held a council and talked over plans for a surprise attack, inspired by a vision of the wounded brave, Black Hair.

Indian testimony differs as to who planned the Camas Meadows raid. Samuel Tilden states that White Bird did. Yellow Bull intimates Looking Glass was responsible. However, both Yellow Wolf and Wottolen, tribal historian, declare the older men did the planning. The raiding party was divided into three companies, led by Chiefs Alokut, Looking Glass, Tuhulhutsut, Espowyes, and Teeweeyownah. Others mentioned as members of the group were White Bull, Two Moons, Peopeo Tholekt, and Wottolen. Joseph was not along, according to Yellow Wolf, himself a participant. As usual, Looking Glass's idea for the plan of attack prevailed—it was his decision to go mounted. The Indians declared this chief always opposed any plan not first thought of by himself.

Nez Perce scouts had been watching the troops all day, and soon after sunset the raiding party of thirty or more warriors started on the eighteen-mile trip to Howard's command. Under cover of darkness, just before reaching the encampment, they paused to hold their final council. After Looking Glass's plan was agreed on, some active young men dismounted, silently worked their way around the sleeping enemy, and stealthily crept between the picket lines. These scouts succeeded in getting among the mules (mistaking them for horses) to cut their hobbles and remove the bells from the lead mares. The mounted

---

[7] Howard, *Chief Joseph, His Pursuit and Capture*, p. 225.

Indians remained waiting for the signal shot before advancing.

According to Howard's account, upon hearing the clip-clop of horses' hoofs and seeing the dark forms of men and mounts dimly outlined in the starlit night, the sentry thought them Bacon's detachment returning. He allowed them to approach very close before he issued the challenge. As he did not receive the correct answer, he fired. But the Indians assert the premature shot came from Otskai, one of their "nervous" members, and was the prearranged signal for the raiders to charge.

At once the Nez Perces replied with a war whoop, deployed, and dashed among the mule herd—about 150 in number. Fortunately for the troops the scouts did not have time to locate and cut the picket ropes of the horses. Thus the Indians only stampeded the pack mules by waving buffalo robes in their faces. As they did so, other braves poured a melting fire into the camp. Several warriors rode ahead of the mules, ringing the bells to direct the stampeding herd toward the Indian village.

For a while the army camp was a scene of confusion —rifles firing, horses neighing, Indians shouting war whoops, and bewildered soldiers hunting for pants and guns and cartridge belts in the darkness. Howard issued immediate orders for three troops of cavalry to give chase and recapture the mules.

The men quickly recovered from their suprise and dressed hastily. In obedience to the "Boots and Saddles" call of the bugle they were soon ready to mount, but had to wait for dawn. Then, in the chilly air of early morning, the orderly gallop shortly turned into a race for half an hour between the companies of Captains Carr, Norwood, and Jackson.

As the troops approached the first ridge of some foothills, they could dimly make out the Indians and the stolen herd four or five miles ahead. Captain Carr, leading the advance, charged the warriors who were driving the mules.

But the leaders were forewarned by scouts of the pursuit and they prepared for it. Eight miles from the army camp they divided their forces, one group galloping ahead with the mules, another company dismounting as skirmishers. These stood behind their ponies to check the cavalry's advance and attacked on three sides among the lava beds. A flanking party of Indian riflemen crouched behind the rocks where they did "good shooting." Peopeo Tholekt, one of the flankers, explained that in battles each warrior "watched and fought" wherever the most harm could be done to the enemy.

As the head of Carr's company dashed up, his men received a hot fire from a thousand yards and were forced to pull up their horses. Norwood, immediately behind Carr, "went into position nearly abreast [of him] . . . while Jackson with his company came up on the right."[8] The cavalrymen dismounted and deployed along the ridge, exchanging shots for twenty minutes. Lieutenant Benson stood up for a moment and received a bullet that entered his hip pocket and passed entirely through both buttocks.

When the skirmish became general, Major Sanford's left flank was turned by the Nez Perces. To protect himself, he ordered retreat. Warriors soon completely surrounded Captain Norwood's company, which had become separated from the others. The Indians next turned Sanford's right flank, and threatened to cut him off from camp. Not knowing the fate of Norwood and his men, the other troops promptly retreated after losing possession of the mules once more to the Indians. The animals had been captured in Carr's first charge.

According to Howard's report, Norwood "began to fulfill the order simultaneously with the rest, when, finding himself pressed too hard to do it with safety, he selected a defensive position and remained, repelling the enemy from every side."[9] The captain himself admits in his report to the Secretary of War of having received the order to withdraw. But he refused to obey because, as

[8] Howard, in *Report of Secretary of War*, 1877, I, 612.

[9] *Ibid.*

he explains: "My company would have been slaughtered from my first position, an exposed one, if, as it proved, the enemy moved around my flanks."[10]

Norwood's men quickly realized that they had "no ordinary Indians to deal with, for, while we had been frolicking with the skirmishers in front," writes Sergeant H. J. Davis, Second Cavalry, "Chief Joseph had engineered as neat a double flank movement as could be imagined, and we were exposed to a raking fire coming from right and left."[11]

Captain Norwood had then ordered his trumpeter to blow "Recall." When the men had dismounted in the beginning of the fight, the horses had been taken into a grove of cottonwoods, five hundred yards away. Now, as the soldiers began to retreat they could not see their steeds, and for a time panic seized them. Davis relates:

> The race to that thicket was something never to be forgotten, for a cavalryman is not trained for a five hundred yard sprint. Luck was with us, however, and no man was hit in that mad race for safety. . . .
>
> We all reached the horses and found the place an admirable one for defense; it was a sort of basin an acre or so in extent, with a rim high enough to protect our horses, and filled with young cottonwoods in full leaf. It was oval in shape, and we deployed in all directions around the rim. For two hours it was a sniping game and our casualties were eight. The Indians crawled very close, one shooting Harry Trevor in the back at about fifteen feet, as we knew by the moccasin tracks and empty shells found behind a rock after the engagement. Poor Trevor's wound was mortal as was that of Sam Glass, who was shot through the bladder; a bullet hit Sergeant Garland's cartridge-belt and drove two cartridges from it clear through his body; his wound never healed and he blew out his brains a few years later. Will Clark had his shoulder partly torn away by an explosive ball; Sergeant Wilkins, a head wound, and Farrier Jones, a "busted" knee; a

---

[10] *Report of Secretary of War*, 1877, I, 573. Report of Captain Norwood.

[11] Sergeant H. J. Davis, "The Battle of Camas Meadows," in Brady, *Northwestern Fights and Fighters*, p. 196. Instead of Joseph these were probably Peopeo and his companions.

citizen attache, a bullet through the foot, and the lieutenant [Benson], wounded as told above. This was the amount of damage done to us, and what we did to the Indians we never knew, as they retreated in good order taking their dead or injured with them, after they found they could not dislodge us. Three dead ponies and some pools of blood were all the records we found of their casualties.[12]

Sergeant Hugh McCafferty proved the hero of this skirmish. Within close range of the Indians he concealed himself in the foliage of a cottonwood tree, and kept Norwood posted on the Nez Perces' movements "by passing the word to a man stationed under the tree."[13] For this daring act he received a certificate of merit and a medal from Congress.

While Norwood's men continued to put up a gallant fight, Howard had been receiving messages from the front. He, with Captain Wells's company of infantry, Wagner's cavalry, and the howitzer battery under Lieutenant Otis pushed out to reenforce the troops in action. The general met Major Sanford's retiring cavalry and at once noted the absence of Norwood's company. Howard asked the captain's whereabouts, and Sanford admitted that he didn't know. So the general ordered the combined force, with the infantry column on the right, to move slowly forward to locate Norwood's position. The cracking of rifles soon led them to the beleaguered captain, from whom the Indians had recently withdrawn. Scouts had probably warned them of the approaching reenforcements.

Howard learned from Norwood that his casualties were Lieutenant Benson and six enlisted men wounded. Two of the latter died of their injuries. Young Brooks, the orderly and favorite bugler of Captain Jackson, had been killed in the raid on the camp as he attempted to blow "Boots and Saddles." Carr's company had one man wounded.

---

[12] *Ibid.* The Indians admit two men were slightly wounded.

[13] *Ibid.*

The column returned to camp about 3:00 P.M. On the way the troops recovered twenty mules abandoned by the Indians. "The others," Davis writes, "were never retaken, but were worn out or died before the final surrender. . . .[14] Howard sent the wounded men and the volunteers to Virginia City. When his artillery unit and the rest of the infantry overtook his command, he marched on after the Indians. Upon leaving Camas Meadows, a small force of Bannock scouts under Captain Bainbridge of the Fourteenth Infantry, and scout S. G. Fisher, joined the general.

Joseph declared after his surrender that forty of his youngest men (meaning tribesmen) had "made all the noise and firing of the first attack." He explained that he was tired of having General Howard so close on his heels and planned to "set him afoot." He was greatly disappointed to find that the cavalry horses had been picketed for the night, as he would have preferred the horses to the mules, although he had hoped to get both, for, he observed, "You didn't picket your horses other nights, so I didn't expect it this time."[15]

J. W. Redington,[16] a scout with Howard's command, says Joseph personally conducted the column of fours.[17] As already narrated, McWhorter's Indian informants, who actually took part in the raid, including Joseph's nephew, Yellow Wolf, all deny it. Probably here again the whites mistook Alokut for his brother Joseph.

The night following the raid, the soldiers went into camp on the North Fork of Snake River in a stand of heavy timber. Rumors filtered among the troops that the Indians were nearby, waiting to spring another night

[14] *Ibid.*

[15] Wood, "Chief Joseph, the Nez Percé," *Century Magazine*, May, 1884, p. 140.

[16] Redington was a traveling printer at the outbreak of hostilities, and offered his services to the governor of Idaho. He had had military experience in Massachusetts.

[17] The soldiers claimed the Indians approached the camp by columns of fours like cavalry, but the Nez Perces denied this. A detailed account of the raid from the Indian viewpoint is given in McWhorter, *Hear Me, My Chiefs!*, pp. 417 ff.

attack. Consequently the tired men kept nervously wakeful during the long hours of darkness.

Since nobody was very sleepy, Howard started the column at 2:00 A.M. in the hopes of overtaking the Nez Perces before they got beyond Henrys Lake. But at eight o'clock scouts reported the Indians had passed through Tacher's (Targhee) Pass. As the general's troops sorely needed supplies of every kind, he ordered them to make camp and they lay over four days while awaiting the stores.

Although the plan did not completely work out in the way Joseph had hoped, the surprise raid was no failure. Before Howard could renew the pursuit he had to replenish his packtrain by buying mules from settlers in Virginia City some seventy miles away. The foray produced another significant aftermath because the general lost his last opportunity to catch the fleeing foe. Joseph and his tribesmen, meanwhile, marched merrily along without interruption into Yellowstone Park, for, after two days of fruitless waiting without seeing any signs of the enemy, Bacon had returned to the command.

Lieutenant Colonel Gilbert was reconnoitering in the park with two troops of cavalry from Fort Ellis near Bozeman. However, he feared to intercept the Nez Perces because of their superior numbers. Thus the chiefs' strategy in the Camas Meadows raid gained them three days.

Gilbert's force was acting as an escort to General W. T. Sherman, who, as General of the Army, was making an inspection tour of the western forts. Sherman left the park shortly before the arrival of the main band of Indians. Asks Francis Haines:

> It is interesting to speculate on the unique situation which would have developed had he been captured by the Nez Perces and held as a hostage while they negotiated terms with his subordinates. Do you suppose they could have traded him for the Wallowa?[18]

[18] Haines, *Red Eagles of the Northwest*, p. 287.

When Howard reluctantly took up the chase again on August 27, by order of the General of the Army although he was far beyond the limits of his Department of the Pacific, it led him through forest and canyons, over mountains and across gorges, where his wagons had to be let down almost perpendicular walls with ropes hand over hand for sometimes two hundred feet.

In speaking of the difficulties the army faced, Howard wrote to the Secretary of War:

> Though under known interpretation of law our campaign against hostile Indians is not recognized as war, yet as it has been a severer tax upon the energies of officers and men than any period of the same length of our late civil war, surely some method must be found to encourage and properly reward such gallantry and services hardly ever excelled.[19]

[19] Howard, in *Report of Secretary of War*, 1877, I, 613.

CHAPTER XIX

The Attack on the Cowan and Weikert Parties

It is always the innocent bystander who suffers most, and so it was with a party of tourists who were enjoying the freakish wonders of Yellowstone Park that summer of 1877. Frank Carpenter, a young man of twenty-seven, had originally conceived the idea of exploring the "wonders of geyser land." He had induced his friends, Albert Oldham, William Dingee, A. J. Arnold, and Charles Mann to go sight-seeing with him. The party left Helena, Montana, on July 29, and were joined at Radersburg by Mr. and Mrs. George Cowan, and Frank's thirteen-year-old sister, Ida. Emma Cowan, who died in Spokane, Washington, December 20, 1938, was two years married, and twenty-four years old at the time. She was also a sister of Frank's. Henry Myers had charge of the team.

Frank kept a diary of their memorable trip and wrote a highly colored account of their adventures, which was published in 1878 under the title of *The Wonders of Geyser Land.* The party were peacefully encamped in the Lower Geyser Basin before they heard rumors of the Nez Perce War. They had decided to remain a day or two longer and then return home.

But their decision came too late, for on the night of August 23, five Indians discovered the Cowan camp. These warriors were members of a scouting party under the leadership of Yellow Wolf, Joseph's nephew. The next morning they debated what they should do with the tourists, since they felt that all the whites whom they met in the park were enemies. Yellow Wolf wanted to kill them and solve the dilemma, but a half-breed interpreter, Henry Tabador, said that instead they should take them to the chiefs and let them dispose of the whites.

This decision reached, three of the Indians walked into camp without any warning and surprised the tourists at their morning fire building. One of the white men advanced and shook hands with Yellow Wolf. This simple friendly gesture, he later admitted, changed his mind about killing the party. The hearts of these whites were good, he reasoned.

The half-breed Henry, acting as interpreter, asked for flour, bacon, and sugar. Instead of immediately granting the request, the whites questioned the Indians. Henry explained that Joseph's band was three days' march toward Henrys Lake in advance of the bands of Looking Glass and White Bird.

A parley then ensued, during which the Nez Perces insisted they were friends and meant no harm, but that "Joseph's Injuns heap bad." Again they requested food. This George Cowan refused them, so one Indian walked toward the timber and tried to whistle through his thumbs. Cowan, probably fearing he was trying to call up a large band of Nez Perces that the scouts said were camped nearby, picked up his gun and ordered, "Keep your hands down!"

Members of the Cowan party report that by this time they were surrounded by Indians who had stopped to view the geysers. In growing anxiety Frank Carpenter and George Cowan held a council, and decided to visit the camp and ask the chiefs' permission to leave the park unmolested. They made this intention known to the scouts.

When about to start, Mrs. Cowan, who had remained in the tent until then, made her appearance and begged her husband not to go. Ida Carpenter also emerged and joined her sister. The presence of the white women drew the fascinated gaze of the Indians. George Cowan objected to the manner in which they watched his wife. Again he picked up his gun and waved it threateningly.

To relieve the growing tension, other members of the party calmly proceeded to get breakfast. Two of the white men gave the Indians all the bacon and flour to appease them. After the group, including the scouts, had filled up on flapjacks, Oldham and Frank harnessed the horses.

Then the cavalcade of buggy, wagon, and mounted men started for the Indian village, accompanied by the five Nez Perces. Upon leaving the timber the whites saw the main band "moving abreast in an unbroken line ten or fifteen deep, driving ponies and constantly riding in and out of line. We could see about three miles of Indians. . . ."[1]

A group of thirty or forty warriors, on catching sight of the captives, dropped out of the main band and charged up to them, but were stopped by the half-breed interpreter upon Cowan's demand. The braves pulled up their ponies and stared with great interest. The Cowan party halted and went into a huddle, but decided to push on. Soon they were surrounded by another large group of curious braves, who finally ordered them to stop. The excellent condition of the whites' horses and the assortment of firearms had not missed the sharp eyes of the Nez Perces. The warriors rode about the party and also eyed the women. Then a messenger joined the scouts and told the interpreter that Looking Glass wanted the whites brought back to him, apparently to save them from Joseph's "bad Injuns."

In a spirit of mischief, a group of young braves galloped up to the wagons, yelling and throwing lariats at the harnessed horses to frighten them. The Cowan party, anxious to reach the protection of Looking Glass, set out on the run, accompanied by the prankish red youths. They laughed gleefully and, hoping to increase the alarm of the captives, shouted that Joseph was coming.

When they were unable to continue on the trail with their wagons because of fallen timber, the whites aban-

[1] Guie and McWhorter, eds., *Adventures in Geyser Land*, by Frank D. Carpenter, p. 97.

doned the vehicles. While the Indians watched them unhitch, Frank left the party, escorted by a warrior, to contact Looking Glass. On the way to the village the Indian dropped behind him, Frank reports, and treacherously maneuvered so as to shoot him in the back, but he "got the drop" and forced the Nez Perce to guide him to the chief. He describes Looking Glass as:

> . . . a man of medium height, and is apparently forty-five years of age, his hair being streaked with grey. He has a wide, flat face, almost square, with a small mouth running from ear to ear. His ears were decorated with rings of purest brass, and down the side of his face hung a braid of hair, adorned at the end with brass wire wound around it. The ornament worn by him, that was most conspicuous, was a tin looking-glass, which he wore about his neck and suspended in front. . . . He wore nothing on his head and had two or three feathers plaited in his back hair.[2]

Looking Glass turned young Carpenter over to Poker Joe, who took charge of him and Shively, a prospector, captured the night before. Poker Joe (Lean Elk), together with his small band, had joined his tribesmen on their march up the Bitterroot Valley. After the Big Hole battle it was his duty to direct and regulate the march of the Indians as camp leader and guide.

In the meanwhile, immediately after the whites had abandoned the wagons, the Indians plundered and then wrecked them beyond further use. The captives then proceeded on horseback and were permitted to join Frank at Poker Joe's lodge during the noonday halt. This chief told the whites that the Indians wanted guns, cartridges, blankets, and horses. The Nez Perces did not pass up the opportunity to extract some fun out of the situation by forcibly trading the Cowan party out of their fine horses for their own jaded mounts. In explanation of the seizure Poker Joe said they needed supplies because they were going to the buffalo country. He mentioned the Big

---

[2] *Ibid.*, p. 103. Yellow Wolf's account of the episode is given in McWhorter, *Yellow Wolf: His Own Story*, pp. 172 ff.

Hole fight, but assured the Cowans that the Nez Perces were not hostile to Montana people.

During the horse swapping Poker Joe led A. J. Arnold into the forest, and then told him to mount the gray horse which he was leading and to keep in the woods. Arnold joined William Dingee, and the two of them made their escape through the heavy, fallen timber, although warriors shot at them five times after they abandoned the horses. By keeping in the dense forest they made their way to Howard's command encamped by Henrys Lake.

While Arnold and Dingee were making their escape, the Indians brought up some worn-out ponies which the rest of the Cowan party were told to mount. Poker Joe told them to start for home and to keep in the timber.

When they had traveled a short distance they were again surrounded by young warriors, who allowed them to continue, however. Soon they heard shots in the direction where they supposed Arnold and Dingee to be in hiding. Again the young men, bent on mischief, laughed and threatened them with guns. The whites decided to return and seek protection from Joseph. But the young braves stopped them and traded the party out of their saddles and bridles, which they had been permitted to keep until then.

Once more the whites proceeded on their way, encircled by the unwelcome escort of warriors, when another group of Indians came dashing toward them on the trail. George Cowan, riding in the lead, reported that eight or ten feet away these young men suddenly pulled back their ponies on their haunches. One Indian rode close to him and deliberately shot him in the thigh. Cowan jumped off his horse and ran for the brush alongside the trail, but he stumbled and fell over some bushes.

At this time Albert Oldham was riding with Cowan and the two sisters. He had been permitted to retain his gun since he had only three cartridges, and the Indians had none to fit it. Coincident with the shooting of Cowan, the Indian nearest Oldham swerved his pony suddenly and fired at him, the bullet penetrating his left cheek and coming out under his right jawbone. The shot knocked Oldham off his horse, and he fell in a ravine beside the trail. He got onto his feet and tried to shoot his attacker, but fortunately the gun misfired. Otherwise the entire party doubtless would have been massacred in revenge.

Duncan MacDonald,[3] in a newspaper account published in 1879, sheds light on this unprovoked attack. After the war he talked about it with Nez Perces who told him that a party of reckless young men bent on revenge were responsible for attacking the Cowan party. Of the two Indians who charged the whites for the purpose of shooting them, one was Um-til-ilp-cown, youngest of the three Idaho murderers who were responsible for the outbreak of hostilities. It was he who shot Cowan.

Oldham managed to keep the warriors covered until they joined the group surrounding the injured Cowan. He then hid in the bushes for thirty-six hours, suffering intensely all the while. When the forest around him rang with silence—so quiet it was after the Indians' passing—he crawled forth to the spot where Cowan had been wounded. But he could not locate his friend's body, and so he followed down the Madison River, his tongue becoming so badly swollen he was unable to eat and could scarcely breathe. Fortunately he met two white men who gave him first-aid treatment and brought him to Howard's command, where he found Arnold and Mann.

At the moment of the attack, Frank Carpenter was riding behind the other members of his party. Seeing an Indian point a gun at him and believing he would be shot, he made the sign of the cross. The warrior immediately lowered the weapon, but denied that he spared

[3] Duncan MacDonald, *New Northwest*, 1879, Deer Lodge, Montana. An extract from MacDonald's *The Nez Percés in 1877—the Inside History from Indian Sources*. Duncan MacDonald's father was a Scotch trader with the Hudson's Bay Company, and his mother was a Nez Perce. MacDonald lived on the Flathead Reservation in Montana until his death. In McWhorter, *Yellow Wolf: His Own Story*, p. 44, Um-til-ilp-cown is given as Wetyetmas Wahyakt (Swan Necklace). He was also known as John Minthon. Regarding the attack on Cowan, Yellow Wolf explains that it was the "bad boys" who tried to kill the white men.

Frank because of the religious gesture. They had been told by the chiefs, he explained, not to injure the whites. However, it seems likely that the non-Christian Nez Perces did associate the idea of "strong medicine" with Christian ritual, even though they would not openly admit it. Be that as it may, the Indians impressed Frank into service as a guide for that section of the park to get them back on the trail. It seems that the Nez Perces were lost for a while, as none of them was familiar with the country, their route to the buffalo hunting grounds being much farther north.

After Cowan had fallen in the bushes, his wife ran to him and asked where he was hurt. He told her he thought his right leg was shattered. The wound was bleeding profusely. A curious crowd of warriors had quickly gathered about them. Emma Cowan held her husband's head in her arms and cried.

Ida, half hysterical from fear, pushed through the throng and joined her sister who was by then struggling with Henry, the interpreter. He wanted to kill Cowan and finish his suffering. The frenzied young wife argued and pled and fought with the scout. Another Indian leaned close and fired a revolver, the bullet crashing against Cowan's forehead. He relaxed as with the stillness of death. Sobbing wildly, Emma Cowan and her young sister were led away to Joseph's camp, where they were given the most humane treatment. Mrs. Cowan herself is authority for the statement.

In the meanwhile, according to Duncan MacDonald,[4] when the chiefs learned of the attack upon the whites, they dispatched Poker Joe to protect the tourists. He succeeded in controlling the vicious young men, but, believing Cowan dead, brought only the women and their brother back to the village. Frank thus describes the scene:

The Indians had encamped on the outer edge of a circular basin about three-fourths of a mile in circumference,

---

[4] *Ibid.*

and were building their camp fires about every twenty or thirty feet apart. The ponies, a thousand or more, were in the basin encircled by the fires. Others were constantly coming, and we could hear their "yip, yip," as they drove the ponies in for unpacking.[5]

That night the captives were placed under the personal protection of Chief Joseph, to whom Frank was introduced. The chief "has a high forehead," he wrote, "a straight prominent nose, high cheek bones, and when he speaks he sets his lips together with a firmness that showed he meant what he said. He talked but little, but I noticed that when he spoke to an Indian, there was no hesitancy about obeying him."[6]

A warrior came over to Joseph's fire and began telling him about the events of the day and the attack on the whites. "Joseph listened for a moment," relates Frank, "then with a motion of disgust got up and went over where his squaw and . . . daughter were. He was evidently displeased with the actions of the Indians, in the shooting of our party."[7]

In writing of the experience Mrs. Cowan also gives an interesting, if brief, portrait of Joseph as he appeared to her in camp. It likewise throws light on the essentially humane character of the man, for what was to prevent him from having the entire party put to death in the wilderness? Mrs. Cowan writes:

My brother tried to converse with Chief Joseph, but without avail. The chief sat by the fire, sombre and silent, forseeing in his gloomy meditations possibly the unhappy ending of his campaign. The "noble red man" we read of was more nearly impersonated in this Indian than in any I have ever met. Grave and dignified, he looked a chief.

A squaw sat down near me with a babe in her arms. My brother, wishing to conciliate them, I suppose, lifted it up and placed it on my lap. I glanced at the chief and saw the glimmer of a smile on his face, showing that he had a

---

[5] Guie and McWhorter, *op. cit.*, p. 129.

[6] *Ibid.*, p. 135.

[7] *Ibid.*

In the face of Joseph, the chief, were registered all his pride, courage, and enduring strength; his sorrow, and discouragement, and disdain; his wisdom, patience, and dignity.

heart beneath the stony exterior. The squaw was all smiles, showing her white teeth. Seeing that I was crying, the squaw seemed troubled and said to my brother, "Why cry?" He told her my husband had been killed that day. She replied, "She heartsick." I was indeed.[8]

Frank and his two sisters, like Joseph, rolled up near the fire in the blankets given them. Unlike the chief, though, who stretched out with his feet to the blaze, they sat up all night.

In the morning Poker Joe rode through the camp, issuing orders to the people for the line of march that day. He mounted Emma Cowan behind him and rode off, while Frank accompanied an Indian to the horse herd where the young men were lassoing the ponies they wanted to ride. It was the white man's chore to assist the women in packing, and to carry water at the noonday camp, for which he earned the warriors' jibes of "heap squaw."

While his wife sorely grieved for him, George Cowan lay unconscious for two hours. Then he came to and tried to find water. As he started to crawl he noticed an Indian on horseback watching him. He attempted to hobble into the brush, but the warrior shot him above the hip, the bullet passing out in front of his abdomen. He remained motionless, waiting for the Nez Perce to finish the job. The brave evidently thought him dead, however, and rode away. Later a party driving loose horses passed nearby, but did not discover him.

Then it was that George Cowan displayed great fortitude and stamina. Although seriously wounded and weak from loss of blood, he managed to crawl back to the abandoned wagons, making the nine miles in sixty hours and without food. Certainly a record of human endurance! Groups of Indians passed him in the timber while he lay still in the bushes. He found his faithful dog guarding the

[8] Mrs. George F. Cowan, "Reminiscences of Pioneer Life," *Contributions: Historical Society of Montana*, IV (1903), 173. The babe referred to by Mrs. Cowan was probably Joseph's infant daughter, born before the White Bird battle.

wrecked remains of the wagons. She followed him as he painfully dragged himself on his elbows to the Lower Geyser Basin to search for some coffee that he remembered had been spilled. Much to his relief he found it and managed to boil the coffee in a tin can. After drinking it he felt greatly refreshed. He then believed himself strong enough to crawl through the Firehole River, fortunately only a few inches deep, but the effort drained his strength. Exhausted, he lay in the brush where two scouts from Howard's command, Captain S. G. Fisher and J. W. Redington, found him. The sight of white men filled him with new hope and courage.

They fed Cowan, gave him a blanket, and advised him to remain there as the army would come by the next day and care for him. He believed the rest of the party to be dead, except for his wife and Ida, so the scouts went on to find and bury their bodies. The men had built him a campfire which was fanned into a conflagration by a sudden wind that arose. Soon the timber became a blazing menace to the injured man. To save his life he was forced to seek refuge in the Firehole River. After the forest fire had burned itself out, he crawled back into the blackened ashes and lay by his camp until discovered by General Howard and his staff. He was placed in an ambulance after being told that the rest of the party, except his wife, Frank, and Ida, had safely reached the Montana settlements.

At noon one day the Indians held a council to decide whether the captive sisters and brother should be retained or freed. It would seem that the whites were something of a problem to the Nez Perces, partly because of the two women in the party. Joseph, in accordance with his code of civilized warfare, did not countenance unnecessary killings, nor the murder of noncombatants. Above all he would not tolerate the violation of white women prisoners by his reckless young men. So, what to do with them? Hunting and scouting parties abroad from the main band had their own ideas in reference to the whites, which accounts for the several changes of attitude in evidence during the preceding days. Perhaps Joseph feared if the party were given their liberty that they would be violated before they could leave the vicinity. This seems very probable in view of the treatment accorded the prisoners, and the manner in which their escape was finally contrived by the Indians.[9]

There are conflicting accounts in various histories as to how the whites made their escape. According to Mrs. Cowan,[10] the Nez Perces held the council within three days after the attack. The Indians proposed to release the women, along with Irwin, a discharged soldier who had been captured in the park. She refused to go unless her brother was also released, as she felt safer in the Indian camp. This was granted her and "two old worn-out horses were brought" for the journey.

We clasped hands sadly with our good friend Shively, promising to deliver some messages to friends in Philipsburg should we escape. His eyes were dim with tears. In reality, I considered his chances of escape better than our own, and so told him. The Indians needed him for a guide. "We may be intercepted by the warriors out of camp," I said. "No," he replied, "something tells me you will get out safely."

We crossed the river [the Yellowstone] again, my brother riding behind Poker Joe, who went with us a half mile or more, showing us presently a well defined trail down the river. He told us we must ride "All Night, All Day, No Sleep—we would reach Bozeman on second day." He reiterated again and again that we must ride all night. We shook hands and set out, not very rapidly. My brother walked as the horses we rode were worn out. It seemed folly to think we could escape. Furthermore, we placed no confidence in the Indian. I regret to say that as

[9] White Bird is generally credited with ordering the release of the Cowan party, but it is Sam Tilden's opinion that they were freed by order of Joseph. The confusion on this point may have arisen from the fact that White Bird was sometimes called "Joe Hale," and that Poker Joe actually did guide the Cowans away from the Indian encampment. Mrs. Cowan herself is not specific on this point.

[10] Mrs. George F. Cowan, "Reminiscences of Pioneer Life."

soon as he was out of sight we left the river trail and skirted along in the timber.[11]

The Indians had refused to give Frank a horse in order to prevent the whites from reaching the settlements too quickly and then telling the location of the Nez Perces. A squaw had prepared lunches for the three of them. According to Frank, Poker Joe left them at the river after making a long plea for peace between the Nez Perces and the citizens of Montana.

After they struck into the timber, Frank kept a sharp lookout for young braves who might be pursuing them. Emma Cowan wanted to return to her husband, whom she still believed dead, but was prevented by her brother. They traveled cautiously through the forest by day and shivered in the chilly mountain air all night. If they built a fire they feared their presence would be revealed to scouting parties of Nez Perces.

Upon reaching Mammoth Hot Springs they found Lieutenant Schofield encamped with L troop of the Second Cavalry. His detail formed part of Lieutenant Colonel Gilbert's command. The troops were returning to Fort Ellis near Bozeman to report "No Indians coming into the park," Mrs. Cowan relates! From Mammoth the little group of brother and sisters made their way to Bozeman and thence home.

After George Cowan's rescue by Howard's command the surgeon dressed his wounds, and the next day a scout brought word that his relatives were safe. From that moment his interest in life quickened, and his recovery became speedy.

A. J. Arnold, in his account of the capture,[12] criticized the general, his staff, and the surgeons for going off to view the geysers instead of giving immediate attention to

---

[11] *Ibid.* Shively was the prospector who had been captured. The Nez Perces impressed him into service as a guide through the park, but treated him well and finally permitted him to escape.

[12] Guie and McWhorter, *op. cit.*, pp. 222-24.

the wounded Oldham and Cowan. It seems that the old army game of "passing the buck" was in vogue even among the medical staff. Each of four surgeons to whom Arnold went to ask for aid told him it was the next doctor's duty to care for civilians! Finally one surgeon grumblingly agreed to attend the injured men, but paid scant attention to them afterward, and the job of nursing them devolved upon Arnold. He praised the teamsters who contributed old, but clean clothing for the patients.

While the soldiers were encamped between the Yellowstone River and the Lower Basin, Bannock Indian scouts with Howard's command ran off all the teamsters' loose horses. It became necessary to use pack mules for several days, although the general held the Bannock chief, Buffalo Horn, as a hostage until the missing horses were returned. Cowan, though, was transported over the rough terrain in an army wagon which was lowered over precipices with ropes. He survived every danger and was reunited with his wife at Bottler's ranch on the Gardiner River, not far from Mammoth Hot Springs. From there the happy couple returned to Helena, where his recovery became complete.

Besides the Cowan tourists another party had left Helena on August 13 to see for themselves the wonders of the park. The original group was composed of Andrew J. Weikert, Richard Dietrich, a music teacher, Fred Pfister, and Joe Roberts. In most accounts of this Yellowstone episode the assertion is made that these two parties were together, which was not true. Also, Howard in his book *Chief Joseph, His Pursuit and Capture* is apparently the authority for the statement that one man of the Cowan party was killed, and other historians accepted the fact without investigating it. That fate did befall two of Weikert's friends, as will be related presently.

At Mammoth Hot Springs the group was joined by the other members of the party, who included Leonard Duncan, August Foller, Jack Stewart, Leslie Wilkie, Charles Kenck, and Ben Stone, a colored man and cook. Although they knew the Nez Perce Indians to be on the warpath, they did not expect to see any of them. Indeed, they loaded their pack horses and penetrated farther into the park to get a view of the Upper and Lower Falls. Then, on the morning of August 25, Weikert records in his diary,[13] they left camp and struck off in the direction of the Mud Geyser. When they had almost reached that place they detected a moving caravan, which on closer inspection proved to be Indians. The white men held a brief conference and decided to backtrack, as the ten in their group would be no match against what Weikert estimated as three hundred Nez Perces.

They turned their horses about and galloped back into the timber, the Indians doing likewise in the opposite direction, not knowing, apparently, how large a force opposed them. Although the whites feared that these Indians were Joseph's hostiles, the forest seemed so peaceful they concluded it would be safe to camp between the forks of a creek about a mile and a half above the Upper Falls. After lunch Weikert and Wilkie rode back to investigate the trail left by the Indians. Since they had not been attacked, and did not see any more signs of the Nez Perces, their confidence was restored.

When their curiosity was satisfied they started for camp, and hoped to continue their sight-seeing journey to Yellowstone Lake. Near Sulphur Mountain and Alum Creek they espied an Indian pony about a mile from the trail, and supposed it to be abandoned. Wilkie suggested catching it and taking it "to camp for luck." They managed to rope the pony, but it was a colt and would neither lead nor be driven, so they released it and went on their way.

After a short distance had been covered Weikert detected the heads of several Indians bobbing above fallen logs. Instantly he suspected an ambush. He called a

[13] Andrew J. Weikert, "Journal of a Tour through the Yellowstone National Park in August and September, 1877," *Rocky Mountain Magazine*, Vol. IV, No. 1, March, 1902. Same in *Contributions: Historical Society of Montana*, Vol. III, 1900.

warning to Wilkie and the men wheeled their horses as the Nez Perces leveled their guns and fired. The whites, Indian-fashion, crouched low on the backs of their running ponies, but one bullet creased Weikert's shoulder-blade. Strewn about the ground were fallen logs, and presently Weikert's horse tripped over one and fell, throwing its rider, who still gripped his gun. The Indians came, leaping lightly over the tree trunks as Weikert sprang to his feet, shot at the warriors, mounted and galloped away. Each action had been so speedily accomplished that the braves were nonplussed and stood with their mouths open.

Weikert soon overtook Wilkie and the pair gained dense timber in time to conceal themselves in thick underbrush. Wilkie had been in the lead and so was unharmed. They rode cautiously through the forest to the camp, intending to warn the others. But they found their peaceful camp deserted and in a shambles. At first they thought the others had heard the shooting and retreated into the brush, so they shouted their companions' names. They received no answer.

The Indians had pillaged the camp, taken provisions to replenish their own and appropriated fourteen head of horses. Besides, they had wrecked the shotguns, and taken all the blankets, tents, and saddles. What they did not want, they set on fire.

Weikert learned later that Ben Stone, the darky cook, had been lighting the fire for dinner and the rest were lounging about the camp when the Indians suddenly fired upon them. Stone thought Wilkie and Weikert were playing pranks to frighten them, and paid no attention to the shots. At the second volley, though, all the tourists scampered into the brush. Fred Pfister struck for the Yellowstone River; Dietrich fell into a hole in the creek and lay there for perhaps four hours, being concealed by the high grass surrounding the water. Roberts and Foller ran through the timber, followed by the bullets of the Indians, none of which, fortunately, found their mark. They made their escape to Virginia City, one hundred and fifty miles away. Leonard Duncan also made a hurried exit, via the woods, and reached Mammoth Hot Springs. Stewart and Kenck were closely pursued by the warriors, Stewart receiving a wound in the side and leg. They killed Kenck and took Stewart's money, a large roll of bills, but spared his life.

As they received no answer to repeated hails, Weikert and Wilkie believed the others had escaped the attack, so they filled their saddlebags with ham and other food spurned by the Indians and started for Mammoth Springs, distant fifty miles. Stewart and Ben Stone had made their getaway after the braves left and were overtaken by Weikert and Wilkie. Stone, too, had hidden in the water. Near the Springs the party met a white man who told them that Pfister had reached Mammoth safely, and also Mrs. Cowan, Ida and Frank Carpenter.

Upon their arrival they were soon joined by Duncan and Dietrich, who was nearly exhausted. Weikert and Jim McCartney, a settler who owned an interest in the Springs and store, set out with pack horses to search for the rest of their party. Dietrich decided to stay at Mammoth and await the return of the others.

After the soldiers and other whites left Mammoth, a raiding party of eighteen or twenty Nez Perces appeared. They were at first mistaken for Weikert and the missing members. At the time Dietrich was about a mile from the house, repicketing his horse. He was warned by Stoner, a hunter, to take refuge in the brush because the Indians had stopped at the Springs.

Apparently the next day Dietrich ventured back to the house shortly before the raiding party returned with horses they had stolen from a Montana rancher down the river. A short time later the troops who pursued the Indians found Dietrich's body near the steps of the house. He had been shot through the heart and was still warm.

When the Nez Perces had appeared Ben Stone ran out the back door and up the gulch, hotly pursued by a brave. He had the presence of mind to climb a tree, and as his dusky hue blended with the shade of approaching darkness he managed to escape detection.

In the meantime Weikert and McCartney reached the place where the party had been attacked. They found and buried Kenck's body and salvaged the ruins of the camp. Unable to locate the bodies of the others, they started for Mammoth. Before they left an Indian spied them, evidently a scout from the raiding party, but they galloped away in the timber.

About eighteen miles from the Springs they suddenly ran into a party of Indians on the trail. The white men dashed aside into the brush, pursued by the warriors who blazed away at them. One bullet hit Weikert's horse. As the animal sank beneath him, he dived for the underbrush. McCartney's saddle slipped, which caused his horse to buck. The settler was thrown and his mount galloped away. Once the whites gained the shelter of thick brush the Indians withdrew, contenting themselves with taking Weikert's saddle and bridle.

They made their way on foot to Mammoth, but found only Dietrich's body where the soldiers had left it inside the house. Having nothing to eat, they decided to continue on to a ranch seven miles away toward the Gardiner River. In the darkness they stumbled on the soldiers' camp, where they were reunited with Ben Stone. Weikert later returned with a wagon and brought the bodies of Kenck and Dietrich to Helena for burial. The troops, pursuing the Indians, had had no time to bury Dietrich, they explained.

Major General Hugh L. Scott, then a lieutenant in the Seventh Cavalry, but attached to Lieutenant Doane's detail which pursued the eighteen Nez Perces, states that the soldiers' chase had

"momentous consequences we little dreamed of and surely never intended, since with us it was mostly a lark. None of us had thought that with ten men we could beat the Indian force that had nearly overcome the Seventh Infantry; we had only wanted to drive in their advance guard and maybe get back to the horses, if we were quick enough, and we actually were quick enough to get back nineteen. It was months afterward that I learned what had really resulted.

"Chief Joseph, on various occasions since, has repeatedly told me that they had intended to go out to the buffalo country, down the Yellowstone Valley, leaving the mountains where the river turns northeast—now the site of the town of Livingston, Montana. But they were diverted by seeing us in front. They had been surprised by General Gibbon and the Seventh Infantry in their front at Big Hole. . . . The Nez Perces had enough to think about with General Howard on their trail, and they did not wish to encounter any more troops on their front, with the risk of being caught between two forces.

"The eighteen we chased back were Joseph's scouts, feeling far in his advance, who returned and reported meeting troops down the river. No one could imagine that we would chase them that way unless we had a strong support behind us. The Yellowstone Valley here is hemmed in between high mountains with little room to maneuver. If both ends of the valley were closed by troops, the Indians could never hope to save their women, children, and horses, and so, instead of trying to go on down the river, as originally intended, they crossed the Yellowstone at the Mud Geysers just below the outlet of the Yellowstone Lake, and went up Pelican Creek, across the mountains and down Clarks Fork of the Yellowstone, which they recrossed at the mouth of Cañon Creek, just above Billings. . . . I was first told of this by Joseph in 1877, and his information was confirmed by a signed statement obtained by the Nez Perce agent at Nespilem, Washington."[14]

General Scott further states that this change of direction put the Indians "more than a day's march nearer" Miles, thus losing them several days of valuable time and making it possible for Miles to overtake and defeat them. McWhorter's Indian informants deny Scott's theory, declaring their route had been selected long before the brush with Scott's detail.[15] In addition McWhorter points out: "Unfortunately for this theory, the Nez Perces had crossed the Yellowstone and made their way up Pelican

---

[14] Scott, *Some Memories of a Soldier*, pp. 64-65.

[15] McWhorter, *Hear Me, My Chiefs!*, p. 442.

Creek no later than August 26, a week before Scott's little clash with isolated raiders on September 2."[16]

No supporting evidence has been found in the reports or later writings of the other military commanders to corroborate General Scott's claims. It must be remembered that Poker Joe (Lean Elk) was the Nez Perces' camp leader and guide at this time, and that he, being thoroughly familiar with the country, was doubtless well aware of the settlements along the Yellowstone in Montana, and of the existence of an army post (Fort Ellis) near Bozeman. Besides, Looking Glass, it will be recalled, was most desirous of reaching the Crow Indians' territory to the southeast. Thus, it would appear illogical for the tribal leaders to guide their people northward through a settled region. Nor is it reasonable, because, as McWhorter states, the clash between Scott's party and the Indian raiders took place a week after the five bands had left the park. On the other hand, it is entirely possible the Yellowstone route had been discussed in a chiefs' council and rejected as unfeasible upon learning of the presence of other troops in the field besides those of Doane's detail and of Sturgis' and Howard's commands. They may well have secured such information from Irwin, the discharged soldier they captured in the park.

At any rate, while war parties attacked all tourists and prospectors whom they found in the park, the main body of Nez Perces pushed on across the Yellowstone River, passed around the north shore of the lake, and then took off along a tributary stream called Pelican Creek in the direction of the Stinking Water (Shoshone), a wilderness area.

Meanwhile, Howard was forced to build roads through the park for his wagons. Finally, near the eastern boundary, he abandoned them because the rainy days and cold nights made the march so fatiguing for the horses, and the soldiers encountered so many precipitous canyons and fallen timber that eventually they could no longer find

[16] *Ibid.*

even a faint apology for a road. So the general placed his wagons in charge of Captain W. F Spurgin, Twenty-first Infantry, who brought them to Fort Ellis. The command continued the chase with a packtrain.

At the Baronet Bridge over the Yellowstone, a war party of Nez Perces partially burned the structure to delay Howard's troops. The bridge was a flimsy affair, fifty feet above the river, and it took the soldiers two hours to repair it. The command then crossed safely and marched twenty miles down the Yellowstone to Mammoth Falls, where the general learned he had just missed Lieutenant Colonel Gilbert.

Joseph later admitted that he "did not know what had become of General Howard, but we supposed that he had sent for more horses and mules."[17] And we can imagine a faint smile flitting across the handsome features of the chief whenever he thought about the Camas Meadows raid.

---

[17] Wood, "Chief Joseph, the Nez Percé," *Century Magazine*, May, 1884, p. 140.

CHAPTER XX

The Battle of Canyon Creek

COLONEL Samuel D. Sturgis had the Seventh Cavalry in the field, scouting the valley of the Yellowstone about twelve miles from Miles City. The regiment, composed of recruits and young and inexperienced officers, had been reorganized following the terrible disaster of the Custer Massacre the year before. There has been so much controversy over this phase of the military campaign that it is illuminating to examine the official reports.

Colonel John Gibbon states that he sent two dispatches to Colonel Sturgis "to move with all speed to Fort Ellis [near Bozeman, Montana], hoping to get him there in time to move up the Yellowstone River, and head off the Indians before they crossed to the eastward of that stream; but my dispatches did not reach him until he had arrived on the Musselshell [after the battle of Canyon Creek was over.]"[1]

Part of Sturgis' cavalry, though, left at once for Fort Ellis, and upon arriving there August 27, Gibbon writes:

Lieutenant Doane was ordered by telegraph to push up the Yellowstone to the bridge at the mouth of East Fork, cross that, and feel for the Indians up the right bank of the Yellowstone.[2]

In the park Doane's force overtook Lieutenant Colonel Gilbert of the Seventh Infantry, escorted by Captain Norwood's cavalry, which had been detached from How-

[1] *Report of Secretary of War*, 1877, I, 505. Report of Colonel Gibbon.

[2] *Ibid.*

ard's column and was returning to its headquarters post. The combined detachments later struck the trail of the general's command in the Lower Geyser Basin and followed it down the Clarks Fork, but failed to overtake him and so returned to Fort Ellis.

While in camp at the Lower Basin, Howard dispatched Captain Cushing to Fort Ellis with three companies of the Fourth Artillery on August 24, with the intention of their operating from the Crow Agency in advance of the hostiles. The general hoped Cushing would form a junction with Colonel Sturgis, and so prevent the Nez Perces from continuing their northward march.

Sturgis, then at the old Crow Agency on the Big Rosebud above its confluence with the Little Rosebud and southeast of Fort Ellis, received orders from Gibbon on August 27 "to push up to the head of Clarks Fork," one source of which rises on Sunset Peak near Cooke City, Montana, at the northeast boundary of Yellowstone Park. But instead of leaving immediately, Sturgis remained at the agency to await word from his Crow scouts as to the movements and line of travel of the Nez Perces.

Because of subsequent events, Sturgis blames Lieutenant Doane for not following his orders to guard the lower canyon of the Yellowstone, and for not keeping him posted through Doane's Indian scouts as to the route taken by the Nez Perces. The full responsibility, however, falls on Gibbon for countermanding Doane's orders. Gibbon made a second serious mistake in countermanding Howard's orders to Cushing. This point will be discussed at the end of this chapter. To complicate matters still further for Colonel Sturgis, his two mountain men, Groff and Leonard and an Indian boy with them, whom he had sent to reconnoiter, were discovered and killed by Nez Perce scouts.

Still not knowing the whereabouts of the Indians, Sturgis left the agency on August 31 with Companies H, I, F, M, G, and L of the Seventh Cavalry, commanded respectively by Captains F. W. Benteen, Nowlan, Bell, and French, and by Lieutenants Wallace and Wilkinson. About thirty Crow scouts later joined the command. The column marched toward Clarks Fork Canyon and encamped at the eastern base of the mountains, a strategic site as it guarded the outlets of the Stinking Water and Clarks Fork rivers. The former stream, now called Shoshone, flows in a general northeasterly course to empty into the Big Horn a few miles south of the Montana boundary. The Clarks Fork rises in the Absaroka National Forest not far from the park's northeastern border, flows southeastward into Wyoming, where it makes a big bend to the north around Sawtooth Mountain, and forms a confluence with the Yellowstone at the present site of Laurel, Montana.

Sturgis' movements were hampered here because he had been unable to obtain any reliable guides for the strange country in which he found himself, nor could he get any accurate information as to the topography of the region.

Since he found no trail through the Clarks Fork Canyon, the colonel left his wagon train and artillery, intending to continue his march with pack mules toward the North Fork of Clarks Fork in the direction of Soda Butte Pass. When ready to start, however, a party of Crow scouts, with a Frenchman as leader, rode into camp and reported no trace of the Nez Perces and no trail leading to Soda Butte Pass, which is in the northeastern section of the park. So Sturgis unpacked again and went into camp on the spot.

He had the foresight to warn prospectors near the Pass at "Miner's camp" that Indians might attack them. His messengers fell in with Howard's command and apprised the general of Sturgis' location about fifty miles away. Heretofore, every courier sent by Howard to communicate with the colonel had been killed by the Nez Perces, which effectively prevented the two forces from uniting or exchanging information.

Howard at once telegraphed General McDowell that the Indians were then between his command and that of Sturgis, and he "could not see how it was possible for them to escape." Nor could they, that officer agreed, if he had known the whereabouts of the general, and if the couriers between the two commands had not been intercepted and murdered. The last dispatch from Howard on August 24 had come to the colonel from Virginia City.

Sturgis' camp was located on the east escarpment of the mountains. His troops had to guard the various passes through them from the lower Yellowstone Canyon over a wilderness of rugged hills for approximately two hundred and fifty miles. It was then that Lieutenant Doane could have rendered valuable aid to his colonel, had he not received counterorders at Fort Ellis.

On September 6, Sturgis dispatched Lieutenant Varnum, the quartermaster, and a force of twenty-five men to pick up supplies at the old Crow Agency. He then moved his command toward Hart (Heart) Mountain (located north of the present Cody, Wyoming), and encamped in a canyon. From here he detailed two scouts to reconnoiter the country between the Stinking Water (or Shoshone) and Clarks Fork. Since they failed to return to camp, Sturgis sent Lieutenant Hare and twenty men on September 8 to make a reconnaissance in the direction of the Stinking Water by way of Hart Mountain. Lieutenant Fuller and twenty more men scouted the region along the North Fork "if possible," Sturgis writes, "to discover a way by which the command might reach the Miners' Camp."[3]

Lieutenant Hare returned in the afternoon to report that he had found the two scouts sent previously, one dead and the other dying, about sixteen miles from camp. According to the pony tracks he estimated about thirty Nez Perces had attacked them. Lieutenant Fuller returned later and reported the hostiles to be moving on the Stinking Water trail about eighteen miles away. His men had discovered the Indians' pony herd two miles from them. The animals had just been taken to water, and were being driven up one of the numerous ravines by

[3] *Report of Secretary of War,* 1877, I, 509. Report of Colonel Sturgis.

some half-naked boys. The young herders were unaware of the soldiers' presence, for they made no attempt to conceal the herd.

Fuller's prospector guide assured Sturgis that the country was too rough and broken for the Indians to cross over to the Clarks Fork, and that they must debouch on the Stinking Water River.

When the Nez Perces found themselves cut off between the two commands, they feigned flight along the Stinking Water—a stratagem which McWhorter ascribes to Poker Joe.[4] The Indians passed by Sturgis' right flank, and then, after a short detour south they turned north toward the Clarks Fork, gained a heavily timbered ridge and passed through a narrow chasm, which opened into a towering canyon with cliffs scarcely twenty feet apart. This gorge abruptly opened into the Clarks Fork Valley after a course of three or four miles, not far from Sturgis' former camping place. By forced marches the Nez Perces then avoided the colonel completely. Howard writes:

> The Indians left the Stinking Water trail, doubtless, because Joseph heard that the prairie ahead of him had been set on fire and was burning, and that some of General Crook's troops [Sturgis' Seventh Cavalry] were coming up from that direction. By this information my command was saved nearly a hundred miles of circuitous following, the toughest journey which this pursuit occasioned, for we traced the chord of the arc which the astute young chieftain was forced to describe.[5]

While the Nez Perces were eluding Sturgis on the

[4] McWhorter, *Hear Me, My Chiefs!*, p. 454. Sam Tilden states that Looking Glass and White Bird planned this strategy. Joseph makes no mention of it in his own story. The supposition is that the chiefs held a council and jointly agreed to the move. McWhorter also disagrees with other accounts that Looking Glass "went to the Crows for help and was rebuffed." *Op. cit.*, p. 460. However, Yellow Bull reports: "After we reached the Crow country, a Crow chief, son of Double Pipe, came and talked to Looking Glass, telling him that the Crows who were with the soldiers would not shoot at us with the intention of hitting us, but they would aim over our heads." Curtis, *The North American Indian*, VIII, 167. Later, a Crow shot a Nez Perce and then the latter regarded them as enemies.

[5] Howard, *Chief Joseph, His Pursuit and Capture*, p. 243.

Clarks Fork, Looking Glass reportedly rode ahead to hold a conference with the Crows, for the purpose of seeking refuge among them. However, their attitude toward the Nez Perces had undergone a change, as they were friendly to the whites and did not wish to offend the latter by giving succor to the Nez Perces. The Mountain Crows decided to remain strictly neutral, but the River Crows became allies of the army. When Looking Glass brought back this discouraging news to the village, the other chiefs realized that they would have to find sanctuary in Canada, the "old woman's country," as the Nez Perces referred to it.

In the meantime Sturgis decided it would require too much time to go in direct pursuit of the hostiles. He determined to try for the outlet of the Stinking Water trail in advance of the Indians, hoping to head them off, or throw them back on Howard, wherever he was at the moment. (Actually, the general was moving toward the colonel and was surprised to find that the Seventh Cavalry had decamped from Hart Mountain.) Advice from Miles, which reached Sturgis at this time, confirmed the latter's judgment. The colonel did not divide his command to watch both rivers simultaneously because he had been informed that "the Nez Perces had 400 warriors, well mounted and well armed." He feared the division would weaken his strength and lead to disaster against a superior force of hostiles. The colonel sent his wagon train and artillery back to the old Crow Agency, and moved his command south along the Stinking Water trail in hot pursuit of Joseph and his tribesmen.

According to Lieutenant C. E. S. Wood, Howard's aide-de-camp, if Sturgis had remained at Hart Mountain, abiding by his orders (although whose orders from higher authority Wood fails to state), Joseph's escape would have been blocked, since the Nez Perces made their exit through "the dry bed of a mountain torrent, with such precipitous walls on either side that it was like going through a gigantic rough railroad tunnel." During the night, Wood explains, Joseph sent a few of his young men "around Sturgis' force toward Hart Mountain. There, at daybreak, they stirred up a great dust by tying sagebrush to their lariats and riding furiously, dragging the bundles of brush along the ground."[6]

Sturgis, completely fooled into thinking he was chasing the main band, flew south after them. This ruse left the mouth of the pass to the north clear and the Nez Perces marched through. The young men who executed the strategy made a long circuit and rejoined their tribesmen on the plains between the Yellowstone and Missouri rivers.

Howard, once again close on the Indians' heels, explains:

> My command, discovering Joseph's ruse, kept the trail which Sturgis had been so near, but had not seen, and finally slid down the canyon, many a horse, in his weakness, falling and blocking the way. The mouth of this canyon, which debouches into Clarke's Valley, was not more than twenty feet across from high wall to high wall.[7]

The Nez Perces, meanwhile, took cover in a dense forest then and, keeping a mountain between them and Sturgis' command, managed to escape from between the two forces (Howard and Sturgis) by following the Clarks Fork Valley and crossing the Yellowstone in the direction of the Musselshell Basin.

On September 10 Sturgis arrived at the point "where the Indians had turned back and headed for Clark's Fork," which they reached contrary to the assertions of his guide, the colonel grimly notes in his report to the Secretary of War.

It was then Sturgis realized the trick the enemy had pulled on him. Theodore Goldin, one of his men, relates:

> We knew our old Colonel was hopping mad that the savages had outwitted him, and as we returned to camp

---

[6] Chester A. Fee, *Chief Joseph: the Biography of a Great Indian*, p. 320. From the account by C. E. S. Wood. This maneuver was also noted and described by scout S. G. Fisher in his "Journal," *Contributions: Historical Society of Montana*, II (1896), 277.

[7] Howard, *op. cit.*, p. 255.

we heard the old veteran, with many an explosive adjective, declare that he would overtake those Indians before they crossed the Missouri river if he had to go afoot and alone. He wound up his impromptu oration with an order for reveille at half-past three and an advance at five o'clock.[8]

Sturgis faced his cavalry about and by long marches over rugged and precipitous mountain country tried to catch the elusive Nez Perces. He was now surprised to find himself within a mile or so of Howard's camp. The general rode over and mutual explanations were exchanged between the two officers. They decided that Sturgis should continue the pursuit by forced marches, since his horses were fresher than Howard's. The latter loaned Lieutenant Otis to the colonel with the howitzers on pack mules, accompanied by fifty men from Major Sanford's cavalry under the command of Captain Bendire of the First Cavalry. The commanders further decided to apprise Colonel Miles of the situation by courier, giving him plenty of time to head off the Indians if Sturgis failed to stop them. The latter sent duplicate dispatches on to Miles, which he duly received.

A stretch of rainy weather set in, which made the trails slippery and, in addition to numerous swollen fords, delayed Sturgis' march, although he moved his troops forward with all feasible speed. Several days later on September 13, ten miles north of where the Clarks Fork empties into the Yellowstone near the present site of Billings, Montana, the colonel had about given up the chase. He had called a halt when one of his scouts, Pawnee Tom, rode wildly into camp, shouting, "Indians! Indians!"

As the command quickly remounted they could see a large column of smoke down the valley. They proceeded about seven miles toward Canyon Creek at a trot, Major Lewis Merrill's battalion being in the lead with Lieutenant Wilkinson's L troop as advance guard. On reaching

[8] Theodore Goldin, "The Seventh Cavalry at Cañon Creek," in Brady, *Northwestern Fights and Fighters*, p. 214.

the crest of the first ridge they found that they had overtaken the Indians at a rest camp. Sturgis immediately dismounted and attacked with 350 soldiers. These included his reenforcements from Howard's command.

The Indians evidently had discovered the troops about the same time as the soldiers sighted them. According to Yellow Bull, the chiefs held a hurried consultation and Looking Glass dispatched young warriors to check the cavalry, while the women and children began a hasty retreat. The Nez Perces quickly collected in force along the ridges on both sides of the canyon. S. G. Fisher, Howard's chief of scouts, describes Canyon Creek as "a narrow 'wash,' with banks from ten to twenty feet high. At this season of the year there is no water running in it, and only occasional pools of alkali water."[9]

A series of gallant charges by Captains Bell and Nowlan with Companies F and I drove the hostiles from this position back upon the main body. As the warriors retreated, though, they fought hard to delay the troops in order to give the women, children, and old men a chance to escape through the canyon, which would furnish admirable defense for whoever gained possession of it first. Its course, three or four miles distant, lay through a gradually narrowing valley, seamed with gullies, ravines, and side canyons, and protected by overhanging rock ledges. An armed force of even fifty could hold it.

When his men topped the first ridge Sturgis ordered Captain Benteen's cavalry, which had been held in reserve, to detour to the left in order to gain an open plain running along the base of some farther hills, so that he could "charge across the front of Merrill's battalion, cross the creek, and cut off the herd before it should enter the canon,"[10] at this point 1800 yards wide at the bottom.

At the same time that Benteen was executing his orders, Sturgis directed Major Merrill to gallop forward "so as to get beyond and in rear of Benteen" as soon as

---

[9] "Journal of S. G. Fisher," *Contributions: Historical Society of Montana*, II (1896), 278-79.

[10] Sturgis, in *Report of Secretary of War*, 1877, I, 511.

the latter's troops had passed. Merrill was supposed to protect the captain's left flank from the fire of the Indians "who had by this time occupied the mouth and sides of the canon in strong force."[11]

Theodore Goldin, a trooper in Captain Benteen's battalion, thus describes the fighting race to capture the canyon:

> On we went at a mad gallop. The Indians seemed to divine our purpose and redoubled their efforts. For a few moments it was doubtful which would win. An instant later and our flankers were assailed with a murderous fire from the bluffs, and we realized that an advance-party of the Indians were in the canon ahead of us. The fire was so fierce that our men were compelled to draw away from the hills and rejoin the main body of the battalion. It was apparent, now, that our only hope lay in heading off the main body, which was by this time dangerously near the entrance to the pass.
>
> On we galloped and a little later, sheltered from the enemy on the bluffs, we were dismounting in a deep ravine. Our loss so far had been only two men. Leaving our horses in charge of the horse holders, we scrambled up the bank, deployed as skirmishers and were soon hotly engaged. In the meantime, so far as we could see, the other two battalions, as dismounted skirmishers, were moving up the valley, keeping up a running fight with the Indians. Just about this time up came Lieutenant Otis with his "jackass" battery. Pushing well out to the front he opened fire on the enemy, apparently doing considerable damage. By this time the first and second battalions had joined us and the fight was raging fiercely, the Indians gradually drawing into the canon in spite of our efforts to restrain them. The first and second battalions had been pushed out toward the hills, and from the incessant firing in that direction we knew they had their hands full.[12]

Merrill's troops, who had been skirmishing on foot for nearly three miles across broken and rough country, were

[11] *Ibid.* Apparently in this battle Joseph did some active fighting, for Philip Williams, a Nez Perce, reports seeing him "with the rest of the warriors on Canyon Creek." McWhorter, *Hear Me, My Chiefs!*, p. 506.

[12] Goldin, *op. cit.*, p. 216.

too exhausted to reach Benteen in time to support him. This enabled the Nez Perces to get the main herd of their ponies into the shelter of the canyon, but Benteen pushed the animals so closely that the Indians had to abandon four hundred of their most worn-out horses.

Benteen's third battalion, strengthened by Bendire's detachment of cavalry and the howitzer loaned by Howard, received orders to make a flank movement and clear the heights on the west side of the canyon. The troops put spurs to their tired mounts, keeping them at a gallop as they swung up the valley toward a narrow ravine at right angles to the former line of battle. No sooner had the cavalrymen entered its narrowest part, however, when a fusillade of rifle shots zipped past them from the cliffs on their right and thudded into the banks on the opposite side of the canyon. Those at the column's head spurred their horses and soon got out of range. The soldiers in the rear were taken unawares, and two recruits became panic-stricken and fled to the shelter of a ravine.

Captain French's arrival with M troop checked the threatened rout, "and with a mad cheer the men rushed up the steep hillside, some mounted, some dismounted, in a wild effort to reach the enemy," Goldin continues. "The head of the column soon rejoined the charging lines, and a few moments later we stood on the top of the plateau, but not an Indian was in sight."[13]

After taking a breathing space, the troops reformed their ranks and advanced cautiously across the plateau, from where they could peer through the grass and sagebrush into the valley below. They observed some thirty or forty mounted Indians in a huddle and fired into the group, presumably killing or wounding most of them and their horses, although Yellow Wolf says only one man was slightly wounded and two animals were slain. The others fled on their ponies in wild haste. Preceded by a skirmishing line, the cavalrymen then advanced into the valley. Hardly had they reached level ground when

---

[13] *Ibid.*, p. 217.

the Indians poured a volley into them from the bluffs across the canyon. Their position being dangerously exposed the soldiers dismounted and took shelter under a rock ledge. Both sides then indulged in a game of sniping.

All afternoon until sunset the Indians hotly contested every foot of ground, and forced the exhausted troops to withdraw at nightfall and camp at the mouth of the canyon. The raw winds of September that whistled through the ravines at evening did not add to the comfort of either side. The air grew chill and the ground was damp from recent rains.

Having won the race to the canyon the main body of Nez Perces continued their successful retreat after a short rest during the night while young men blocked the passageway behind them with logs and brush. All next day they kept up a running fight with a large party of River Crows, gaudily arrayed in war paint, who had reenforced Sturgis. So vigorously did these scouts pursue the Nez Perces that the latter abandoned more weary ponies, Sturgis placing the loss at nine hundred in all—a costly price for escape after a running battle of two days' duration. Amply satisfied, the Crows then gave up the chase within forty miles of the Musselshell River. This loss of stock was another serious blow to the Nez Perces, and no doubt counted heavily in the troops' favor at the final conflict. The Indians' casualties, as reported by Sturgis, were twenty-one killed, whereas the soldiers had three killed and eleven wounded.[14] The Nez Perces denied having any mortalities, and scout S. G. Fisher affirmed that he found no dead Indians at Canyon Creek.

The cavalrymen, mostly recruits, for the first time were engaged under fire and fought with "coolness and courage." In his report, Major Merrill commends the enlisted men:

---

[14] These figures are based on Sturgis' official report in *Report of Secretary of War*, 1877, I, 512. However, Yellow Wolf declares only three warriors were wounded, one of them being hit when a cavalyman fired on them from the bluffs. Three braves were killed later during the running fight with the Crow and Bannock scouts. McWhorter, *Yellow Wolf: His Own Story*, pp. 186-87.

They fought on foot over some eight miles of difficult and intersected ground, on the heels of a forced march of 80 miles, almost without rest and on half rations, and this preceded by two days of severe exertion, during which 70 miles, chiefly of mountain climbing, had been covered, and men and horses were pushed to the very verge of physical endurance, yet there was not seen a falter or a moment's need of urging forward.[15]

At dawn the next day Sturgis grimly continued the pursuit, hoping the Crows could check the enemy until his command could close up. But the Nez Perces did not linger by the wayside, and fought the Crows for every mile they covered in their flight to freedom. By night the army column was scattered for ten miles, with many cavalrymen on foot, which forced the colonel to go into camp after "a weary march of 37 miles." Trooper Goldin reports the men feasted on "pony steaks and rib roasts," that night, so famished were they that they surreptitiously killed the weaker horses.

Still without rations, as his supply train from the agency had been unable to overtake him, Sturgis' force wearily resumed the chase in the morning. On reaching the Musselshell River the colonel found the distance between himself and the Indians had increased, so, in disgust, he gave up the pursuit. In any case, his cavalry was too worn out to continue. For a week men and horses had been pushed to the limit, making long, weary marches, sometimes fifty and sixty miles a day, on half rations and with very little rest. "Hungry, tired and discouraged," writes Goldin, "it was not a good-natured crowd to say the least, but officers and men were on an equal footing."[16] Besides, a disease of the hoof had broken out among the animals, which placed the men on foot and rendered it impossible to overtake mounted Indians.

Here, on the banks of the Musselshell, Sturgis held another conference with Howard, who merged the two

---

[15] Report of Secretary of War, 1877, I, 571. Report of Major Merrill.

[16] Goldin, *op. cit.*, p. 221.

forces upon his arrival. The colonel then accompanied the general's brigade on to the Missouri River.

In a dispatch to Miles, Sturgis, greatly chagrined, explained the reason for the failure of his campaign:

. . . The absence of a single guide who had ever been in the country in which we were operating, taken in connection with our ignorance of it, and its exceeding rough and broken character, and my inability to learn anything of Howard's position, enabled them to elude me at the very moment I felt sure of success. This is extremely mortifying to me, I assure you, and we are doing all that human endurance can possibly accomplish to circumvent them yet. . . .[17]

In his report to the Secretary of War, Howard places the blame on Colonel Gibbon for the Indians' escape at Hart Mountain, and for Sturgis' failure. The general accused Gibbon of countermanding part of his order to Captain Cushing. Howard had ordered Cushing to operate from the old Crow Agency, to push up the Clarks Fork and join Sturgis. It seems that Gibbon, without a full cognizance of the facts, acted on his own responsibility, held Cushing at Fort Ellis, completely detached Norwood's company from Cushing, and did not strengthen the captain's force with Lieutenant Doane's troops. Gibbon held Norwood's cavalry at Fort Ellis to act as couriers, but, Howard complains, "the real or perhaps additional reason was probably a desire to give Lieutenant-Colonel Gilbert a command while en route to join me and to meet a supposed emergency in the direction of Mammoth Springs, where the Indian raid, before described, had just occurred."[18] (The raid when Dietrich, of the Weikert party, was killed.) Regarding Gibbon's action, Howard writes:

I was exceedingly annoyed at this conflict of orders, for it certainly prevented Cushing from being at Clarke's Fork with sufficient force to take either the offensive

[17] Sturgis, in *Report of Secretary of War*, 1877, I, 74.

[18] Howard, in *Report of Secretary of War*, 1877, I, 625.

against the crossing Indians or from cooperating effectively with Colonel Sturgis at Heart Mountain. Had Cushing been at Clarke's Fork with the force I had directed him to have, the escape of the enemy across the Yellowstone in the direction he took, without an engagement, would have been absolutely prevented. Indeed, Captain Cushing reported to me that Lieutenant-Colonel Gilbert had treated him with marked official coldness, and when he, at Fort Ellis, asked him for the means of complying with my orders, and said, "What, sir, is my status?" Colonel Gilbert replied, "You have no status, sir," and directed him to report to the commanding officer at Fort Ellis for duty, which, if he had been constrained to do, would have cut off my expected supplies.[19]

Cushing loafed around the fort for several days. Then, since no one there seemed to know much about anything, least of all the Indians, he acted on his own responsibility and tried to carry out part of Howard's orders as best he could. He brought the general his expected supplies to the Clarks Fork, rejoining the command on September 14.

Meanwhile, just prior to the Canyon Creek conflict, the Nez Perces had captured a stagecoach in which a party of young men took a wild drive, and then dismantled it and destroyed the mails. The passengers and station tender had hied themselves into the brush, whither they were rescued by Howard's men. To complete their escapade the young braves burned the stage buildings to the ground. Other depredations had more tragic aftermaths when raiding parties killed four civilians, burned buildings, and ran off stock.

By outwitting and outdistancing Sturgis, Joseph's tribesmen once again had earned their freedom.

---

[19] *Ibid.*

CHAPTER XXI

The Skirmish at Cow Island

AFTER leaving Sturgis' command behind, the Indians retired up the Musselshell River, well knowing now that their people could expect no help from the Crows. They circled west of the Judith Mountains, and on September 23 crossed the Missouri River at a point called Cow Island, the head of fall navigation where a freight depot was located. Twelve soldiers under Sergeant William Moelchert of the Seventh Infantry and four citizens were guarding the fifty tons of supplies which had just been unloaded from the steamer *Benton.*

A guard of twenty warriors stood by while the families and the herds crossed from the river's south bank, watched by the little garrison. Yellow Wolf affirms the chiefs had told the braves "not to shoot unless the soldiers fired first."[1]

After all the five bands had moved on to encamp two miles away up Cow Creek, two scouts approached the entrenched stronghold near the supplies. They parleyed with Sergeant Moelchert, asking for food and offering to pay for it. Moelchert refused their request as he was not authorized to sell government freight, but he gave them some bacon and hardtack.[2] However, it was insufficient for several hundred people.

Apparently the scanty amount of food disgruntled some of the hot-blooded young men who commenced

---

[1] McWhorter, *Hear Me, My Chiefs!*, p. 471.

[2] "Moelchert Correspondence Regarding Cow Island Affair." Manuscript in possession of Montana Historical Society, Helena, Montana.

shooting from the bluffs while the soldiers were getting their supper. After dark, a recent historian states, the Indians slipped up to the freight piles where they found four kegs of whiskey "and soon became a drunken and savage mob. They made at least three attempts to capture the entrenched defenders, the leaders taunting the bucks in 'Indian talk' "[3] This spree is confirmed by Josiah Red Wolf who recounted in the *Spokesman-Review Inland Empire Magazine* (November 17, 1963): "Joseph made the men break up the barrels with axes. As the whiskey flowed (from one axed-barrel) to the ground Zon [Red Wolf's warrior brother] got down and lapped up that whiskey. (Red Wolf laughed and laughed as he recalled the scene.) Joseph told him 'You will be shot if you get half shot.' "

During the eighteen hours of the attack one Indian and two volunteers were wounded. In the interim the Nez Perce women replenished their stores, taking such badly needed food as flour, sugar, bacon, beans and coffee, also cooking utensils. Afterward, some "bad boys," in Yellow Wolf's words, burned the rest of the government and private freight at the landing during the night. "It was a big fire!" he commented.

The chiefs stopped the shooting the next morning and at ten o'clock the camp moved on in the direction of the pass between the Bearpaw Mountains and the Little Rockies.

Upon learning that the hostiles were probably headed for the freight landing, a company of the Seventh Infantry under command of Major Guido Ilges had set out several days earlier from Fort Benton before the Indians reached Cow Island. The major traveled overland with thirty-six volunteers on horseback, while Lieutenant Hardin brought the troops down the river in boats. The parties united at Cow Island shortly after the Indians had left.

On the morning of September 24, Major Ilges and the

[3] Oscar O. Mueller, "The Nez Perce at Cow Island," *Montana, the Magazine of Western History*, April, 1964, p. 52.

mounted volunteers started after the Nez Perces, on a trail which led up Cow Creek Canyon from the freight depot. They had proceeded ten miles when an advance scout discovered the Indians' camp. The warriors had surrounded a party of teamsters and their wagon train near the mouth of the Judith Basin. When the braves learned of the approach of Ilges' men, they set the train on fire and killed two of the teamsters, the other seven escaping into the hills.

Meanwhile, about seventy-five mounted Indians, acting as rear guard, came charging down the canyon toward the command. At one thousand yards they halted and divided into small parties, all of which disappeared. Ilges disposed of his men behind any available natural cover and awaited the attack. It began after high noon and lasted for two hours. The major writes:

> The Indians held the high ground above the high hills on right flank; they did very excellent shooting without exposing themselves. After the Indians had ceased firing and had withdrawn from the immediate front, Major Ilges fearing that they were trying to get to his rear and left, and on account of his unfavorable position for defense, slowly withdrew and returned to the pits at Cow Island, where he arrived at 6 P.M.[4]

These warriors held the detachment at bay until the main band made their escape. One citizen with the troops and one horse were killed, and the Indians had two wounded. Major Ilges returned to Fort Benton on September 29, leaving Lieutenant Hardin in command of the force at the freight depot.

The fact that these braves did not give pursuit and annihilate the detail seems to indicate that Joseph and Looking Glass were sincere when they said they didn't want to fight, that they only wanted to go to the buffalo country. They felt secure now, believing that they had an open march across the Canadian border.

Some time during the day of the skirmish, Looking

[4] *Report of Secretary of War*, 1877, I, 557. Report of Maj. Ilges.

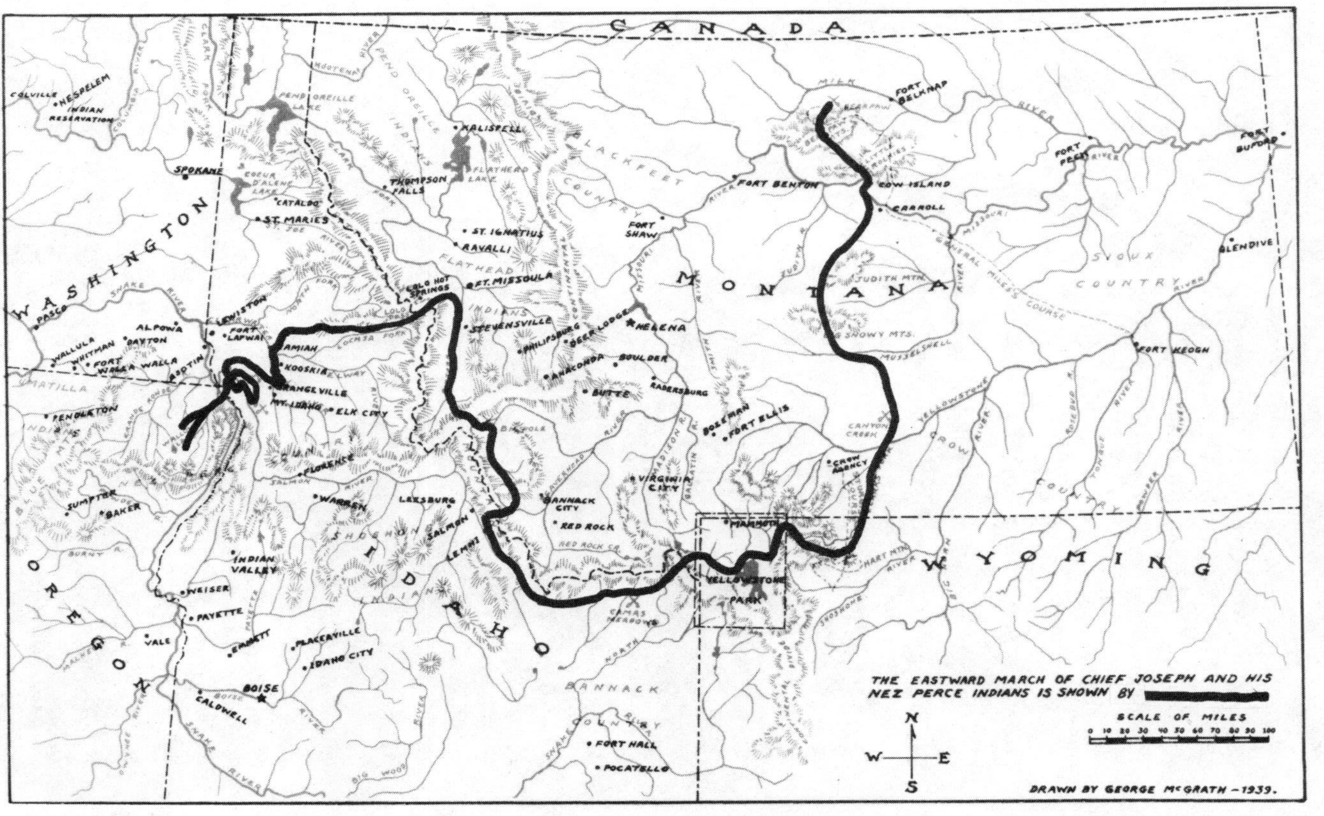

CANADA
WASHINGTON
MONTANA
IDAHO
OREGON
WYOMING
COLVILLE
NESPELEM
INDIAN RESERVATION
SPOKANE
PASCO
WALLULA
WHITMAN
ALPOWA
DAYTON
FORT WALLA WALLA
PENDLETON
SUMPTER
BAKER
LEWISTON
FORT LAPWAI
AMIAH
KOOSKIA
GRANGEVILLE
MT. IDAHO
ELK CITY
FLORENCE
WARREN
LEESBURG
SALMON
LEMHI
INDIAN VALLEY
WEISER
PAYETTE
VALE
EMMETT
PLACERVILLE
IDAHO CITY
BOISE
CALDWELL
CATALDO
ST. MARIES
COEUR D'ALENE LAKE
PEND OREILLE LAKE
THOMPSON FALLS
KALISPELL
FLATHEAD LAKE
ST. IGNATIUS
RAVALLI
FT. MISSOULA
LOLO HOT SPRINGS
STEVENSVILLE
PHILIPSBURG
DEER LODGE
HELENA
ANACONDA
BOULDER
BUTTE
RADERSBURG
BOZEMAN
FORT ELLIS
VIRGINIA CITY
BANNACK CITY
RED ROCK
FORT SHAW
FORT BENTON
COW ISLAND
CARROLL
FORT BELKNAP
FORT PECK
FORT BUFORD
GLENDIVE
FORT KEOGH
JUDITH MTS.
SNOWY MTS.
CANYON CREEK
CROW AGENCY
MAMMOTH
YELLOWSTONE PARK
CAMAS MEADOWS
FORT HALL
POCATELLO
BLACKFEET COUNTRY
SIOUX COUNTRY
CROW COUNTRY
GENERAL MILES'S COURSE
SNAKE RIVER
THE EASTWARD MARCH OF CHIEF JOSEPH AND HIS NEZ PERCE INDIANS IS SHOWN BY
SCALE OF MILES
0 10 20 30 40 50 60 70 80 90 100
N
W
E
S
DRAWN BY GEORGE McGRATH – 1939.

Glass replaced Poker Joe (Lean Elk) as caravan leader. Many Wounds says the former remonstrated with Poker Joe for hurrying all the time, and he (Looking Glass), as ranking chief, again took over the leadership. To this the other chiefs consented.

Meanwhile, Howard had sent a written order down the Yellowstone by boat to Colonel Nelson A. Miles to intercept the Nez Perces. To provide against emergencies, he also dispatched a duplicate letter overland by mounted messenger notifying Miles of Joseph's escape from Sturgis. Howard then delayed his pursuit deliberately, knowing from past experience that the wily Nez Perces would only keep a day's march or so ahead of the troops.

Colonel Miles's temporary headquarters was at the cantonment on Tongue River, Montana, later known as Fort Keogh, near Miles City. Upon receipt of Howard's dispatch on the evening of September 17, the colonel immediately notified his superior, General A. H. Terry, commanding the Department of Dakota and in command of Fort Buford, that he would leave nine companies of infantry and one of cavalry at that point on the Yellowstone to keep the peace among the Indians of the region. With the remainder of his command he would "strike across by the head of Big Dry, Musselshell, Crooked Creek and Carroll, with the hope of intercepting the Nez Perces in their movement north,"[5] as he presumed Howard and Sturgis would follow them to the Missouri.

That night all of Miles's available force was ferried over to the north bank of the Yellowstone. The morning of the eighteenth, the colonel's command of Troops A and D of the Seventh Cavalry, Companies B, F, G, and I of the Fifth Infantry, mounted, with D and K of the Fifth marching on foot as escort to the wagon train, began the pursuit. Other troops were picked up along the route of march.

The country from the valley of the Clarks Fork to the Bearpaw Mountains is rolling plateau land, cut by bluffs

[5] *Report of Secretary of War*, 1877, I, 73. Report of Col. Miles.

and gashed with crooked ravines or coulees. Prickly-pear cactus and sagebrush dot the plains, while cottonwoods cluster along the river bottoms. Although the water is alkaline, bunch grass which nourished the buffalo for centuries grew in abundance and supplied nutritious forage for Indian pony and cavalry charger.

Unaware of another army in the field, the Nez Perces moved along in leisurely fashion after their skirmish at Cow Island. They reached the northern slope of the Bearpaw Mountains within an easy day's march of the Canadian line—and the blessed freedom for the lack of which they had suffered so much and would have to suffer much more. On Snake Creek, a tributary of Milk River, Looking Glass halted to give the exhausted people and horses a chance to rest, the wounded to recuperate, and to take advantage of the excellent hunting. Here, thirty miles southwest of Fort Belknap, he located his camp in a sheltered valley abounding in game, for he and Joseph both believed themselves safe from pursuit.

This belief is evidenced in an interview held in 1900 with Indian Inspector James McLaughlin, in which Joseph said:

> I sat down in a fat and beautiful country. I had won my freedom and the freedom of my people. There were many empty places in the lodges and in the council, but we were in the land where we would not be forced to live in a place we did not want. I believed that if I could remain safe at a distance and talk straight to the men that would be sent by the Great Father, I could get back the Wallowa Valley and return in peace. That is why I did not allow my young men to kill and destroy the white settlers after I began to fight. I wanted to leave a clean trail, and if there were dead soldiers in that trail I could not be held to blame. I had sent out runners to find Sitting Bull, to tell him that another band of red men had been forced to run from the soldiers of the Great White Father, and to propose that we join forces if we were attacked.[6]

The last sentence indicates that either Joseph antici-

[6] James McLaughlin, *My Friend the Indian*, p. 362.

pated possible pursuit by American troops into Canada, or his memory was confused as to the *time* when he sent out runners. In any event, he and Looking Glass made a fatal pause—the stop at the camping spot in the Bearpaw Mountains, like a siren, lured the five bands of Nez Perces to their final downfall. And the chief was big enough to admit his error. McLaughlin reports that Joseph almost wept when he spoke of this fatal blunder.

"I knew that I had made a mistake," he told McLaughlin, "by not crossing into the country of the Red Coats, also in not keeping the country scouted in my rear."[7]

Despite the fact that Joseph took the blame, Yellow Wolf declared it was Looking Glass, camp leader after crossing the Missouri River, who ordered the layover in the Bearpaw Mountains. There, as in the Big Hole, Yellow Wolf placed the responsibility for the Nez Perces' disastrous final battle upon this chief's dilatoriness.[8]

---

[7] *Ibid.*, p. 363. Joseph's memory is vague, apparently, on this point, for Miles reports that the chief had kept the country scouted directly to his rear, but his (Miles's) force approached the Indian camp from an angle.

[8] McWhorter, *Yellow Wolf: His Own Story*, pp. 204-5.

CHAPTER XXII

Battle of the Bearpaw Mountains

ALL the while Colonel Miles was secretly approaching the Nez Perces with three troops of the Second Cavalry under command of Captain George Tyler; three of the Seventh commanded by Captain Owen Hale; four companies of the Fifth Infantry, mounted on captured Sioux Indian ponies, Captain Snyder in command; a breech-loading Hotchkiss gun and a 12-pound Napoleon cannon, besides a wagon train guarded by the two unmounted companies of the Fifth Infantry under Captain Brotherton—375 men in all. Miles advanced rapidly and reached the Missouri at the mouth of the Musselshell on September 23.

Upon learning two days later that the Nez Perces had crossed at Cow Island and burned the supply depot on the twenty-third, Miles commandeered the last river steamer for the season and ferried his troops across the Missouri. The colonel then left his wagon train in command of Captain Brotherton, and pushed on with all speed by the northern side of the Little Rockies to intercept the Indians. These mountains are a range fifty miles in extent, running northwest and southeast. About ten miles beyond their northern spurs are the Bearpaw Mountains, with a low divide connecting the two. Miles could make rapid progress because his course led over the foothills and grassy plains.

He kept his Cheyenne scouts on the west side of the Little Rockies to keep him apprised of the Nez Perces' movements. These spies brought him word that the Indians' trail led over the pass between the two ranges. Miles kept the Little Rockies between his command and the Nez Perces' line of march. Thus he continued to approach them from an angle, and managed to keep his presence concealed from the Indians. To guard his movements further, the colonel ordered the soldiers not to hunt or disturb the vast herds of buffalo, deer, antelope, and elk which they frequently encountered.

On reaching the northern end of the Bearpaw Mountains, fifty miles northeast of Fort Benton, the Cheyenne scouts discovered the Nez Perces' camp, eight miles away. Miles reported to the Secretary of War that he broke camp at four o'clock on September 30. The command struck the trail near the head of Snake Creek and followed it to the Indian village, which they reached at 8:00 A.M. after a forced march of some two hundred miles.[1]

It is thus described by Lieutenant, afterwards Captain, Henry Romeyn, of the Fifth Infantry:

> The camp was located on a small stream called Snake Creek, as it proved in an excellent position for defense in a kidney-shaped depression covering about six acres of ground, along the western side of which the stream ran in a tortuous course, while through it, from the steep bluffs forming its eastern and southern sides, ran "coulees" from two to six feet in depth and fringed with enough sage brush to hide the heads of their occupants. Here the Nez Perce chieftain had pitched his camp and here he now made his last stand for battle.[2]

According to the Indians a boy went out to secure his pony about the same hour (eight o'clock), and discovered Miles's Cheyenne scouts. The youth gave the alarm. Part of the warriors had time to hide behind a steep bank, and to take refuge in the entrenchments which it was customary for them to build at each important camp after the Big Hole battle. The Indians, however, had no time for concerted action, and they were unaware of the size of the opposing force.

---

[1] *Report of Secretary of War*, 1877, I, 514. Report of Col. Miles.

[2] Lieut. Henry Romeyn, "The Capture of Chief Joseph and the Nez Perce Indians," *Contributions: Historical Society of Montana*, II (1896), 287.

Yellow Wolf states that scouts had warned the camp earlier about seeing buffalo stampeding, and the Indians supposed soldiers were coming. But Looking Glass told the people to take their time packing and not to worry. Later, another scout waved the blanket signal of imminent danger, causing a "wild stir." Yellow Wolf also reports his uncle, Chief Joseph, ran into the open and his voice could be heard above all the noise as he shouted, "Horses! Horses! Save the horses!"

Meanwhile, Miles's cavalry approached the village at a trot over the rolling, grass-covered prairie. In the crisp air the trot soon quickened to a gallop. As they rode over low ridges, Miles threw his troops into line of battle while in motion. "This gallop forward, preceding the charge, was one of the most brilliant and inspiring sights I ever witnessed on any field," the colonel writes. "It was the crowning glory of our twelve days' forced marching."[3]

"My God!" cried Captain Hale, who commanded the Seventh Cavalry, "have I got to go out and be killed in such cold weather!" He was the personification of the dashing cavalry officer, with slouch hat jauntily perched to one side, and mounted on a mettlesome gray horse.

As they swept over a rise part of the leading battalions of the Seventh Cavalry and Fifth Infantry, preceded by Cheyenne and Sioux scouts, broke into a charge. With a pounding of hoofs over the turf, a creaking of saddles and jingle of bits they struck directly at the village.

The Indians were not completely surprised this time, though, and withheld their fire until the cavalry was within one hundred yards of their rifle pits. Then, instead of breaking and fleeing before the blue-coated soldiers thundering down on them, the Nez Perces stood up to the cavalry charge and poured a cool, deadly volley into the oncoming ranks. They were no ordinary red foe. Soon an empty saddle, and another, and another, appeared among the cavalrymen until the loss became alarming, and the soldiers had to retreat before the withering fire.

---

[3] Nelson A. Miles, *Personal Recollections of General Miles*, p. 268.

Within five minutes the Nez Perces had repulsed the first attack at the southwestern end of the camp. They were still fighting for their freedom, for their right to live as free-born human beings, and they must have realized, in desperation, that it would be their last fight.

When part of the cavalry took the bluffs east of the village, the Indians had to abandon a steep butte from which they had first directed their fire against the attacking force. As the mounted Fifth Infantry charged up behind the cavalry, they executed "left front into line" and halted at this crest. They had come up to the valley's edge where the camp was located. Dismounting, the men held their ponies by means of lariats. These troops with their long-range rifles delivered a murderous fire on the village. Their captured Sioux ponies, so accustomed to the firing of guns, stood quietly, and many began nibbling the grass! From the coulees, fifty yards away, the Nez Perces also poured a hot fire, picking off infantrymen and horses.

Captain Hale's K troop had first engaged the Indians, who were ranged on "cut-banks," or bluffs, twenty to thirty feet high. Curiously enough that officer, according to Miles, was the first one killed in the battle! His gray horse fell beside him with a mortal wound. Lieutenant Biddle was the next to fall—a singular coincidence that the only two bachelors at the post should be the first to die! It was the young lieutenant's first battle, too. Hale's ranks were almost decimated.

The battalion of Second Cavalry under Captain Tyler had swung slightly to the left, to attack in the rear and cut off the herds grazing on a high plateau behind the village. In the running fight that followed, Lieutenants Jerome and McClernand succeeded in capturing most of the horses and mules, about eight hundred to a thousand in number. The animals were corralled in a small valley in the rear of the command.

The Seventh Cavalry became separated. Captain Godfrey placed himself between his men and the Indians, and promptly his horse was shot under him. The animal pitched to the ground in a heap, stunning the officer.

Trumpeter Herwood ran to his captain and fought off the advancing squad of warriors until Godfrey recovered consciousness and rejoined his troops.

The casualties among the soldiers became fearful. Lieutenant Baird, adjutant of the Fifth Infantry, had his left arm shattered and one ear shot away while he was carrying orders. Captain Moylan of the Seventh Cavalry received a wound in the thigh. Another officer "had one shot through his belt, another carried away his field glass, while a third took off his hunting knife and cut the skin from an ear," writes Lieutenant Romeyn. "Creeping carefully up to the edge of the bluff to look over, a bullet instantly lifted the hat and a lock of hair for a Sergeant, and another went through the head of a comrade at his side."[4]

So fierce and close was the fighting that the battalion of the Seventh had only one officer unwounded after the first charge. This man, Lieutenant Eckerson, remarked to Colonel Miles, "I am the only damned man of the Seventh Cavalry who wears shoulder straps, alive."[5] That battalion had 53 killed and wounded out of 115, while the loss suffered by Captain Hale's troops amounted to over 60 percent.

The reason so many officers were killed and wounded was because the warriors deliberately picked them off, for "wherever the Indians heard a voice raised in command there they at once directed their fire. . . ."[6]

Mortality ran high among the Indian leaders also. Yellow Bull reports: "In the first day's fighting were killed Tuhulhutsut . . . Looking Glass, Alokut [Joseph's beloved brother], and Pile of Clouds."[7] Yellow Wolf adds that Hush-hush-cute (Husishusis Kute) killed three of his tribesmen, mistaking them for enemy Indians. Poker

[4] Romeyn, *op. cit.*, p. 288.

[5] Nelson C. Titus, "The Last Stand of the Nez Perces," *Washington Historical Quarterly*, VI, No. 3, July, 1915, 149.

[6] Romeyn, *op. cit.*, p. 287.

[7] Yellow Bull's account appears in Curtis, *The North American Indian*, VIII, 168. Yellow Wolf's account appears in McWhorter, *Yellow Wolf: His Own Story*, p. 209 and p. 214.

Joe (Lean Elk) likewise was slain in error by a Nez Perce the first day of the battle. However, Yellow Wolf stated Looking Glass died on the last day of the fighting. In describing the latter's death, Yellow Wolf relates that the chief stood up from his rifle pit to view a mounted Indian, mistaken for a friendly Sioux from Sitting Bull. A sharpshooter, apparently, killed him with a single bullet in the forehead.

At the beginning of the attack, according to Romeyn, "a portion of the lodges had been struck and about one hundred ponies packed for the day's march."[8] This band of women and children, defended by fifty or sixty warriors, drove the pack horses and made a bold dash for freedom. They were pursued by G troop of the Second Cavalry under Lieutenant McClernand. After galloping five miles from the village, the warriors halted to fight. The cavalrymen were busy keeping the captured ponies closely herded to prevent them from stampeding back to the Indians. Thus the Nez Perces were able to take the offensive "and forced the soldiers back toward the main body, although they failed in their attempts to retake the stock."[9] Some of the warriors succeeded in reaching the shelter of the Indian camp again, where they aided in its defense. The others escaped, and probably made their way into Canada.

When the first attack began, Joseph was on the opposite side of the creek from the village. This is one of those rare instances in which we have any definite knowledge of his personal activities in battle. It is also unusual for an Indian chief to describe such experiences in his own words. He said:

> We had no knowledge of General Miles' army until a short time before he made a charge upon us, cutting our camp in two, and capturing nearly all of our horses. About seventy men, myself among them, were cut off. My little daughter, twelve years of age, was with me. I gave her a rope, and told her to catch a horse and join the

[8] Romeyn, *op. cit.*, p. 287.

[9] *Ibid.*

others who were cut off from the camp. I have not seen her since, but I have learned that she is alive and well.

I thought of my wife and children, who were now surrounded by soldiers, and I resolved to go to them or die. With a prayer in my mouth to the Great Spirit Chief who rules above, I dashed unarmed through the line of soldiers. It seemed to me that there were guns on every side, before and behind me. My clothes were cut to pieces and my horse was wounded, but I was not hurt. As I reached the door of my lodge, my wife handed me my rifle, saying: "Here's your gun. Fight!"

The soldiers kept up a continuous fire. Six of my men were killed in one spot near me. Ten or twelve soldiers charged into our camp and got possession of two lodges, killing three Nez Perces and losing three of their men, who fell inside our lines. I called my men to drive them back. We fought at close range, not more than twenty steps apart, and drove the soldiers back upon their main line, leaving their dead in our hands. We secured their arms and ammunition. We lost, the first day and night, eighteen men and three women.[10]

At one o'clock in the afternoon Miles ordered a second charge, the object being to cut off the Indians' water supply. Companies A and D of the Fifth Infantry had lost every officer in the first assault, so Lieutenant Henry Romeyn was placed in command and ordered to attack the Indians on the southwest. Part of the Second and Seventh Cavalry closely engaged the Nez Perces in desperate fighting in broken ground intersected by draws on the north and east. While they did so, Captain Carter, Lieutenant Woodruff and the detachment of the Fifth Infantry under Romeyn "charged down the slope, along the open valley of the creek, and reached the west end of the Indian village."[11] But, Miles reports to the Secretary of War, "the deadly fire of the Indians with magazine guns dis-

[10] "An Indian's Views of Indian Affairs," *North American Review*, April, 1879, p. 428. According to Sam Tilden this daughter was Sarah Moses, whose Nez Perce name meant "Walking-in-crushed-snow." She was married to George Moses on July 21, 1879, at Lapwai, Idaho. Sarah returned to Idaho from Canada in 1878 with a small group, including Yellow Wolf, that slipped back to join their reservation brethren.

[11] Miles, in *Report of Secretary of War*, 1877, I, 528.

abled 35 per centum of his [Romeyn's] men, and rendered it impossible for them to take the remainder of the village."[12]

The Nez Perces had too strong a defensive position, Romeyn explained. Because of their withering fire the soldiers could not break through their lines. But fourteen men of Company I under Captain Carter of the Fifth Infantry did succeed in crossing the coulee and reached the lodges. It was these men whom Joseph engaged. His warriors immediately killed five outright—a third of their number—and the others concealed themselves in the draws and gullies until nightfall, when they were able to rejoin their comrades. Lieutenant Romeyn was shot through the lungs in this skirmish, but not mortally wounded.

The troops held their ground until Miles ordered them to withdraw. This proved to the colonel that any more charges would be accomplished at further severe loss to his men.

The soldiers, though, forced the Indians back to the ravines or "coulees" behind their camp. Here the Nez Perces entrenched themselves and easily defended their position against the troops. Indian women assisted in the work of increasing the entrenchments. In many cases they did all the digging by using knives and shovels made of frying pans with sharpened edges. This was accomplished after the first day, according to Yellow Bull. Some of the pits were dug separately and connected by underground passages. These trenches explain why the Indians' casualties were not greater, and why they were able to hold off the superior force of soldiers for five days.

Being unable to dislodge the Indians and suffering fearful losses, Miles withdrew his men at 3:00 P.M. and laid a siege after throwing a thin line of troops completely around the village. He was considerably worried by the fear that Sitting Bull would come to the Nez Perces' aid

---

[12] *Ibid.*

and stage another Custer Massacre before Joseph's surrender could be effected.

And, in truth, Joseph did try to establish contact with the Sioux. That very evening he sent six of his most trusted warriors to get reenforcements from Sitting Bull. The unfortunate messengers, though, stopped at a village of Assiniboines, by whom they were all murdered, probably for their fine guns. It was apparently Joseph's plan to withstand the troops until Sitting Bull could come to his aid. When some of the former's messengers eventually did arrive, however, it was only to discover that the Sioux had learned hearty respect for the U. S. Army. Instead of gallantly joining the beleaguered Nez Perces, Sitting Bull and his people packed up bag and baggage and scampered forty miles farther north from the Canadian border! Perhaps the timely approach of Howard's brigade may have lent speed to their heels.

However, McWhorter's Indian informants told him a Sioux war party led by Sitting Bull actually did start for the Bearpaw battlefield, but upon meeting White Bird's group of refugees they learned of Joseph's surrender, and so all turned back to the Sioux village.[13]

Although fighting with their usual grim fearlessness, the Nez Perces did not harm any of the soldiers who fell within their lines, but only relieved them of arms and ammunition. "They even gave some of the wounded water after nightfall when it could be done with safety," writes Lieutenant Romeyn.[14]

The weather turned stormy on the evening of September 30. Snow fell thickly, driven by a high wind that developed into a blizzard. This caused much suffering in both camps, especially among the wounded soldiers who were on higher ground and had no tents or shelters of any kind to protect them from the raw wind, snow, and cold. Nor could they have the comfort of a fire, for every

---

[13] McWhorter, *Hear Me, My Chiefs!*, p. 513.

[14] Romeyn, *op. cit.* A graphic account of conditions within the Nez Perce camp during the battle is given by Yellow Wolf in McWhorter, *Yellow Wolf: His Own Story*, pp. 211 ff.

light attracted the marksmanship of Indian sharpshooters. It was not until the next evening of October 1 that Captain Brotherton's wagon train arrived, bringing medical supplies, tents, blankets, and food.

Miles had brought his artillery into action and shelled the Indian camp with telling effect. He also sent a dispatch to Howard, saying he had the Nez Perces corralled.

The general had reached Carroll on the Missouri on October 1, and took a boat up the river to Cow Island, leaving Sturgis in command of the column. October 3, Howard dashed on to join Miles, being accompanied by two aides—one, his son, Lieutenant Guy Howard, the other, Lieutenant C. E. S. Wood—and seventeen men, including the two faithful Nez Perce scouts, Old George and Captain John. Arthur Chapman, who had a Umatilla wife and was said by the whites to be a good friend of Joseph's (this, however, was denied by the Indians), also rode with the general in his capacity as official interpreter.

During the evening of October 2, Colonel Sturgis received a note by courier from Miles, informing him of the Bearpaw battle and asking for reenforcements. So Sturgis ferried his and Howard's command over the river and started to the relief of Miles with all the troops. Sturgis continued until he was within a two hours' march of the battlefield, when a courier from Howard apprised him of Joseph's surrender. Then he went into camp to await the general's return.

On the morning of October 1 Miles had started negotiations for surrender with Joseph and some of his warriors. Joseph sent Yellow Bull, a subchief, as his representative to meet the messenger of Miles, who entered the Nez Perce camp under a flag of truce. The report of this first interview and subsequent ones we have in Joseph's own words as follows:

Yellow Bull understood the messenger to say that General Miles wished me to consider the situation; that he did not want to kill my people unnecessarily. Yellow Bull understood this to be a demand for me to surrender and save blood. Upon reporting this message to me Yellow Bull said he wondered whether General Miles was in earnest. I sent him back with my answer, that I had not made up my mind, but would think about it and send word soon. A little later he sent some Cheyenne scouts with another message. I went out to meet them. They said they believed General Miles was sincere and really wanted peace. I walked on to General Miles's tent. He met me and we shook hands. He said, "Come, let us sit down by the fire and talk this matter over."[15]

Joseph was accompanied by some of his warriors, for Miles states in his official report to the Secretary of War that at first the Indians seemed willing to surrender and brought along eleven rifles and carbines, but he thought they became suspicious "from some remarks that were made in English in their hearing,"[16] and so hestitated to lay down their arms. At any rate, Miles, in his own words, "detained" Joseph in his camp overnight. Meanwhile, he dispatched Lieutenant Jerome of the Second Cavalry to "reconnoiter" the Indian village, which is military parlance for orders to spy on the camp.

When that officer appeared in the village and there was no sign of Joseph, the Indians became distrustful. Yellow Bull himself seized the bridle of Jerome's black horse and pulled the lieutenant out of the saddle. Some of the young men wanted to kill him, but were restrained by Yellow Bull. While Joseph was held as a hostage in Miles's camp, Jerome was likewise "detained" as a prisoner, being confined in a damp, cold, underground passage. His Indian guards had to dance to keep warm in the freezing air. The battle continued intermittently, and they finally left him, saying, "We must fight again pretty soon to get warm."

Joseph was not as well treated by his civilized captors, he reported later. Miles had him "hobbled" hands and feet, rolled in a double blanket and quartered with the

[15] "An Indian's Views . . . ," *op. cit.*, p. 428. Miles was a colonel at this time, although holding a brevet of major general.

[16] Miles, in *Report of Secretary of War*, 1877, I, 528.

mules. These indignities were heaped upon the chief after the colonel had deliberately violated the flag of truce.

Just why Miles "detained" Joseph he never made clear. Perhaps he hoped to speed up the surrender by depriving the Nez Perces of their chief, or perhaps he feared that Joseph might attempt to slip away if given his freedom. Ambitious officer that he was, Miles may have hoped to score a decisive victory before Howard could arrive to take over command as ranking officer and thus defeat the colonel's desire to win national acclaim (and a promotion) for the capture of the Nez Perces.

In any event, Yellow Bull came into "Bear Coat's" camp to find out if Joseph was still alive and why he had not returned. Joseph complains:

> General Miles would not let me leave the tent to see my friend alone.
>
> Yellow Bull said to me: "They have got you in their power, and I am afraid they will never let you go again. I have an officer in our camp, and I will hold him until they let you go free."
>
> I said: "I do not know what they mean to do with me, but if they kill me you must not kill the officer. It will do no good to avenge my death by killing him."[17]

Yellow Bull was permitted to return to the village where he then made good his word about holding Jerome. The next day mutual confidence was restored when Miles showed good faith by releasing Joseph, exchanging him for the lieutenant under a flag of truce midway between the two camps.

In later years Yellow Bull related the affair, from which we can infer that the Indians were almost starving while negotiations were under way:

> After we kept Captain [Yellow Bull's mistake; Jerome was a lieutenant.] Jerome in our camps for a day and night he wanted something to eat. I and Tom Hill [a half-breed Indian] told him that we had nothing he could eat; that he had better write a note to General Miles and ask

---

[17] "An Indian's Views . . . ," *op. cit.*, p. 429.

him for something to eat. He wrote a note to General Miles, and Red Wolf's son took the message to General Miles, and we made an exchange of prisoners. . . .[18]

Upon Joseph's return to the village he held a council with the surviving chiefs and found them divided about surrendering. "We could have escaped from Bear Paw Mountain," he says, "if we had left our wounded, old women, and children behind. We were unwilling to do this. We had never heard of a wounded Indian recovering while in the hands of white men."[19]

Again the battle was resumed amid chilling snow flurries.

---

[18] Report of Secretary of Interior, 1911. *Senate Executive Documents, No. 97, 62nd Congress, 1st Session,* XXX, 44. "Memorial of the Nez Percés Indians." From the notarized statement of Yellow Bull.

[19] "An Indian's Views . . . ," *op. cit.*, p. 429.

CHAPTER XXIII

Joseph's Surrender

GENERAL HOWARD approached Miles's camp after dark on a cold, snowy evening of October 4. He could see flashes of rifle fire from the pits of both sides. Miles, bringing his adjutant, Lieutenant Oscar Long, an orderly, and two or three soldiers, all mounted, advanced across the prairie to meet the general's command.

Both parties dismounted, and Howard held out his hand, saying heartily, "Hello, Miles! I'm glad to see you. I thought you might have met Gibbon's fate. Why didn't you let me know?"[1]

Instead of answering the question Miles replied with a cold, formal greeting to his superior officer, and asked the general to his tent while another was being prepared for Howard.

With his characteristic kindness and consideration for those beneath him in rank, Howard requested Miles to have the two Nez Perce scouts and Chapman well cared for, and then the others went on to the colonel's tent.

In the presence of his aide-de-camp, Lieutenant Wood, Howard promised to give Miles the credit for capturing the Indians. The colonel, Howard well knew, was ambitious for a brigadier generalship. Miles's wife was a niece of General W. T. Sherman, then General of the Army. Howard further promised not to take over command until after the surrender—a promise which he kept. Then, Wood recounts: "Colonel Miles' entire man-

[1] Fee, *Chief Joseph; the Biography of a Great Indian*, p. 324.

ner changed; he became cordial, thanked the General for all he had said...."[2]

Wood reports there was much bitterness against Miles among the men of Howard's command over Joseph's surrender. It would appear that messages from Miles to Howard keeping the latter informed of Miles's movements against the Nez Perces apparently failed to reach the general, since he had left his command under Major Edwin Mason and Colonel Sturgis. It turned out later, however, that Major Mason did receive the messages, but he was unable to communicate with Howard. So, not hearing from Miles, Howard began to fear that the colonel had suffered Gibbon's fate. Wood states he privately told Howard that he distrusted Miles, but the general defended his subordinate officer. However, the opinion was prevalent, Wood writes, that "Miles did not want Howard to close up for fear Howard, as senior officer, would by operation of military law, supersede him in full command." No mention of this resentment appears in Howard's book or in his official report to the Secretary of War, although he makes a veiled allusion to "garbled dispatches" sent to General Sheridan in Chicago.

The officers consulted that night on the details of bringing about a surrender. The general suggested that his two Nez Perce scouts, Captain John and Old George, who had accompanied him from Idaho and both of whom had daughters in the Indian camp, should be sent as emissaries to Joseph.

In their own tent later that night, Lieutenant Wood reproached Howard for his generous gesture, and reiterated his distrust of Colonel Miles. Again the general expressed implicit faith in Miles, and there the matter rested. Miles had been Howard's aide during the Civil War, and Howard had secured for him his first regiment. At a later date Wood further accused Miles of changing the dispatch sent to General Sheridan in Chicago which gave credit to Howard for his part in the surrender.

[2] *Ibid.*, p. 326.

Miles's version of the capture (giving all the credit to himself) was published in a Chicago newspaper. Upon reading it, Wood wrote a true account, which was also published and drew forth Sheridan's anger because he had not been consulted first by the general. But Howard, although deeply hurt by the matter, refused to be a party to a public criticism of Miles. Wood declared that Miles never alluded to his (Wood's) open criticism of him whenever they met in later years.[3]

However, on the Bearpaw battlefield during the surrender negotiations, a seeming appearance of harmony prevailed among the officers. The next day (October 5) before noon, the two Nez Perce scouts parleyed in the village with the surviving chiefs and other headmen in council. After much "running to and fro between the camps," Joseph sent his reply, to which White Bird agreed, saying, "What Joseph does is all right; I have nothing to say."[4]

Joseph realized that further resistance was futile and that his hope for aid from Sitting Bull was vain. The terms of surrender as the chief understood them are best explained in his own words:

> I could not bear to see my wounded men and women suffer any longer; we had lost enough already. General Miles had promised that we might return to our country, with what stock we had left. I thought we could start again. I believed General Miles, or I *never would have surrendered.* I have heard that he has been censured for making the promise to return us to Lapwai. He could not have made any other terms with me at that time. I would have held him in check until my friends came to my assistance, and then neither of the generals nor their soldiers would have left Bear Paw Mountain alive.[5]

According to Lieutenant Wood, when old Captain John

---

[3] *Ibid.*

[4] *Report of Secretary of War*, 1877, I, 630. Report of Brigadier General Howard.

[5] An Indian's Views of Indian Affairs," *North American Review*, April, 1879, p. 429.

brought Joseph's message, "his lips quivered and his eyes filled with tears as he delivered the words of his chief."[6]

This famous speech of surrender has been quoted and misquoted so often in history that it is illuminating to note Howard's comment in his official report to the Secretary of War: "This reply . . . was taken verbatim on the spot by Lieutenant Wood, Twenty-first Infantry, my acting aide-de-camp and acting adjutant-general, and is the only report that was ever made of Joseph's reply."[7] Contrary to the statements of some writers, Joseph's surrender speech was not spoken to Howard and Miles on the battlefield but was delivered orally to the officers by old Captain John.

In the simplicity of its dramatic intensity the speech is without parallel in aboriginal oration:

Tell General Howard I know his heart. What he told me before I have in my heart. I am tired of fighting. Our chiefs are killed. Looking Glass is dead. Too-hul-hul-sote is dead. The old men are all dead. It is the young men who say yes or no [that is, vote in council]. He who led on the young men is dead [Joseph's brother, Alokut]. It is cold and we have no blankets. The little children are freezing to death. My people, some of them, have run away to the hills, and have no blankets, no food; no one knows where they are—perhaps freezing to death. I want to have time to look for my children and see how many of them I can find. Maybe I shall find them among the dead. Hear me, my chiefs. I am tired; my heart is sick and sad. From where the sun now stands I will fight no more forever.[8]

True to his word, Joseph made a formal surrender at 2:20 P.M. on October 5, and all firing ceased.[9] Around 4:00 P.M. of that raw, windy, overcast day with a dim sun visible, he rode from his camp, accompanied by a guard of five warriors, including Chief Hush-hush-cute,

---

[6] Wood, "Chief Joseph, the Nez Percé," *Century Magazine*, May, 1884, p. 141.

[7] Howard, in *Report of Secretary of War*, 1877, I, 630.

[8] *Ibid.*

[9] Miles, in *Report of Secretary of War*, 1877, I, 515.

who walked beside him talking in low tones. The chief's hands clasped the saddle pommel, his rifle lay across his knees, and his head was bowed. His scalp lock was tied with otter fur, and the rest of his hair hung in thick braids on either side of his head. He wore buckskin leggings and a gray woolen shawl, containing four or five bullet holes. His head and wrist also showed scratches from bullets.

Stolidly he rode, looking neither to right nor left. Slowly the group ascended the hill to a halfway spot between the lines on the snow-covered plateau where General Howard and Colonel Miles were waiting. A little aside stood the aides, Lieutenants Wood, Guy Howard, and Long, and, farther away, an orderly and Arthur Chapman, the interpreter. At some distance a courier waited beside his horse that nervously pawed the snowy ground. The soldiers observed that the chief's clothes were pierced by more than a dozen bullet holes.

Reaching the officers, Joseph straightened himself in the saddle, and then with a graceful dignity swung off his horse. He flung out his arm to its full length in an impulsive gesture and offered his rifle to General Howard. The latter, with a smile, generously motioned to his subordinate officer, who accepted the token of surrender.

The officers then shook hands with Joseph, whose worn face lit up briefly with a sad smile, as he silently took each proffered hand. Afterwards he turned away and entered the tent provided for him. Lieutenant Wood visited him and offered to make him as comfortable as possible.

From then on a straggling line of Indians, wounded, sick, half-starved, came into Miles's camp on Eagle Creek, bringing their guns and the remnants of their ponies in miserable condition—lame, thin, and bone-weary.

After the early winter dusk had fallen that night, according to Howard's report to the Secretary of War, White Bird and a band estimated variously at twenty to fifty, and later officially established at 104, escaped through the pickets' lines and joined Sitting Bull.[10] Later, Black Eagle told McWhorter that 233 Nez Perces in all slipped away and that only six of White Bird's warriors surrendered. Three of these were Yellow Bull and his two brothers. Howard states that thirty warriors, twenty of whom were wounded, and two hundred ponies were reported by the Red River French half-breeds to have crossed the Canadian border.

Joseph, likewise, could have escaped, but he chose to become an honorable prisoner of war and remain with his people as their tribal guardian. Other fugitives sought refuge among the Gros Ventres and Assiniboines. The Nez Perces were either murdered by them or driven to the hills, whither Miles's Sioux scouts could not be induced to pursue the fleeing remnants of the hostiles. Some time later White Bird's band returned to the Lapwai Reservation in Idaho. According to McLaughlin, White Bird himself continued to live in the land of the Redcoats until his death a few years before 1900.[11] The

---

[10] Sam Tilden relates: "After this capture I got away with Chief Poker Joe [Tilden was in error; Poker Joe was killed at Bearpaw] and some other Indians. Some of us had kept horses saddled since early in the morning.

"We got away and camped with the Sioux. Sitting Bull let us stay with his people a few months. Then we came over toward home by way of Canada and some of us came back four or five at a time. We stayed near Fort McLeod three years.

"We had a sort of ranch and stayed with some other tribes, and after a while we came over to the Flathead reservation—although it was an open place then. We stayed there about three or four years, and there was no trouble in Idaho. That is how I got home.

"After a while we took up some allotments—that is where my home is now—Lewiston."

[11] R. G. Bailey, formerly Nez Perce County historian for the Idaho State Historical Society, states in his volume, *River of No Return—the Great Salmon River of Idaho*, on pp. 195 ff., that White Bird was working in the motion pictures in Spokane, Washington, in 1920. He met there Felix Warren, a dispatch carrier during the Nez Perce War. After escaping into Canada, White Bird supposedly returned to the United States during the Bannock Indian War in 1878. Felix Warren maintains that White Bird told him that he (the chief) and fifty other renegade Indians from Northwestern tribes had returned for reprisal raids on the settlers. But Warren claims that he dissuaded them. Felix Warren offers no proof for this fantastic tale.

In a letter to the author, dated July 12, 1939, Mr. Bailey clarifies the above:

"The picture in my book is that of young White Bird—chief by

"He flung out his arm to its full length in an impulsive gesture—"

Escape of Chief White Bird

chief sought refuge in Canada because he evidently expected to face a firing squad if he surrendered as it was his young men who had commenced hostilities.

In the last analysis the real test of greatness is how an individual bears defeat. Joseph acquitted himself well in his darkest hour—a hero with moral courage—and in his last stand fought a brave battle, causing casualties of 20 percent among the troops. He had lost twenty-five killed, and of the eighty-seven warriors who surrendered, forty were wounded.[12] Besides these, there were 184 women and 147 children, a total of 418 prisoners out of the original 800 who fled from Idaho. The troops lost twenty-six killed, including two officers, and of the forty-two wounded, four were officers.[13]

Joseph, his older wife and daughter Sarah in exile with White Bird, had left only his younger wife and his baby girl, less than five months old.[14] He had come to the end of the trail, but behind him he and his tribesmen left an illustrious record. The Nez Perces never at any time had more than three hundred warriors, and their fighting strength was diminished with each battle, yet they had engaged in all some two thousand soldiers. The troops' casualties for the campaign were 126 killed and 140 wounded, whereas the Nez Perces' fighting force lost

---

courtesy. He was the son of the sister of old Chief White Bird. At the battle of the Big Hole, he was holding the hand of his mother, and both were running for the bushes. A bullet from one of the army men's rifles, struck his thumb and cut it off as well as a finger of his mother."

Old Chief White Bird was murdered by one of his own men about 1882, according to Yellow Wolf, after he, in the role of medicine man, unsuccessfully treated the small son of another Nez Perce medicine man. The dying boy stated that it was White Bird's "power" killing him. When another son died making the same claim, the father shot the old chief. He was buried near Fort McLeod. McWhorter, *Hear Me, My Chiefs!*, p. 524.

[12] Miles states, in *Report of Secretary of War*, 1877, I, 655, that twenty-five were killed and forty-six wounded.

[13] These figures are based on Brady, *Northwestern Fights and Fighters*, p. 39. Haines, *Red Eagles of the Northwest*, p. 318, lists 127 killed and 147 wounded. He compiled his own list.

[14] Joseph's younger wife had been wounded at the Big Hole but she recovered. He mentions her in his own story. See p. 320 of this text.

151 killed and 88 wounded, which does not include the loss of women and children.[15]

The Nez Perces had fought eleven engagements, five of these being pitched battles, of which they had won three, tied one, and lost one. Howard's troops marched in pursuit some 1,321 miles in seventy-five days, and the Indians about 1,800 miles, since they had to double and loop and backtrack. Judged by any standard, the fighting Nez Perces had accomplished a military exploit of the first magnitude. Although McLaughlin observes that Joseph had made "one of the greatest campaigns in the history of the world's wars," the credit properly belongs to the five nontreaty bands. When McLaughlin asked him where he got his military knowledge, Joseph replied, "The Great Spirit puts it in the heart and head of man to know how to defend himself."[16]

The chief admitted, however, that he and his people had watched the cavalry drill "and they could maneuvre as the white troops did in time of peace."[17] This keen observation, intelligently applied, enabled the Nez Perces to use "every obstructive and offensive device known" to the science of military tactics. From his conversations with Joseph, McLaughlin brought out that in each engagement the chief knew accurately the number of troops opposing him until the final battle. Had the Indians spread a chain of scouts, they might have avoided the last fight.

Both Howard and Miles paid admiring tribute to the great chieftain. In his report to the Secretary of War, Miles states:

The Nez Perces are the boldest men and best marksmen

---

[15] Brady, *op. cit.*, p. 39. A revised list, compiled later by McWhorter, gives the Indian losses as ninety-six killed, including thirty-six women and children. While these figures may be too low, they seem more reasonable than the number of dead given in Brady as the Nez Perce mortalities were consistently fewer, except at the Big Hole, than were the troops' casualties. McWhorter, *Hear Me, My Chiefs!*, p. 501.

[16] McLaughlin, *My Friend the Indian*, p. 352.

[17] *Ibid.*

of any Indians I have ever encountered, and Chief Joseph is a man of more sagacity and intelligence than any Indian I have ever met; he counseled against the war, and against the usual cruelities practiced by Indians, and is far more humane than such Indians as Crazy Horse and Sitting Bull.[18]

Probably because Joseph had struggled through diplomacy and arms for thirty-three years for his Wal-lam-wat-kin's tribal liberty, and because he was the only head chief of the original five warring bands to surrender, the whites' legend grew around him as having been the supreme military leader who planned the campaign and masterminded the retreat. As the Nez Perce evidence clearly shows, though, Looking Glass and Poker Joe (Lean Elk) served as war chiefs on most of the march. The Indians had no overall plan of campaign and they fought a defensive war. Their strategy and tactics on the retreat were worked out in numerous councils of the chiefs to suit the immediate exigencies as they arose. Yet Joseph became the symbol of the fighting Nez Perces' skill and courage, and through no overt act on his part. Although not a military genius, Joseph is still outstanding as a peace chief, as a great diplomat among warriors, as a guardian of his people, and he is distinguished for his Lincoln-type humanity toward friend and foe as well as for his integrity of character.

---

[18] Miles, in *Report of Secretary of War*, 1877, I, 529.

PART IV
Later History

CHAPTER XXIV

Prisoners of War

AFTER Joseph's surrender on October 5, the troops were busy stacking the Indians' guns, burying the dead, and preparing the wounded for their long journey to the fort hospital. General Howard left Miles at the battlefield on October 7, and rejoined him on the thirteenth at the Missouri River for a conference at the colonel's request.

Miles took charge of the Nez Perces, now prisoners of war. The officers agreed they should be taken to the colonel's headquarters post on Tongue River. On the seventh his command began its slow march over the snow-covered plains to the Missouri River. Lieutenant Maus had been sent north to try to overtake the escaped Nez Perces, especially Chief White Bird. He did capture a few stragglers and then returned to the command.

The troops met up with Sturgis' Seventh Cavalry which remained in the field to watch any movements of the hostile Sioux. Several of the wounded soldiers and Indians died on the way and had to be buried beside the trail. At the Missouri River as many wounded as possible were sent down on the steamer. General Howard, with his infantry and artillery battalions, embarked on the steamer *Benton* for St. Louis. His troops went back to their headquarters post at Fort Vancouver, Washington. The cavalry the general had dispatched overland on September 27 to its various headquarters posts in the Northwest. From St. Louis, Howard continued to Chicago for an interview with General Sheridan.

Escorted by Miles's column the Nez Perce prisoners continued their march to the Yellowstone. "There were three battalions of well-equipped, hardy resolute soldiers, with artillery," the colonel writes, "besides upward of four hundred prisoners; and on the opposite flank, some distance away, were driven over six hundred of the captured stock, while in the rear were the travois and ambulances, bearing the wounded, followed by the pack-trains and wagon trains, and all covered by advance guards, flankers, and rear guards."[1]

The thirty Sioux and Cheyenne scouts attached to Miles's command were each permitted "to select five captured ponies," nor did they pick the poorest ones. The scouts then hurried on and reached the fort ahead of the troops, causing much consternation, as the families of the officers and men feared for their safety. Their fears were put to rest, however, when the interpreter arrived and disclosed the first accurate news of the Bearpaw battle.

Three days later the command made its appearance in full force on the buttes to the west. The cantonment, later called Fort Keogh, lay on the south bank of the Yellowstone near the mouth of Tongue River and the present site of Miles City. The soldiers and Nez Perces descended the winding trail down the bluffs to the waiting ferry.

A royal welcome awaited the returning victorious troops. It is best described in Colonel Miles's own words:

> The families of the officers and soldiers and all the other people at the garrison, including the band of the Fifth Infantry, citizens and Indians, lined the bank of the Yellowstone; and as some of the principal officers, including myself together with Chief Joseph and one or two of the principal Indians, stepped into the boat, and it moved from the northern shore, the band struck up "Hail to the Chief," and then as we neared the other shore, it suddenly changed to "O, no! no! not for Joseph," which it played for a short time, and then went back to the former strain.[2]

Miles reports that the "Nez Perce Indians were given

[1] Miles, *Personal Recollections of General Miles*, p. 277.

[2] *Ibid.*, pp. 278-79.

a comfortable camp on the right bank of the Yellowstone, and it was my purpose to keep them there during the winter and send them back to Idaho in the spring."[3]

---

[3] *Ibid.*, p. 279.

CHAPTER XXV

"Somebody Has Got Our Horses"

JOSEPH and the remnants of the five warring bands became another problem to the War Department. What should be done with them now that they were captured? It is true they had surrendered with the agreement that they should return to their own country, but how to get them there? Miles had already written to the Secretary of War:

> As I received no reply to my request for orders or information that should govern my movements, I acted on what I supposed was the original design of the government to place these Indians on their reservation, and so informed them, and also sent assurances to the war parties that were out, and those who had escaped, that they would be taken to Tongue River and retained for a time, and sent across the mountains as soon as the weather permitted in the spring. They cheerfully complied.[1]

The nation's press of the time had dubbed the Nez Perces "Howard's Indians," since he had been originally sent to round them up and remove them to the Lapwai Reservation. He used his official discretionary powers and issued the following written order to Miles:

Headquarters Department of the Columbia,
In the Field, Battle-field of Eagle
Creek, near Bear Paw Mountains,
Montana, October 7, 1877.

Col. Nelson A. Miles,
Fifth Infantry, Commanding District of the Yellowstone.

[1] *Report of Secretary of War*, 1877, I, 529. Report of Col. Miles.

Colonel: On account of the cost of transportation of the Nez Perces prisoners to the Pacific coast, I deem it best to retain them all at some place within your district, where they can be kept under military control till next spring. Then, unless you receive instructions from higher authority, *you are hereby directed* to have them sent under proper guard to my department, where I will take charge of them, and carry out the instructions I have already received. . . .

O. O. Howard,
Brigadier-General, Commanding Department.[2]

All of which is evidence that the two officers were working for the best interests of the Indians—an important point because of the suffering and misery that the Nez Perces later went through, due to "higher authority" breaking the promises and countermanding the orders of Howard and Miles. But more of that later.

Within ten days after the Nez Perces' arrival at Fort Keogh, orders came from "higher authority" to send them eight hundred miles by steamer to Fort Lincoln near Bismarck, Dakota Territory, the reason given being that subsistence would be cheaper there. And Joseph's medley of bands were fairly launched, like the Cherokee Indians, on their own "trail of tears."

Since it was low-water season on the Yellowstone, fourteen flatboats were used to transport the Nez Perces from Fort Keogh. These barges had been used to carry garden truck from Livingston to the post for the soldiers' mess. Each boat could accommodate from twenty to twenty-five people, and in them the wounded, the aged, the sick, and the children were placed. One white man took charge of each boat to handle the tiller, dole out the rations, and guard the prisoners. The able-bodied warriors, including Joseph, and a few women marched overland to Fort Lincoln, escorted by a detachment of the Seventh Cavalry and a wagon train under command of Colonel Miles.[3]

---

[2] Wood, "Chief Joseph, the Nez Percé," *Century Magazine*, May, 1884, p. 142.

[3] Major General (then Lieutenant) Scott's Troop I, Seventh Cavalry, and a company of the First Infantry were detailed to con-

Those on the flatboats drifted down the current during the daytime and tied up to the bank at night, always on the alert, however, for roving hostile parties of Sioux. The weather remained sunny with cool, frosty nights. Rations were supplied by the army commissary at Fort Keogh, and were supplemented by game killed along the riverbanks. To the Nez Perces' credit be it noted, the lone white guard had no hesitation in loaning his gun to the hunters, and he permitted the older boys to fashion bows and arrows.

Years afterward Nelson Titus recalled how one flatboat taking the Nez Perces down the Yellowstone to the Missouri was so heavily loaded that the deck was near waterline. An Indian woman with a papoose strapped to her back stooped over to dip drinking water, and the child fell into the river. The mother immediately jumped in after it. The boat, however, did not stop, and that was the last seen of either.[4]

In passing the Mandan Agency, the officer in charge of the prisoners stopped for two hours to get supplies. During the interval, according to Miles, the Mandans and Nez Perces curiously investigated each other. One of the latter tribe, an old man of seventy named "George Washington," told the officer when they were again floating down the river, "Those Mandans back there are bad

---

duct the Nez Perce prisoners from Fort Buford, near the mouth of the Yellowstone, to Bismarck, 225 miles away. He rode in the wagon with Joseph together with Interpreter Chapman. General Scott's comments on Joseph and the Nez Perces are in line with the consensus of all other Army men who had contact with these unhappy Indians. He writes that "Joseph was then a tall, stalwart, active, fine-looking young man of great force and dignity. His life in Kansas and the Indian Territory, where many of his people died, did much to break his body and spirit; this was quite patent at the times I saw him in Washington in after years. He and his people were among the finest Indians America produced, but they were treated most unjustly by the government, first as to their lands, and secondly in their deportation to Oklahoma, where they could not live. These Nez Perces received Lewis and Clark, Bonneville, and many other white men with great hospitality and kindness, but their treatment by the white man is a black page in our history." Scott, *Some Memories of a Soldier*, p. 84.

[4] Nelson C. Titus, "Last Stand of the Nez Perces," *Washington Historical Quarterly*, VI, No. 3 (July, 1915), 152.

Indians." The officer inquired why, and the old man answered, "Because they stole two Nez Perce blankets." Now the Nez Perces had lost nearly everything on their long march from Idaho, and had given up all their guns and horses. So the officer was properly sympathetic, and then the thought struck him to ask George Washington if the Nez Perces had taken anything that belonged to the Mandans. "Oh, yes," came the truthful reply, "we got away with four buffalo robes."[5]

However, Fred Bond, in charge of one of the flatboats, relates a very different reception from the Mandans, who lined the shore ready to start hostilities, possibly fearing the Nez Perces were a raiding party's advance guard.

> Two middle-aged Indians kept crowding in the river towards the boat. I halted them but still they pressed towards the boat then I thought of what Billy Edwards the light weight champ of years ago had taught me at Woodhaven, L. I. A good upper cut to point of chin the result would be a knock out blow, so I stept quickly towards those two and gave each of them a good upper cut. They each fell in the river knocked out. . . . Then I backed to the boat and stood there with folded arms. I heard a small moan behind me and I knew it was Shades of Night [a woman captive so named by Bond] ready to sink her eight inches of sharp steel to the hilt on the first one who toutch our boat, then I seen two young bucks trying to work their way with a bull boat to our stern. . . . I plunged out into deeper water and shoved their bull boat out into swifter water and they was carried further down stream. . . .[6]

Finally, the official in charge of the post convinced the Mandans that the Nez Perces were present by authority of the United States government. The boat then "pushed off safely except the small Mandan boys pelted us with rocks on our way till I got my gun. That bluff them away."[7]

On arrival at Bismarck, Joseph was the guest of honor

[5] Miles, *Personal Recollections of General Miles*, p. 280.

[6] Fred G. Bond, *Flatboating on the Yellowstone*. A pamphlet.

[7] *Ibid.*

at a dinner given jointly by the ladies of the town and those of Fort Lincoln. The Bismarck *Tribune* for November 21, 1877, reprinted the following invitation:

To Joseph, Head Chief of Nez Perces.
Sir:—Desiring to show you our kind feelings and the admiration we have for your bravery and humanity, as exhibited in your recent conflict with the forces of the United States, we most cordially invited you to dine with us at the Sheridan House, in this city. The dinner to be given at 1½ P. M. to-day.

Joseph and the other chiefs named, about twelve o'clock, held a reception in the Sheridan Parlors, and all were presented to a number of the ladies of the house. The Indians were told that this respect was on account of "their humanity to our soldier prisoners."

Joseph, half starved for months during the campaign, gave evidence of his pleasure when his favorite dish of salmon was served to him.

Apparently Miles was distrustful of the government's attitude toward the Nez Perces and feared they would not be given a fair deal, for in his report to Secretary McCrary he warmly urged:

As these people have been hitherto loyal to the government and friends of the white race from the time their country was first explored, and in their skilful campaigns have spared hundreds of lives and thousands of dollars' worth of property that they might have destroyed, and as they have, in my opinion, been grossly wronged in years past, have lost most of their warriors, their homes, property, and everything except a small amount of clothing, I have the honor to recommend that ample provision be made for their civilization, and to enable them to become self-sustaining. They are sufficiently intelligent to appreciate the consideration which, in my opinion, is justly due them from the government.[8]

And did the Secretary of War faithfully fulfill the conditions of surrender, and hearken to his military experts

[8] Miles, in *Report of Secretary of War*, 1877, I, 529.

in the field? Assuredly not! With seeming governmental perversity McCrary ordered the Indians to Fort Leavenworth, Kansas, in November, after a short time at Bismarck, Dakota Territory. They made this stage of their journey by train. Here, amid unhealthful conditions, they remained until the Indian Bureau could assume jurisdiction over them.

The entire responsibility for not honoring Howard's and Miles's promises did not rest wholly on McCrary's shoulders, however. It would appear that General W. T. Sherman, acting in his capacity of General of the Army, shared some of it, for he had written to the secretary: "They should never again be allowed to return to Oregon or to Lapwai."[9]

Yet, in that same document, Sherman admitted that the Nez Perce War was "one of the most extraordinary Indian wars of which there is any record. The Indians throughout displayed a courage and skill that elicited universal praise; they abstained from scalping, let captive women go free, did not commit indiscriminate murder of peaceful families, which is usual, and fought with almost scientific skill, using advance and rear guards, skirmish lines, and field fortifications."[10] But admiration did not prompt him to respect this honorable foe in deed—not even to the extent of making restitution of their property.

However, General Philip Sheridan, as commander of the Division of the Missouri with headquarters in Chicago, had issued the first order for the Indians' removal to Fort Lincoln or Fort Riley, thus transferring them from Howard's departmental authority. The general was unable to persuade Sheridan to execute his and Miles's plan for the prisoners.

What explanation was made to Joseph after he had acted in good faith, had laid down his arms, given up over eleven hundred horses and more than one hundred

---

[9] Sherman, in *Report of Secretary of War*, 1877, I, 15.

[10] *Ibid.*

saddles? He was told that if he were permitted to go back to his own country more bloodshed might occur between the Nez Perces and the relatives of the murdered whites. Settlers in the Wallowa Valley and around Lapwai had been flooding the government with petitions to keep the Indians out of the Northwest, fearful, perhaps, that the lands they had seized from those Indians might be given back to their original owners. Yet it was White Bird's band, not Joseph's, which had brought on the war!

When the terms of surrender were violated by the government, Joseph did not dig up the tomahawk and go on the warpath again. No, he, the red savage, spoke with a straight tongue, and was a gentleman of his word! Nor did he blame Howard or Miles for what his people suffered. He remarked only, "Somebody has got our horses." From the time the Indians relinquished their ponies in 1877 until 1885—eight long years—one gross injustice followed another. But Joseph never gave up hope that some day a repentant government would carry out the pledged word of Colonel Miles.

Meanwhile, at Leavenworth, the Nez Perces sickened and died in a climate entirely unsuited to their constitutions. Acclimated to a mountain plateau country, they were now forced to live in the hot, malarious lowlands of the Missouri River bottom, with only river water for drinking and cooking purposes. Joseph vainly protested; like the humanitarian he was he always had the interests of his people at heart. Says he, "I cannot tell how much my heart suffered for my people while at Leavenworth. The Great Spirit Chief who rules above seemed to be looking some other way, and did not see what was being done to my people."[11]

Miles used his influence in Washington to have his promise kept to the Nez Perces—likewise in vain.

In July of 1878 they were ordered onto a reservation in the Indian Territory, which Congress had apportioned for them on both sides of the Salt Fork of the

[11] "An Indian's Views of Indian Affairs," *North American Review*, April, 1879, p. 430.

Arkansas. By then but 410 persons remained of the 431 sent to Leavenworth. Three more died en route to their new home. Two hundred and sixty were ill, and shortly thereafter one fourth of the survivors died.[12] This appalling mortality was due largely to malaria contracted at Fort Leavenworth.

They were first located with the Quapaws, but here again they found the climate very unhealthy—so much so that the Commissioner of Indian Affairs, E. A. Hayt, visited the band and asked Joseph to travel with him to search for a healthier reservation, or at least one suited more to the Nez Perces' liking.

Like all other officials who came in contact with him, the commissioner was duly impressed with Joseph and the justice of his cause. Hayt wrote a testimonial in his annual report to that effect:

> I traveled with him in Kansas and the Indian Territory for nearly a week and found him to be one of the most gentlemanly and well-behaved Indians that I ever met. He is bright and intelligent, and is anxious for the welfare of his people. . . . The Nez Perces are very much superior to the Osages and Pawnees in the Indian Territory; they are even brighter than the Poncas, and care should be taken to place them where they will thrive.[13]

Joseph reported that he liked the land on the Ponca Reservation, although it had no mountains or rivers and the water was warm, and he feared all his people would die since the Indians already in possession of the country were constantly dying.

At this time Joseph got permission to go to Washington to plead his own case before the Great Chief Father, President Hayes, and on down the line of bureaucrats to Congress. He took along his friend, Yellow Bull, and an interpreter. Can you wonder that his head was in a whirl over the innumerable chiefs the white men had, who

---

[12] *Annual Report of U.S. Commissioner of Indian Affairs*, 1878, pp. 32-35.

[13] *Fourteenth Annual Report, Bureau of American Ethnology*, Part II, 1892-93, p. 715.

were all allowed "to talk so many different ways, and promise so many different things?" The chief's impression of the white man's government might be summed up in the sentence: "It makes my heart sick when I remember all the good words and all the broken promises."[14]

While in Washington Joseph gave an interview on his life, published in the *North American Review* for April, 1879, under the title of "An Indian's Views of Indian Affairs"—a rare and valuable document.

His intelligent mind was fully cognizant of the red man's problem, and he expressed his views to Bishop Hare who reported the interview. The chief said:

> I know that my race must change. We cannot hold our own with the white men as we are. We only ask an even chance to live as other men live. We ask to be recognized as men. We ask that the same law shall work alike on all men. If the Indian breaks the law, punish him by the law. If the white man breaks the law, punish him also.[15]

And that, you may recognize, as the principles on which our country was founded; the justification for our Revolutionary War; and one of the underlying causes of our terrible Civil War. But Joseph had yet to learn that our American nation has two sets of ideals—one a set of ideals which are rammed into the heads of schoolchildren, and the other a working set of practical purposes that are twisted and warped by politicians to fit the circumstance and the occasion.

Joseph went on to voice the cry of our forefathers in 1775, the cry of all oppressed men throughout the world, in an impassioned speech lyrical in its rhythm:

> Let me be a free man—free to travel, free to stop, free to work, free to trade where I choose, free to choose my own teachers, free to follow the religion of my fathers, free to think and talk and act for myself—and I will obey every law, or submit to the penalty.[16]

---

[14] "An Indian's Views . . . ," *op. cit.*, p. 432.

[15] *Ibid.*, p. 433.

[16] *Ibid.*

In closing he expressed his own idea of an Utopia that white man and red might share alike:

> Whenever the White man treats the Indian as they treat each other, then we shall have no more wars. We shall be all alike—brothers of one father and one mother, with one sky above us and one country around us, and one government for all. Then the Great Spirit Chief who rules above will smile upon this land, and send rain to wash out the bloody spots made by brothers' hands upon the face of the earth. For this time the Indian race is waiting and praying. I hope that no more groans of wounded men and women will ever go to the ear of the Great Spirit Chief above, and that all people may be one people.
>
> In-mut-too-yah-lat-lat has spoken for his people.[17]

In discussing the Indian problem with Miles, Joseph summed it up with shrewd logic:

> The greatest want of the Indian is a system of law by which controversies between Indians, and between Indians and white men, can be settled without appealing to physical force. [He went on to deduce that] the want of law is the great source of disorder among Indians. They understand the operation of laws, and, if there were any statutes, the Indians would be perfectly content to place themselves in the hands of a proper tribunal, and would not take the righting of their wrongs into their own hands, or retaliate, as they now do, without the law.[18]

And what was the outcome of all this impassioned oratory? Why, simply that the Nez Perces were removed to the Ponca Reservation in June of 1879, and given a reserve containing 90,735 acres!

They made valiant attempts to become civilized and to adapt themselves to their new country. In time, with government assistance, they acquired a small herd of cattle and horses, raised their own vegetables and considerable grain. In February, 1880, a day school was

[17] *Ibid.*

[18] Miles, "The Indian's Problem," *North American Review*, 1879, p. 312.

opened, conducted by James Reuben, a Christianized Nez Perce who journeyed from the Idaho reservation to help his people in exile. Two others who came with him soon took ill and returned to Lapwai. In May of 1883 the school was closed, and, securing the permission of the War Department, Reuben took twenty-nine Nez Perces, the majority widows and orphans of the war, back to Idaho.

Their homecoming is thus described by an eyewitness, Kate McBeth:

> After him [James Reuben] rode the weariest, dustiest, most forlorn band of women with blankets and belongings behind each woman on her horse. Two men besides James were with them. But the ponies! The poor ponies, after such a journey of perhaps three hundred miles! But they and the captives had been well drilled. A half circle was formed by them facing the agent's office. Their friends ranged themselves behind. James Reuben, from his saddle, with the oratory for which he was noted, made the opening speech, gracefully guiding his horse's head this way and that, as he addressed the now well formed half-circle. He pathetically described their sorrows in that far-off land, the hardships of the journey home, and the many they had left sleeping among strangers. The agent responded. James Reuben dismounted, drawing his horse's bridle over his left arm, leaving his right hand free to extend to his friends. Each captive did the same. Hundreds of friends gathered around, took them by the hand, and oh! such weeping and wailing in remembrance of the graves in that distant land! Doubtless there was great joy in their hearts, but just then, the sorrow exceeded.[19]

The captives remaining in Indian Territory did not find the Ponca country any healthier than Joseph had feared, for Agent Jordan reported in 1881 that the tribe numbered 328, and there had been few births. They had no houses and were insufficiently sheltered in tepees from the heavy rains. Because of the lack of a church they

---

[19] Kate McBeth, *The Nez Percés Since Lewis and Clark*, pp. 100-101. Since the railroad did not extend beyond Boise at the time, the Indians had to complete the journey to Lapwai by horseback.

were compelled "to meet under an arbor covered with branches and leaves." Agent Jordan continues:

> They keep the Sabbath-day holy, abstaining from all kinds of work, and the service at the arbor is attended by every member of the tribe, whether a communicant or not. ... Poor as they are they have contributed $45 with which to buy the lumber, etc., necessary to build a house for their pastor....
>
> Love of country and home, as in all brave people, is very largely developed in this tribe, and they long for the valleys, the mountains, the streams, and the clear springs of water of their old home. They are cleanly to a fault, and most of them have adopted the dress, and as far as possible the habits, of the white man. They keep their stock in good order, and are a hard-working, painstaking people. I hope by the time winter comes on, to have them all in comfortable houses.[20]

Certainly the criminals in our penitentiaries were given far more humane treatment! At least, the Indians had one consolation—they had a sympathetic agent.

---

[20] *Annual Report of U.S. Commissioner of Indian Affairs*, 1881, p. 94.

CHAPTER XXVI

Return from Exile

IT TOOK four long years yet of "recommendations" on the part of agents, and pleadings on the part of white friends, before an apathetic Congress could start its august machinery into motion to remedy the situation. The Indian Rights Association "and other Eastern philanthropists were active on behalf of the Nez Perces and the Presbyterian church took up their cause." In May, 1884, Congress received fourteen petitions "from groups of citizens from Kansas to Connecticut, ranging from mass meetings to private individuals, all demanding the return of Joseph's Nez Perces to Idaho."[1]

Finally in the spring of 1885 a remnant of the five bands—268 souls—were returned to the Northwest over the Union Pacific and Oregon Short Line. They were met at Pocatello by Captain Frank Baldwin, who was acting judge advocate of the Columbia Military Department. Here the Nez Perces were divided into two parties, one group of 118 persons going under military escort to the Lapwai Reservation in North Idaho. Due to local prejudice there, Joseph and the remaining 150 of his people proceeded to the Colville Reservation at Nespelem, Washington, where the chief located his home on the banks of the river.

In the *Report of the Commissioner of Indian Affairs*, 1885, the reason given for sending the majority of the Nez Perces to Colville was "on account of indictments said to be pending in Idaho against Chief Joseph and some of

[1] McWhorter, *Hear Me, My Chiefs!*, pp. 536, 538.

Photo by courtesy of Miss Mary M. Crawford

Joseph at Lapwai in 1895

his immediate followers, for murders committed by them before their removal to Indian Territory in 1878, and numerous threats were made that, in the event of their return to Idaho, extreme measures would be taken by the citizens to avenge wrongs alleged to have been perpetrated by these people over eight years ago." Yet, two of the three guilty young men—all were members of White Bird's band—had themselves paid the supreme penalty, and the third, young Swan Necklace (John Minthon) had sought refuge among the Sioux. Their chief had died an exile in Canada in 1882!

The Indians were in a destitute condition, thinly clad, without cattle, tools, or farming implements, even without sufficient food. Colonel Miles writes that some of the soldiers were moved to pity and shared their rations with the unfortunates.[2]

The other bands of Nez Perces at Lapwai most heartily welcomed the returned exiles. Old friends met again, families were reunited, and the absent faces were mourned with loud wails.

Somewhat different was the reception accorded Joseph's group by old Chief Skolaskin of the San-poil tribe, who resented the Nez Perces' presence as an unpardonable intrusion on his inalienable domain. It was necessary for the Indian Agent, Major Gwydir, to call for troops from the fort at Spokane before Skolaskin would consent to Joseph's peacefully occupying his share of the reservation.[3] That Joseph did not come by choice made no difference to Skolaskin.

So Chief Joseph, warrior and diplomat, settled down to spend most of his days in meditation and brooding, growing old and gray.

Judge Lippincott[4] recalled a meeting with him on the train about September of 1885. At the time he was in

[2] Miles, *Personal Recollections of General Miles*, p. 412.

[3] Fuller, *A History of the Pacific Northwest*, p. 276.

[4] Judge William I. Lippincott, of Butte, Montana, recounted this anecdote to the author and Dan McGrath in a personal interview at Los Angeles, California, in 1934.

white man's clothes, but wore moccasins and had his hair in two long braids. He was still broad-shouldered and deep-chested despite the years of suffering he had gone through. The chief was then around forty-five, and impressed the judge as being very reserved and democratic in manner, and expressive of countenance rather than as stoical as the proverbial Indian. Although he appeared to be depressed, he was glad to meet everybody and shook hands with anyone who spoke to him. He was generally recognized on the train, but did not converse at length with any of the whites. He had his hands full, as three or four Indian women who accompanied him were ill. So far as the judge could learn they were not related to Joseph, but, of course, were Nez Perces. All were wrapped in blankets, and Joseph exercised tender care and gentleness in looking after them. The judge gave each woman a dollar apiece, at which the chief smiled, and his feminine companions beamed their pleasure.

Ex-Sergeant Martin L. Brown told in an interview his impressions upon meeting the Nez Perce chieftain:

I never met Joseph personally until after the war was over. I was on a detail that took nineteen Indian prisoners to Fort Lapwai, Idaho. To return them to Joseph, who was then in the Indian Territory, we had to sail down the Snake and Columbia rivers to Portland, re-ship to San Francisco, then take the Union Pacific to Fort Leavenworth, Kansas, and finally a stage-coach to the Indian Territory. This round-about journey was necessary as the Union Pacific was the only railroad in the west at that time.

When we delivered the prisoners to Joseph, he shook hands with each one of our detail, and appeared quite friendly. He apparently felt no resentment toward the soldiers. His manner was grave, and he had the air of one used to being respected. All the Indians in the camp showed deference toward him and seemed to like him. Joseph was an honest man, and really believed the government unjustly took his land from him. As for the war, he thought he was doing right by fighting for his ancestral lands and finally for his liberty.[5]

[5] Addison Howard in *Sunday Missoulian*, June 14, 1925, Missoula, Montana. From a newspaper feature article.

In 1889 Joseph went to Portland, Oregon, to sit for a bas-relief plaque of his head by the sculptor, Olin L. Warner. Copies of this plaque now hang in the Portland Art Gallery and the Metropolitan Museum in New York.

Colonel C. E. S. Wood, Howard's aide-de-camp during the Nez Perce campaign, was practicing law in Portland in 1892 when Joseph invited his thirteen-year-old son, Erskine, to visit him at Nespelem. This incident illustrates the tolerance of the chief, and the trust placed in him by the boy's father.

Erskine left Portland by himself, July 3, 1892, and spent five months alone with Joseph and his band. So greatly did the lad enjoy himself that he returned the next year for another three months. According to Erskine's diary, he accompanied Joseph and his tribespeople into the mountains on their annual fall hunt after deer, and was present at the Indian dances and feasts, being the only white boy so honored. Under the old chief's teaching, Erskine learned the Nez Perce customs and arts.

During the summers, he records, Joseph's people spent much of their time in horse racing, accompanied by the inevitable gambling which that sport always prompts. The boy's description of the domestic life of Joseph's people at Nespelem is interesting:

> The Indian camp is usually in two or more long rows of tepees. Sometimes two or three families occupy one lodge. When they are hunting and drying meat for their winter supply, several lodges are put together, making one big lodge about thirty feet long, in which are two or three fires instead of one. They say that it dries the meat better.[6]

After the hunt Joseph divided the meat equally among his people.

The following excerpt shows the lasting influence of the *tewats,* or medicine men, on the chief, despite his increasing contacts with white civilization:

[6] Erskine Wood, "A Boy's Visit to Chief Joseph," *St. Nicholas Magazine,* September, 1893, p. 816.

I was sitting with Joseph in the tepee once, when a lizard crawled in. I discovered it, and showed it to Joseph. He was very solemn, and I asked him what was the matter. "A medicine-man sent it here to do me harm. You have very good eyes to discover the tricks of the medicine-men." I was going to throw it into the fire, but he stopped me, saying: "If you burn it, it will make the medicine-men angry. You must kill it some other way."[7]

Erskine's boy companion was Niky Mowitz, whose father had been killed in the Nez Perce War. Niky was the nephew of Joseph and had been adopted by the chief. This speaks eloquently for Joseph's inherently humane nature and for his grief over the loss of his own four sons.

---

[7] *Ibid.*

CHAPTER XXVII

The Trail to the Setting Sun

TWELVE years passed before Joseph again left his beloved Northwest. When he did so in April of 1897 he made a voluntary visit to New York City for the dedication of Grant's tomb as a guest of Buffalo Bill, and rode beside the former scout in the parade. While visiting the metropolis Joseph stayed at the old Astor House and dressed, by request we may well presume, in the full Indian regalia of buckskin, which caused quite a furore among the fashionable guests. They must have been rather disillusioned, though, by the great chief's gentlemanly manners and his sly sense of humor. He gave an exhibition of the latter when a young woman, wearing a hat decorated with an artificial aviary and garden, asked him, "Did you ever scalp anybody?"

Joseph cogitated on the matter for a while, then turned to the interpreter and replied quietly, pointing to the young lady's hat, "Tell her that I have nothing in my collection as fine as that."

Of course, he was besieged by Easterners who were thrilled to get sight of or talk to a genuine, "honest-to-gosh," red Indian chief out of the wild and woolly West, who had actually led his tribespeople on the warpath against the American army. And the obliging chief graciously submitted to various interviews. In one of these he gave his impressions of Gotham, and if he were something of a curiosity to New Yorkers, they and their ways were no less queer to him. He said:

This East is strange to me. I do not understand it at all. The green of the trees and the grass is not here. The quiet of the woods is missing. It is all dirt and noise and hurry and the people are strange. I notice many things as I walk, and they puzzle me. The white men have put up buildings which one cannot see the top of. They tell me people stay there and labor during the day. I have had white men who know the ways of their fellows tell me many strange things. I can understand a little English myself, but I cannot speak any. The white men are very wonderful and skilful, to do some of these things. They send the cars along on a rope [trolley-cars] and the buildings up into the sky. They have railroads in the air [the elevated trains], and they go up and down the buildings [elevators] without moving themselves. I have heard much of these wonders in Washington, and one or two of them I saw in Portland once. But here in New York it is all wonders, and I do not understand how the people live. It is good for me to see these things before I die, and so I must see them now, for I do not ever expect to leave my people for so long again.[1]

On this trip Joseph was accompanied by a subchief, an interpreter, and a young Sioux. G. O. Shields, who was acquainted with the chief, relates another incident of the visit. It seems that he invited Joseph and the other Indians to a dinner at the Camp Fire Club, to be held on a Saturday night. On the Monday preceding he told the chief that he would call for his party on Saturday afternoon, and take them to the hotel where the dinner would be given. Mr. Shields continues:

On Wednesday, I went down to call on Joseph and remind him of the engagement, lest he forget. When I told the clerk I would like to see Chief Joseph, he said, "He is not here any more."

I said, "Not here? How is that?"

"They all left here yesterday morning."

"Why that's strange. I understood they were to stay through the week and they promised to dine with the Camp Fire Club."

"Yes, but Chief Joseph said he wanted to get where he could see some trees."[2]

---

[1] Edward S. Ellis, *Thrilling Adventures among the American Indians*, p. 240.

[2] Shields, *The Blanket Indians of the Northwest*, p. 117.

Comparatively happy again back among his beloved trees in Washington State, Joseph devoted himself to his people—that remnant of his band living on the Colville Reservation. He was a progressive Indian in that he had always evinced the greatest interest in the white man's education for Nez Perce children.

The aging chief's fame had so far spread that he was considered a proper subject for a master of letters thesis. The young student, Edmond S. Meany, who became interested in this living topic for his academic study while attending the University of Wisconsin, was destined to become chairman of the History Department at the University of Washington in Seattle. The young man became acquainted with the old chief and paid him several visits. Through the kind permission of the late Professor Meany the following chapter is quoted from his master's thesis:

The week beginning with June 21, 1901, was devoted by the writer to a trip to Nespilem, on the Colville Indian Reservation, State of Washington, for the purpose of visiting Chief Joseph and his surviving warriors and to learn something of their present conditions. . . .

The Colville Reservation has been cut in two. The Government has thus far neglected to pay the Indians the $1,500,000 agreed upon for the northern half. The southern half has also been thrown open for mineral entries and the familiar haunts and pasture lands of the Indians are now being overrun by a constant stream of prospectors. The writer visited one mining camp within two miles of Chief Joseph's tepee where the herds of Indian ponies are startled twice a day by the blasting of the rocks. At the sub-agency are two stores where these miners procure supplies. . . .

Chief Moses of the Columbians had been located on the Nespilem before Chief Joseph's band was brought there. He had gone to Washington City and secured many favors for his people such as a saw-mill, grist-mill, physician, blacksmith and school and a yearly salary for himself of one thousand dollars. He also procured certain allowances of agricultural implements.

Chief Joseph got no salary but the Government has issued his people regular rations of food, clothes and agricultural implements. From this fact and from the fact that he and the members of his band are supposed to ask permission if they wish to leave the reservation it is construed that Joseph's band are still practically prisoners of war.

The best agriculturalists in this vicinity are the remnants of the original Nespilems, who first occupied the land. They live in frame houses, till the soil and, with unusual pride, refuse to receive aid from the Government. If they get a reaper from the Government store-house they insist on paying for it in hay or labor.

Joseph's band, on the other hand, being supplied with everything they need, do not progress in the industrial activities. It is claimed that this idleness is a bad influence on the other Indians and the agents have been asking the Government to curtail and finally discontinue all rations to the Nez Perces.[3]

In order to get lumber for houses, barns or other purposes, the Indians go to the hills and cut the logs, which they haul to the mill. Then they assist the Government sawyer to cut the logs into whatever shape is desired. They mark their own logs and keep track of all the details carrying the finished product to their homes.

The Government built for Chief Joseph, a small, rough-board, battened house and a barn on the farm he selected about four miles from the sub-agency. The Chief will not live in his house and the roof of his barn is broken in. He prefers to live in the traditional tepee, winter and summer, and this tepee he has pitched near the sub-agency so he can be near his people and the school.

The teacher of the school, Barnett Stillwell, who has been there for four years, says that Chief Joseph has manifested great interest in the children. He often visits the school, at which times the Indian children would remain almost motionless. On several occasions he administered light punishment to some of the little ones, who were not progressing to suit him.

Not far from the school house is the Nez Perce burial ground. The headstones consist of poles set in the ground with bells or feathers ornamenting the tops. It forms a weird picture of mingled savagery and civilization. Chief Joseph presides at every Nez Perce funeral with great and solemn dignity.

The interior of Chief Joseph's tepee presents a model appearance of neatness. Indian mats cover the floor and

---

[3] *Annual Reports of U.S. Commissioner of Indian Affairs*, 1888, p. 223; 1890, pp. 217-18; 1891, p. 442; 1892, p. 493; 1893, p. 321; 1894, p. 311; 1897, p. 290; 1898, p. 298; 1899, pp. 354-55.

in huge rolls around the edge are buffalo robes now quite scarce among the Indians, and blankets. From one of these rolls the Chief brought a small leather trunk in which were bundles of letters he had received from white men, and photographs of Indian and white friends. He knew each face and seemed glad to call up memories of his friends and relatives. At the bottom of his trunk were the eagle hat and saddle robe with which his high rank is proclaimed on all gala days.

The Indians were making great preparations for the approaching Fourth of July when they would have a celebration extending over one or two weeks. Joseph would not allow his picture to be taken until that time when his wardrobe would be in better condition for such an important operation. The Indians of this whole region show their respect for Chief Joseph by according him, without any questioning, the principal place of honor on all great festivals or celebrations.

Chief Moses had a great reputation among the Indians and whites of this section but he was dissipated. The Indians will manage at times to get liquor and Moses brought on his own death by a protracted spree. Chief Joseph never drinks intoxicants. "Nica Halo Bottlum," as he puts it in Chinook (meaning, "I never touch the bottle").

Moses had two wives who survive him. Joseph is now the only Indian on the reservation who has two wives. His wives are Wa-win-te-pi-ksat, aged forty-six, and I-a-tu-ton-my, aged thirty-nine. Joseph's Nez Perce name is Hin-mah-too-yah-lat-kekht meaning "Thunder rolling in the mountains." He claims that he is fifty-three years old but General Howard estimated his age at thirty-seven at the time of his war, which would make him sixty-one years old now.

Henry M. Steele, the sub-agent at Nespilem, says that Joseph's wives do all the work about the home and always call for the rations on issue day. He says that Joseph is appealed to when there are harnesses or other such goods to give out to the Nez Perces. The Chief will designate the ones to be thus favored but he usually begins the process by claiming one of the articles for himself.

On our visit to the tepee, the writer saw Joseph unharnessing his team and on another day he was saddling a pony. The sub-agent said on both occasions that it was unusual. The wives or his helpers usually did such things for him.

The Government has built for Joseph two small "ietas" houses in which are kept his many precious properties. In one are four rifles. One of these is old and worn. Joseph says it is the one he carried through the war. Here is also seen nicely framed the certificate of Chief Joseph's appointment as an aid in the New York parade at the dedication of the Grant memorial monument on April 27, 1897. On that occasion he marched side by side with his friend Buffalo Bill.

Joseph was asked what Indian chief he considered the greatest and he answered that he thought his father, also a Chief Joseph, was the greatest. To another question he said he thought his brother Ollicutt was the next greatest chief.

Joseph has had nine children, five girls and four boys, but they are all dead. One died since living at Nespilem, two died in Indian Territory and the rest died in Idaho. One daughter grew to womanhood and was married. He seems especially fond of her memory and tells what a good girl she was while showing her picture. On the back of this tintype picture is written "for Chief Joseph from his loving Daughter Sarah Moses."

Bereft of his children the Chief now leads a quiet life sustained by the Government against whose authority he waged a long and bitter warfare. His last effort to regain the Wallowa Valley has been investigated by Inspector James McLaughlin who has reported strongly against the request.[4] But Joseph still longs for that old home the "Valley of Winding Waters." In a dictated letter to the writer, dated at Nespilem, May 27, 1901, he says: "My old home is in the Wallowa Valley and I want to go back there to live. My father and mother are buried there. If the Government would only give me a small piece of land for my people in the Wallowa Valley, with a teacher, that is all I would ask."

The white people in Wallowa Valley have named one of their towns Joseph and their newspaper was called Chieftain but there the sentiment ends. They enter strong protest when it is talked of sending any of the Nez Perces back to that home of their forefathers.[5]

---

[4] Seattle, *Post-Intelligencer*, July 8, 1900; Chicago *Record*, August, 8, 1900.

[5] Meany, "Chief Joseph, the Nez Perce," Master of Letters thesis, University of Wisconsin, Madison. A manuscript copy of this thesis was kindly loaned to the author by the late Dr. Meany.

A vain dream which Joseph was never to realize. So set was his heart, however, on returning to the ancestral land of his people that in 1903 he went to Washington again, this time to petition President Theodore Roosevelt to grant his tribe the Wallowa Valley. Since the land was taken up by white settlers the request was once more denied. On this occasion Joseph stayed East long enough to join Cummin's "Indian Congress and Life on the Plains," then exhibiting at Madison Square Garden. An anecdote is told of him that he was given a stiff measure of whiskey, as some whites were anxious to see what effect it would have. The chief swallowed the contents in one gulp and said nothing!

Twenty-seven years after the Nez Perce War, in 1904, Joseph attended the commencement exercises of the Carlisle Indian Industrial School in Pennsylvania, and sat at the same banquet table with his former enemy, Major General O. O. Howard. A queer prank indeed of fate, that a red fighter and a white general should toast each other! Howard called his one-time foe "the greatest Indian warrior I ever fought with," while the said warrior made a speech that was reported in translation by a special correspondent of the *Inter Ocean:*

Friends, I meet here my friend, General Howard. I used to be so anxious to meet him. I wanted to kill him in war. Today I am glad to meet him, and glad to meet everybody here, and to be friends with General Howard. We are both old men, still we live and I am glad. We both fought in many wars and we are both alive. Ever since the war I have made up my mind to be friendly to the whites and to everybody. I wish you, my friends, would believe me as I believe myself in my heart in what I say. When my friend, General Howard, and I fought together I had no idea that we would ever sit down to a meal together, as today, but we have, and I am glad. I have lost many friends, and many men, women and children, but I have no grievance against any of the white people, General Howard or any one. If General Howard dies first, of course I will be sorry. I understand and I know that learning of books is a nice thing, and I have some children here in school from my tribe that are trying to learn something, and I am thankful to know there are some of my children here struggling to learn the white man's ways and his books. I repeat again I have no enmity against anybody. I want to be friends to everybody. I wish my children would learn more and more every day, so they can mingle with the white people and do business with them as well as anybody else. I shall try to get Indians to send their children to school.[6]

Following his visit to Carlisle, Joseph went to Seattle at the invitation of James J. Hill, the railroad magnate, who was attempting "to enlist public opinion for the restoration of Wallowa." The largest auditorium in Seattle was filled to capacity. Joseph and another chief, Red Thunder, were introduced by Professor Meany, who says they took so long making themselves presentable that he had to extemporize for twenty minutes on Nez Perce history and the war until the chiefs appeared on the platform.

The next day Joseph gave a short talk before the students at the University of Washington and shook hands with members of the faculty and each of the students. In the afternoon he attended a football game where he created as much interest as the game did! He followed the plays with deep absorption, and excitedly got to his feet to watch intently whenever the players would pile up in scrimmage after being tackled. Then, when they untangled themselves, he would draw a long breath and sit down again.

Once only did Joseph return to his beloved valley—the last time he would ever see that place so hallowed in his memory. It was during June and July of 1900 in company with Indian Inspector James McLaughlin, whom the government had appointed to investigate the feasibility of restoring part of the Wallowa country to its rightful owners. For Joseph it was a kind of pilgrimage to his ancestral home. When he gazed once more upon the grave of his father, preserved by a white friend who

---

[6] Wood, *Lives of Famous Indians*, p. 525.

Photo taken by the author, August, 1940

Monument at the grave of Chief Joseph, Nespelem, Washington

Photo taken by the author, August, 1940

Monument at the grave of Chief Joseph, Nespelem, Washington

had enclosed it with a fence, the tears brimmed over in the old chief's eyes.

McLaughlin's adverse report decided the government never to remove the Nez Perces to Oregon. With the fulfillment of that desire still cherished in his heart, Joseph went on his last journey over the trail to the setting sun that led to the Spirit Land of Indian religious belief. Toward the end he sat beside his campfire, gazing long and earnestly at the tawny hills as he murmured, "Halo manitah," meaning that he would not live to see another winter. Silent and brooding he would stoically sit whole days without speaking or moving. So sitting before his fire on September 21, 1904, he fell forward on his face. Dr. Latham, the agency physician, said, "Joseph died of a broken heart."

The Anaconda *Standard* of September 25, 1904, stated that his surviving relatives were a brother at Lapwai; a nephew, Amos, the son of his sister; John Moses, the son of his brother; Red Thunder, a nephew, and Ollicutt, another nephew, but makes mention of only one wife.[7]

Joseph was quietly laid to rest, but the following year on June 20, 1905, when the monument to his memory was unveiled at Nespelem, he was "reburied" with great ceremony.

The monument is a white marble shaft, standing seven and a half feet high. A fine likeness of the famous warrior-chief is carved on the front, and below it appears his name in raised letters, "Chief Joseph." On another side his name is carved both in Nez Perce and in its English translation, "Thunder-rolling-in-the-mountains." On still a third side is the inscription: "He led his people in the Nez Perce war of 1877. Died 21 September, 1904, age, about 60 years."[8] On the back of the monument is

[7] The author can find no supporting evidence for this statement. However, according to a newspaper clipping in J. H. Horner's possession, Joseph's wife, Wa-win-tip-yah-le-ka-set, died near Nespelem in February, 1929, aged nearly one hundred years.

[8] Joseph was nearer sixty-four.

inscribed: "Erected 20 June, 1905, by the Washington University State Historical Society."

The young men of the tribe dug a new grave and placed the remains in it with the head toward the east and facing the monument. When the coffin was reopened so that relatives and friends of the old chief could look upon his face for the last time, "the Nez Perces circled around the body of Joseph," while the whites stood respectfully in the background. Tears came into the eyes of the old warriors, and the widows of the war "gave voice to the wail of the grieving Indian."[9]

Late in the afternoon whites and Indians reassembled to dedicate the monument.[10] Among the principal speakers were the nearly blind Yellow Bull, the newly elected chief, Albert Waters, Ess-Kow-Ess (Espowyes—Light-in-the-Mountain), a prominent spokesman of the tribe, and Professor Edmond Meany, who delivered the main address for the whites on behalf of Samuel Hill, donator of the monument, and of the Washington University State Historical Society.

The next day, following the banquet at noon, a huge potlatch or gift feast took place, being the greatest affair of that kind of which there is any record. A very large council lodge was filled to capacity with Indians, whites, and the heaps of Chief Joseph's worldly possessions which were guarded by his three nephews, Ollicutt and Black Eagle of Montana, and Chief Tow-at-way of the Umatillas. According to a reporter from the Seattle *Post-Intelligencer*, who covered the dedication:

In the only chair in the lodge sat the official announcer, Pio-pio-mox-mox, "Yellow Bird," who is one of the noted men of the tribe. At his right hand on the ground sat Joseph's younger widow. Back of these relatives sat the blind chief, Yellow Bull. From this end of the long tepee

[9] Seattle *Post-Intelligencer*, June 25, 1905.

[10] While on a field trip to the Wallowa Valley in August, 1940, the author was told of a plan being organized to have Joseph's body again removed and reburied beside that of his father at the foot of Wallowa Lake. The movement was strenuously opposed by the last survivors of the chief's band at Nespelem.

or council lodge were ranged the men, all reclining on reed mats and robed in brilliant blankets . . . for nearly half the length of the lodge, and beyond the men were the women and children.[11]

Before the distribution of Joseph's property, Chief Yellow Bull delivered the principal address for the Indians. He recited the speech on horseback while riding three times slowly around the outside of the council lodge on Joseph's horse. "Besides that dignity," notes the reporter, "he wore all of Chief Joseph's war clothes, including the famous eagle-feather war-bonnet."[12]

Yellow Bull's speech was interpreted by Camille Williams, an educated full blood Nez Perce. It is a characteristic example of the older Indian oratory:

I am very glad to meet you all here today, my brothers and sisters and children and white friends. When the Creator created us, He put us on this earth, and the flowers on the earth, and He takes us all in His arms and keeps us in peace and friendship, and our friendship and peace shall never fade, but it will shine forever. Our people love our old customs. I am very glad to see our white friends here attending this ceremony, and it seems like we all have the same sad feelings, and that fact helps to wipe away my tears and the loss of our dead chief.

Joseph is dead, but his words are not dead; his words will live forever. This monument will stand—Joseph's words will stand as long as this monument.

We [the red and the white people] are both here, and the Great Spirit looks down on us both; and now if we are good and live right, like Joseph, we shall see Him. I have finished.[13]

At the distribution of Joseph's possessions nearly every Indian was given something. According to the reporter:

The great war bonnets and war clothing went to the three nephews. A dozen watches were among the gifts, three fine guns and an endless array of blankets. One of

---

[11] Seattle *Post-Intelligencer,* June 25, 1905.

[12] *Ibid.*

[13] *Ibid.*

the three buffalo robes was given to Three Knives, or Professor Meany.

Only fourteen of Chief Joseph's horses were given away. The others were left for his two wives. The bands of horses are large enough to keep these two widows all their lives. The widows will be protected and the horses cared for by Red Star, a relative.[14]

On Saturday morning all of the late chief's household goods and food supplies, including sacks of flour, meats, bread, syrup, dishes, and table utensils were likewise distributed. The newly elected chief, Albert Waters, was presented with Joseph's large bass drum. Then the potlatch closed with a war dance, enacted by young men, and a final oration in the Nez Perce language given by an old warrior who was dressed in furs and feathers and carried a calumet, a peace pipe, in his hand.[15]

So concluded the funeral ceremony of Chief Joseph, warrior and statesman. In the words of Mrs. Eliza Spalding Warren, "his name will . . . take a place in history with those of Tecumseh, Brant, Black Hawk, Pontiac, and Sitting Bull; and by many he is considered the greatest of all the Indian warriors."[16]

It is gratifying to know that a Monument of Contrition was erected to Chief Joseph on the Bearpaw battlefield in northern Montana. The Honorable Lew L. Callaway, former Chief Justice of the Montana Supreme Court, in a letter to the author, dated January 8, 1947, related how this unique and appropriate idea originated: "When Chief Justice of Montana I spoke on the Bear's Paw Battlefield on two occasions; first in 1928 on the desirability of having the field set apart as a National Monument. . . . The Great Falls *Tribune* printed a report of the meeting . . . saying . . . 'Monument of Con-

[14] *Ibid.* Only four or five of Joseph's original band were still alive and residing on the Colville Reservation in 1939.

[15] *Ibid.*

[16] Mrs. Eliza Spalding Warren, *Memoirs of the West: The Spaldings*, p. 142. Mrs. Warren was the daughter of the Reverend H. H. Spalding who conducted the mission for the Nez Perces at Lapwai at the time of the Whitman massacre.

trition for Failure to Keep Faith with Chief Joseph Urged. Walsh (then U.S. Senator), Leavitt (Congressman) Promise Aid in Creation of Chief Joseph Battlefield Memorial.' That object having been attained, on [*sic*] Oct. 1931, a huge stone with a bronze plaque thereon was dedicated in commemoration of the surrender."

Speaking of monuments, L. V. McWhorter, in a letter under date of "Hunting Moon 25, 1942," wrote the author that he and the well-known sculptor, Alonzo V. Lewis of Seattle, Washington, accompanied by three Nez Perces—Peopeo Tholekt, Black Eagle, and Many Wounds—toured the five major battlefields in the summer of 1928 to place markers at each site. These small monuments of synthetic stone, bearing a "bronze plate on the shaft . . . dedicatory to Chief Joseph and his Warriors," were located at the White Bird, Cottonwood, Clearwater, Big Hole, and Bearpaw battlegrounds.

Since the chief's death many other honors have been bestowed by white Americans upon his memory. A few among them include a Liberty ship built at Portland, Oregon, during World War II which was christened the *Chief Joseph* on March 28, 1943. Erskine Wood, Portland attorney and son of Colonel C. E. S. Wood, delivered the launching speech. A dam on the Columbia River in Washington was dedicated in June, 1956, as the Chief Joseph Dam, one of the world's largest hydroelectric developments. An elementary school in Great Falls, Montana, constructed in 1962, was named the Chief Joseph School. On December 18, 1964, the *Daily Missoulian,* Missoula, Montana, reported: "State highway commissioners . . . approved Chief Joseph Pass as the name for a cut through the mountains between U.S. 93 and Montana 43." All of which recognition the chief would have gladly exchanged for the privilege of living and dying in his beloved Wallowa—the valley of winding waters.

Appendices

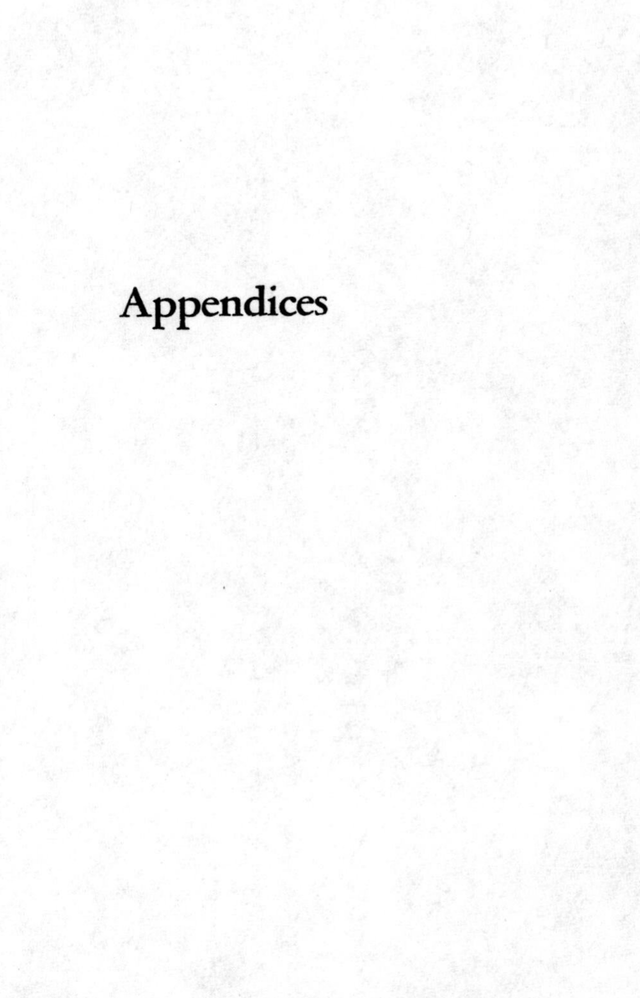

GENEALOGY CHART

- Wa-la-mat-kin and Nez Perce Woman
  - Old Joseph (Tu-eka-kas)
    - —Nez Perce Woman (Arenoth?)
      - Young Joseph
      - Alokut
      - Sarah Conner
        - —Gilbert Conner*
        - —Lizzie Conner*
        - —David Conner*
        - —Paul Lawyer*
      - Celia
        - James Black Eagle
          - Joseph Black Eagle*
    - —Walla Walla Woman
      - Peo-peo-mox-mox-low-e-ax
        - Annie George
    - —Cayuse Woman
      - Wa-la-mat-kin, junior
      - Ho-um-ya-she-moo-to-lien
        - David Young Chief
          - Louise Martin*
          - Winnie Crane*
        - Young Chief
    - —Ip-as-ship-ap-la-chon-my
      - Pa-ca-ta-le-cot-sat
        - White Wolf
          - Julia White Wolf*
          - Elizabeth Halfmoon*

*These were the living relatives (in 1935) of Chief Joseph through his father's marriages.

Some writers have erroneously stated that Young Joseph's mother was a Cayuse. Were this true, Young Joseph would have been known as a Cayuse and not as a Nez Perce, since it is customary among the tribes of the Columbia River Basin for tribal descent to be traced through the maternal side of the family. The grandfather of Young Joseph was Chief Wa-la-mat-kin of the Cayuse tribe. He had two wives, Nez Perce Woman, and Cayuse Woman. As we are concerned only with the genealogy of Young Joseph, the descendants of Chief Wa-la-mat-kin and Cayuse Woman have not been included, but only those known through his marriage to Nez Perce Woman.

Among the original letters of John B. Monteith, agent of the Lapwai Reservation, which are preserved in the Idaho State Historical Library in Boise, the author found one letter to H. Clay Wood, dated April 24, 1876, in which Monteith states that old Joseph's father was a Cayuse chief and his mother a Nez Perce. "Old Joseph was born near the mouth of Grand Ronde," the letter continues. "Old Joseph took his wife from a band living on the Snake river near the mouth of the Ashotin. She was the mother of several children including Young Joseph. The Indians say she was only part Nez Perce. I am unable to ascertain of what other blood she was. It could not have been Snake as the Nez Perces and Snakes were always enemies."

Young Joseph's own family, treated in the text, is not included here as there are no living direct descendants of the chief. The genealogy chart above* was given to Mr. Omar L. Babcock, Superintendent of the Umatilla Agency, Pendleton, Oregon, by Mr. Philip Jones of the Umatilla Reservation. Through the courtesy of Mr. Babcock, it is reproduced here for the first time.

---

* This chart is at variance with the testimony of several old Indians. For example, Toy-Wate was the father of old Joseph (Tu-eka-kas), according to Young Alokut, son of old Alokut. Young Alokut made the statement to J. H. Horner, Wallowa County historian, Enterprise, Oregon. Old Indians also told Mr. Horner that old Alokut's mother was not Nez Perce Woman, but a sister of hers. This would make Alokut a half-brother to young Joseph. However, when questioned by the author, Joseph Black Eagle, grand-nephew of the chief, could give no definite information on this point. He stated, though, that Sarah Conner was a sister of Alokut's, not a daughter; Celia, also a sister of Alokut's, became the mother of James Black Eagle, who became the father of himself, Joseph Black Eagle (Blackeagle).

SIDELIGHTS

Other sidelights on the chief are furnished by Mrs. Frances G. Hamblen of Spokane, Washington, an artist who modeled a bust of Joseph in bas relief. As a girl of about eighteen she wrote the following perceptive description of the chieftain immediately after he had visited her father's house in 1893:

Moderately tall and heavily built. Hand that felt as big as a ham when shaking hands. Eyes small but particularly bright. At first one doesn't notice his eyes (when he is apparently looking one's way) but suddenly you perceive these bright, searching, direct little eyes riveted upon you. The first few times I met him, I could seldom detect him looking my way (except at meeting or parting) and it seemed as if he was oblivious to everything in the room. Knowing however, that Indians seemingly have no eyes and yet see—we observed the Chief carefully, soon finding that when we looked he did not, and visa [*sic*] versa. Being perhaps the most interested party, I sat next to him. He leaned back in a Morris chair with legs extended to the fire warming first this side then the other. As he also insisted on retaining his large overcoat in a house at summer heat, we asked him if he was sick. He shook his head and slapping his knee said, "Him cold."

An Indian's expression is hard to analyze. It is such a combination of childlike simplicity, of cunning, of directness and evasion, of sadness and sternness, of cruelty. Then with all savages comes the smile, which in Joseph's case I do not hesitate to describe as winning. This has also been the criticism of many others. The labial fold is always strongly marked. Then the development of the masseter make more strong lines about the corners of the mouth. So there is that expression on an Indian's face that just before becoming a broad smile changes into austerity and grimness. Then the long development of certain muscles about the eye from squinting in a strong light and observing objects at a distance has given a look of almost grief to the face. But here again the expression is not perfect. These expressions are peculiar to the Indian and do quite as much toward making the Indian face as do the high cheek bone, big nose and long upper lips, low forehead. (All usually found.)

Joseph does not speak good English. Mixes in a number of Nez Perce words but it is almost possible to understand him by his gestures, without any words. In these he is perfectly free and unconscious, moving with a native grace that is very pleasing. Several times he stood to better illustrate a climax. When any numbers were required he would lean forward, sit up in his chair, plant the elbow of his left arm on the chair arm and with forearm and wrist held up straight, fingers extended; and then with his right hand count off from these human digits exactly the number he wished. We asked him if he had hunted lately. Yes, he had killed a hi-u (big) grizzly this winter. He measured the height the bear stood from the floor. The grizzly were ferocious—"killed Boston man's cow." Had long claws and sharp teeth. Here Joseph's sound teeth came together in a perfect snap as he bent his fingers claw shape. He shot with Boston man's gun—not bow and arrows, and he pointed to several different spots on his own breast to show where he had hit the bear. I should not have liked to be Joseph's enemy in battle. Upon my questioning him about bows and arrows he drew back and carefully aimed an imaginary bow at me with such a look in his eye that in an instant all civilization was gone and there stood the fearless savage pausing ere he sent the swift arrow on its message of death.

Among the Indian pictures in the house was one of Joseph taken just at the close of the war. He expressed decided interest in this and explained about the bead ornaments he then wore. "Young man then," he said. And then, pointing to himself, "Me old," fifty-three snows.

One of the ladies present—a physician—rose to go. Joseph's manner is quite courtly. He at once rose and extended his hand nodding his head and smiling. I told him this was a medicine woman, whereat he and Dr. C. both laughed heartily. But he seemed to take it as all joke, so Dr. opened up her case and Joseph looked surprised to see these many bottles.

He told us how he lived away from his people—how his wife had died, his children, all his family and putting his hand on his heart, he shook his head, "Sick-sick."

I asked him to tell me his Indian name—he merely grunted and shook his head. I asked again and he must have concluded that I was in earnest, for suddenly he leaned towards me in his chair and told his name, waiting for me to repeat each syllable after him. "Hin-mah-too-yah-lat-kekht." The last syllable in true Indian style between a cough and a spit. When we had done this together several times, he told us what it meant, "Hi-u-mountains," he said "Li-u (Thunder)," "Li-u Thunder in mountains," and with his arm he described the course of the thunder which reached from the base, to the very summit of the mountains. His voice, too, was deep and full.

About this time, Win brought in some sweet cider and Scoty [*sic*] said, "Joseph never drinks," but after he explained to him that it was apple juice, Joseph took a glass—which he drained in one gulp.

Here is something Joseph did—which every time made us all start in our chairs. The fireplace screen was drawn away from the fireplace about 6 inches on the side where Joseph sat. Every time he wished to expectorate, he did so—without changing his position and his unerring aim at the fire was surprising. I think he did not miss once—but we expected it every time just the same.

This ended the notes of that evening visit, but Mrs. Hamblen also jotted down in her notebook another account of Joseph told her by a family friend:

Mr. Law has spoken much of Joseph, admiring him unstintingly. Mr. Law is connected with the N. P. Ry. and was in charge of moving Joseph and his band as prisoners of war at the close of the Nez Perce war. . . . The Indians were much crowded in the cars—and their thirst was merely mocked by the tin reservoir in the car ends. So stops were made at water tanks where the Indians filed out and drank by the bucketfull [*sic*]. Finally the train stopped for supper. Joseph was invited to the private car to eat with the white chiefs. He might have been awkward—but he ate with knife and fork. Shortly after leaving this station it was reported that Joseph was missing. A thorough search was made through the train—but unsuccessfully. This was a loss not to be overlooked. The only plausible theory being that he was left at the place the train stopped for supper and the train was slowly backed up.

Before long a figure was descried on the track. It was coming toward the train then Joseph was recognized. In one corner of his blanket he was carrying something which proved to be pies, rather dilapidated, but food for the sick squaws—as Joseph explained. After he had entered the car again he threw off the blanket. He stood there in nothing but a breech clout steaming with perspiration. "A more magnificent specimen of manhood I have never seen," said Mr. Law. "He was the Apollo Belvedere." Joseph's intention was to overtake the train but he had already realized his incapability, for he said, "It is harder for me to catch this train than it was for General Howard to catch me." Which shows that even a defeated Indian is capable of a pun.[8]

---

[8] Reprinted through the kind permission of Mrs. Grace Bartlett from her booklet, *Wallowa, the Land of Winding Waters*, Joseph, Oregon, 1967.

BIBLIOGRAPHY

ALCORN, ROWENA L. AND GORDON D. "Albert Moore: Patriarch of the Nez Perce," Seattle *Post-Intelligencer Pictorial Review*, October 6, 1963. A one-hundred-and-one-year-old Indian recalls the fighting in Idaho.

———"The Nez Perce Retreat," *Montana, the Magazine of Western History*, XIII, Winter, 1963. Sam Tilden, aged Nez Perce, tells his childhood memories of his tribe's flight toward Canada.

"An Indian's Views of Indian Affairs," *North American Review*, April, 1879. An interview with Chief Joseph.

ARNOLD, R. ROSS. *Indian Wars of Idaho*. Caldwell, Idaho: The Caxton Printers, Ltd. 1932. Chapters VII-IX, pp. 107-68; 296-353.

BABCOCK, OMAR L. Genealogy Chart of Chief Wa-la-mat-kin. (Chart prepared by Mr. Babcock through information furnished by Philip Jones, Umatilla Reservation, Pendleton, Oregon.) n. d.

BAILEY, ROBERT G. *River of No Return—The Great Salmon River of Idaho*. Lewiston, Idaho: Bailey-Blake Printing Co., 1935.

BAIRD, MAJOR G. W. "General Miles Indian Campaigns," *Century Magazine*, July, 1891.

BANCROFT, HUBERT HOWE. *Works of H. H. Bancroft*. San Francisco: The History Co., 1890. Vol. XXXI, Chapters IV-V, pp. 481-526.

BARTLETT, GRACE. *Wallowa, the Land of Winding Waters*. Joseph, Oregon, 1967.

BEAL, MERRILL D. *"I Will Fight No More Forever": Chief Joseph and the Nez Perce War*. Seattle, Wash.: University of Washington Press, 1963. A well-documented chronicle offering some new perspectives on the nontreaty Nez Perce bands.

BOAS, FRANZ, ed. *Folk-Tales of Salishan and Sahaptin Tribes*. Lancaster, Pa.: American Folk-Lore Society, 1917.

BOND, FRED G. *Flatboating on the Yellowstone*. New York: American Library Association, 1925.

BRADY, DR. CYRUS TOWNSEND. *Northwestern Fights and Fighters*. New York: The McClure Co., 1907. Chapters I-XIV.

BROSNAN, DR. C. J. *History of Idaho*. New York: Scribner's, 1918. Second edition, 1926.

BUCK, AMOS. *Review of the Battle of the Big Hole*. Helena, Mont.: Historical Society of Montana, State Publishing Co., 1910. Vol. VII.

CATLIN, GEORGE. *Letters and Notes on the Manners, Customs, and Condition of the North American Indians*. London: Published by the author, 1841. 2 vols.

CATLIN, J. B. "Battle of the Big Hole," in *Historian's Annual Report, Society of Montana Pioneers*. Helena, Mont., 1927.

CAVE, WILL. *The Nez Perce War of 1877*. Missoula, Mont.: 1926. A pamphlet. Clark Memorial Library, Los Angeles, Calif.

CHITTENDEN, HIRAM MARTIN, AND RICHARDSON, ALFRED TALBERT. *DeSmet's Life and Travels among the North American Indians*. New York: Francis P. Harper, 1905. 4 vols. References made to Nez Perces.

CLARK, ROBERT CARLTON. "Military History of Oregon, 1849-59, *Oregon Historical Quarterly*, Vol. XXXVI, No. 1, March, 1935.

CLARK, STANLEY J. "The Nez Perce in Exile," *Pacific Northwest Quarterly*, XXXVI, July, 1945. An exhaustive study of the nontreaty bands in exile.

CLARKE, R. D. *Works of Sitting Bull*, Part II. Knight & Leonard, Printers, 1878. Republished by Library of Congress.

CLARKE, S. A. *Pioneer Days of Oregon History.* Portland, Ore.: 1902. 2 vols.

CLOUGH, J. P. "Recollections of the Nez Perce Indian War of 1877, and Their Entrance into Lemhi Valley." Manuscript in Idaho State Historical Library, Boise.

CONE, H. W. "The White Bird Battle." Manuscript in Idaho State Historical Library, Boise.

COWAN, MRS. GEORGE F. *Reminiscences of Pioneer Life.* Helena, Mont.: Historical Society of Montana, State Publishing Co., 1903. Vol. IV.

COX, ROSS. *Adventures on the Columbia River.* London: H. Colburn and R. Bentley, 1831. 2 vols.

CRAWFORD, MARY M. *The Nez Percés Since Spalding.* San Francisco: Presbyterian Bookstore, 234 McAllister St., May, 1936.

CRUIKSHANK, ALEXANDER. "Reminiscence of Alexander Cruikshank." Manuscript in Idaho State Historical Library, Boise.

CURTIS, EDWARD S. *The North American Indian.* Norwood, Mass.: Published by Edward S. Curtis, 1911. Vol. VIII.

DE SMET, PIERRE JEAN. *Oregon Missions and Travels over the Rocky Mountains.* New York: E. Dunigan, 1847. Same in Thwaites's *Early Western Travels.* Cleveland: A. H. Clark Co., 1906. Vol. XXIX.

DRURY, CLIFFORD MERRILL. *Henry Harmon Spalding.* Caldwell, Idaho: The Caxton Printers, Ltd., 1936.

———*Marcus Whitman, M.D.* Caldwell, Idaho: The Caxton Printers, Ltd., 1937.

DUNN, J. P., JR. *Massacres of the Mountains.* New York: Harper & Bros., 1880. Chapter XIX.

ELLIOTT, T. C. "The Indian Council at Walla Walla," *Washington Historical Quarterly*, Vol. I, No. 4, July, 1907.

ELLIS, EDWARD S. *Indian Wars of the United States* New York: Cassell Publishing Co., 1892. Chapter XXXIX.

———*Thrilling Adventures among the American Indians*, Philadelphia: John Winston Co., 1905. Chapter XX.

FEE, CHESTER ANDERS. *Chief Joseph; the Biography of a Great Indian.* New York: Wilson-Erickson, Inc., 1936.

FINERTY, JOHN FREDERICK. *Warpath and Bivouac.* Chicago: John F. Finerty, 1890.

FISHER, S. G. *Journal of S. G. Fisher.* Helena, Mont.: Historical Society of Montana, State Publishing Co., 1896. Vol. II.

FORSE, LIEUT. ALBERT G. "Chief Joseph as a Commander," *Winners of the West*, Official Bulletin National Indian War Veterans, St. Joseph, Mo. November, 1936.

FORSYTH, GEORGE A. *Story of the Soldier.* New York: D. Appleton & Co., 1900. Chapter XV.

FULLER, GEORGE W. *A History of the Pacific Northwest.* New York: Alfred A. Knopf, 1931.

GIBBON, GEN. JOHN. "The Battle of the Big Hole," *Harper's Weekly*, December 21, 1895.

GOODSPEED, WESTON ARTHUR. *The Province and the States.* Madison, Wis.: Western Historical Association, 1904. Vol. IV.

GRINNELL, GEORGE BIRD. *The Indians of Today.* Chicago: Herbert S. Stone & Co., 1900.

GUIE, HEISTER DEAN, AND MCWHORTER, LUCULLUS V., eds., *Adventures in Geyser Land.* Caldwell, Idaho: The Caxton Printers, Ltd., 1935. Reprinted from *The Wonders of Geyser Land*, by Frank D. Carpenter, edition of 1878.

HAINES, FRANCIS. "The Nez Perce Delegation to St. Louis in 1831," *The Pacific Historical Review*, Vol. VI, No. 1, March, 1937.

———*Red Eagles of the Northwest.* Portland, Ore.: The Scholastic Press, 1939.

———*The Nez Perces.* Norman: University of Oklahoma Press, 1955. A revised version of *Red Eagles.*

Harper's Weekly, New York, Oct. 27, 1877. Vol. XXI. No. 1087, pp. 840, 842, 843.

HARRINGTON, J. A. "Copies of telegrams, letters, manuscripts, collected from originals in possession of Mr. Harrington," Idaho State Historical Library, Boise. These mostly relate to the preparations made by volunteers for reception of the Nez Perces.

HAWLEY, JAMES H. *History of Idaho.* Chicago: S. J. Clark Publishing Co., 1920. Vol. I.

HEROLD, HELMA. "Battle of the Big Hole, Twenty-fifth Anniversary." Manuscript in Clark Memorial Library, Los Angeles, Calif.

HORNER, J. H., AND BUTTERFIELD, GRACE. "The Nez Perce-Findley Affair," *Oregon Historical Quarterly*, March, 1939.

HOWARD, MAJOR GENERAL OLIVER OTIS. "Famous Indian Chiefs," *St. Nicholas Magazine*, Part XI. June, 1908.

———*Famous Indian Chiefs I Have Known.* New York: Century Co., 1908. Chapter XI.

———*Life and Experiences among Our Hostile Indians.* Hartford, Conn.: A. D. Worthington & Co., 1907.

———*Chief Joseph, His Pursuit and Capture.* Boston: Lee & Shephard, Publishers. 1881. The most valuable source account of the military campaign.

Original Dispatches of General O. O. Howard. Three of these are dated, respectively, 1876, 77, 78, and were in Spokane Public Library in 1940.

HULBERT, ARCHER BUTLER, AND HULBERT, DOROTHY PRINTUP. *Overland to the Pacific.* Denver: 1935-37. Vols. IV, V, VI.

HUMPHREY, SETH K. *The Indian Dispossessed.* Boston: Little, Brown & Co., 1905.

HUNT, GARRETT B. "Indian Wars of the Inland Empire." Unpublished manuscript at Spokane Community College, Spokane, Washington. It is based upon government documents and participants' accounts relating to the Columbia Basin Indian War of 1856-58. Written in 1908 it has been privately printed by Spokane Community College Library, September 1966.

HUNTER, COLONEL GEORGE. *Reminiscences of an Old Timer* San Francisco: H. S. Crocker & Co., 1887.

IRVING, WASHINGTON. *Adventures of Captain Bonneville.* New York: G. P. Putnam's Sons, 1880.

———*Astoria.* New York: G. P. Putnam's Sons, 1880.

JACKSON, HELEN HUNT ("H H"). *A Century of Dishonor.* New York: Harper & Bros., 1881.

JOCELYN, STEPHEN PERRY. *Mostly Alkali.* Caldwell, Idaho: The Caxton Printers, Ltd., 1952.

JOHNSON, HENRY C. "Volunteer Survivor Recalls Battle with Indians East of Cottonwood." Manuscript in Idaho State Historical Library, Boise.

JOSEPHY, ALVIN M., JR. "The Last Stand of Chief Joseph," *American Heritage*, IX, February, 1958. Gives a brief resumé of the war.

KAPPLER, CHARLES J. *Indian Affairs, Laws and Treaties.* Washington, D.C.: Government Printing Office, 1904-9. 4 vols.

KIP, COLONEL LAWRENCE. *Indian Council at Walla Walla, 1855.* Eugene, Ore.: Star Job Office, 1897. A pamphlet. Clark Memorial Library, Los Angeles, Calif.

KIP, LAWRENCE. *Army Life on the Pacific.* New York: Redfield, 1859.

LAUT, AGNES C. *The Blazed Trail of the Old Frontier.* New York: Robert M. McBride & Co., 1926. Part III.

MCBETH, KATE C. *Nez Percés Since Lewis and Clark.* New York: Fleming H. Revell Co., 1908.

MCLAUGHLIN, JAMES. *My Friend the Indian.* New York: Houghton Mifflin Co., 1910.

MACLEOD, WILLIAM CHRISTIE. *The American Indian Frontier.* London: Kegan, Paul, Trench, Trubner & Co., 1928.

MCWHORTER, LUCULLUS V. *Hear Me, My Chiefs!*, edited by Ruth Bordin. Caldwell, Idaho: The Caxton Printers, Ltd., 1952. Presents the "entire story of the Nez Perce tribe," including the War of 1877 from Indian sources.

MCWHORTER, LUCULLUS V. *Yellow Wolf: His Own Story.* Caldwell, Idaho: The Caxton Printers, Ltd., 1940. A Nez Perce warrior's personal accounts of events leading up to, and including the war of 1877. A good supplementary volume to this text.

MANNYPENNY, GEORGE W. *Our Indian Wards.* Cincinnati: Robert Clarke & Co., 1880.

MEANY, DR. EDMOND STEPHEN, "Chief Joseph, the Nez Perce." Master of Letters Thesis, University of Wisconsin, Madison, 1901.

———*History of the State of Washington.* New York: Macmillan Co., 1910.

MILES, BRIGADIER GENERAL NELSON A. "Future of the Indian Question," *North American Review*, January, 1891.

———"Chief Joseph's Surrender," New York *Tribune* Supplement, August 4, 1907.

———"The Indian Problem," *North American Review*, April, 1879.

———*Personal Recollections of General Miles.* New York: The Werner Co., 1896.

———*Serving the Republic*. New York: Harper & Bros., 1911.

———"On the Trail of Geronimo," *Cosmopolitan Magazine*, July, 1911.

MONTEITH, JOHN B. "Letters: Lapwai Indian Agency, Idaho." Vol. IV, August 27, 1875-December 30, 1876. U. S. Indian Agent. Original letters in Idaho State Historical Library, Boise. Additional copies of his original letters are in Spokane Public Library, which cover period from October 1, 1871-June 27, 1874.

MONTEITH, MRS. FRANCES WHITMAN. "Original Papers of Mrs. Frances Whitman Monteith." Spokane Public Library. She is the daughter of Perrin Whitman, the widow of Charles Monteith, and sister-in-law of John B. Monteith.

MOODY, CHARLES STUART. "The Bravest Deed I Ever Knew," *Century Magazine*, March 1911.

MORRISON, EDMUND. "The Misfortunes of Joseph—A View of the Nez Perce War," Parts I and II, Southern Branch, University of Idaho, Pocatello. Manuscript in Idaho State Historical Library, Boise.

MUELLER, OSCAR O. "The Nez Perce at Cow Island," *Montana, the Magazine of Western History*, Vol. XIV, April, 1964. The incident is based on newspaper accounts, but contains some errors of fact.

"Nez Perce War Diary of Private Frederick Mayer," George F. Brimlow, ed. *Seventeenth Biennial Report, Idaho State Historical Society*, 1939-1940. Boise, Idaho, 1940.

"Nez Perce War Letters to Governor Mason Brayman," Eugene B. Chaffee, ed. *Fifteenth Biennial Report, Idaho State Historical Society*, Boise, Idaho, 1936.

NORTHROP, HENRY DAVENPORT. *Indian Horrors*. Oakland, Calif.: Pacific Press Publishing Co., 1891.

NOYES, AL J. *The Story of Ajax*. Helena, Mont.: State Publishing Co., 1914.

Oregon Adjutant-General's Report 1866. Salem, Oregon, 1866.

PALMER, JOEL. *Journal of Travels over the Rocky Mountains 1845-1846*. Same in Thwaites's *Early Western Travels*, Cleveland: A. H. Clark Co., 1906. Vol. XXX.

PARKER, SAMUEL. *Journal of an Exploring Tour Beyond the Rocky Mountains under the Direction of the A. B. C. F. M. Performed in the Years, 1835, 36, 37*. Ithaca, New York: Published by the author, 1838.

PATERSON, ARTHUR. *The Daughter of the Nez Perces*. New York: George Bottberger Peck, 1894. A factual account, fictionized in many respects.

PAXSON, FREDERIC LOGAN. *The Last American Frontier*. New York: Macmillan Co., 1913.

PHILLIPS, PAUL C., ed. "The Battle of the Big Hole," *Sources of Northwest History*, No. 8, State University of Montana, Missoula. A pamphlet.

———ed. "Historical Reprints," *Frontier Magazine*, November, 1929.

PHINNEY, ARCHIE, ed. *Nez Percé Texts*. New York: Columbia University Press, 1934.

POND, GEORGE E. "Nelson A. Miles," *McClure's Magazine*, November, 1895.

QUAIFE, M. M., ed. *"Yellowstone Kelley," Memoirs of Luther S. Kelly*. New Haven, Conn.: Yale University Press, 1926.

"Redfield's Reminiscences." *Pacific Northwest Quarterly*, Vol. XXVII, No. 1, University of Washington, Seattle, January, 1936.

REDINGTON, J. W. "When We Fought Chief Joseph," *Sunset Magazine*, February, 1905.

———"Scouting in Montana in the 1870's," *Frontier Magazine*, November, 1932.

RHODES, MAJOR GENERAL CHARLES D. "Chief Joseph and the Nez Perces Campaign of 1877," *Proceedings of the Annual Meeting of the Order of Indian Wars of the United States*, Washington, D.C., February 18, 1938.

RICHARDSON, JAMES D. *Messages and Papers of the Presidents.* Washington, D. C.: Published by Authority of Congress, 1897. Vols. VI, VII, X, XI.

ROBERTSON, FRANK C. *On the Trail of Chief Joseph.* New York: D. Appleton & Co., 1927.

ROMEYN, CAPTAIN HENRY. "The Capture of Chief Joseph and the Nez Perce Indians," *Rocky Mountain Magazine*, Vol. IV, No. 2. April, 1902. Same in Vol. II, *Contributions: Historical Society of Montana*, Helena, 1896.

ROOSEVELT, THEODORE. *Winning of the West.* New York: G. P. Putnam's Sons, 1889-94. 4 vols.

ROSS, ALEXANDER. *Adventures of the First Settlers on the Oregon or Columbia River.* London: Smith, Elder & Co., 1849. Same in Thwaites's *Early Western Travels.* Cleveland: 1905-6, Vol. VII.

RUBY, ROBERT H. "Josiah Red Wolf Tells His Story," *Spokesman-Review Inland Empire Magazine*, November 17, 1963. A ninety-two-year-old Nez Perce's boyhood recollections of the War of 1877.

RUSSELL, CHARLES M. *Back-Trailing on the Old Frontiers.* Great Falls, Mont.: Cheely-Raban Syndicate, 1922.

SASS, HERBERT RAVENEL. *Hear Me, My Chiefs!* New York: William Morrow & Co., Inc., 1940. A picture of the United States before the white man's domination, not only of the Indian way of life, but of the abundance of wild animal and bird life.

SCOTT, MAJOR GENERAL HUGH LENOX. *Some Memories of a Soldier.* New York: The Century Co., 1928.

SEYMOUR, FLORA WARREN. *The Story of the Red Man.* New York: Longman's, Green & Co., 1929.

SHERRILL, THOMAS C. *Battle of the Big Hole in August, 1877*, written by Ella C. Hathaway, July, 1919. n. p.

SHIELDS, G. O. *Battle of the Big Hole.* New York: Rand, McNally Co., 1889.

———*Blanket Indians of the Northwest.* New York: Vechten Waring Co., 1921. Subscribers' edition.

SPINDEN, HERBERT J. "The Nez Percé Indians," *Memoirs of the American Anthropological Society*, Lancaster, Pa.: New Era Printing Co., 1908. Vol. II, Part 3.

SPLAWN, A. J. *Ka-mi-akin: the Last Hero of the Yakimas.* Portland, Ore.: 1917.

STANLEY, EDWARD J. *Rambles in Wonderland.* New York: D. Appleton & Co., 1878.

STEVENS, HAZARD. *Life of General Isaac I. Stevens.* New York: Houghton, Mifflin & Co., 1901. Vol. II.

SUTHERLAND, THOMAS A. *Howard's Campaign against the Nez Perce Indians 1877.* Portland, Ore.: 1878.

TALKINGTON, DR. H. L.. "Manuscript History of the Nez Perce Reservation." State Normal School, Lewiston, 1938. Manuscript in Idaho State Historical Library, Boise.

THOMSON, ORIGEN. *Across the Plains in 1852.* Greensburg, Ind.: 1896.

THWAITES, REUBEN GOLD, ed. *Original Journals of Lewis and Clark Expedition, 1804-1806.* New York: Dodd, 1904-6. 8 vols. A primary source and the most important work dealing with the Lewis and Clark expedition.

TITUS, NELSON C. "Last Stand of the Nez Perces," *Washington Historical Quarterly*, Vol. VI, No. 3, University of Washington, Seattle, July, 1915.

TOWNSEND, JOHN KIRK. *Narrative of a Journey across the Rocky Mountains to the Columbia River and a Visit to the Sandwich Islands.* Philadelphia: Perkins, 1839.

VICTOR, MRS. FRANCES F. *Early Indian Wars of Oregon.* Salem, Ore.: Frank C. Baker, State Printer, 1894.

WARREN, ELIZA SPALDING. *Memoirs of the West; The Spaldings.* Portland, Ore.: The Marsh Printing Co., 1916.

Washington, State of. *Washington Territorial Journal*, House of Representatives, Olympia, Washington, 1854. Pp. 15-22.

WEIKERT, ANDREW J. "Journal of a Tour through the Yellowstone Park in August and September, 1877," *Rocky Mountain Magazine*, Vol. IV, No. 1, March, 1902. Same in Vol. III, *Contributions: Historical Society of Montana*, Helena, Mont.: 1900.

WHEELER, OLIN D. *Trail of Lewis and Clark.* New York: G. P. Putnam's Sons, 1904. New Edition, 1926. 2 vols.

WOOD, C. E. S. "Chief Joseph, the Nez Percé," *Century Magazine*, May, 1884.

WOOD, ERSKINE. "A Boy's Visit to Chief Joseph," *St. Nicholas Magazine*, September, 1893.

———"Diary of a Fourteen Year Old Boy's Days with Chief Joseph," *Oregon Historical Quarterly*, Vol. LI, No. 2, June, 1950. A source account giving a detailed description of a white boy's experiences hunting and trapping among the Nez Perces, and of the reservation life of Chief Joseph and his tribespeople in the 1890's.

WOOD, HENRY CLAY. *Status of Young Joseph and His Band of Nez Percé Indians under the Treaties between the United States and the Nez Percé Tribe of Indians and the Indian Title to Land.* Portland, Ore.: 1876. Photostatic copy in Portland Public Library.

WOOD, NORMAN B. "*Lives of Famous Indian Chiefs.* Chicago: L. W. Walter Co., 1906.

WOODRUFF, GENERAL W. A. "Battle of the Big Hole," *Contributions:*

Historical Society of Montana. Helena, Mont.: State Publishing Co., 1910. Vol. VII.

UNITED STATES DOCUMENTS

HENSHAW, H. W. "Nez Perce Vocabulary Secured," *Tenth Annual Report, Bureau of American Ethnology.* Washington, D.C., 1888-89.

HODGE, FREDERICK W. *Handbook of the American Indian, Bureau of American Ethnology.* Washington, D.C.: Government Printing Office, Bulletin 30, Part I, 1907. Bulletin 30, Part II, 1910.

MALLORY, GARRICK. "Pictographs of the North American Indians," *Fifth Annual Report, Bureau of American Ethnology,* Washington, D.C., 1882-83.

MOONEY, JAMES. "The Ghost Dance Religion," *Fourteenth Annual Report, Bureau of American Ethnology,* Washington, D.C., 1892-93. Parts I and II.

———"Kiowa," *Seventeenth Annual Report, Bureau of American Ethnology,* Washington, D.C., 1895-96.

ROYER, CHARLES C. "The Cherokee Nation of Indians," *Fifth Annual Report, Bureau of American Ethnology,* Washington, D. C., 1883-84.

SHERIDAN, LIEUTENANT GENERAL P. H. "Engagements with Hostile Indians within the Military Division of the Missouri, compiled at Headquarters Military Division of Missouri from Official Records." Washington, D.C.: Government Printing Office, 1882.

TEIT, JAMES A. "Salishan Tribes of the Western Plateau," *Forty-fifth Annual Report, Bureau of American Ethnology,* Washington, D.C., 1927-28.

Commissioner of Indian Affairs. *Annual Reports of Department of Interior,* 1878, 1881, 1888, 1890, 1891, 1892, 1893, 1894, 1897, 1898, 1899.

Executive Documents. No. 93, 34th Congress, 1st Session.

Executive Documents. No. 39, 41st Congress, 3rd Session.

Executive Documents. No. 198, 42nd Congress. "Treaty with the Nez Perce Indians."

Executive Documents. No. 307, 42nd Congress, 2nd Session.

Executive Documents. No. 156, 43rd Congress, 1st Session. "Nez Perce Indian Reservation in Idaho."

Executive Documents. No. 386, 48th Congress. House of Representatives Report, "Nez Perce and Bannock Indian Wars."

Executive Documents. No. 12. "Langford Land Claim against Indian Agent at Lapwai."

Executive Documents. No. 70, 51st Congress, 1st Session, 1889-90. "Agitation to Arouse the Nez Perce Indians."

Executive Documents. No. 552, 56th Congress, 1st Session. "Claims of the Nez Perce Indians."

Executive Documents. No. 97, 62nd Congress, 1st Session. "Memorial of the Nez Perces Indians," 1911.

Report of the Joint Special Committee. "Condition of the Indian Tribes," Congressional Report, Appendix, 1867. Pp. 8-11.

Executive Documents. No. 1, 36th Congress, 2nd Session. Report of Secretary of Interior, 1859-60; 1872-73 (Report of Special Commission). Also each *Annual Report* to 1877 in *House Executive Documents.*

Reports of Secretary of War, 1854-55; 1858-59. Also each *Annual Report* to 1876-77.

Report of Secretary of Interior, *Executive Documents,* No. 4, 1867. Report to the Senate.

Report of Secretary of War, *Executive Documents,* No. 2, 46th Congress, 2nd Session. Letter to the United States Senate.

NEWSPAPER ACCOUNTS

Anaconda *Standard,* Anaconda, Montana, September 25, 1904. "Chief Joseph Was a Good Indian before He Died."

Bismarck's *Tri-Weekly Tribune,* Bismarck, Dakota Territory, November 21, 1877.

Chicago *Record,* August 8, 1900.

Frank Leslie's Illustrated Newspaper, New York, October 27, 1877. Vol. XLV, No. 1, p. 152.

Lewiston *Teller* [Extras], June 16 ff., July, August, 1877. Lewiston, Idaho. A source account of the day-by-day happenings during the hostilities in Idaho.

Sunday Missoulian, Missoula, Montana, June 14, 1925. "An interview with Sergeant Martin Brown," reported by Addison Howard.

Sunday Missoulian, Missoula, Montana, February 1, 1925. "When Charlot Changed," by Addison Howard.

Sunday Missoulian, Missoula, Montana, August 5, 1934. "Last Indian Survivor of Big Hole tells Story," reported by Ralph R. Wayne.

New Northwest, Deer Lodge, Montana, 1879. Extract from Duncan MacDonald's *The Nez Perces Wàr of 1877—the Inside History from Indian Sources.*

New York *Sun,* September 25, 1904. An account of the death of Chief Joseph reprinted in Dr. C. T. Brady's *Northwestern Fights and Fighters.*

Rocky Mountain Husbandman, Denver, Colo., February 26, 1942.

Seattle *Post-Intelligencer,* June 25, 1905. Reburial of Chief Joseph and the Potlatch Ceremonies.

Seattle *Post-Intelligencer,* July 8, 1900.

Weekly Oregonian, Portland, Oregon, March 31, 1877.

HISTORIES, COMPILED

History of Montana, Chicago: Warner, Beers & Co., 1885.

History of North Idaho, San Francisco: Western Historical Publishing Co., 1903.

ORIGINAL CORRESPONDENCE WITH

Chief James Allocott, Umatilla Indian Reservation, Pendleton, Oregon.

Mr. Omar L. Babcock, Superintendent of Indian Affairs, Umatilla Indian Reservation, Pendleton, Oregon.

Mr. Joseph Blackeagle, Nez Perce Reservation, Lapwai, Idaho.

Mr. T. C. Elliott, Historian, Walla Walla, Washington.

Mr. J. H. Horner, Enterprise, Oregon.

Mr. Corbett Lawyer, Nez Perce Reservation, Lapwai, Idaho.

Mr. L. V. McWhorter, Historian, Yakima, Washington.

Mr. Samuel Tilden, Flathead Indian Reservation, Arlee, Montana.

Mr. W. Joseph Williams, Umatilla Indian Reservation, Pendleton, Oregon.

Mr. Erskine Wood, Portland, Oregon.

Report of Judge William I. Lippincott. (His investigations conducted under the auspices of the late W. A. Clark, Jr.)

PERSONAL INTERVIEWS

The names of those persons engaged or present at the time of hostilities can be found in the notes.

Index